WICCA

The Encyclopedia Of Modern Witchcraft.

6 Books in 1:

Wicca for Beginners, Wicca book of Spells, Wicca Candle Magic, Wicca Moon Magic, Wicca Crystal Magic, Wicca Herbal Magic.

ESTHER ARIN SPELLS

COPYRIGHT © 2019, ESTHER ARIN SPELLS
ALL RIGHTS RESERVED

No part of this book may be reproduced in any form or by any electronic or mechanical means, including information storage and retrieval systems, without permission in writing from the publisher, except by reviewers, who may quote brief passages in a review.

In no way is it legal to reproduce, duplicate, or transmit any part of this document in either electronic means or in printed format.

Recording of this publication is strictly prohibited and any storage of this document is not allowed unless with written permission from the publisher. Respective authors own all copyrights not held by the publisher.

We control the copyright and other intellectual property rights in this book. Subject to the licence below, all these intellectual property rights are reserved.

LICENCE TO USE THE BOOK

You must not in any circumstances:
a) publish, republish, sell, license, sub-license, rent, transfer, broadcast, distribute or redistribute the book or any part of the book;
b) edit, modify, adapt or alter the book or any part of the book;
c) use the book or any part of the book in any way that is unlawful or in breach of any person's legal rights under any applicable law, or in any way that is offensive, indecent, discriminatory or otherwise objectionable;
d) use the book or any part of the book to compete with us, whether directly or indirectly]
e) use the book or any part of the book for a commercial purpose.

DISCLAIMER

The information provided in this book is designed to provide helpful information on the subjects discussed and content herein are provided for educational and entertainment purposes only

Although the author and publisher have made every effort to ensure that the information in this book was correct at press time, without any errors and/or omissions, the author and publisher do not assume and hereby disclaim any liability to any party for any loss, damage, or disruption caused by errors or omissions, whether such errors or omission results from negligence, accident, or any other cause. Further, changes are periodically made to this book as and when needed. Under no circumstances will any legal responsibility or blame be held against the publisher for any reparation, damages, or monetary loss due to the information herein, either directly or indirectly. You agree that by continuing to read this book, where appropriate and/or necessary, you shall consult a professional (including but not limited to your doctor, attorney, or financial advisor or such other advisor as needed) before using any of the suggested remedies, techniques, or information in this book. The information contained in this book and its contents is not meant to be used, nor should it be used, to diagnose or treat any medical condition and is not designed to replace or take the place of any form of medical, financial, legal or other professional advice or services, as may be required. Nothing in shared in this book is intended to be any kind of advice. The reader is responsible for his or her own actions and agrees to accept all risks of using the information presented inside this book.

TABLE of CONTENTS

WICCA FOR BEGINNERS 1

INTRODUCTION 2

CHAPTER 1: THE HISTORY OF WICCA 4

CHAPTER 2: WHAT IS WICCA AND HOW TO BECOME A WICCAN 14

CHAPTER 3: WITCHCRAFT 26

CHAPTER 4: ESSENTIAL INFORMATION ABOUT WICCA 36

CHAPTER 5: ESSENTIAL GUIDE TO HERBAL MAGIC, OILS, AND CRYSTALS 53

CHAPTER 6: ESSENTIAL GUIDE TO CANDLE MAGIC 68

CHAPTER 7: ESSENTIAL GUIDE TO SPELLS, RITUALS, AND MAGIC 83

CONCLUSION 98

WICCA BOOK OF SPELLS 101

INTRODUCTION 102

CHAPTER 1: WHAT IS A SPELL? 103

CHAPTER 2: THE STRUCTURE OF A SPELL .108

CHAPTER 3: COMPONENTS OF A SPELL.....123

CHAPTER 4: TIMING A SPELL PROPERLY ...135

CHAPTER 5: A SELECTION OF SPELLS.......142

CHAPTER 6: WHERE TO GO FROM HERE....216

CONCLUSION 219

WICCA CANDLE MAGIC......... 221

INTRODUCTION 222

CHAPTER 1: ORIGIN OF WICCA BELIEFS AND THE IMPORTANCE FIRE 224

CHAPTER 2: CANDLE COLORS AND THEIR MEANINGS 236

CHAPTER 3: SELECTING THE PROPER CANDLES, PREPARING YOURSELF, AND PREPARING YOUR SACRED SPACE 246

CHAPTER 4: PREPARING YOUR RITUAL CANDLES 263

CHAPTER 5: SINGLE COLOR CANDLE SPELLS 282

CHAPTER 6: MULTIPLE COLOR CANDLE SPELLS 315

CONCLUSION 344

WICCA MOON MAGIC 347

INTRODUCTION 348

CHAPTER 1: WHY THE MOON IS MAGIC 349

CHAPTER 2: THE WICCAN MOON 373

CHAPTER 3: PHASES OF THE MOON 396

CHAPTER 4: MAGICAL PROPRIETIES OF THE LUNAR CYCLE 398

CHAPTER 5: MOON'S CONNECTION WITH OCEANS 401

CHAPTER 6: PREPARING FOR YOUR SPELLS AND RITUALS 403

CHAPTER 7: ALTAR AND TOOLS 419

CHAPTER 8: LUNAR GRIMOIRE - SPELLS .. 427

CHAPTER 9: MEDITATION AND DREAMS ... 452

CHAPTER 10: TABLES OF CORRESPONDENCE 462

CONCLUSION 465

WICCA CRYSTAL MAGIC 469

INTRODUCTION 470

CHAPTER 1: HISTORY OF CRYSTALS AND STONES 472

CHAPTER 2: USE OF CRYSTALS IN VARIOUS ANCIENT CULTURES 482

CHAPTER 3: CRYSTALS IN WITCHCRAFT ... 508

CHAPTER 4: PROGRAMMING YOUR CRYSTALS 531

CHAPTER 5: GUIDELINES FOR SUCCESSFUL SPELLCASTING 547

CHAPTER 6: CRYSTAL SPELLS 560

CHAPTER 7: CRYSTAL HEALING. HOW CRYSTALS INFLUENCE AND ENHANCE YOUR LIFE 580

CONCLUSION 594

WICCA HERBAL MAGIC 596

INTRODUCTION 597

CHAPTER 1: WHAT IS A HERB? 598

CHAPTER 2: WHAT IS HERBALISM? 610

CHAPTER 3: WICCA AND HERBAL MEDICINAL

MAGIC 616

CHAPTER 4: HERBS – MEDICINAL QUALITIES
.... 631

CHAPTER 5: HERBS – MAGICAL QUALITIES
.... 646

CHAPTER 6: GROWING A GREEN WITCH GARDEN 664

CHAPTER 7: HARVESTING AND PREPARING HERBS 671

CHAPTER 8: BEGINNER SPELLS 680

CHAPTER 9: INTERMEDIATE AND ADVANCED SPELLS 693

CHAPTER 10: SPELL BOOK 701

CHAPTER 11: SPELL WRITING 726

CONCLUSION 752

WICCA

Wicca For Beginners

The Ultimate Guide to Witchcraft, Wiccan Beliefs, Traditions, Rituals & Magic. Starter kit for the solitary practitioner (Candles & Herbal Spells, Magical Herbs, Oils & Crystals)

ESTHER ARIN SPELLS

INTRODUCTION

Congratulations on downloading Wicca For Beginners and thank you for doing so. You have taken the important first step in discovering the art of Wicca and what it takes for you to become a Wiccan yourself.

We appreciate you choosing our book as your stepping stone into your practice and we hope that you will find that our book has streamlined and made the process easy in discovering more about the Wiccan culture. In our book, we will take you step by step to discover what Wicca is, starting with its history and work you all the way through sample spells and knowing how to use candles, herbs and crystals when practicing your new Wiccan faith.

The following chapters will begin discussing the origins, the new and old versions of Wiccan religions, the spirituality of Wicca and an introduction to The Great Rite. We will then delve into the stories of both the known and the unknown, the traditions and core beliefs of the Wiccan culture. Next, we will cover the history of witches and witchcraft, magic and science and the differences between what was old and new about magic. We will wrap up covering essentials guides for Wicca tools, living a magical life, simple spells, and different lists of things you can use in your practice such as the meanings of colors, how to make your own candles, and how to make a circle in step by step instructions.

We know that there are plenty of books on this subject on the market, thanks again for choosing this one! We hope that you find yourself elated with your choice in books to represent this topic and getting to know it on a deeper level. We have made the best effort to bring you the most up to date and researched information so that your journey through Wicca ... is Magical.

CHAPTER 1: The History of Wicca

I Wicca is commonly referred to as the "Old Religion". Many believe that Wicca is a custom that has survived in cultures through many years, as it was kept concealed during the time that was considered the shady years in the Christian Church's oppression of the Pagans until it was once again able to rise into the everyday life of light during the modern times.

The idea that Wicca has an ancient tradition is what initially attracts a lot of people to the practice. In a day and age that is noisy, dedicated to materialism, and industrialized a lot of people can feel a deeper connection and desire for the elder wise and more spiritual life to live. Most of what people hear about Wicca is hearsay, but what can we say we really know as fact about Wicca?

Wicca is known to be an ancient practice of our ancestors and a very old religion, but this simply is not true. The earliest known date of Wicca is back in the mid-20th century, though it has been said that its influences can be drawn from dates that are much older than that.

Usually, the history of Wicca is known through two different stories. The first is that, of the actual story, where it was founded in the years between 1940 and 1950 in the country of England. The second is rather more of a legendary story in that it is an eternal mission to comprehend and join with a foundation of the godly at the core of Nature's secrecies and ideologies. The first version of the story can be backed by the facts that have been written down in history; both are equally important in truly understanding how the

Wiccan religion came about.

The birth of Wicca is attributed to an English town's worker, who was also known to be an author and an occultist. His make was Gerald Gardner. Gardner was born in 1884 and traveled all over during his young years, and became absorbed with the subjects of folklore, anthropology, and archaeology, and eventually a level of spiritualism and different topics that are enthusiastically accredited to the occult. He spent a lot of time during his life in Asia, which is the place in which he came to know of occult principles and enchanted practices. Gerald was known to be a member of a lot of different groups and civilizations that were known to like these interests, which included the Order of the Rosicrucian that he became a member of in 1939. It was in this group that he met some of his friends that were members in an even more private deep-rooted circle who were told to have exposed to Gerald that they were actually a small witch coven. He began his initiation in September of that year into that same coven.

Early in the 1920s, which was several years later, a popular theory came about and was traveling in the anthropology circles. It was about an ancient religion of the pagans that had been nearly wiped out due to the increasing popularity of Christianity, but it was still known to be in practice in clandestine among small groups of people throughout the western part of Europe. An anthropologist at the time pushed the theory forward, called this religious a "witch-cult" and continued to assert that the persisting people who practiced were organized into covens that likely had 13-members.

When Gerald met the group known as New Forest, he was certain that this group was one of the outstanding covens of this early faith that predated Christianity, and he wanted to do whatever he could make sure that the cult of witches could survive into and through the coming century.

Covens, which ideally have anywhere from 10-15 members are entered through a ritual of initiation and typically bring into line with one of numerous group relations.

As the members of a coven get good at the rehearsal of magic and are becoming more conversant with the rituals, they graduate up to two different levels of a required initiation. There is also a level three of initiation, and this is reserved for those who are interested in entering priesthood. In the system known by Gardner. Importance is assumed to the priestess, and the privileged in this community trace their own level of expertise through a linage of priestesses back to the group in which Gardner was a member.

Although there is a level of difference within the community of Wiccans, many supporters of the religion share a universal list of practices as well as beliefs. They believe in the female Goddess, hold nature in a respective light, and grasp both polytheistic and pantheistic opinions.

There is also a Wiccan Rede, which most Wiccans accept as a code of ethics that says that "if it harms none, do what you will." Wiccans also believe in meditation, and they also have yearly rituals they partake in, celebrating the phases of the moon, and the solstice of summer and the vernal equinox, and most commonly known to outsiders as Halloween, which is commonly referred to as Samhain.

Wiccan rites include asking for help from the deities, practicing magic in a ceremonial way, and sharing a ritual meal. Wiccans typically refer to themselves as witches, which is very controversial to outsiders. Witches is a term that most people from the western world identify with Satanism.

Historic Satanism, which is also referred to as worship of the devil contains the certainty and adoration in the Devil and does not believe in God or Jesus Christ. As a result of this, Wiccans are continuing to completely deny any linking with Satan or any type of devil adoration. Wiccans also have tried to start relationships with other polytheistic and nature orientated spiritual communications such as that of Hindu and Native American cultures. Being Wiccan or practicing the Wiccan religion has nothing to do with the devil or evil worshiping despite what many outsiders of the religion believe.

This myth has been attached to the Wiccan culture for many generations, and it has not been until recently that you are going to begin to see that ideology shift as more people are becoming knowledgeable about what Wicca really is and what it stands for.

There were a projected 50,000 Wiccans in the western part of Europe and North America by 1980. There was a slowdown in the growth rate as the decade came to an end, but Wicca added an increasing communal reception, and it began to diversify to include many distinctions of Gerald's first traditions and rites. Because of this, more Wiccan group began to pop up that were autonomous of the Gardnerians, which included one Alexander Sanders led, who were the Dianic Wiccans and were known to see Wicca as a women's religion, and the equivalent Neo-Pagan crusade, as they had a Goddess to worship and was known to practice witchcraft but did not have the designation of witch for its people. There was a major controversy to develop in in United States in the 1960 and 70s which happened when a section of the Wiccans pulled away from Gardner's principles that clothes repressed magical mechanisms, and they decided that they were no longer going to practice without clothes on. Instead of being nude, they decided to wear robes and said that their beliefs came from the time that predated Gardner, and called wanted to start calling their group Traditionalists.

Wicca's ritual format shows influence from the late Victorian era occultism. There is not much within the rituals that do not show some kind of influence from earlier existing foundations. The mystical information of Wicca however, is stimulated by older Pagan convictions, an instance of which is the worship of past pagan gods, but it also has influences from the Buddhist and the Hindu religions. This is shown in the Wiccan principle of reawakening. It has been said by many novelists including in the works of Aidan Kelly and Francis X that Gardner actually made up the religion he said he had found. He changed the rituals of older traditions of witchcraft as he saw fit, and incorporated fundamentals from the theory of Margaret Murray, and the ideas that came from magic performed for ceremonies.

The workings of the original ceremonies that were brought about by Gardner is not consistent; it is more like a patchwork of substitutions or expansions within the unoriginal material. One element that is characteristic is the use of ritual binding and scourging as a way of accumulating a delighted daze for magic being able to work. One author claims powerfully that this type of Wicca is not a reflection of sad, sexuality that is masochistic but that it is simply a technique of exertion that is a substitute to medicines or other more energetic approaches. Heselton is another author who believes that Gardner did not author the rituals of Wicca himself but received them as a show of trust from source that was unknown. Gardner admitted the rituals he did get from Old Dorthey's coven were very disjointed, and in order to make them make sense within the religion, he had to make them make sense with other ideas. So, as you can see there is a lot of criticism and bath and forth in regard to the real history of Wicca and how it came about, but there are facts that have been authenticated in which we are able to follow in order to trace back a certain amount of time in order to see the true history of how Wicca came about.

Moving through its second generation of practice, the belief was beginning to fade that Gardner had gotten the set of witchcraft ceremonies and observations that had been given on through custom with ties that were continuous to the pre-Christian paganism.

Many Wiccans were known to cite work from Margaret Murray to support their belief in the early roots of their belief; most now understand that Wicca began with Gardner and those who were there working with him. As the 21st century started, Wiccans were located through the Western world that was English-speaking d across most of Europe in the northern and western parts. There are two worldwide partnerships that serve the larger Wiccan community, the Pagan Federations and the Universal Federation of Pagans.

There is a timeline in which we can follow to get a better understanding of the development of Wicca. Hereditary Witchcraft began in the 1950s. Gardner was not the only person at this time who was claiming to be a member of the surviving cults that were practicing Wicca or witchcraft at the time.

They claimed to have been brought into a cult by their familial people and labeled themselves as following "Hereditary" or "traditional" forms of Magic, while Gardner, was talking about a contemporary and unacceptable form of Witchcraft. The politics and practices were very similar to Gardner though, and some of the contemporary groups label their belief as being a system of Wicca, while others in the religion claim it is dissimilar and it is more along the lines of traditional witchcraft.

Within a limited number of years of Gardner bringing about the craft, Wicca had expanded out of England into neighboring countries of Scotland and Ireland. Though, in the 1960s, it also because to reach out a lot farther around the world, in the countries of Australia and the United States that were also English-speaking. Wicca was accessible in Australia because of the established presence and knowledge of the indigenous philosophy with its pagan beliefs and practices.

Wicca found its way to the United States by way of Englishmen who migrated to the United States. The first coven was founded in New York by a couple who began to be a correspondent for Gardner. The coven was later managed by another twosome who are known to have grown the Book of Shadows and added additional levels of initiation than there were previously essential. Wicca would not get a footing in other countries until the 2000s, and these countries were places such as India and South Africa.

One of the most commonly known Wiccan rituals is that of the Great Rite. This is a Wiccan ritual involving symbolic sexual intercourse with the sole purpose of drawing energy for the powerful connection between men and women. It is not a very common ritual as it is used when the coven is in need of a powerful spiritual intervention to help them through a problematic or difficult time. Most often this ritual is performed by the High Priest or the High Priestess, but other people are able to be elected to perform the Rite. There are a variety of occasions in which a coven may feel the need for the Great Rite ritual to be performed. This includes the festival of Beltane on or about May 1st in the northern hemisphere and also on November 1st in the southern hemisphere. In some traditional of Wicca holy sex is a part of the divine practice.

The original Wicca brought out by Gardner is absolutely a fertility religion in its first form, so it is comprehensible that at someplace along the way you may meet situations to sexual activities, whether they are physical manifestations or just symbolized. Implied in terms of these acts means symbolic.

An example of this would be the linking of an athame with a chalice. The Great Rite is the most common ritual sex that is often referred to. It is the ritualized sexual connection between the god and goddess.

Although the Great Rite is the most commonly known idea of sex that is ritualized, not all sex done in ritual is the Great Rite. Ritual sex has many different drives outside of the Great Rite as it can be used to raise the liveliness, create enchanted influence or find a renewed sense of mystical closeness with a companion. If all acts of love and pleasure are ceremonies, then positively sex in ritual can be seen as a sacramental performance of love.

It should also be known that in some charming traditional, sensual release such as masturbation is a flawlessly lawful way of raising the enchanted vigor. Because ritual sex is known to be a holy performance, any form of this type of sex should be consensual.

In many traditions, it is likely to be performed in private and in all societies, it is solely performed by adults. Some traditions of Wicca require actual contact to be achieved as part of what is referred to as a Third-Degree elevation, in which it is only performed by a high priest and high priestess.

However, in other civilizations, the act is almost always symbolic and never portrayed. Usually, if ritual sex is being completed, it is between two individuals who are already a part of a consensual sexual current bond and are of equal power to one another within the coven. It is practiced this way because the ritual sex between two Third Degree people would have very good schism to it but ritual sex between a Third Degree and a Neophyte, for example, would stretch the balance of power too far. A good example of this would be if two teachers were in a consensual relationship and a teacher in a relationship with a student.

Ritual sex is never usually a part of an initiation into a coven. It is uncommon for a coven to demand sensual initiation as a way to gain membership. There are, naturally, a number of different issues as play in this situation. Consent is at the forefront of this.

Think about it, if somebody is being forced into sex as a need of being initiated, can one say that they are really consenting? It is important to keep in mind that ritual sex- the Great Rite or some other kind- is typically a precise, sacred act that is done only by persons within the coven who have considered and educated enough about the ritual to feel relaxed about acting it and only performing it with a partnering which they are trusting.

In the symbolic version of the Great Rite ritual, there are several items that can be used to represent the Goddess. A ritual cup is usually the most common, but a ritual bowl or even a cauldron can be used. The item that is corresponding to the God in the symbolic ritual is usually an athame, a wand, or sword. There are many different variations that can be used and conducted for this ritual.

There is no single right away to have a symbolic Great Rite ritual.

One final thing to note about the Great Rite is that the concept of straight or gay is not an issue within the Pagan communities in general. Same-sex encounters are common in nature and being that they believe humans to be a part of nature, it is seen as common practice to everyone. The Great Rite is not about the "physical" aspects of a man and women but rather their expression of energy as a God and Goddess. This can easily be accomplished between couples that are of the same sex just as it can be expressed through couples that are heterosexual.

For an extended time, Wicca was understood as just being a cult. However, in recent rise with the rise of private practitioners who are describing themselves to be Wiccan, the belief went from simply a cult of unknown to being known as a widespread and publicly recognized religion. Groups began to form the characterize the Wiccan communal, such as one named the Covenant of the Goddess, founded in 1975.

Wiccans are also now appearing on various television documentaries. In the USA, the court case of Dettmer v. Landon in 1986 recognized Wicca as an official religion, and consequently must now be preserved as such in lawful circumstances.

Wicca has come a long way in terms of once being known as a devil-worshiping cult to a full-fledged and recognized religion, and many only see the religion growing from there. When Wicca is held in the eyes of those who see it as a way to give thanks to nature, Wicca is brought into the light in which Gardner wanted it to be. Not all magic is dark magic, and Wicca helps outsiders understand that there is more to magic and spells than putting hexes on people who have wronged you. You probably found your way to this book because you are interested in learning more about how to become a Wiccan yourself, and in the following chapters we will help you do just that.

Chapter 2: What is Wicca and How to Become a Wiccan

All around us nowadays, there are millions of people and collections which are working numerous methods of the Wiccan religion through the United States as well as the entire world.

There are many different names by which the Wiccan religion has come to be known by including "The Craft," "Wicca," "Benevolent Witchcraft," and "The Old Religion." It is also known to be a varied and regionalized faith that is now a part of what is known to be contemporary Paganism or Natural Spirituality. There are also many different forms of the Wiccan religion.

Some of these include Hereditary Tradition, Gardnerian, Alexandrian, Celtic, and British Traditionist, just to name a few. Within the Wiccan culture, much like other Pagan traditions, religion is practiced by individuals as well as a variety of different types of groups.

Groups are known to differ in scope, purpose, construction, alignment, ritual performs, symbology, and many additional ways. There is known to be even more difference in those that are practicing individually compare to those who are active in groups.

Some Wiccan civilizations are initiatory while many others are not. Initiatory performs can vary from custom to custom and include beginnings that are done by divinities and mystical assistants through things like dream expeditions, dreams, self-initiations, and those initiations that are done by educators and collections.

Although there are a lot of alterations, there are also a lot of similar performs and attitudes that Wiccans and other Pagan groups tend to have in mutual.

Each group is known to have a deep admiration and respect for nature, and all group seeks to live in agreement and peace with the rest of the world. A lot of members are known to have personal relationships with various animals, plants and different life forms outside of humans. They are all known to respect the cycles of nature.

Many of these groups and also individuals are known to do rituals at the New Moon as well at times of the Full moon and also have rituals that are done during the eight different seasonal festivals that are known as Sabbats.

Sabbats are usually spaced up to six or seven weeks apart throughout the year and are usually known to coincide with the Solstices, Equinoxes and sometimes the days in the middle that are typically called the "Cross Quarters." Halloween, which is recognized to the Wiccan community as Samhain, is the New Year in most of the Wiccan and usually many Pagan civilizations.

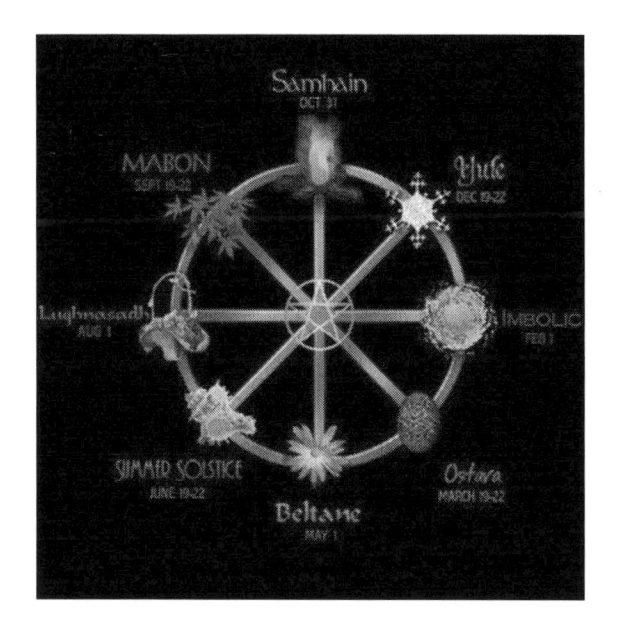

The Wiccan faith is described as being pantheistic because the Divine is seen to be the presence that is everywhere and within everything. Since they take on a natural existence, they can also be seen as animistic in that every human, animal, rock, tree, stream, and other beings that are known to be within wildlife is also seen to have the Divine Spirit inside them.

Wiccans are known to reach deep within themselves and their rituals to feel like they are closer to the surrounding earth in a way to feel like they are getting closer to the spirits they believe in living among them.

This is an element of the Wiccan religion that most closely resembles the Native American tribe religions in which they also believed the spirits lived within nature and did they best to preserve their relationship with the beings around them.

Wiccans are known to honor the Natural Elements, that of Earth, Air, Fire, Water and Spirit, and the directions that are associated with them, North, south, east, west, and center.

They are honored in the sacred circle in which most of the rituals are held. They are honoring the elements because they are the spirits that help guide the rituals of being successful. There are a variety of different rituals that honor the elements such as reflection, requests, music of movement as well as the thoughtful use of the enchanted tools.

Wiccans are able to develop their abilities within intuitive realms as part of their spiritual practices. They are able to practice magic as well as direct psychic energy that helps with healing and other helpful purposes both for themselves as well as the coven as a whole.

In the Wiccan religion all of the Wiccans who partake in the practicing of the religion all abide by the Wiccan Rede, which is their own form of what we can consider the Golden Rule, in that it is a central ethical law for everyone who is practicing, "An it harm none, do what you will"

Essentially what it means is that so long as the religion and rituals you are practicing are only helpful and never hurtful, you are free to do as you wish when you are in your practices of the Wiccan faith. Contrary to popular belief, there is never a time that Wiccan would consider using their rituals and magic practices in order to hard someone or something intentionally.

Wiccans are all about using their power and religion for the good of the world, and only practice what brings them peace and connection to the natural world.

Most Wiccans believe in the idea that whatever enchanted power is sent out comes back to the dispatcher in a magnified state. As mentioned above, Wiccans do not use their powers to perform wicked magic, and they definitely do not respect the Devil, which is known to be the Christians anti-God. The Wiccan religion is known to come to us as a pre-Christian religion; it is not an anti-Christian religion. Many people who only know the myths of religion tend to get this confused as they still believe that those who are practicing Wiccans only do so because they believe in the anti-God and only worship him. We all know by now that this is simply not true. Luckily there are a lot more people out there in the world who are beginning to realize the true identity of those who call themselves Wiccans, and they are much more socially acceptable to be forward with their believes than they ever have been in the past.

Although a lot of the practices within the Wiccan religion draw from their ancient roots, which are especially Europe that was around before Christianity, they also exemplify a lot of the modern.

Numerous of those people who are practicing Wiccans are creating their own new chants, meditations, and rituals so that they are developing on what the religion once was and carrying it through the new world with new needs. They are also sharing them with the others who are practicing either on their own or with their own covens, through publications and written corresponding or even face-to-face gatherings of covens at festivals, conferences and conventions that bring all of those people who are believers in the Wiccan faith closer together so that they can expand on one another's knowledge and grow stronger together. This is something that has become new to the faith as before many Wiccans did not have the ability to interact with others that were of the religion outside of their own coven. If they were to move away from their previous coven it would be harder for a Wiccan to find out about other covens as there was not much correspondence going on initially. Now with technology, it makes it a lot easier for all covens to connect and make each other feel welcome. It also helps those who are practicing individually to find local covens by them if they feel as though they are needing the strength that numbers can provide them.

The Wiccan society have their own view if the Deity that they know of as the God and Goddess. To those that are Wiccan, the God and the Goddess are the male and female essences of the life force that is all encompassing and responsible for all creation. This includes the cycles of life and death on Earth as well. They are typically flattered at the table during all the Wiccan rituals and usually quite frequently throughout enchanted effort as well because they are the supreme deities. Ancient cultures are known to have worshiped a Sky Father and an Earth mother, and the same is true for a modern-day Wicca as well, to a certain degree. Wiccans believe that each deity has power over certain aspects of existence, and it is through their union together, as god and goddess, that life on Earth is created and sustained. Wiccans believe that both are powerful on their own as they each are responsible for giving us one part of the earth on their own, but they also believe they are so much stronger together. They are worshiped so devoutly because without the god and the goddess the world would not be what it is today, and it would also not be sustained like it is without the power of them working together.

This is also part of the reason why the Wiccans believe in the highest members of the coven to be both male and female so that the joining of the two together in ritual ceremonies will be at peak power and do the most good for the community.

The Goddess is the feminine half of the all-encompassing force of life, and she is related to both the Moon and the Earth. Because she is related with the moon, the Goddess of Wicca rules the evening and in turn the ocean currents, as well as the procreative sequences of all the females and the realm of the human essence. In most of the Wiccan traditional readings, the Goddess is known to take a three-fold form, which is how she has also been come to be known by the name Triple Goddess.

Each of the three individual aspects, all with their respective names of the Maiden, the Mother, and the Crone, are aligned with the phases of the Moon cycle as well as its orbit with the earth.

These phases are known as the waxing, full and waning phases. In this water element, the Goddess is also associated with human elements like emotion, intuition, and wisdom that comes to us when we are practiced in engaging with our shadow side.

These essential aspects of human life come from being able to get in touch with another side of ourselves that is not necessarily always shown to the people around us. Intuition also comes with some level of experience in which you are able to feel if you are getting into a situation in which you are in danger, or you can tell if a person is lying to you.

Wisdom also comes with time age and experience and the mother Goddess allows us to hold onto what we have learned and use it in our future selves to move forward and be successful while also sharing what we have learned from our experiences with others.

As she also represents the earth, she signifies the beached and bodily vigor that all of natural life in all its different forms to take a deep root into the earth and flourish. This includes domesticated animals, fields, and crops as well. The Goddess is known to be both the mother and partner of the God, and together in their earthly series of establishing, growth and return to death save the Wheel of the Year continues to turn, and the clear away the old in order to make room and bring forth the new.

This is a timeless co-creation between what we know to be the divine pair of the Goddess and the God. This is usually why a lot of religions refer to the Earth as Mother Earth, and Wiccans and other religions alike always refer to the earth as a female entity.

Typically, as the Mother or the female entity it is the ruler of the elements of human beings that are softer and more fragile. That is why Wiccans believe she controls emotions as well as the reproductive cycles because giving life to a new being can be a fragile experience to some. By controlling the moon, she also controls the tide cycle that allows the earth to ebb and flows as needed to nourish the surrounding life forms that rely on the water from the oceans to survive.

On the masculine essence side of the divine, the God is typically associated with the Sun, whose ever robust light is measured to be one of the aspects of male vigor and energy that is essential for the development of all life as we know it.

The God, however, is also known to be associated with all of the animals in the forest that are horned, and with the masculine energy of hunting game that is traditionally needed in order for survival in the wild. The God can also be represented fully by two aspects of twins which are named the Oak King and the Holly King, in some Wiccan traditions.

These two known figures take turns ruling the year as they are representing the waxing and waning of the Sun as each season turns into another. The Oak King is known to rule during the light half of the year, as we refer to it as Spring and Summer, and the dark half of the year belongs to the Holly king, which we refer to as Autumn and Winter.

Being the ruler of the Sun is essential to the lives of all living beings as we know that if it were not for the sun we would not be able to survive life on Earth as we know it. This is why it is so clear to see that as we referenced above the God and Goddess are so powerful on their own as we need each of them in order to survive, but they are also much stronger together because we cannot have one without the other and expect total survival of all living beings, as all Wiccans believe to be true and strive for in their practices.

For many Wiccans, including those who are now practicing in modern days, within these God and Goddess energies that are all-encompassing there are countless ancient deities who had also existed since long before what is the recorded history of Wicca and when it began.

Gods and Goddess like Venus and Osiris, who predate the modern god and goddess of Wicca by more than a thousand years, have been essentially reclaimed over the past hundreds of years by those people who feel connected to them as a deity that is a living presence in their lives as they know it today.

Traditionally, these types of ancient gods and goddesses are incorporated into parts or what we know as smaller aspects of the God and Goddess. There are however some eclectic Wiccans who are more polytheistic in their practice than others, and these Wiccans may worship the ancient gods and goddesses in addition to the ones that are known to a Wiccan as the divine pair.

That is why we have mentioned many different aspects of the known and unknown of the Wiccan culture because there are many people who practice in their own way, but there are essential traditions and norms of Wicca that all those who practice partaking in.

It is important to remember the past of what Wicca came from originally but it is good of those who are transforming the religion to become more modern and in tune with the lives of the people who worship today, so that the religion can stand the test of time while also being brought to the light in a positive way so more people are accepting of it.

If you are interested in becoming more involved in the Wiccan community there are a few things that are suggested to do that will help you in your journey to discovering more about the Wiccan community on a more personal level.

First, off you should definitely begin by reading, watching and listening to the Wiccan publications, blogs, podcasts and videos on social media that are offered for free from a variety of very knowledgeable sources and are people who are respected within the Wiccan community.

There are many books about Wiccan that you might also enjoy, starting with The Spiral Dance by Starhawk; Drawing Down the Moon by Margot Adler; Paganism: An Introduction to Earth-Centered Spirituality by River & Joyce Higginbotham; and Wicca: A Guide for the Solitary Practitioner by Scott Cunningham.

These are just a few of the many books that are available from a very wide variety of sources. You should also consider looking into the Circle Sanctuary's online if you are looking for a more technology-based way of getting to know more about Wicca. You should also look into attending Pagan festivals, which is a great way to meet and mingle with a very wide range of people who practice the faith and are from dissimilar Wiccan trails.

One of the main, and the oldest recognized festival that is very well known between people who practice and even those who don't is the Pagan Spirit Gathering which is typically held around the summer solstice. You should also look into contacting others in your range who are practicing through your social media accounts, email and even maybe making in-person contacts. If you are not lawfully a grownup yet, you will want to get tangled with mature practitioners and also inform your parts first to get their permission.

Most groups, educators and festivals are not exposed to those who are under the age of 18 unless they get parental permission. This not only protects the child but the Wiccan community as well.

It is also good for you to take part in the offered classes, seminars and retreats to get a better understanding and new education involvements. Workshops and other training like it are offered by the Circle Sanctuary live and also online through podcasts as well as at centers you can travel to.

There are plenty of ways to get involved in the Wiccan and Pagan communities nowadays because of the popularity that the Wiccan community has gained in recent years. It is much easier as an adult to get in contact with those who are practicing in your area so that you can get with like-minded people who can answer any question you may have about joining the religion and maybe even a coven of your own.

It really depends on your preference on how you want to receive your information, but technology has made it really easy to get it both online and connecting you with people to get it in person as well.

It is also really a good idea to become a member of the Circle Sanctuary. Association is exposed to Pagans and those on pathways that are related to Nature Spirituality and those people who exercise methods of spiritually that include respect and respect for wildlife.

They also want someone who follows the Wiccan Rede, which is the code of morals that indorses the well-being for self, others, and the planet. If this is not something you feel like you want to do early on in your journey, you should consider spending time getting into nature and spiritually communing with it in your own way.

When you are ready and are feeling more connected with the earth and the elements, you should start doing some meditations and rituals that are published online and usually available for free. It is a good idea to keep a journal handy, so you can record your experiences at the moment while you are going through them, so you know what feels right and what you can change the next time you go to do that meditation or ritual.

Practice makes perfect and if you are ever feeling stuck or that you are in a low place, reach out to other Wiccans to help bring you up and back to your level of self so that you can continue on being the best Wiccan you can be while giving back to nature and connecting with it on a deeper level with your whole self.

As we mentioned above there are so many resources out there for you to get a better understanding of how to become a Wiccan and we hope you take the time to do the best research you can do so that you are fully prepared when it comes time for you to partake in your own meditations and rituals of the Wiccan faith.

It is important to immerse yourself in whatever information you can find so that you do not feel overwhelmed in your new religion and always know there are many Wiccans out there who are happy to help and lead you through the beginning initiations so that you stay on track with your practices.

The power is within you to grow and understand, and we believe that starting with this book is the right first step to getting to know Wicca for what it is and everything that it can be in your life if you allow it to be.

Chapter 3: Witchcraft

Witches have been illustrated in various forms throughout the world's history. They began as evil women with warts on their noses who were always hanging out around a cauldron of boiling liquid hexes. They then appeared to us as hag-faced, cackling terrifying beings who could be seen riding through the sky during the night on their trusty brooms while they donned their pointed hats.

In more recent years when pop culture took a stab at the group, enchantresses have been a compassionate, twitchy nosed residential housewife, a teenager in her awkward years learning how to control all of her new-found powers, and a trio of sisters who were charmed with needing to battle the forces of evil together, one demon at a time.

The more real version of the history of witches, however, is much darker and usually a lot more deadly, especially for the witches themselves. Witches never had a good reputation, and they are only brought into a good light in some of the more recent films that have been made about them.

One of the most positive views of witches in recent years within a film has been that of Practical Magic, which is a movie based on a family of female witches who learn and grow together as they learn how to handle both their human lives as well as their magical lives.

It has a very positive view of witches because it takes the time to debunk a lot of the myths that have been brought up about witches over the years and takes the time to show that most people have a little magic in them and it just makes a difference on how you choose to use it. The witches in this film never used their powers for evil; they actually use them to save themselves against the evil forces that are after them.

It is a great adaptation of a book about witches, and it's a great introduction on what it is like as a witch living among mortals and trying to keep a normal routine and schedule as a witch.

This movie was made back in the 90s, and since then there have been a lot more positive reactions to those who see themselves and identify as witches. As we mentioned before, though, this has not always been the case for witches throughout our history. We will begin by discussing the origin of witches.

The earliest witches we know of are those who were known to practice witchcraft. They castoff enchanted incantations and called upon their higher power spirits to help them solve a problem or to bring about change to a situation.

Most of the time, witches were just seen as Pagans who were worshipping the devil and doing spells to do the Devil's work for him in the human world. Many witches, as well as Pagan, were actually not doing anything at all like that. They were simply trying to be natural healers and were referred to as the wise women who were simply misunderstood for their chosen profession. Most witches who are true to their nature are not evil at all.

They simply feel a deeper connection to the spirit world as well as nature, and they use this connection to help rectify situations that have gone wrong, or to bring about the spirits power to make a negative situation a more positive one.

Early witches were seen to be truly horrific people and were often avoided by those who did not practice witchcraft. Usually, witches kept to themselves to avoid the unwanted attention, and that's how covens came about so that they had a group of like-minded people who they could worship with and not be judged for their practices.

It is not exactly clear when witches first came on the scene in our history, but there is one of the initial archives of a witch. It is in the Bible in the book of 1 Samuel, which was believed to have been printed between 931 B.C and 721 B.C.

This idea that was written in the Bible tells of King Saul when he went and sought out the Witch of Endor to help him beckon the dead fortuneteller Samuel's soul so that he could get the help he needed to defeat the Philistine army. Even in times as old as these witches were used to help others out in times of need when they were not strong enough to do it on their own.

It also shows witches in a positive light which is interesting because of all of the negative press they had gotten years after. The witch had the ability in this story to rouse Samuel, who then had the opportunity to prophase that Saul and his lads would expire. The following daytime, rendering to the story that was told in the Bible, Saul's sons both perished in battle and Saul was told to have committed suicide.

It is interesting that this is the story that was first discovered about witches because they are shown as someone who can resurrect the dead, which is not something that is commonly done by witches.

This is just typically a myth of the religion and not many Wiccans or witches for that matter are able to do such thing, and even if they were, typically they advise against it because of the bad things that can come along with it. Witches typically live by a rule that they should not mess with the natural course of life, so bringing someone back from the dead can only mean that something else has to happen in order to keep the universe in balance.

However, there are other Old Testament verses within the bible that convict witches, such as the often talked about Exodus 22:18, which speaks "thou shalt not suffer a witch to live." There are other instances in the bible to which it heeds a warning when it comes to witches and the powers that they possess.

The additional verse in the bible caution again divination, chanting or using witches to contact those who have already died and are gone beyond the earth. This shows the earliest times of the Bible as seeing witches negatively as well, so the story from above can be seen both as a positive thing and a negative one depending on how you look at it.

This is probably why those who were condemning witches in the early years took this approach because many people were Christian at that time and advised against any such religion that was not of the same faith. Witches stirred a lot of controversies because they did not believe in the Christian God like so many others did at that time.

It is important to note that even if you are of a different religion, everyone should be accepted as well as their beliefs. With this being the oldest written record of any such type of witches, the next history marker of witch history would likely be the hysteria that took over Europe during the mid-1400s.

This hysteria was brought on by a writing known as Malleus Maleficarum.

This was a time in our history that everyone was accusing everyone of being a witch. When many of the suspect witches admitted, it was frequently under torment. They likely confessed to a diversity of wicked performances that they were not even guilty of partaking in. Within the next century witch hunts became the new normal and most of the people who were accused of being witches, many who had not confessed to any wrongdoing were executed by either being burned at the stake, or they were hung in the town square for public executions.

This scene is one that is widely depicted in all of the stories and movies we have today in the early history of witches.

The Salem witch trials were absolutely the most popular of that time, as Salem was known to be the headquarters for most of the witches that were around at that time. There were so many people being accused of witches in that town and during that time that they were holding public executions on the regular.

This is an interesting point in our history because usually when there is a group such as witches who threaten the way of life that people enjoy, they are often punished in the most public and critical ways.

If you are reading this book, it is safe to say that you believe witches were around during that time. Think back to this time and how it would feel to be a witch during one of the most horrific times in the history of witches. Since then we have obviously grown from this and have been become more accepted, but we should all learn where the history of witches because so that we can take the opportunity to build a better future.

Between 1500 and 1660, there were up to 80,000 different people who were suspected of being witches and were eventually put to death during these years. More often than not, those that were accused of being witches were women, and hardly any men although some were, were accused. Around 80 percent of the female population was accused and were supposed to be working with the devil and filled with desire and other undignified emotions. Within Europe, Germany had the uppermost witchcraft execution amount while Ireland was known to have the lowest.

Although the Salem witch trials happened in the united states, it was also known to have a high rate of execution, especially for just one town inside of an entire country. What we learn from this information is that the more populated an area was, the more accusations they had of people being involved in witchcraft. It was commonplace for women to be the most accused because at that time it was not really popular for men to be known to dabble in witchcraft or performing spells.

This type of behavior was often accused of women who lead a more promiscuous lifestyle at that time.

With the book of Malleus Maleficarum, which was printed by two very well-respected German Dominicans in the year 1486, this was known to have been the starting point of the stirred witch mania to go viral across many different countries.

The book was written as the guidelines for someone to be able to identify a witch, hunt a witch, and also interrogate them into admitted of the witch activities.

This probably spurred this hysteria because many people would read the book and determine that all of their friends and neighbors had the same characteristics as the witches described in the publication and therefore they would go on a rampage accusing everyone of being a witch because of it.

The mass hysteria that was caused was so detrimental, and no one was honestly safe from being accused of being a witch during this time. The mass hysteria started in Europe before it made its way to the New World.

This publication was known to have labeled witchcraft as heresy, as it that it was not necessarily true. This also rapidly developed as the expert for both Protestants and Catholics in their regions to begin to try to flush out witches that could possibly be living among them and they just do not know who it was. For more than what seemed like 100 years, the book retailed more reproductions than any other book in Europe other than the Bible.

It was so widely popular that it was continued to be in print for a very long time was translated into a lot of different languages which added to the widespread ideology of the witch trials and executions. It was definitely a crazy time in our history to be alive and living in.

To cover more information about the Salem Witch Trials in the new world, it became a phenomenon here as the hysteria about witches began to die down in Europe. The Salem Witch Trials are one of the most well-known trials to take place in Salem, Massachusetts in 1692.

There are so many books and writings and movies about this time in our history that many did not even realize that it actually started in Europe many years earlier.

The Salem witch trials were known to have begun when two girls became extremely ill. They demanded to be witches and were suspect by many of their fellow citizen of practicing and meddling in witchcraft. Ultimately during the entire length of the Salem witch trials, 150 were accused of being witches and practicing magic, and 18 of those 150 were actually put to death. When the 300th anniversary of the Salem witch trials came around there was an event held in 1992 to honor the dead of the trials, as a park was devoted in Salem and a dedicatory was held in Danvers, a nearby town.

In 2016 the University of Virginal announced a new projected called the Gallows Hill project which was a team of people who were determining the exact execution place in Salem, where 19 of the witches were hanged. The town owns the place of the hangings, and they are establishing a commemorative site for the dead.

Massachusetts was not the first of the original 13 colonies that were obsessed with the idea of witches, however. In the city of Windsor which was located in the state of Connecticut in the year 1647, Alise Young was one of the first people in America who was accused and executed for being involved in witchcraft. Before the final execution in Connecticut was conducted in 1697, forty-six persons were suspect of sorcery in this state, and 11 of those people were put to death for the crime.

This information shows us how easy it was for the hysteria of witches to spread through the colonies of the new world. Many were affected, some more than others. While Massachusetts is the most well-known, places like Connecticut as well as Virginia saw their own fair share of accusations that lead people to their death alone with social annellation and many other things.

In Virginia, people were known to be far less frantic about the idea of their family members and neighbors being witches and practicing magic. In fact, in Lower Norfolk County in the year 1655 a law was approved making it delinquency to incorrectly blame someone for sorcery without having any proof of the fact that they were actually practicing magic. Still though witchcraft was definitely a concern for this population, but at least the law stopped any mass hysteria among the people, saving a lot of innocent people from getting executed for something they may not have had any part of. Out of all of the witch trials that happened in the new world, about two dozen of them took place in Virginia and may of them were for women between the years 1626 and 1730.

Although many of these women were accused, none of them were actually executed for the crimes in which they were accused.

One of the most famous witches of the time was Grace Sherwood, who lived in Virginia. She was accused by her neighbors of killing their pigs and putting hexes on their cotton crops. When more and more accusations were brought upon her, she was eventually brought to trial for witchcraft in 1706.

While the trial proceeded, the court decided to use a test of the water, which at that time was very controversial, to determine whether or not she was guilty. Her arms and legs were tied and then she was tossed into the river. This test determined that if she sank she was acquitted and if she hovered she was guilty of the crime. Once she was thrown into the water, she did not sink, and therefore she was considered guilty and was sentenced to being a witch.

Although she was not murdered for her accusations, they did however through her in jail, and she was in there for 8 years. As you can see, each state in the new world took their own approach to their witch trails while many were extreme not all of them took part in the executions of those that were accused of being witches.

There was also an ironic article that was allegedly inscribed by former president Benjamin Franklin about a witch trial that took place in new jersey. The article was printed in 1730 in the local paper at the time known as the Pennsylvania Gazette. This article that was written brought light to the ridiculousness of some of the accusations that came about of people practicing in witchcraft. After this article was published, whether it had some influence or not, it did not take long for the mania to die down regarding accusing neighbors and friends of being witches.

There were many laws eventually passed in the new world that helped persons from being incorrectly suspect and sentenced to crimes they did not commit. These laws were the protection that a lot of people needed so they did not get executed during the trials or that they help keep people from looking at one another in an accusatory way.

Even today a lot of modern-day witches have a really hard time shaking the historical stereotype away from what they are trying to accomplish through their worship and rituals.

Many witches in today's age practice Wicca, which is now accepted as an official religion in both the United States and Canada. Wiccans, as we know, evade wicked and the arrival of evil at all costs.

The motto the uphold stand for damage nobody, and they all strive to live nonviolent and stable lives that are accepting and in tune with what nature delivers to humankind. Current day witches are still known to practice witchcraft, but there rarely is anything that can be considered menacing about it. Their spells and chants that they perform are often from the Book of Shadows, which is a 20th-century gathering of the understanding of sorcery and can be likened to the act of a prayer in other faiths.

Chapter 4: Essential Information about Wicca

Just about every known religion around the would typically use sacred objects regularly in its observances and practices. It could be a special outfit that is worn by the religious leaders or officiants, statues of the gods that are honored at shrines, candles of different colors, amulets, chalices or many other symbolic items that people have been using and creating and utilizing artifacts, or tools, in order to create and maintain the spiritual energy that surrounds them and to help keep the focus in their ritual practices.

Usually the use of different types of ancient artifacts helps those who are practicing believe that it will be easier to wake the spirits because many think that the artifacts still carry the souls of those whom they are trying to get in contact with. It is often said that they typically are enchanted because they were once used by the higher-ups in the society and they have kept their mark on the relics so that they can be passed down through the generations of people who will need them in order to perform a ritual or spell correctly.

Wicca rituals and spells often involve the use of several different types of tools which all have their own significance and related symbolic preferences, particular uses and even a specific placement in which it is used to be on the Wiccan altar during the ritual.

It has been said that a relic that is placed in the wrong position can either cause a ritual to not be successful or even bring about the opposite effect wanted by those that are partaking in the ritual. This is how important these sacred objects are to the success of the ritual.

Most of the Wiccan tools are used to focus and direct the spiritual energy that is being evoked for the purpose of connected directly to the divine spirit of choice. This is an understated but really important difference between the practice and the use of symbolic objects in other religions, however.

Wiccans are known to believe that they share in the co-creative powers of nature that are embodied by the God and Goddess, rather than feeling as though they are completely subject to the will of what the higher power wants. This means that the tools that are used by Wiccans in the ritual practices are both symbolic and practical, as each of these objects and each action that is performed within the circle of sacred energy with these objects is deliberately intended to direct and harness the force that is co-created between the divine power and the person performing the ritual.

Tools are used to both evoke and welcome the deities and the energies that are brought from the Elements. They are used to preformed magical work and also to protect against any type of energy influences that are unwanted just to name a few different uses of them. It is important to understand and recognize that the tools do not have powers themselves, but they only work to help as in being conduits of the person power the Wiccan has and uses.

The exact set of ritual tools are considered to be at the very core of the Wiccan practice and it will likely vary depending on the tradition. Some covens and those who practice in solidarity observe the highly elaborate rituals using a diverse array of different kinds of objects, while others usually like to keep things relatively simple, using some of the tools for multiple practices and functions in the ritual practice.

The most commonly talked about tools used in the basic rituals of both types of Wiccans are the cup, or the chalice as it is referred to, the want, the pentacle, the athame, which is a ritual knife, the censer, which is typically used for incense, and one or more candles that can vary in size shape and color.

An altar is found in a variety of different types of religious traditions. It is essentially a solid physical structure that serves as a place to honor the deities and/or ancestors, to make various ritual offerings, and to keep the sacred objects that are used in rites and rituals visible as well as safe. In the Wiccan tradition an altar has the chief purpose of being used to serve as a focal point in the ritual celebrations at the eight different Sabbats and the thirteen different Esbats, which are also known as the full moons, on the wheel of the year.

The Wiccan altar can be used at other times however such as during the times in which a Wiccan is working on their spells, during their meditation time, as well as in instances of prayer. Depending on how the Wiccan likes to practice and what part of their traditions they are working on. The altar may be used in a variety of different functions throughout the practice of the Wiccan. Usually Wiccans can spend a great deal of time at the altar in their practices, and it usually is a valued resource amongst all of them.

Since Wicca is typically practiced in a home or even outdoors, the Wiccan altar is often tucked in the corner of a room, where it can be easily accessed and pulled out to stand in the center of a created sacred circle during a ritual. The ritual tools that are being used vary depending on the ritual that is being performed, but they are always typically residing on the altar or stored somewhere close by then they are not being used.

An altar in its true form can take shape in many different forms. Depending on your circumstances, it might be a permanent structure in your home, or it very well could be a piece of furniture that can work as double duty in your home as a desk or a table.

When you are not doing your rituals and spells. The only real requirement is that it has a flat surface in which you can place your tools. Many Wiccans prefer an altar that is round in shape which can lend itself easier to move within the sacred circle. But square and even rectangle altars also work just as good and are just as popular.

Ideally most Wiccans like their altars to be made of natural materials like wood or stone but they do use metal as well. Wood is usually the most traditional material used, and it is generally inexpensive and very easy to come by in terms of locating it to make an altar for yourself. If you can find something that is oak or willow, these are the ideal type of woods to make a wooden altar.

This is a great resource to sue become most people do not have the affordability of going out and buying an expensive piece of furniture to use solely as an altar.

Do not worry if you need to temporarily use your coffee table or any other table in your house to begin doing your rituals. You can also find a very well price Wiccan altar kit online if you wish to do so. Remember going forward that any physical object charged with magical energy will be there to contribute its power to your ritual work. If you can get the object to be closer to nature, the better it will be, so try to avoid using objects that are made of plastics or other types of synthetic materials if you can.

Also, along these lines, if you are able to hold all of your rituals outdoors, you can think to use a large rock, an old tree stump, or some other natural feature outside that can be made into a makeshift table quickly can be used as your altar.

To many Wiccans this is the ideal situation to be in when performing magic and rituals.

Elemental Magic

The four elements are an essential part of Wiccan magick. Working within the elements can bring about very different effects as well as different results to your spells and your meditations. Elemental magic can be very tricky however if you are unfamiliar and you do not know what you are doing. As a reminder, the four elements are fire, water, air, and earth. In the Wiccan practice, the four elements each provide their own unique energy and power.

Since the beginning of Wiccan magic, people who practiced Wicca have attempted to harness and control the powers of each of the elements. This is not really what we want to achieve when we are working with elemental magic, however.

Wiccan should strive to be at peace with the elements, allowing them to flow through each of them and to give more internal power to us as being in our magical workings.

Air is all around us and a necessity for life on earth as we know it. It is usually the easiest element to begin working with because it is something that we are widely accustomed to. This does not mean that all the air in the world is friendly! We have all seen or at least experienced the force of hurricanes, tornados, and large gusts of wind but air can also be a gentle breeze or a light wind coming off of the ocean. Air is fluid in which it is constantly and easily change. It is known as the manifestation of intelligence, new beginnings, and freshness.

A change in the wind can be known at the beginning and end of new seasons, and it typically lets us know when there is going to be changed in the weather as well. If you want to connect to this element, you should find a place where you are able to breathe cleanly and deeply. Focus on what you expect to be the freshness of the air and the feeling you get deep within you when you get a deep breath in your lungs. There are different properties that the element of Air possesses. It comes from the direction of the East which is the place in which the sun rises. It has a projective energy style.

The color that is associated with it is yellow, think like the color of the sun and the sky when the sun rises in the morning. There are different rituals to perform using air. They can be associated with travel, study, freedom, and recovering lost items.

The forms in which it takes in rituals include throwing objects into the air, fanning objects and the art of positive thinking.

The season associated with the Air element is spring because this is the time of new beginnings and usually fresh starts as the weather gets nicer and the days start to get longer. The magical tool associated with it is the want. The symbols of it are the feather, incense smoke, and flowers.

The Earth element is in the world all around us. It is on the ground, mountains, dirt, trees, and grass in which we are surrounded by every day. The Earth is known to be a stabilizing force that grounds up, and upon that stability it also offers us prosperity and richness. "Mother" Earth is a place in which all of life as we know it comes from, and it is a working element that is important during rituals of business, stability, fertility, and knowledge. Any rituals, spells or workings that require the ground to be stable and firm or energy should call upon the element of Earth. It is also associated with darkness and quietness and can be called upon when the person doing the ritual is seeking those out. The direction of the earth is the north, and it has receptive energy.

The colors associated with this element is the color green. You can think of it as the color of the lush green plants that surround us. Rituals that can be performed using the Earth element should be centered around money, fertility, grounding, and employment. Ritual forms of the element of Earth including building in the sand as well as burying items in the ground. It is associated with the season of winter. The magic tool used to pull out the energy of this element is the pentacle.

Symbols that represent the earth usually include soil, wheat, leaves plants as well as salt. Using the energies form the Earth element are great for rituals in which you are looking to feel more grounded in your life if you've had sudden changes that were out of your control.

The element of water is another element that we cannot live without. It is an essential necessity for all human life to be sustained. Water comes straight out of the earth, and it can provide beginnings as well as endings. It can bring life as it turns mere seeds into plants, and it can end it with natural disasters and major storms, but no life can be continued and sustained without proper hydration from water. Water is known to cleanse, heal and it can also be a way to provide magical people a way to peer into the physic realm of the world in which we live.

Water is an element also known as the love element. It is known to ebb and flow, it can be poured over us, it supports us as we move through it to swim, and it can also be a power to keep businesses running. Water can be known to be emotional as well as purifying, and it should always be used in rituals that are for healing, cleansing, happiness, reflection and being able to obtain a psychic ability. The direction of water is from the west. It also has receptive energy.

It is associated with the color blue. This is likely because water as we know it can take on the color of the sky as it is reflected upon it on large bodies of water. Rituals to perform using air include purifying, love, dreams, sleep as well as relationships. Ritual forms of water include placing an object in water, which can include yourself by taking a bath or going for a swim or using water to dilute any other substance. It is associated with the season of Autumn. The magic tool that is commonly used with this element is the cup or a cauldron. The symbols associated with this element are shells, a cup of water and seaweed as well.

Fire is the final element and sometimes seen as the most powerful as well. Fire is destructive as well as creative. It is known to provide light. Heat, motion, and it is constantly active and always moving. We use fire to keep our houses warm, to cook our food, and use its light to keep the darkness away.

Fires are known to transform matter into ash and smoke, and it should be used in rituals of transformation. You can feel and sense the element of fire by standing in the sun.

Listening to the cracking and popping of a campfire and by watching the flame of a candle flicker with each passing wind. You need to be able to control the element of fire because it has a destructive aspect. This is very important when working with this element. If you lose control over the element of fire when you are working with it, not only can it bring negative results to your rituals, it can cause a lot of physical damage as well.

Fire is known to promote passion, change, creatively power and sensuality. Its direction comes from the south, and it has projective energy.

It is associated with the color red as we know most fires have the red elements to them. Rituals that you can perform using air are related to sex, courage, authority, remove negativity and add strength.

Ritual forms of fire include burning and or smudging. IT is associated with the season of summer. The athame is its magic tool. Symbols of fire include lava, flames and any object that has been heated.

With all of these ideas in mind, we want to remind you to start out slowly when you are working with the elements. You can start y getting to know the elements better in a way in which you are not using them during a ritual or spell. Begin by feeling the Earth beneath your feet and appreciate the grass between your toes. Feel the water flows over you when you are in the shower. Once you are comfortable with your connection with the elements you can start to introduce the elements in your rituals. There will definitely be extra power added to your workings when you do, and you will likely be surprised with the results of your rituals once you being to add elements to them.

Kitchen Witchery

Kitchen Witchery is a new form of Wiccan magic that has been infectious in new years as a new magic trail that can be taken, but it is actually one of the eldest kinds of magic known to mortals and Wiccans alike. Envision an ancient lady soaking basils for medicines or contribution thank you to the soul of the animal that she is cooking to eat, mindfully scattering salt crossways the edge of her home to shove off the spirits who are known to do evil and stoking the fires of the sacred earth as she invites the Goddess into her home for blessings. She would have been known to help her surrounding community with her skill set, and the shoe would also pass down what she knew to her daughter to keep this way of life alive. Kitchen witchcraft is also known as cottage witchcraft. It is known to combine hearth and the home with magic as well as enchantment.

The liens between the enchanted and the ordinary are usually indistinct as the Witch transports her magic into every lifecycle and the terrible everyday chores we all have to do.

It is not a ceremony use of magic in wildlife, but it is about hitting that trigger of magic int all you do, even if it includes your domestic duty of keeping your house clean each week.

Kitchen witches are known to rehearsal ways that have been approved down through generation to them, typically down their own domestic contour or if they are fortunate through a counselor. Many witches of the kitchen in modern days are self-taught because we today have much easier admittance to records and the internet and we can also find ways to encounter and say easily with others in its place practicing in secret.

Most kitchen witches these years are some form of the Wiccan culture because this religion typically embraces charmed as a part of flora as well as a share of lifetime. There are some kitchen witches who not exercise one exact belief but instead following their own trail and matching to their own mystical beat as they see fit. Kitchen witches have usually been womanly.

There is no law to say a man cannot be a kitchen witch however, it just naturally turn out this way since up till the more recent periods the women have been known to be the ones who tended the home-based and kept the fires red-hot. You do not have to be a permanent housewife or mother to be a kitchen witch, and you definitely do not need to be a woman.

Menfolk can be kitchen witches just as effortlessly as women. It all originates down to bring in love with being in your home an wanting to bring magic into your everyday rituals of life.

Kitchen witches are typically related to the outdoors – someone in a small village with a cabin out of the way of the town and into the woods somewhere. You can adapt the concepts of kitchen witchery however even if you live in the city.

It does not matter where you live your work with the things you have within your home. Age does not apply to kitchen witchery either. You can be ancient or new aged. With old-time traditional illusionists offspring would typically be skilled in both the domestic and the enchanted works from a really early age.

Totaling a vigor or forming a spell over the work they are doing becomes second nature for them and usually adds a bit of surprise to work that is rather boring in its own right. The home is the temple of the kitchen witch. The core of the internal sanctuary is obviously the kitchenette, and the core of the outside sanctuary is the garden. Some kitchen witches do like to ultimately set up a memorial or a working table in the kitchen or in the garden where they can easily troupe incantations and honor their divinities, but not everyone's does this.

In universal, the working countertops and benches can be your altars. Your cutting blades can work as your athame. Your pots and pans are your caldrons and your spoon of wood is your wand. You do not need anything more formal than that to be a successful kitchen witch. The home is not always seen as jus the physical house but it is more of a mystical home of sort, a type of priory in which you live the otherworldly life every day.

As of this, kitchen witchery inclines to succeed in keeping the home-based and the shrubbery in decent direction. He or she usually takes conceit to keep a sincere and happen home that is enchanted with magic. Do not think that you need land to garden however.

If you want to become a kitchen witch you can follow these easy guidelines. Begin by becoming more watchful and make yourself more current in the instant in which you are successful in your housework dusting and tasks. Become conscious of how charmed and vigor are going on in an instant.

Start to study magic more extremely, practice green magic, fold magic and vigor work. All magic is known to b engrained in the same philosophies and works within the same values but it just mainly contingent on how to request to use it. You should also begin to clean up your household and shrubbery more frequently.

It does not have to be a demonstration home but it should be a residence in which you feel warm and contented and somewhere that you find attractive. Your home should be considered your slight nature preserve in the large ecosphere in which we live. You also should start to plant a garden.

If you do not have land don't worry. You can keep a few posts on shelves and hang hangers around the border of a doorway with some sun contact. Grow heaps of aromatic plants and floras and potted plants and garden vegetables like tomatoes and cucumbers and peppers. These are the most planted in storage containers and coffee cans you already have lying around your house. Even if all you have access to is a windowsill, you can grow some herbs to get started. Be grateful for your nourishment.

Give thanks more often than just at anniversaries but for every suppertime and nosh you are allotted. Thank the essence of the animal in which you eat end be conscious of their authority as you take it in your form. Once you do these things more regularly before you distinguish it you won't be looking at the almanac speculating when the following Esbat is.

All in your life develop portion of your activities into enchanted and this can be a profusion of sanctifications and happiness into your life as well as your magic performs.

Wicca Moon Magic

The relationship between the moon and magic can be approximately labeled as a cycle of waxing and waning. As the moon produces we can work magical for increases but as it wanes we can work magic for the decrease.

If you are looking for to bring somewhat into your lifetime, you work with the waxing moon and if you want to get rid of something that is unwelcome in your life you will work during the waning phase.

These are a change point between these two contraries which is the full moon, a time of the yield as we rejoice what we have grown and established over the primary half of the lunar series. We then essential begin to freshen up after it is over and we identify and release what is no longer wanted in the additional half of the year.

WICCA

A Step by Step Guide on How to Make a Circle

The required tools need would be a casting tool. It can be a wand, athame, staff sword or even a finger. You will want to follow the following steps

Prepare your space. You will want to clean up the area from any debris and purify it by casting a simple spell

You will want to mark out of the physical area in which your circle will be or just keep in mind where you will want it to be. Some usually mark out with chalk of mark out the four corners of the elements with a candle or symbol.

Prepare yourself by becoming grounded and center and calling the quarters or just simply by taking deep breaths and spending a new minute meditation on what you are about to do. Then you will want to stand in the center of the circle area. Invite anyone you want to have in the circle with you who are planning to stay the entire time the cycle is there.

Raise your casting took and declare your intention to cast a circle all while declaring the purpose of what you are creating the circle. This can be to create a sacred place, to protect people within the circle, to create a realm between works, or to contain the energy raise during the ritual

Point your casing took toward the ground and start the point of your circle. Allow the energy to flow from your center through your casting tool and "draw" the circle on the ground turning your whole body clockwise as you do so.

When you have completed the work, you need to raise your casting tool once more and declare your intention to get rid of the circle. Point it at the same starting point and suck the energy back into it and return it to your center.

Return yourself and the space you are in back to normal by reversing your quarter call and grounding and centering yourself again by taking a few breaks or by walking away to get something to eat.

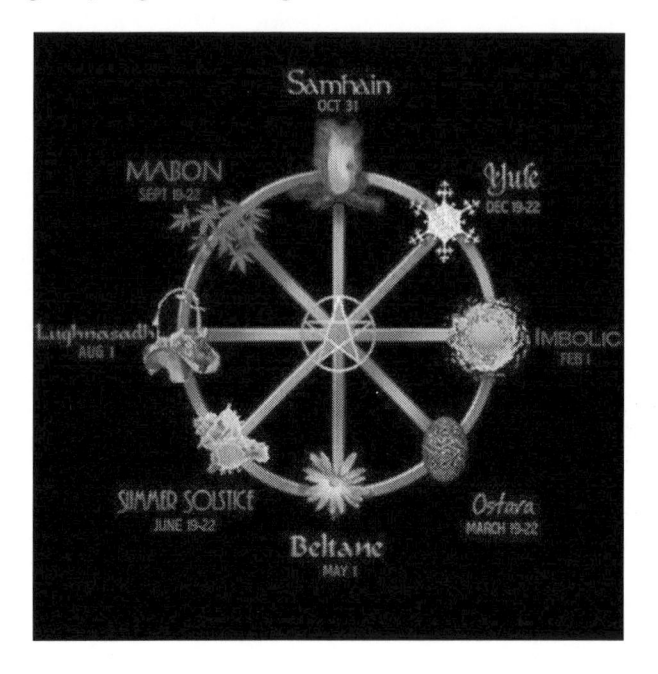

You will use a similar guide to the above when you are working to call out the elements.

Each callout begins with mediation and grounding, you will set your intentions, call the elements to the quarters, cast the circle, then you will evoke the elements, and then once you are done in your ritual you will close out just as we described above.

Chapter 5: Essential Guide to Herbal Magic, Oils, and Crystals

It can be said that because the Earth as we know it was originally developed as a plant kingdom long before the evolution of humans and animals, herbs are the oldest form of magic tools that are currently in existence. Plants have been known for generations to have healthy beneficial properties for both the spiritual and physical wellbeing of a person, and many different species and types of plants have been known to be used into the practices of those who are called healers, shamans and other types of medicine men and women. This is the origin of herbal magic as we know it.

In the times before medicine and magic were treated as separate instances, the times that physical healing was taking place was often most commonly also done with a ritual and prayer, so that the person who was being healed might be treated with an herbal concoction, likely a tea, as well as a ritual that was done with smudging and an incantation that would life the person up to the spirits and asking for a quick recovery from the illness or pain. In today's age, enjoying a cup of your favorite tea can still have more benefits than just those that are nutritional. Drinking tea can have emotional and spiritual effects on you as well.

The combination of both the healing and magical properties of herb make them incredibly powerful additions to modern-day magic and spells.

The study and the practice of herbal magic can prove to be one of the most rewarding forms of witchcraft one can hope to discover.

When speaking about the symbolism within magic, the plant embodies the power of the four classic elements of Wiccan spells as they work together to create as well as sustain life on earth for animals, plants and humans alike. Think of it as the beginning of a seed in the soil on Earth, where it will be embedded into the minerals needed to sustain themselves and find life from within. They will interact with the warmth and "fire" of the sunlight that is given to them which makes the process possible to convert carbon dioxide into oxygen, which is a direct reflection on the quality of air within the area in which the plant is growing.

Air has the ability to continue to foster more life in the form of win at it both stimulates the growth of things like stems and leaves and it also aids in scattering the seeds around to continue on the cycle of fertilization and developing new opportunities for growth.

All plants obviously need some amount of water to survive as well, even the cactus in the hot desert needs water from time to time in its growth and development. They will also play a really critical role in the regulation of the water cycles of the Earth as it has the opportunity to purify the water and help to move it from the soil and back into the atmosphere.

There truly is no better way to give an illustration of how the elements of the world can come together than in what is known as the magical existence of plants and what they have to offer.

There was one a very famous Greek philosopher of ancient times named Aristotle, who believe that plants had their very own psyches, which is typically a word that only describes a human quality of the soul or of the spirit. Many Wiccans and other types of witches today agree with his line of thinking and believe that plants can have human-like qualities.

Scientists themselves are even beginning to realize that plans actually have what can be considered to be a level of consciousness in which they can be aware of what is going on around them in the world to a certain degree. This is true because plants are known to be able to communicate as well as cooperate with one another when they are out in the wild, even if they are among different species. This meaning a bunch of wildflowers are able to grow within the same space as evergreen trees.

In a forest setting trees bushes and other plants are able to spread information and use their own form of communication with each other through the network they have created underground that contains a network of their roots as well as developing different types of fungi. This can be considered similar to what would be known as a natural internet as plants are allowed to exchange their nutrients with one another who are in need of it, which in turn is them helping one another to make up for any types of shortages in things that they need to survive.

This happens at various types of the growing seasons depending on the plans you see with one another. This is very similar to having to borrow eggs from your neighbor and then returning the favor to them later on with milk on top. Plants are also known to be able to warn one another about predators that may be lingering nearby.

An example of this would be that if there is a leaf that has been bitten by a predator insect, the plant will release specific chemicals that will be used to both repel the insect away from it as well as prompting the nearby similar plants around it to do the same, so they do not become prey to the predator as well.

The things that we are able to discover in this day and age service as wonderful types of pictures of now the plants on earth share intelligence with Mother Earth. Whether it be working with the roots or leaves of the plant, or maybe even the bark of a tree, a witch can trap the magical energy from within when incorporating herbs into their daily magical practice.

Cinnamon is the primary herb for love spells, but you can also use jasmine. Red peppercorns are the primary herb for sex spells, but you can also use chili. Mandrake is the primary herb for fertility spells, but you can also use patchouli. Irish moss is the primary herb for work relates spells, but you can also use thyme. Basil is the primary herb for money spells, but you can also use pennyroyal. Cloe is the primary herb for Protection spells, but you can also use mustard seeds. Bergamot is the primary herb for curse-breaking spells, but you can also use wild garlic. Nutmeg is the primary herb for luck spells, but you can also use red clover.

A Spell to Be More Open to Love

What you are going to need:

6 entire pieces

1 teaspoon of dehydrated mugwort

1 teaspoon of St. John's wort

1 teaspoon of jalopy ointment

¼ cup of chamomile florae

1 tablespoon of rose petals

A small bowl

1 pink candle

Instructions:

You will need to gather all of your ingredients and then place them on your altar, or whatever surface you are working with. Begin by illumination your candle and take a few deep smells into tranquil your attention. IN the boule, you will insert the mugwort, lemon balm and St. John's wort with the chamomile and mix it mildly with the tips of your fingers.

Then you will dispense the combination into a packet. Shake in the cloves and then the rose petals, you will then pull the packet shut. Holding onto the allure you will want to shut your eyes and begin to envisage your whole complete form being enclosed with white light, commencement in your core and dispersion out to the rest of your body. When you have held this vision of yourself for a few instants, let a easy pink light to begin to glow from your core as it circulates with the white light. Perform the next words three times:

As underneath, so overhead,

I release all hidden blocks to love.

As overhead, so underneath,

My healthy heart lets love to stream.

You will want to let the candle scorch out on its own. Keep your pouch near you as much as possible particularly when you are in bed at evening. When you are able to feel its vigor has helped its resolution for you, you can bury the magic or shake the herbs back onto the soil.

HERBS AND SPELL INTENT	Love	Sex	Fertility	Work	Money	Protection	Friendship	Curse breaking	Luck
Primary herb	Cinnamon	Red pepper	Mandrake	Irish moss	Basil	Clove	Valerian	Bergamot	Nutmeg
Secondary herb	Jasmine	Chili	Patchouli	Thyme	Fenugreek	Mustard	Gardenia	Wild garlic	Red clover
Crystal	Rose quartz	Garnet	Emerald	Tiger's eye	Malachite	Amethyst	Amber	Onyx	Obsidian
Color	Pink	Red	Green	Brown	Gold	White	Yellow	Black	Silver
God	Eros	Pan	Amun	Lugh	Ra	Atlas	Baldr	Osiris	Odin
Goddess	Aphrodite	Venus	Cerridwen	Demeter	Osun	Artemis	Hestia	Persephone	Athena

For many modern-day Wiccans essential oils are a staple element of ritual and in their magical practice. When they are using magical oils in their spells it is a traditional way of working with the dynamism of Nature to bring about the change you desire in your life. Since before the history of Wicca was being written down, many shamans and healer were known to use scented oils in the rituals as well as the magic and medicine. Oils were often used as ointments, Charms, incense and tinctures for almost every purpose you can think of. These oils were sacred and were made by heating the fragrant plant matter, like the leaves and flowers for example, in hauler oils made from olives and sesame seeds.

Some of the earliest oils that were fragment were made in this way were frankincense, which is known to help with pain, myrrh, and cinnamon, and they are all very classic scents that are still used today in many forms of the modern craft.

Oils are known to be more of a supplement than a main feature in a spell, unlike many other ingredients that are used. Witches are known to used oils to anoint their ritual tools, their crystals, as well as their own bodies. Oils are often used when trying to create an incense, which is particularly excellent for use in candle magic rituals and charm making.

Anything you want to do within your magical being can be enhanced when you incorporate oils. You can use a single sent or even blend different oils together to create your own unique smell. Scented oils are that derived from plants are powerful components in ritual and spell work for two main reasons.

One reason why is because they can contain the magical energies of the plants from which they are made, like flowers for example, as they are transformed into a state of liquid from a solid. Plants are living and breathing beings and with their own intelligence that is working in peace and harmony with the nature that surrounds them. Plants have magical properties as well, which can become highly concentrated when they are in the form of essential oils. This cannot be said about synthetic fragrance oils however.

They smell very similar to the real deal, but they do not have the natural ingredients are contained in the botanical oils. Many witches have used synthetic oils in the practices over the past few decades, but most agree the true power comes from the natural botanicals.

The second thing that we can gain from magic oils is the power of scent and the effect it can have on your mind. We understand this because we all have a favorite smell that can instantly turn us into a happy and relaxed mood.

The scents of myrrh and cedarwood or blends of lavender and clove seem to be known to instantly awaken something within us that is beyond our ordinary sense of smell and puts us into a different mind frame, one that can be considered more In touch with the invisible powers the universe has to offer and we are there for more able to become in control of them and have these powers achieve what we are aiming to get. The botanical oils can provide a tie that is directly between the natural world and the spiritual one in this way.

Eucalyptus is one of the most widely known healing oils and most varieties of it are natural to Australia. Koalas are known to eat the leave and the vital oil is widely prevalent for aromatherapy and herbal medicines.

A of lot people are acquainted with eucalyptus oil because it is an active element in cold medicines like VapoRub. Because the greeneries are very fibrous, it has also been studied to be used as a renewable fabric foundation. Eucalyptus is known to be available to witches as a dehydrated herb. An essential oil, as well as a smearing oil.

Typically, they do not use synthetics because it is not very expensive to produce. In magic, eucalyptus is known to bring new vigor to a state, to be able to settle doubts and qualms, and to also dismiss cerebral tightness and tiredness. It is the known herb to use if something or somebody has been worrying you. It is often mixed with other curative herbs for respite from both bodily as well as expressive cares and anxieties.

Eucalyptus greeneries can safely be scorched, filled, scattered and bloated into cushions and sachets. Smearing oils with eucalyptus are really good for purging ritual tools. There is a protecting magic within eucalyptus that is quick survived but is known to be really potent. It has the ability to remove all of the negative influences from the immediate surroundings as well as people.

Unlike some of the other known protective herbs, witches are known to use, eucalyptus gently makes a wall without aggressive or hurting others.

Eucalyptus is known to be used for a variety of different things even as healing properties for people who do not consider themselves as witches. Many candles are infused with the essential oil and are known to have stress relief properties especially when it is mixed with mint essential oil as well.

Many people use this combination of oils right before they go to bed, so it gives themselves an opportunity to rest before sleep and not have to stress about the next day or the things that did not get done earlier. Eucalyptus and mint are also known to have healing properties and people often use the oils when they have aches and pains in the joints as well as headaches.

Spells and Formulas with Eucalyptus

One way to include eucalyptus into your daily chores and activities is to make a brew of the leaves from eucalyptus, mint, and hyssop for cleaning your floors and doorsteps. Hyssop is known to be cleansing of evil, eucalyptus is known to heal the past, and mint is known to invite good luck. You can also put the leaves into therapeutic sachets and also eye cushions to reduce inflammation.

If you are looking to start the day with a new and optimistic viewpoint, polish a few drops of eucalyptus oil amid your palms and inhale in very intensely for a few moments. You can also do this in the shower as you let the steam fold around your body.

To relieve a cold:

Circle green candles with greeneries and husks and burn them into a hole, imagining the person or you as being totally well. It also helps to hang a small division of eucalyptus over your bed if you are sick as breath in deeply as you envision yourself waking up in the morning completely healed.

Healing Spell with Candle

You will need:

1 blue candle

1 smidgen of ground ginger

5 droplets of eucalyptus oil

The Spell:

Run a warm soak and then add in the ginger and eucalyptus. Light the blue candle and turn off all the illuminations. Enter the bath and immerse your body in the bathwater. Touch the waters emptying your body of all of the poisons as you say:

"Isis, Goddess who reconciles all

Releases this ___(cold, flu, etc.) from me and make me healthy again."

Chant this as you feel the poisons departure your form. When you are feeling wobbly, as you will, trough the tub and imagine all of the sickness wash down the gutter. You will then want to rinse your body as well as the tub with cool water as you think about the poisons washing off of your form and you sensation unrestricted of the poisons that were making you unwell. You will want to transport the candle into your area and directly go to bed, but keep your candlelit for a few more moments because you will want to think about yourself waking up in the morning feeling much better than before. Make sure to blow out the candle before completely falling asleep.

You can also add a few droplets of the eucalyptus lubricant to a cotton puff and keep it next to your bed for added measure.

If you have ever had the opportunity to hold a real crystal, you may have nee able to feel the mysterious sense of wonder and light that these stone tend to awaken within us. It almost seems like they are able to speak to a different part of ourselves that we do not get to see very often.

Crystals have been known for over a few thousand years and are used as talismans and in jewelry since well before our time. Today, crystals and other stones are also used as a form of alternative healing as well as for enhancing the energy in physical spaces, such as our homes, and for a wide variety of many other magical purposes. The term crystal in Wiccan refers to a wide variety of solid minerals not all of the mare truly crystals however. They all fall under the crystal magical realm however.

Only a few of the crystals that are known to be used in healing and magic. Wiccans and other types of witches are known to be able to understand the power of crystals and stones as they are with the power inherent in other natural happens like wind and a river that is continuously flowing. All matter whether we can see it or not has energy and all of the energy is somehow connected. The energy can be harnessed and sent out into the world through the energy field that is within crystals and those that are chosen to do magic with.

In the practice of Wicca, crystals and stones are used to mark the sacred circle before a ritual begins. They are also used to honor the gods. Magical tools like wants and pentacles are often decorated with crystals and they also have magical jewelry of all kinds. In magic, crystals are used to heal, and it can also be used to manifest wealth and love. They are still used as good luck charms, which keeps with the ancient traditions.

Crystals can be a very powerful element in spell work, whether it is with other ingredients or the main focus of the spell. Crystal magic also takes advantage of the fact that the stones are naturally colored, unlike candles and cloth that need to be dyed. Colors as they are vibrations of different lights, resonate with different aspects our of lives, such as love health and matters of money. Pink is the color of rose quartz, which is a color that is harmonizing, loving, and it makes a powerful force to draw love into your life. Likewise, the color green is known to be in association with abundance and making green stones like bloodstone or jade are really good with spells that involve money or matters of prosperity.

Spell to Reach a Goal

When to set your mind to achieving a specific goal, quartz is a powerful magic partner to help you crystallize your will and intent to succeed. Whether your goal is related to love your career or your health, quartz can accelerate the fulfillment of your wants and desires by boosting the energy that is being put into it. As you perform the spell below, it is important to not only think about the end result of your goal but to direct your energies of feeling successful and satisfied with your manifestation into the stone itself.

You will need:

1 pure clear quartz crystal

A small slip of paper

Small drawstring bag

Instructions:

Spend some time breathing deeply and clearing your mind. Focus on your goal. Write down the goal that you have on the small piece of paper. Remember you will ant to be very specific on what you want to achieve, and this will help to concentrate the energy on the true outcome you are wanting. If you want to get a new job for example, do not simply write down new job. Focus on the type of job you are looking for, and even write a brief but very specific description. Wrap the quartz up in the slip of paper. Hold the paper and the quartz in your hands. You will want to begin concentrating on your goal by seeing it in your mind completed. When you have imagined the most detailed and positive visualization, place the paper wrapped quartz stone in the bag and tie it shut while reciting the following words:

With the Stone of Earth and the power of Fire,

I manifest my heart's desire"

Always have the quartz close to you when you are working on activities that are putting you closer to your goal. This can be at your desk or in your purse or in any room of your house. Repeat this spell with every new goal and with a new quartz whenever you are needing it.

Chapter 6: Essential Guide to Candle Magic

Many believe that the use of candles in magic is one of the oldest forms of magic in the history of humans. This may not be technically correct, but it is certainly true that fire itself was sacred to pagan ancestors, who were known to honor their gods not only with candles but with torches, bonfires and even wheels that were lit with flames. The fire was one of the only original resources that were available which not only provided heat, but it also illuminated the surrounds when it was too dark to see on your own. Besides the sun and the moon for light, fire was really the only other constant reliable source for these things. It is easy to see why fire has become a symbol of a sacred power throughout history for everyone. The idea that fire has its own energies has long continued even after modern electricity was invented and became a way of life for all of us. Many religions around the world still continue to make their own candles and make use of them in formal services or even if they are just practicing lighting the candles for different reasons.

Even in the world around us that are not practicing Wiccans, they use the power of fire in their own ways often by wishes on candles on the birthday cake before blowing them out.

Since this custom is so familiar, this is probably why people drift to candles when they are interested in learning more about magic. There is something in the idea of the flame of a candle that brings about a happy surrounding and feeling of comfort.

People often fee at peace and enjoy watching the flickering light dance around on the walls and surfaces around it. Lighting a candle is actually one of the easiest ways to shift your reality and connect with the energies that are not seen around you, even if you are not interested in doing any type of spell work.

People often invoke a new sense of good feeling when they light a candle, and often it becomes a ritual for some just to do this simple task in order to wind down at the end of the day or add some relaxing scents to their evening bath. Depending on what smells you like there are a variety of different candles you can bring into your daily routine in order to start getting familiar with candles before incorporating them into your magic and spells.

There are many candles that are often infused with essential oils as well, and from what we learned above, it is a great way to infuse those oils into your life even if you are not interested in directly using the oils on your skin.

If you are someone who is just beginning on your journey through spell work, candle magic really is one of the best starting points. Wiccans who practice all types of magic are usually very happy to use candle magic whenever they can. It is a simple and straightforward use of magic, and basic candle spells can help you build confidence in your spell casting as well as strengthen your ability to focus and direct your energy right into what you intend to accomplish.

Honestly, it really is the power thought that is underneath both the most complex as well as the most simple forms of magic.

Specifically, we know that magic is the art of sending one particular though into a spiritual realm to be manifested and return backed to us on the physical plane. For someone who is just starting out in mafic, candle magic makes for helpful messengers. Your intention is the request you are making in the spell and you can send it into the candle to be the medium.

As the candle continues to burn the intention will disappear, leaving the material plane and joining into the spiritual one as it carries your message. This should give you a better illustration of how useful candles can be in your magic and spells.

Using a candle as a symbolic element, the candle is a well-balanced item that is a good representation of the Elements. The base and the wick of the candle represents the element of Earth, which is necessary to keep the flame grounded and able to stay lit for as long as you need it.

The wax, which turns into a liquid from a solid, and then eventually a gas, represents the characteristics of the Water element, in that it too has shapeshifting abilities.

The air element is in the form of oxygen and it too is necessary to keep the flame continuously burning and it is often visible to the eye through the smoke that is released when blowing the flame out. The flame itself is obviously the representation of fire. If you want, you can add in the element of spirit in that you are charging the candle with your intention and you have a tool within a magic real that embodies the whole universe in one simple and easy to manipulate item.

This is one of the main reasons why witches love to use candles in the practice because you can bring all of the elements into your spell with just one item, rather than having to bring multiple and maintaining them throughout your practice. Candles are easy to use and easy to store so they do not need to be kept out and taken care of in an intrusive way.

Along with the symbolic qualities of the candle, candles also allow us to work with the magical properties that color provides in a direct and focused way. For many years certain colors have been associated with different qualities or events, like love luck wealth and death. It does seem that even though all of the centuries of candle magic that the color red has always been associated with love and passion, which is the color of blood and therefore it comes from the heart. The color green is also almost always associated with abundance, which is usually in reference to money or the Earth during the time in which it is growing season. If you are looking to up your game in your spell casting by bringing in the color that is associated to your intention to direct the focus and spell, candles of color as designed specifically for this purpose. They are actually often called spell candles because of this. They can be found in just about any color and they are usually very affordable and easy to get. Some Wiccans have taken to making their own candles, but this is definitely not something you have to do, especially when you are just starting out.

In addition to choosing a color to enhance your spell work, you can also think about adding in essential oils to your candles as well.

Anointing a change with an oil that is magically charge, which can be a single oil or an oil blend of your choice, is really a long-standing tradition and it adds the magical benefit of scent to your ritual. Some people who are devoted to this kind of practice also like to roll their candles in the herbs themselves as a way to heighten the smell of the oils even more than before. You can also consider scribing into the sides of your candles with something that allows you to illustrate symbols that are known to correspond with your intention and what you are trying to accomplish.

These are just a few of the different things that you can do with candles in a simple way to bring more energy to your incantation and really focus solely on your intention without any distraction. You should see the benefits of doing all of these as it will direct all of the required energy directly into the candle so that it can act as the medium to send your message to the magical plane before it brings its back to your physical world to bring to you what you were looking for.

Once the spell has been spoken and the candle has been lit, a lot of people like to watch the size and shape of the flame of the candle move and shift as it brings about the success of the spell. If the flame is high and strong, that means that the manifestation of the intention will happen quickly, whereas if the flame is low and weak it will indicate that there is not a lot of spiritual energy to back your intention and bring it to fruition. If the wick produces black or a think smoke, it is said that there is active opposition to what you are trying to accomplish. This means that either in the physical world or the spirit world, there is something that is going to get in the way of you having success in your intention. If you find this to be happening with your intentions, you should take a moment to reflect upon what these outside forces could be, and why they are against what you have intending from coming true. It could be that you are looking for a new promotion, but your co-worker is striving to make sure they get it instead. There is a possibility for you to overcome the opposition by either having a conversation with that person or stepping your game up at work to prove you are more deserving than the person who is in completion with you.

When the candle has been burned all the way down to the base, it can be fun to read any of the melted wax that has been left behind. This is called ceromancy, and it is very good for people who are visually creative, as in those who typically see animals in the cloud shapes visions inside crystal balls as well as tea leaves in the bottom of a cup. As you begin to look at and study the wax, look to see if there are any shapes or patterns that you recognize that could be suggesting anything about the unseen forces around you that are moving and taking shape around the request that you have made to them.

Try not to overthink this part of course. You do not want to muddle your own energy with the energy sent out through the spell by trying to hard to look for information that may not even be there yet. You likely will need to do several of your own candle spells before you can get a grasp on understanding the sense of the flames and what the wax is trying to communicate with you.

Always remember to pay attention and practice safety when using candles in your spells. You should approach candle magic with caution and as long as you are sincere and focused in your work so that you are not attempting to harm anyone, you will see great success in all that you are able to explore within candle magic.

There are many options for additional resources if you want to learn more about beginning with candle magic.

Candles of all different colors can be used in magic. They can be a very effective tool used in your spells, mediations and rituals within other types of ceremonies. Below you will find a list of the individual colors of candles and what they mean as well as what ideas are typically associated with that candle color.

White

- The Goddess
- Cleanliness
- Amity
- Virginity
- Higher Self
- Substitutes any other color

Black

- Binding
- Shapeshifting
- Defense
- Banishes negativity

Brown

- Special favors
- To influence friendships

Purple

- Third eye
- Hidden knowledge
- Psychic ability
- Influence people in high places
- Spiritual power

Silver

- The Goddess
- Female energy
- Astral energy
- Clairvoyance

- Instinct
- Thoughts
- ESP

Blue

- Defense
- Element of Water
- Knowledge
- Still
- Good fortune
- Opening up blocked communication
- Spiritual inspiration

Green

- Physical healing
- The Element of Earth
- Monetary success
- Tree and plant magic
- Mother Earth
- Development
- Personal Goals

Pink

- Kind
- Affection
- Romance
- Love
- Development
- Goodwill for the plant

Red

- Element of Fire
- Forte
- Desire
- Fast action
- Career goals
- Envy
- Driving force
- Blood of the moon
- Existence

Orange

- Legal matters

- Fairness
- Vending
- Property deals
- General life success

Copper

- Professional growth
- Desire
- Money goals
- Career maneuvers
- Business fertility

Gold

- God
- Power of the Male
- Contentment
- Winning

Yellow

- The Element of Air

- The Sun

- Reminiscence

- Logical imagination

- Accelerate learning

- Intelligence

- Break mental blocks

If you are looking to make your own candles for your spells we are going to provide you with a step by step guide on how to make your own herbed and oiled candles for your spell casting. The basic ingredients you need to get started are the wax and the wick, and a witch of course!

There are a few options of wax you can use depending on your preferences. You can buy sheets of beeswax that will soften when warmed with a blow dryer or In the heat of the sun.

Once it is pliable you can scatter in crushed herbs and roll it round in the wick to form it into a candle. The beeswax will give your candle a honey scent and it may downgrade the smell of the burns, but you will have a sweet-smelling candle all the same! Since you are not boiling anything in this method you should be able to burn the herbs like smudge. When it is cooled completely you can carve your own images and symbols into the way.

This is definitely the easiest way to make a candle. Another way you can make a candle is by buying the chunks of paraffin or soy wax cubes you can find in your local craft stores. You can melt this down easily in a double boiler. If you do not have a double boiler you can also achieve this by boiling water in one large pot and placing a smaller pot or bowl above it so that the steam from the boil will warm the bowl or pot to melt the wax but will not burn it. Make sure your bowl is heat safe as you do not want to make a mess. To this you will want to add dry powdered herbs for your scent. Be careful as you do this because you do not want to get any water into the wax pot because it will be flammable.

After it has completely melted you can pour the wax into a mold that can easily be made of foil or anything else that is stable that you have laying around. Allow it to cool for a few days before you remove the mold. You can also speed this process up by putting it in the fridge or freezer.

Sometimes it will crack the wax and gives it a really cool look. As the wax forms into a solid, it will create a depression around the wick because there is more tension. You can release the pressure by poking holes or add some extra wax on top after the candle has cooled.

This is a lot prettier! Using this way you will realize that not all herbs are very fragrant. Sage and creosote have been proven to be the most fragrant. You can also add in essential oils rather than actual herbs or both depending on how strong you want to smell to be.

If you want to add decoration to your candle you can definitely inlay stones into the candle wax. You will want to gouge out the shape of the stone so that it can be placed in evenly.

Lay of holding the candle on its side and melt the indented surface of the candle so that it becomes a pool of wax. You can then place your stone of choice into the warmed wax and then smooth out the wax around the stone. You can also do this for things like shells and sprigs of herbs. You can also carve lines into the wax to represent the changing elements and create different patterns depending on our intentions for it.

As a precaution please remember that the herbs within the candles are bound to catch fire themselves. Be aware of burning in places with a lot of clutter because stray flames and embers will definitely catch something on fire. If the watch catches fir while it is boiling, you should smother it with a cloth. Adding water to already burning wax will make it worse. You do not need to have the water boiling really intensely, just enough to make the steam heat up the pot above to melt down the wax delicately. You will also want to keep your wicks trimmed just like a regular candle that you buy from the store. This will help keep the flame controlled as well as not creating as much soot once the candle is blown out. You will also want to make sure that you are dedicating your candles for a specific spiritual use. This means that you do not want to light a candle for a bath if the candle you are using has a very powerful energy. Keep these things separate and you will continue to enjoy your baths as well as the success of your incantation.

The Money Flow Candle Spell

This is a prodigious incantation when you need some additional cash and can't figure out why you are running low. This is also a good starter spell for someone who is just starting to get into candle magic. Give this one a stab and see what occurs. The trick of this spell is to sidestep trying to find out how you are going to get the extra money to show up when you need it in your life. This is going to tell the universe you do not hope it to labor for you. Basil and patchouli are both herbs that are known to be related to cash and wealth as well as the colors of green and gold. IF you do not have patchouli oil on hand, you can always use olive oil in its place.

You will need:

1 gold or green candle

Candle container or a warmth resistant platter

Pin or mineral tip

1-2 drops of patchouli essential oil

A small nip of dried basil

Instructions:

With the crystal tip or pin you will want to draw a pentacle in the center of the candle body. Then you will smear the candle with the oil and then reel it around in the dried basil so that the herb will stick to the form of the candle. You will then place the candle in the receptacle with the representation you drew facing to you.

Then you will spend the next few instants preparation and placing your mind and begin to feel enthusiasm for receiving money in an unforeseen way. You will want to see yourself upright in a graceful river with money and brightly colored bills of cash. When you have this image correctly absorbed say the following words:

With this fire I beckon natures forces,

Currency now streams to me from concealed foundations

Light the candle as the wick begins to flame say "So let it be". You will want to leave the candle in a safe place to burn all the way down to the base.

Most candle spells will want you to burn the candle all the way down on its own. It is never a good idea to leave a candle that is burning unattended. If you absolutely must do so, be sure to put the candle in a sink or tun so that it is far away from any other materials that are flammable. You should also use caution when using anointing pols as well because a lot of them can be highly flammable and you do not want to burn your fingers. If the approach your candle magic with the right cautions you should see very favorable results. There are a variety of different spells you can cast when using candles in your magic and you can learn a variety of different things about yourself as well as your ability to do magic when you start out by using candles.

There are a variety of different resources online that provides candles as well as spells that are already proven to work depending on what your intentions are. Candle magic is a very lucrative force to use when you are simply starting out or you want to learn some simple spells that you can bring into your everyday life. Most people start out with candle magic because it is always an enjoyable feeling to have multiple candles around the house and making your own can be very cost-effective as well as a great hobby to pick up.

Once you get really good at it and finding a variety of different combinations that work for you, you can share you candles with others and help them along their magical journey as well.

Chapter 7: Essential Guide to Spells, Rituals, and Magic

A book of shadows, which is also referred to as a grimoire, is a witch's book of spells. This is where all witches record their magic spells incantations and charms that they use. Book of Shadows comes from the time in which witches needed to hide their craft from others around them in order to avoid being persecuted and tried during the witch trails. Modern witches today are now able to practice freely without fear, but a book of spells is still referred to as a book of shadows and are now available more easily online to the public where witches from all around the world share their spells for free with one another.

Being successful in performing a spell comes with a lot of practice. You must keep your energy and intent aligned with the results that you desire as this is the most important thing. If you do not have this skill, even your most elaborate and powerful spells will not have any effect.

If you do have this ability however, even your most basic spell can have truly extraordinary results. If you are looking to know how to improve your magical skills and casting spells that really work, there is a book referred to as the Essence of Magick and it is a guide that explains the workings behind the magic that Wiccans known and practice. It contains exercises that will teach you how to work with your energy and how to improve your skills in spell casting.

There are 8 known main types of magic. The different types are known to overlap and can be combined. Many of the underlying principles of the eight different magic types are relatively the same. The only change lies mainly in the method in which it is applied. Most people who are casting spells tend to have their own favorite way that they are specialists in and though it is always good to branch out and experiment you should find what works best for you. You are always free to be at anyone that you choose and once you get comfortable in that version of magic you can always move on to another that is completely different or one that is similar but may be harder to grasp initially. You should always work to improve upon your skills as magic is ever-changing you and should want to be prepared for anything that comes your way, even if it is a simple spell that helps you get through your chores this weekend. We will begin by running down the list of the eight different types of magic and given a brief description of each one.

High Magic

This is also known as Ceremonial or Ritualized magic. It is known to be the most formal of all types of magic. It is intricate, complicated, and tremendously influential once you are able to master it. It involves many things like symbolism and complex numerology and astrology and it also summons the entities from other worlds.

The main purpose of high magic is to aim towards spiritual growth and for higher purposes. High magic is something that you should not try to start mastering when you are beginning your Wiccan journey. There are many other different types of magic you can start and master first before you begin your journey through high magic.

It is recommended to leave this one as one of the last types of magic to master because you need everything you would learn in the other types in order to be extremely successful at high magic. Plus, you are more likely to try and fail an eventually get discouraged in your practice because you will not see the results that you want, when you can start small and begin celebrating your successes right away.

Low Magic

Low magic is also known as soil magic. It can also be meant at growing your spirit, but it is generally more troubled with the every-day lifetime and mundane duties we face daily. It can be ritualized or not, though it is not nearly as ritualized as the high magic. You also need to study and practice with low magic, but this type of magic relies more on instinct, spontaneity and creatively unlike high magic that is the exact opposite.

The terms that describe these like high and low are not there to talk about the fact that one of these types is better than the other. It truly just depends on what you are trying to accomplish and that is the type of magic you should use. Most Wiccans tend to practice low magic more than high solely because low magic has the easiest spells and do not require a lot of time to prepare for a ritual or for a spell casting. These are also the spells that are cast you make your everyday life more exciting, so if you are washing dishes and need some music, you can use your low magic spells and make it happen.

You can think of the difference between high magic and low magic like classical music and jazz music. One is definitely not better than the other, it just depends on your preferences and each can be approached with different styles.

Divination

This type of magic involves all of the kinds of enchanted in which the goal of the incantation is to see into the upcoming and see as many responses as possible about what lies in stock. Some people believe that the future is not set in stone, so they use divination to see what is going to happen if they continue down the same path that they are already on.

If the witch does not like the outcome that they see, this give them the opportunity to change course before they reach that point. This is also true for someone taking no action at all. If you are choosing not to act on a certain thing that is happening in your life, you can use divination to see the outcome of your inaction accordingly. Some people refer to this type of magic as having visions or dreams. Some people are able to hold objects or touch people and see brief glimpses into the future about events that may happen, good or bad.

Most people see tarot card reading as a type of divination. This is widely practiced among a lot of people and many people who do not believe in magic are heavy users of tarot because they do not consider telling the future to be magic.

Sympathetic Magic

Sympathetic magic invoices any kind of magic in which one thing is used to be representative of a person and to the degree that the two objects develop related. Afterward, whatever is complete to the object is also done to the individual. The type of magic that immediately comes to mind to most people when they hear this description of sympathetic magic is the Voodoo doll.

Sympathetic magic can be done with a toy or sometimes even a small figurine but it can also be done with a simple object that belongs to that individual, or even as simple as a photo of that person. Most people tie sympathetic magic to hexing thanks to literature movies and likewise, but in authenticity sympathetic magic can really help with attaining goals, therapeutic, wealth and love.

Although there is almost always a negative connotation to what we know sympathetic magic to be, it can really be used to accomplish a lot of good in the world as well. Not all magic is dark magic and the only type of magic that Wiccan perform is magic that is positive and helps everyone out rather than hurting them. You can use sympathetic magic to help out your friends and family in ways you may not have been able to before you started your practice.

Talismanic Magic

This is the type of magic that requires the creation of a talisman or amulet. This talisman or amulet is a thing that has been enchanted. The resolve of this is to draw in or push away exact vitalities depending on what you are trying to do.

Talismans are shaped and then are usually carried around or worn like jewelry. They can be man complete matters or substances that are found in wildlife.

Talismans are usually depicted in movies as objects that are worn around people's necks in order to ward off evil spirits and demons alike. This is a true depiction of what as talisman or amulet is able to do, but they are also used for so many other things as well.

Talismans can be used to bring positive energy to you as well. If you are looking for luck or to gain money or something physical having a talisman with you can help you achieve this. It is best to select an article that is conductive, this is the goal. An instance of this would be if you are trying to draw love closer to you, you should make a talisman out of rose quartz, a sprig of rosemary and a heart necklace, as these all things that are associated with love. Having these things with you at all times allow those energies to flow to you easier and you are likely to see results sooner because of it.

Folk Magic

Folk magic is a type of magic that is often approved down in relatives and philosophies before we can even trace its roots, this is how deeply ingrained it is into the society. Folk magic, is named for being magic that is of the common folk, or the average person, and is the least ritualized form of magic we know. It is also the most spontaneous forms of magic, and is known to involve chants, gestures symbols as well as natural items. It is ready to go and extremely practical for use in everyday life. Some examples of folk magic are drawing a curse sign-on or over a doorway to prevent wicked from walking through, changing a remedial chant over an injury for immediate relief, or scattering lavender around your bed in order to get a more restful night sleep. Folk magic is the type of magic that medicine men and those types alike are known to reform. They are the ones that you would go to for more holistic healing rather than taking pills and medications to solve it. Folk magic and medicine men go hand in hand as they both use elements from the earth to provide aid to whatever situation may need to be attended to.

Elemental Magic

Elemental magic is what it sounds, a type of magic that utilizes the dynamism of the holy fundamentals (Earth, Air, Fire, and Water) in incantations, or used in working with utensils and other mechanisms that are known to represent and characterize them.

This is an influential type of magic but is known to get multifaceted as there are many numerous types of associations that need to be educated as also measured when you are getting ready to perform a spell. This is not the only type of magic that falls until the header of elemental magic however.

There are several other types of magic because they use the dynamism of the exact basics but they have actually become strict magic focusses all on their own:

- Candle Magic
- Herbal Magic
- Kitchen Magic
- Crystal Magic
- Metal Magic
- Musical Magic
- Color Magic
- Rune Magic
- Tarot Magic
- Moon Magic
- Planetary Magic

Not all witches reflect these types of rudimentary magic but most do because they are of the same traditions. In most Wiccan covens, all of these types of magic are powerfully related to one or more types of basics.

Every herb, tarot card, rune, planet, moon and crystal is associated with one or more of the elements. Working with them is just working with the component that resembles it.

Petition Magic

Petition Magic is a type of magic that most closely resembles the act of prayer that takes place in other religions. Petition magic is when you are petitioning for a Higher Power to grant you what you are desiring. You need to ask the higher power; you cannot command them to do what you are asking.

This means that you are relying on your relationship with the higher power so that they are to look favorably upon you to fulfill your wants and need rather than casting you aside because you are demanding. In this however, if the higher power has looked favorably on you in the past, this does not mean you are going to get what you desire each and every time you ask them. You must also be understanding and accepting of hearing a nod from the higher powers as well.

This is countless magic or when you are really not sure if you partake the right within you to change the path of something, but you are feeling in your heart that you should do something and asking for help to see if it is possible to do so. You should not use this type of magic in any negative ways, as it is often known that if magic is used against someone, it has the power to come back on you tenfold.

This is because whatever energies you put out into the universe is always likely to come back at you. This is why Wiccans only practice magic that is good for them as well as others, because they want everyone to be at peace within themselves as well as nature.

What a Wiccan ritual is about will depend on the occasion that is happening. If it is the full moon celebrations, these are solely focused on the Goddess, whereas the Sabbats often honor the co-creative relationship between the God and the Goddess. There are a ton of different variations, despite this, there are a few basic elements that tend to always be included in what can be considered to be a typical ritual. First there is always a purification, both of the people performing as well as the place in which the ritual is help. This can be a ritual bath, a smudging ceremony or likewise to remove any unwanted energy that could be lingering in the ritual space. This can be outside or in any part of the house.

Next you will want to set up your altar. Some Wiccans are able to keep their altar up permanently which is great of those who practice their rituals daily, but many do not have this luxury. The altar should be arranged with various tools, symbols, offerings and they should all be laid out according to whatever type of tradition you are looking to uphold.

Then you will want to cast your circle, which is an act that is known to create a boundary between the sacred space and the ordinary physical world. The circle is marked by seal salt, a long cord stone herbs or more often candles. There are many methods that you can cast your circle with. Once the circle has been cast your invocations will begin. There is no particular order for this but typically the God and Goddess are always invited to join the ritual and well as the four elements.

In other traditions, this step is known as calling the quarters, the four directions are addressed at this point, and they are used instead of the four elements. Once this is complete, the heart of the ritual will begin. First the intent of the ritual should be stated, it is either to celebrate the Sabbat or the Sebat or perhaps you are petitioning the God and Goddess on behalf of someone who is in need of healing or any other kind of assistance. After you state your intent, the main body of the ritual can consist of various different activities. The focal point may be a performance of a ritual drama, or liturgical apteral, depending on the specific tradition of Wicca you follow. You can also read from ancient texts or compose your own poetry.

Chanting, singing, and dancing gestures may also be a big part of what happens, and it might simply be there to bless the season informally. Food and drink are often offered and usually symbolically shared with the God and Goddess, at the end of the body of the ritual. This ceremony connects the spiritual plane with the one on earth and helps keep the grounding and centering of the participants intact before closing the ritual. When it is time to end the ritual, the elements and the God and Goddess are formally thanks and released and the circle is closed.

Waxing Moon Banishing Spell

Banishing spells in one of the essential skills in which very witch should master since it is one of the cornerstones of the craft. This skill can be used to banish all types of unwanted things, from people who are toxic in your life to unwanted spiritual energy or even rid bad situations from your life. This is not to say that banishing spells are easy. It is important to perform a banishing spell in a calm and collected state and it is important that you let go of all anger.

You will need:

Apple cider vinegar

Dried herbs: rosemary, mint and thyme

3 fresh cloves of garlic

A glass jar

Instructions:

You will want to wait until the waxing moon, which is when the moon is growing. Find a space that is quiet and comfortable and gather all of the supplies above. Place the herbs in the jar and cover it with the apple cider vinegar. Make sure you screw the lid on tightly so that it is air tight and nothing can get in or out of the jar unless you open it with intention. Gently shake the vinegar. With your eyes closed you will want to focus your energy on the entity you wish to banish while you are remaining very calm and collected. Try to se the situation as a third party and do not let your emotions get involved. Feel the jar being charged with the energy that you are giving it. Leave the jar in a dark and cool place for 4 to 6 weeks. After that, it should be sprinkled over your doorstep and windows to banish your enemies.

A Spell to Enhance Fertility

Every woman merits the opportunity to give birth to an attractive and well-child if they so desire. If you are struggling to conceive this spell is powerful and it will help improve your fruitfulness and reduce the chances that you have an early failure. In accumulation to that, some women have used this spell in the previous have said that they have been blessed with giving birth to doubles and even trios without any such births running in their relations. One of the main reasons why this incantation is so influential is that it takes both associates to cast it and there is double the energy flow and that in itself increases the chances of success.

You will need:

- Three new candles that are of the similar size
- The father-to-be who needs to be fully existing as well as dedicated to the spell

This spell is to be done over the course of three days. This is to happen the day beforehand ovulation, the day of, which should also be the day interaction in order to get pregnant occurs, as the day after. Each candle is used only once, and one is used on each of the days, separately. On the day before ovulation the father should light the candle and reiteration the subsequent three times while holding the candle:

The cascade of life, the ever-flowing vigor, bless us tomorrow with a well-child.

The days of the ovulation beforehand and afterward any love creation, the father must light up the next candle and both associates will hold the candle together and repeat the following three times:

The originate of life, the ever-flowing vigor, bless us tonight with a well-child

The day after, the mamma should light up the third and last candle and repeat the next three times as she grips the candle:

The source of life, the ever-flowing vigor, may the new life flourish and cultivate inside me.

After each candle is lit, they should be left to burn for a minimum of three hours. If the mother is starting to feel a heating sensation in her abdominal after the final spell the probabilities are very high that the spell has functioned.

Conclusion

You have reached the end of this book, Wicca for Beginners. We hope this book has giving you the opportunity to begin your studies in the magic and enlightenment of Wicca and we look forward to hearing from you if you enjoyed your time reading it. This book is just the beginning of what all you can discover out there in the world and what the religion of Wicca is all about. We encourage you to reach out to other Wiccans in your area to get their tips and insights into how to be a Wiccan and where you should start in your journey.

The next step is to use what you have learned from this book and begin applying it to your study of the Wiccan religion. Remember that you should always start with the basics until you have gotten more comfortable with the craft and all that it has to offer you. We have provided some very easy and basic spells for you to be with and we hope that you have the time and dedication to be practicing with them so that your craft and abilities can grow stronger and you become the best Wiccan you can be. Always remember that the true meaning of being a Wiccan is to become more connected with the earth and living in peace with the energies of the nature around you. Once you have gotten to this harmony you should see that you are in the right frame of mind to begin your incantations and ritual casting.

Wicca is a very powerful religion with a colored past, and we are looking forward to a future in which Wiccans are able to be more and more open about their abilities and working more towards Wicca becoming less ideologized as the workings of the devil. With your help and those like you, this will come to fruition must faster and easier than we could ever think possible Be sure to stand strong in your beliefs and only use the power that is bestowed on you for the good of the world, and never use your gift in the intentions of harming someone or something.

Finally, if you found this book useful in any way, a review on Amazon is always appreciated!

WICCA

Wicca Book of Spells

The Ultimate Guide to Practicing Wiccan Magic Spells and Magical Rituals. A Book of shadows for Wiccans, Witches, Pagans, Witchcraft practitioners and beginners

ESTHER ARIN SPELLS

INTRODUCTION

Congratulations on downloading Wicca Book of Spells and thank you for doing so.

The following chapters will discuss several kinds of Wiccan spells, the tools necessary to perform them, and the rituals ever practitioner needs to safely and effectively perform magical works.

There are plenty of books on this subject on the market, thanks again for choosing this one! Every effort was made to ensure it is full of as much useful information as possible. Please enjoy!

CHAPTER 1: What Is a Spell?

Most people grew up surrounded by spells. Spells can be found in books, in movies, and on television. Magic drives the action in countless video games and serves as the foundation for tabletop gaming.

But none of that magic is real. Special effects and fanciful stories don't create real change. And, for most people, that's the end of it. Spells are nothing but wishful thinking and handy plot devices.

But Wiccans and witches know first-hand that spells extend well beyond the realm of fantasy. No, magic cannot make a broom fly or turn the local bully into a toad. But it can – and does – help witches around the world achieve their goals. And it can help you too.

Spells, at their core, are nothing more than a means to an end. Wiccan spells blend a witch's personal power with the power they call forward from nature and from the Divine. They then focus all of the energy on a single goal or outcome.

It's important to note that spells are a boost, not a solution. They need real-world action is necessary for spells to succeed. Spells are like gas in a car. We can fill a car with all the gas it can hold. But real-world action is the key in the ignition. It lets the energy of the spell take hold. Real-world action ignites all the gas and turns it into energy that powers us to our destination.

A spell will not fix a problem or achieve a goal all on its own. But it will take a witch further, faster, than they would get without the boost from their spellwork.

The Rules of Spellwork

Before a witch casts a spell, however, there are a few rules they must follow. Wiccan spells must always follow the Wiccan Rede, which is a set of rules that governs how Wiccans behave.

Of these rules, the most important is "And it harm none, do what ye will." Because of this rule, most Wiccans refuse to cast spells that may harm someone else. This includes spells that will affect someone else's free will, such as a love spell directed at a specific person.

The Wiccan Rede is also the reason Wiccans will not curse or hex other people. Some witches will, as not all witches are Wiccans. But Wiccans view curses and hexes as, quite literally, against their religion. If they choose to stop a negative person with spellwork, it will be done through defensive spells rather than offensive spells.

Wiccans also believe in the three-fold law, which states that all energy a witch puts out into the world will come back to them three times over. Spells such as curses and hexes would send negative energy out which would ultimately return to the witch three times over. Positive spells, on the other hand, will ultimately bring even more positive energy into the practitioner's life.

So long as a spell follows these rules, there is nearly no limit to the sort of spells a Wiccan Witch may cast. Some witches cast spells to summon creativity, promote communication, or even increase their chances for success. Other witches might cast spells to help with their health, encourage their plants to grow or to banish negative energy from their lives.

The Book of Shadows

When witches find a spell that works very well or one that perfectly suits their needs and preferences, they'll often keep a copy for reference. These spells are then written down in the witch's Book of Shadows. Though the name may sound intimidating, a Book of Shadows is nothing more than a witch's catalog of spells.

Some practitioners may also choose to use their book of shadows as a sort of journal. They will record a spell and then write a journal entry every time they perform the spell. Once the spell has had an impact, they will go in and make a note of that as well.

Many witches use their Book of Shadows as a means of tracking which spells work best for them. Spells often use crystals, herbs, and candles to direct and amplify their effects. By tracking spells and their outcomes in a Book of Shadows, a practitioner can easily see which spells and ingredients work best for them. Over time, these notes may even allow witches to alter spells or write their own.

Although pop culture tends to favor hand-bound leather books for a witch's book of shadows, they can take nearly any form. Some witches do use old fashioned books like they do in the movies. But most witches use a notebook or binder with loose-leaf paper. Other witches prefer to keep a digital Book of Shadows.

These options might not be as aesthetically pleasing, but they're easier to arrange. Many practitioners also find it easier to use a more "casual" Book of Shadows because they can go back and edit their entries without worrying about messy pages. Popular spells – including spells written by the practitioner – can always be copied into a more traditional book at a later time.

Changing and Writing Spells

While anyone can alter spells – or even write them from scratch – it is something that only experienced witches should attempt. Spell writers consider the properties of every herb, stone, and candle they use. They also take moon phases, timing, and the spell's intent into account. Changing even one of these properties can affect how well the spell performs.

Beginners are encouraged to try as many spells as they like. They should track what works and what doesn't, then choose new spells accordingly. But they should avoid writing or altering spells until they have studied the components, their correspondences, and understand the effects of each element on their spell.

The Next Step

Once a practitioner has learned the rules of Spellwork, they can learn the structure of a spell. Spellwork may seem intimidating at first. But as long as practitioners follow these rules, stay aware of their energy levels, and follow the proper procedure when casting a spell, there is very little to be intimidated by.

Chapter 2: The Structure of a Spell

Wiccan spells, no matter how personalized their intent or components, almost always follow a set structure. The process begins with steps to protect the with and the spell, then moves into the spell itself, before ending with a release of all the energy called into the circle.

It is possible to mix up the steps, skip a few, or even create entirely new spellcasting formats. However, only experienced witches should try to change the format of a spell. Beginners will find much more success and comfort in following the prescribed pattern.

Before the Spell

As with all endeavors, spells require a little bit of preparation. A witch must gather their supplies and ensure they have everything they'll need. Then they have to arrange everything inside the space where they will be casting their spell. Most experienced witches strongly advise leaving the protective circle once it has been raised. So, if a witch forgets a spell ingredient, they may have to give up and try another night again, or do without and hope it does not affect the spell too much.

There are also a few optional preparations that practitioners can use if and when it suits them. These are the act of ritual bathing and the donning of ritual clothing.

Ritual Bathing

Wiccans believe that practitioners interact with the energy of everything they touch. And, because of this, they may accidentally bring unwanted energy into a spell if they do not perform a ritual bath prior to entering the protective circle.

Ritual baths do not have to be complicated. They just need to be effective. And, in practice, it's more of a shower than a bath. Many Wiccans believe that bathing in standing water only redistributes the grime of the day and the random energy the practitioner picked up. A shower allows them to rinse the grime and energy away.

For the most part, a ritual bath is little more than a quick shower while the practitioner focuses their intention on preparing for the spellwork ahead. If the practitioner wants to get a little more involved, they may use special products that they reserve solely for ritual bathing. Sandalwood soap is a popular option, as are natural soaps scented with lemon or mint.

Ritual Clothing

Different branches of Wicca have different guidelines on what practitioners should wear when casting spells. A few branches require that their members perform naked, which is also known as Skyclad. These branches make up a relatively small percentage of Wiccans, however. The majority of Wiccans fall into one of two camps. They either don't care what a practitioner wears. Or they suggest the use of ritual clothing.

As with ritual bathing, ritual clothing can be as simple or as elaborate as the practitioner desires. For some, their ritual clothing is an everyday outfit that they only wear during the ritual. Another popular option is a plain white cotton dress or pair of pants and tunic. More complex versions may have multiple layers of clothing, embroidery, cloaks, and jewelry worn only for rituals or spells.

Typically, ritual garb is only put on after a ritual bath so that they remain clean. The clothing is taken off again as soon as the protective circle has been lowered before the practitioner cleans up the physical remnants of the spell.

The Protective Circle

All spells should begin with a protective circle. It can be a physical circle or one created through visualization. If the circle is physical, chalk is the easiest to create and clean up from most surfaces. Salt is also an option, though it will have to be vacuumed or swept clean at the end of the spell. If the witch is working in a secure area, they can also paint the circle permanently onto the floor. They can then raise or lower the protective barrier through visualization.

No matter what the circle is made of, it must contain the entire area a witch will be working in. The circle does not have to fill an entire room, of course. But it must be big enough for the witch to cast their spell in. If the spell involves movement, the witch must take this into account. Similarly, the practitioner should make sure that they have all of their spell materials gathered and arranged before they cast their protective circle.

Physical	**Pros** • Easier for beginners to work stronger and more durable **Con** • More clean up or permanent fixture
Visualized	**Pros** • Can be cast anywhere • No clean up necessary **Con** • Harder for beginners to master

When the circle's size is set and the witch is ready to begin, the witch must visualize the circle around their workspace. In their mind, they must picture the circle becoming a bubble that extends up over their space and down into the ground or floor beneath them.

This bubble will protect the witch from outside influence while also ensuring the energy they raise is properly directed. Without the control of a protective circle, the power's spell could melt away or redirect in a direction that the witch did not intend.

Calling the Quarters or Watchtowers

Once the protective circle has been raised, the witch must call forward the elements and energy of the four directions – called the Watchtowers or Quarters in some Wiccan traditions – as outlined in the table below.

North	Earth	Stability and grounding
South	Fire	Motivation and a point of gathering
East	Air	Breathes in life and blows away obstacles
West	Water	Source of life

The directions can be called in any order, but most witches opt to use the order of "North, South, East, and West." Each of the directions brings in the properties of its corresponding element.

North brings the stability of Earth, which is one reason many witches call North first. Its stability is a groundwork on which the rest of the spell's energy can be built.

South is associated with fire. Calling south second offers a two-fold benefit. Fire is motivational, both its heat and light serving to fuel the witch as they cast their spell. But fires are also gathering places. When the witch calls the element of fire into their circle, they are creating a gathering place for the rest of the energy and elements to come together.

East brings in the element of air. The air breathes life into the fire and clears away obstacles to the witch's spell.

Finally, the witch calls West, which brings with it the element of water. Water is the source of all life on Earth, and it is from water that the spell's life can be most easily drawn.

Many witches take a moment to let the energy of the elements settle before they move onto the next step, which is to invoke the divine.

Invoking the Divine

Most Wiccans view the divine as a Goddess and a God. Together, they bring a balance of masculine and feminine energy so that the spell will follow an even, steady path.

There are several ways that practitioners can call the Goddess and God into their circle. A witch can pray to them, either silently or aloud, by calling the names of the Divine figures and then stating the intention of the spell. A sample quote is provided below.

Oh, glorious Lady, lend me your wisdom and nurture my gift as I embark upon this path.

Oh, glorious Lord, lend me your strength and push me to achieve that of which I can only dream.

Other methods include the use of statues or dolls to symbolize God and Goddess. Witches may also use their chalice to represent the Goddess and their athame to represent God.

Some witches may choose to select specific deities to aid their spells. This is fine to do, so long as the practitioner understands the myths surrounding the deity as well as the culture they come from. There are many cases where witches call on a deity without knowing enough about them, and it negatively impacts the outcome of their spell.

Practitioners should also remember that they must respect any and all energy they call into their circle. It does not matter if the energy if from the elements or from the divine. The energy is not the witch's to demand but is being given by stronger forces. So, all witches must remember to show respect for the elements and the divine.

Casting the Spell

Only when the protective circle has been raised, and the proper energies called into the circle, can a witch cast their spell. A spell can be cast by reciting incantation either aloud or the witch's head. If the practitioner has to be discreet, it is strongly recommended that they either recite the spell in their head or use hand gestures to recite the incantation.

And while most spell rhyme – particularly those seen in pop culture – it's not a hard rule. The most important trait for any incantation is that it outlines the spell's intent clearly and without room for miscommunication.

Spells are driven by energy and intent. So, it is absolutely vital that an incantation clearly state the intent of the spell. If the spell is meant to inspire creativity, for example, the incantation should specify what kind of creativity. Otherwise, someone who normally paints might suddenly have an idea for a play or find themselves interested in trying new recipes!

If, on the other hand, a spell is meant to banish negative energy, it may end up banishing stressful things that the witch actually wants in their lives. Things like complicated personal projects, intense relationships, and work challenges can all bring negative feelings like stress, anxiety, and doubt even if they are otherwise cherished. A banishment spell may target these things instead of the source of truly negative emotions such as a toxic person or situation.

The spells in this book are written with a few intentional blanks that each practitioner can fill in for themselves. This is not the same as altering the spell, of course. But these blank spaces allow each person to tailor the intent and direction of the spell to their exact need.

Some spells will consist of only a small incantation. Others will have multiple incantations as well as some ritual movement, candle lighting, or other small gestures. Some spells even involve dancing, though those are more advanced and none are listed in this book.

No matter the length and content of the spell, however, witches should take their time and make sure they are properly guiding the energy from their circle into the spell. And, if they are speaking aloud, they should make sure to enunciate as clearly as possible. This will keep their focus on the spell so that their minds will not wander and accidentally redirect some of their energy.

Releasing the Borrowed Energy

There will always be energy left over once a witch has fully charged their spell. Some spells will leave the practitioner feeling drained, but that does not mean that all the summoned energy has been used.

This is why it is important for practitioners to release the energies they called into their circles actively. Most witches choose to release the energy by reversing the order they used when summoning the elements and the divine.

The Goddess is released first, then the God, and then the four elements in the opposite of whatever order they were called in.

To release the energies, a witch must thank the deity or the Watchtower for heeding the witch's call and aiding in their spell. The witch then says the power is released to return home. Some witches choose to finish the release with a request that the energy returns the next time the witch calls. A sample quote can be found below.

I thank you, all who lent me your energy this day. My working was done with your blessing and your might. I release now that which you freely gave, that it may return to you and aid your strength.

Opening the Circle

Once all the unused energy has been returned to its source, practitioners must open their circles to end the ritual. This is usually a three-step process, but it is reduced to two steps if the circle was created purely through visualization.

To release a protective circle, the witch must first bring back the visualization they created for their protective circle. Then they must visualize the protective energy receding back into the flat space that the circle takes up on the floor. If a physical circle was used, the final step is clean up whatever was used to create the circle. For witches whose circles are permanent, they symbolically "cut" the circle using their athame.

This final step – cleaning up the circle – leads into the very last aspect of every spell: the cleanup.

Cleaning Up After the Spell

Spells are tools witches use to focus their power. And, like any good workman, they must take care of their tools. In the case of spells, this means cleaning them up after the casting has been completed.

Clean-up will take different forms depending on the ingredients used in the spell. Some components must be held onto, such as charged stones or special candles. Other components, like extra herbs or the burnt incense, can be disposed of.

Wicca is a religion focused, in part, on earth worship. So, when witches clean up from their spells, they try to do so in as sustainable a manner as possible. For example, they will compost or bury herbs they no longer need. Or they may collect up spilled candle wax and melted down later to be used in forming a new non-magical candle.

Spells may seem complicated at first glance. But they quickly become second nature. Until then, practitioners can refer to the flow chart below if they want a quick guide to the steps of a spell.

WICCA

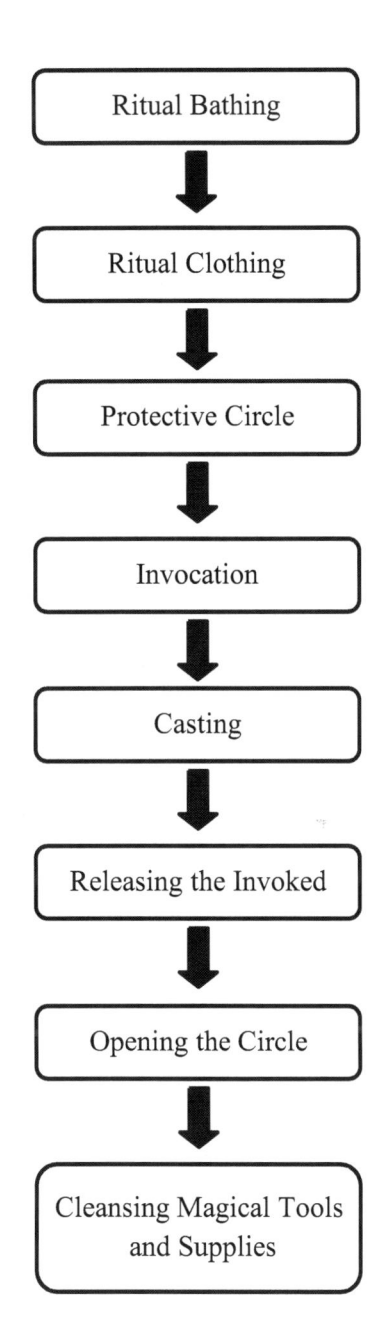

```
Ritual Bathing
     ↓
Ritual Clothing
     ↓
Protective Circle
     ↓
Invocation
     ↓
Casting
     ↓
Releasing the Invoked
     ↓
Opening the Circle
     ↓
Cleansing Magical Tools
and Supplies
```

Cleansing Magical Tools and Supplies

Although cleansing is vitally important in witchcraft, it is not necessarily part of every spell. Rather, most witches wait for the new moon and then cleanse all of their tools and supplies all at once. The new moon, as covered in the Timing section of this book, is a time when the absence of the moon means that energy is easily drawn away into the darkness.

Cleansing may seem a bit surreal at first, but it is by far of the easiest parts of magical practice. Practitioners need only collect everything they need to be cleansed, then lay it out in front of a window whose curtain or blinds are left open all night.

If the moon were visible, the tools would be bathed in moonlight. But, because it is the new moon – or dark moon, as some witches call it – there is no light to be had. Instead, the energy in the tools and supplies is drawn into the darkness to fill the void where there is usually light. When the sun rises, it prevents the energy from returning to the tools. Then, as the moon once again waxes in the sky, the energy is purified and released back into the universe.

There are, of course, other ways to cleanse magical tools. But this the easiest method that is safe to use on all materials and stones, even those that would react poorly to other cleansing methods. Some practitioner prays to the Goddess and God before leaving their tools out to be cleansed, just for an extra measure of assurance. It isn't strictly necessary, however. The practitioner should just be sure they have their tool put away before the sun sets again, or the old energy might find its way back.

Chapter 3: Components of a Spell

Most Wiccan spells feature several different tools and components. It is possible to cast a spell with visualization alone, of course. But most witches find that crystals, herbs, and all the other tools increase their odds of success. These features allow them to focus and concentrate their energy. And each one achieves this in its own way.

Tools

Although some witches may have tools unique to their personal practice, all Wiccan practitioners have the same core tools. The largest of these is the altar, which is any location where they can worship the Goddess and God. A witch's altar will usually contain a ritual knife called an athame, a special cup known as a chalice, an incense burner, a wand, and some sort of divination tool.

The Altar

A witch's altar is as unique as they are. Its size, shape, and contents all change depending on the season, the witch's location, the Divine beings they honor, and the kind of magic they prefer to perform. Generally, an altar is large enough to hold the witch's tools, images of the Goddess and God, and a few offerings. Many witches also like to decorate their altars with flowers, crystals, and tapestries.

The Athame

The Wiccan religion is very fond of symbolism. And the athame is the perfect example of this. Although it is referred to as a ritual knife,", most athames are dull. They're never intended to cut or puncture anything.

Instead, they are meant to represent the male half of all energy. Knives have long been seen as phallic symbols in cultures around the world, and Wicca is no different. Witches often hold the athame when calling forward the energy of their chosen God, as they feel it is a fitting conduit for His power.

The Chalice

As the athame symbolizes God, so the chalice represents the Goddess. The hollow of the chalice symbolizes the feminine body and its ability to hold liquid represents the ability to create life since we require liquid to live.

Although the term "chalice" is very formal, a witch's chalice needs not to be a goblet. All of a witch's tools should fit their needs and personal practice. So, if a witch must be discreet in practicing, they can use regular glass. They just have to cleanse it before using it in spells or rituals.

The Boline

A boline is another kind of ritual knife. Unlike the athame, however, it is sharpened along at least one side of the blade. Its sole purpose is to cut and prepare herbs for use in spellwork. This particular tool is a little less common than either the athame or the chalice because not all witches can grow their herbs. For those that do, however, a boline is specifically blessed to make the herbs as potent as possible for future spells.

The Incense Burner

Incense is very popular among Wiccans and witches. Some practitioners even make their own to ensure the ingredients are specifically suited to the spell or ritual the witch wants to perform. Most witches, however, buy their incense premade.

There is a wide range of incense burners. Practitioners must decide which form of incense is right for them and then buy an appropriate burner. Most witches prefer stick incense, as it is the easiest to find. Others prefer cones because the ash is more easily contained. And yet others prefer loose incense that they sprinkle over a lump of hot coal kept in a protective dish on their altar.

The Wand

A witch's wand is probably the unique thing on their altar. Unlike in the storybooks, there is no limit to what a wand can be made of wood, stone, metal, clay, paper. As long as the wand suits the witch, it is a proper wand. Different materials have different properties, of course. And, for this reason, some wands are better suited to certain spells than others.

Wands allow witches to direct their energy. While some people use their hands to direct the flow of their energy, others prefer the fine-tuned direction that a wand can offer. Many witches find that raising protective circles, calling the Watchtowers, and even moving energy into enchanted objects are all easier when they work with a wand.

Divination Tools

Not all witches practice divination. But those who do usually have a preferred method. And they will be the first to clarify that they cannot tell the future.

Divination is nothing more than a way to find or clarify information that may otherwise stay hidden. And there is a wide range of tools to help witches achieve this goal. The most well-known are, of course, tarot cards. But other forms include rune stones, scrying mirrors, and even the use of books or music. As with wands, a witch's preferred form of divination will ultimately depend on their personal practice and preferences.

Stones

Witches are, as a general rule, very fond of crystals and stones. There are whole libraries on the subject of stones and their magical properties. Witches access these properties when they want to work a spell. When not in use, their stones and crystals are often used to decorate a witch's altar or home.It is important to note that crystals must be cleansed between spells. Cleansing removes residual energy that may muddy the intent and outcome of a spell. Many stones can be cleansed through a ritual washing with plain water. There are stones that react poorly – or even dangerously – to water, however. So, it is vital that witches know the physical properties of their stones as well as the magical.

Talismans and Amulets

Whenever a witch directs their energy into a piece of jewelry, they then wear around, they have created an amulet. Talismans are similar, but they do not need to be worn. Rather, they can be carried around in the witch's bag, car, or pocket.

Some witches will use their amulets once or twice, then cleanse them and get rid of them or return them to mundane use. Other witches will hold on to every talisman and amulet they've made so that they can easily "refill" its energy and jump right back into whatever the item's intended use was.

For both groups, it is important to cleanse amulets and talismans between uses. This will prevent the energy of one spell from leaking into another. Crossovers, even between repeated uses of the same spell, can affect the ultimate outcome and possibly derail whatever the witch had been trying to achieve.

Supplies

A witch's tools will usually stay with them for life, or until they find their energy works better with a new tool. At that point, the old tool is either returned to the earth in as sustainable a fashion as possible, or it is passed to another witch.

There are certain supplies, however, that are only used once or twice before the practitioner discards them. The most common of these is, of course, incense. But herbs and offerings to the God and Goddess may also be used in spells.

Incense

Incense burners have already been discussed. But it is also important to mention the various kinds of incense as well as the impact their contents can have on spellwork. Most witches use store-bought stick incense, the majority of which comes from large chain stores. There is absolutely nothing wrong with using this kind of incense. Practitioners just have to make sure their incense doesn't contain any harmful byproducts.

It is possible to buy handmade stick incense online through sites like Etsy. Many artisans are even willing to create custom-made incense so that practitioners may have the perfect incense for every occasion.

Stick incense is the most common. But it is far from the only type of incense. Cone incense is also relatively popular. It burns in a similar fashion to stick incense in that the user must light the tip and then blow it out, thus creating a smoldering ember. Unlike stick incense, however, there is no stick leftover once the incense has burned down.

A third – and much more uncommon – option is to place loose incense and herbs directly on a piece of hot charcoal. The charcoal usually rests in a pot or tempered ceramic dish that is elevated above the surface of the altar to prevent heat damage.

Stick incense is the easiest to work with, particularly for people who have not used it before. Then, as practitioners become more comfortable with using and handling the incense, they can try new forms until they choose their favorite.

Herbs and Plants

Wicca is a religion centered on the idea of nature worship. This influences several aspects of religion, and spellwork is one area where it is the most obvious. Herbs, leaves, living plants, and flower petals all make frequent appearances in spells.

More complex spells will sometimes call for odd parts of specific plants such as dandelion roots or wood from a particular tree. It all depends on the properties of the plant and the spell's intended outcome.

Spells that call for plant matter will usually tell the practitioner how long to keep the ingredients. When it is time to dispose of the plants, many witches choose to compost them. This returns their matter and energy back to the earth rather than adding to landfills.

Offerings

Of all the spell components, offerings are among the most uncommon. Witches will often leave offerings to the Goddess and God. But they rarely do so in connection to spells. Still, it happens on occasion and thus deserves mention.

Despite what some people think, Wiccan offerings are usually plants or small plates of food. Often, after a time, these offerings will be left outside for local wildlife or composted so as to return them to the earth. Both options allow the energy and sustenance of the offering to return to the earth, which is thought to be holy through connection to both aspects of the Divine.

Energy

A witch's energy is, by far, the most important part of any spell. It is what will call more energy into their work. It is what will drive the spell. And it is what will deliver the results the witch ultimately wants to see. But to use their energy for a spell, a witch must learn to control their energy.

Typically, if a witch is learning from someone more experienced, they're told to practice grounding and centering before they attempt spells. Both practices involve visualization and allow the witch to set limits and controls on where their energy goes.

Once a witch has mastered the basics of both grounding and centering, they are ready to cast their own spells. Their knowledge of visualization will help them raise the protective circle and call other energies to their aid. And, once the energy has manifested, their preferred centering technique will allow them to channel the energy into their spell.

The larger a spell's intended impact, the more energy it will take. Most of the energy will belong to the Divine or the Watchtowers. But witches have to infuse a spell with personal energy as well. It is the only way to tie a spell to the witch's will.

Infusing a spell with their personal power leaves practitioners tired or 'drained' once they release the additional energy they called into their circle. The larger the spell and the more energy they give, the worse their exhaustion will be. Most experienced practitioners make sure they have drinks or snacks ready to aid their recovery as soon as their spell has been cast.

This exhaustion is another reason that inexperienced witches are advised to practice with established spells before they write their own. Until a practitioner knows what spells require from them, they may accidentally cast one that demands more energy than they can comfortably give. Understanding spells, as well as grounding a centering, ensures that the witch knows their limits before they push themselves too far.

Other Energy Sources

Most witches rely solely on the energy gained from the Divine, the quarters, and themselves. There are a few other sources that a practitioner can call on, however. These sources include the practitioner's ancestors, local land spirits, and the Fae.

Unlike Divine and Watchtower energy, however, these other energy sources are tied to spiritual beings that may have intentions of their own. Practitioners should get to know these spirits very well before they allow them into a protective circle. This is particularly true of the Fae who are known to view things differently than humans and, to an extent, align themselves with trickster spirits.

Intention

The intention has already been touched on. But it's such an important factor in every single spell that it must be mentioned again. Without properly focused intention, a spell may never work. Or, worse still, it will work but have utterly unforeseen consequences. Everyone has seen a spell backfire in movies, usually with hilarious results. But witches will be the first to say that an improperly aimed spell rarely ends on a happy note.

It is not that the spell will bring about some horrible event. Usually, the result ranges from a minor annoyance to a severe but manageable problem. However, spells are meant to help the witch, not create more problems. The unfortunate consequences simply add insult to the injury of a miscast spell.

Witches can set the intention of their spell by speaking it out loud after they call on the Divine and the Watchtowers, but before they recite the incantation. Then, while reciting the incantation, they should keep the intention in mind.

Some practitioners find that this is easiest when they create a visual. If the spell is intended to promote motivation at work, they create a mental image of them at work, performing their job quickly and efficiently. Or, if it's a spell to increase creative energy, they will imagine themselves working with their medium of choice, radiating the bright light of creative inspiration.

Other witches find that repeating a single phrase or word over and over is the best way to keep their intention in mind. It could be something as simple as "creativity" or "health." It doesn't have to be specific – that's what the spell's incantation is for. But it does need to keep the practitioner's mind on the goal they ultimately want to achieve.

Real-World Action

This is another component that is important enough to merit several mentions. Spells require real-world action to work. Unlike the spells in storybooks, real magic will not fix a problem all on its own. Spells are meant to support real-world action.

If a practitioner wants to encourage their creativity, for example, they cannot just cast a spell and then wait for a muse to appear. They have to sit down with the medium and begin to work. Rather than causing a sudden burst of creativity, the spell will ease their creative block much more quickly than would have otherwise happened.

The idea of using spells to support real-world action is particularly important when the spells are intended to address a health issue or a real crisis. In both of these cases, the spells act as charms to ease the difficult paths that real action will take the practitioner on.

Because of the real-world impact action has on spellwork, every spell in this book has a few suggested actions listed at the end of the spell. They may not fit every practitioner's particular needs. But they are good building blocks for reader's to find the right actions for their situation.

Space

Witches must have space to work in. But the amount of space they need will vary depending on the spell and how discreet the practitioner must be. Witches who practice openly can take up as much as space as an entire room or as little as a circle around the space they're standing in. There are even spells that use dance or other movements as a way to generate power. These spells, naturally, require as much room as possible.

There are several ways that practitioners can minimize the space they need when their work must be discreet, however. They use miniature versions of their tools that can be kept on their person. This allows them to cast their spell from a sitting position. When casting from this position, the witch's protective circle need only surround the floor space immediately around the witch.

Chapter 4: Timing a spell properly

Timing a spell properly can be a little bit tricky. Some spells can be cast at any time. It does not matter the season, day, or phase of the moon. Other spells can only be cast at very specific times, such as on a new moon in the coldest part of winter.

These time constraints might seem random. But they each have their own impact on certain spells.

The Season

Very few spells are limited to a certain time of year. But timing is essential for those that are. These spells usually tap into either the spirit of a season, its physical traits, or the holidays at that time of year. A spell that calls on the "freezing snows of winter" will have very little power in the middle of summer. Of course, that also depends on the climate in which the practitioner lives.

If the spell does not call on the physical traits of a season, it may call on the spirit of the season. Generally, this means they call on the growing cycle for local vegetation. And, since many Wiccan spells are based on English magical practices, they are centered on the growing cycles in Europe and Britain.

Generally speaking, spring is a time of birth and growth in these areas. Summer is when everything is in full bloom and food is plentiful. Autumn marks the largest harvest season as well as the approach of cold and death. And winter rounds out the cycle of life with a cold spell in which things will not grow, and darkness outweighs light.

Following this pattern, spells meant for springtime will focus on birth or growth. This might refer to creativity, confidence, money, or a more literal idea of birth and growth. Summer spells will highlight heat, warmth, and the idea of abundance that is already all around us. Spells for autumn will refer to the nearness of life to death as well as decay, harvest, and aging. Winter spells, as mentioned above, will usually reference the cold, death, isolation, hope for the upcoming year of abundance, or the warmth of spending time indoors among other people.

Season reliant spells may also need to use the energy generated by holidays in a given season. These holidays will usually be those on the Wiccan Wheel of the Year. In some cases, however, culturally-relevant celebrations may also find their way into spells. These can include the secular celebration of Christmas, national holidays like the Fourth of July or Thanksgiving, and commercial holidays like Valentine's Day.

Every holiday has its own atmosphere, and these spells seek to tap into it. Winter holiday spells might want to use the giving, jolly themes that permeate secular winter holidays. A Fourth of July spell, on the other hand, might tap into the excitement of fireworks and the easy fun of a bonfire or cookout with friends. A Thanksgiving spell would reference a sense of gratitude and fullness. And, finally, Valentine's spell would call on the love – romantic and otherwise – that tends to abound at that time of year.

There are countless other holidays that can be tapped into, of course. But larger holidays tend to get more attention. And this, in turn, lends them more energy. Practitioners will also find the energy of holidays easier to work with if they celebrate the holidays themselves. So, while the energy of an unknown holiday might seem appealing, it might also not work since the practitioner doesn't have a connection to it.

The Day

Spells relying on certain days of the week are a fairly new concept. Humans have used a few different calendars over the years, which means that the days of the week changed names. And when it comes to spellwork, names are wildly important.

Some spells have to be cast on certain days because that day is named for a specific deity. Otherwise, a spell will specify a day because of the social energy that surrounds that day.

The Power of a Name

Most days of the week were named after Pre-Christian gods. Wednesday, for example, is often linked to the Norse All father Odin, since his name is pronounced "Woden" in traditional texts. Similarly, Thursday is "Thor's Day," named for Odin's son Thor, the God of storms and harvests.

Both of these days are heavily tied to attributes associated with Odin and Thor. Wednesdays are ideal for divination, seeking the truth, or seeking knowledge. Thursday, on the other hand, is ideal for spells that want to reap the benefits of something the witch has already done.

Social Energy

The term "social energy" isn't widely used in the magical community. But it is the best term for the way society views certain days of the week and the energy this then projects onto that day. This energy can then be used to fuel, direct, or amplify certain spells.

Productivity spells are an excellent example. They work best when cast on a Monday because, in most cultures, Monday is the beginning of the workweek. If the spell were cast on a Friday, it would not have that unconscious association with work.

On the other end of the spectrum, a tension relief spell works best when cast on a Friday. Even people who work over the weekend still use the phrase "Thank god it's Friday" because of many cultures associate Friday with the beginning of their time off.

Phases of the Moon

The most common time constraint placed on spells is the phase of the moon. Wiccans are generally very attuned to the moon as it represents their Goddess. And as the Wiccan Goddess has her three aspects of Maiden, Mother, and Crone, so the moon can wax, sit full in the sky, or wane. The new moon is also important to Wiccans, but it is seen more as an absence of the Goddess rather than one of Her aspects.

Each phase of the moon channels the properties of its corresponding aspect of the Goddess. Most calendars keep track of new and full moons, which makes it easy to pinpoint where in the cycle a particular day falls. Witches also tend to count the day before and after an "official" full or new moon as part of that particular phase. This is in part to honor the preference for multiples of three within Wicca and also to give practitioners a little more time for spellwork.

The Waxing Moon and the Maiden Goddess

Wiccans associate the waxing moon with the first face of the triple Goddess, the Maiden. Both a waxing moon and the Maiden Goddess are young versions of the larger powers they will one day be. Over time they will grow into their full power and then, eventually, fade. But for now, they are young and vibrant. They represent growth and growing things.

Spells for the waxing moon include any kind of spell meant to increase something the practitioner already has. This could mean creativity, money, friends, confidence. The possibilities are limited only by the practitioner. Gardening spells are also best cast during the waxing moon, as the moon's growing energy will encourage the plants to grow as well.

The Full Moon and the Mother Goddess

Although the Mother Goddess represents a variety of motherly traits, the full moon's connection to Her rests in its resemblance to a pregnant belly. This resemblance also symbolizes all of the untapped promises that a full moon holds. It also represents nurturing energy as well as achieving things after working for them.

Full moon spells tend to be spells that increase the harvest of something a practitioner has worked toward. Practitioners may also use the full moon to support new endeavors, as the promise of unknown potential makes full moons ideal for such things. Such spells may include attempts to find romantic love if the practitioner is not already in a relationship. Or, on the professional side of things, spells meant to attract a new job or new opportunities that the witch does not yet have access to.

The Waning Moon and the Crone

The third and final aspect of the Wiccan Goddess is the crone. She represents old age, wisdom, and experience. The crone may not be as sprightly as the Maiden or as vibrant as the Mother. But she has knowledge neither can match and she has lived through so much more than either can imagine. And, in this, she is connected to the waning moon.

Because the crone has lived through so much, she knows how to overcome nearly any obstacle. And she lends this energy to the waning moon. This makes the waning moon an ideal time to cast protective and banishing spells. The crone's ability to survive, and even thrive, will boost a protective spell. Banishing spells will gain power as the moon grows ever small in the sky, as well. Some witches even time their banishing spells to begin as soon as the moon leaves its full phase and end when the last visible sliver leaves the sky.

The Dark Moon or The New Moon

The final phase of the lunar cycle is not connected to an aspect of the Goddess. Rather, it is more connected to her absence. The new moon, or dark moon as some practitioners refer to it, is a time to delve into shadow work. Truth-seeking spells and spells that connect practitioners to the spirit realm are usually reserved for this phase of the moon.

The new moon is also an excellent time to banish unwanted energies. Witches believe that the energies will be trapped within the void where the moon should be, then be cleansed and released when the moon begins waxing again. This is why many witches will use the new moon as a chance to cleanse their altars and tools. Many tarot deck cleansing spells call for the deck to be set beneath a white quartz crystal under a new moon.

Chapter 5: A Selection of Spells

It is impossible to compile every spell into one single book. There are certain types of spells that beginners tend to favor, however. Each of those categories is represented here with two sample spells for new spell workers. They are excellent building blocks for larger, more complex spells. And they should serve to guide new practitioners as they find the best spells for their particular approach to magic.

Each spell is formatted with a list of necessary components, an incantation, and a selection of real-world actions. It is assumed that practitioners have raised a protective circle and called the necessary energies into the circle before they begin the spell.

Wellness and Health

There as many wellness spells out there as there are afflictions in the human body. This book contains a basic spell to banish a general illness as well as a spell to increase the practitioner's motivation to exercise.

To Banish an Illness

Illnesses sometimes seem to linger well past when they should. If you're ready to kick your cold, give this spell a try. If you intend to cast this spell for someone else, be sure you get their permission first.

Components You Will Need

- A lock of hair from the person you want to heal, tied with black ribbon
- A small black candle (such as a tea light)
- A match and something to strike it on
- A plate or try you can drip wax onto

Follow These Steps

Sit in the center of your protective circle and center the plate in front of you. Next, strike the match and then light a candle. Then set the lock of hair on the plate and set the candle on top of it. With your match and striker, light the candle. Be careful to keep the flame away from the hair, as burnt hair smells awful and can become a fire hazard.

Watch the candle flame for a few minutes and think about the specific symptoms you want to banish. If the illness has a specific name, keep it in mind. Visualize all of the symptoms as energy or vapor in a sickly color. Then, with that image in mind, recite the incantation.

  Illness lingers, bringing misery

  I seek rest for {person's name} in the name of Divinity

  May their health return and bloom

  And illness fade into the gloom

Carefully pick up the candle and tilt it so that the black wax falls onto the hair. The flame will tip upward, so be sure your hand is not in the way. As the candle wax drips onto the hair, imagine a sticky substance moving through your image of the symptoms. This substance collects all the sickly energy together and binds it into one mass.

Set the candle back down on the plate, some distance from the hair. Visualize the person you're trying to help, this time without the sickly energy all around them. Now that the negative energy is gone repeat the following incantation.

  Into their void, I do call

  Energy of the Watchtowers true and tall

  Fill the space and make it shine

  Heal {person's name} with light Divine

Blow out the candle gently, so you do not splatter wax anywhere. The candle is now tied to the symptoms or illness and so should not be used again. Both the candle and the hair should be disposed of as quickly as possible, and any remaining wax scraped off the plate. It is also a good idea to cleanse the plate during the next new moon to ensure no lingering traces of the sickly energy remain.

Real-World Action

- Drink plenty of water and soup broth to keep electrolyte levels balanced
- Be sure to take the proper dosage of all medication
- Clean the room where the sick person has been sleeping and air it out

Exercise Motivation Spell

There are a million reasons to exercise more often. For cardiac health, for the fun of moving, for weight loss. The list is nearly endless. Motivation, however, is not. And the harder some people push themselves to exercise, the less they want to. This spell invites motivation into the practitioner's workout routine.

Components You Will Need

- Nothing but visualization

Follow These Steps

Sit in the center of your circle and close your eyes. Visualize the type of exercise that you normally do. If you dislike your normal workout routine but cannot change it, visualize yourself going through the routine with a genuine smile on your face. If you can change your routine, visualize yourself in the midst of something active that you do like to do or would like to try.

Now flex your fingers and toes in time with the movement in your visualization. Imagine yourself moving in sync with the version of you in your head. While moving, try to focus on how good it feels to control the muscles you're using. While still moving, recite the incantation.

This body is mine

To move as I choose

But my energy wanes

And motivation I lose.

Imagine your movements slowing down. Try to remember what it feels like when you know you should get up and get moving, but your motivation fails you. Imagine the bright energy of the Divine and the Watchtowers sweeping into you and carrying away the sluggish feeling that you've been carrying. Then recite the final incantation.

Lift me up

Energy Divine

Let me move

Let me shine!

Switch your visualization back to the happy and energetic movements you started with. This time, imagine yourself glowing or sparkling with the energy of the Watchtowers and the Divine. Open your eyes and shake off any jitters you may be feeling. Then move into the closing of the spell. Every time you go to exercise, take a moment to repeat the second incantation, and remember the feeling of the light shimmering through you.

Real-World Action

- Find a form of exercise that you like.
- Get rid of any ill-fitting exercise clothes and replace them with comfortable alternatives.
- Set up reminders on your phone and non-food rewards to give yourself small reminders as well as immediate gratification to help set your new habit.

Love, Relationships, and Sex

This is one area where the Wiccan rule to Harm None is immediately obvious. Love spells, when intended to compel affection from a specific person, are strictly forbidden. They are seen as a form of harm since they aim to remove a person's free will.

Instead of compelling a particular person, love spells are meant to attract love into a person's life from whatever source is best. Practitioners should be careful that they specify the type of love they are looking for, as these spells can be applied to platonic, familial, romantic, or sexual love.

Unlike the other sections, this section has three spells. There is one to attract love, one to support communication, and one to boost the practitioner's sexual confidence.

A Spell to Attract Love

This is a general spell to attract any kind of love. Practitioners can fine-tune it through visualization and the real-world actions they take after the spell has been cast.

Components You Will Need

- A rose quartz crystal or petals from a flower that brings love to mind
- A small magnet or a few small hematite beads
- A drawstring pouch

Follow These Steps

Get comfortable in your circle and set the pouch in front of you. Gather the rose quartz or petals in your hand, then add the magnets or hematite. Close your eyes and imagine the energy of all the ingredients swirling together in your hand and pouring over like mist.

This mist combines loving energy with the attraction of a magnet. And, as you are holding the heart of the mist in your hands, it is attracting love to you. Imagine the mist rising up and out into the world, seeking energy that would work well with your own. Hold this image in your mind and say the following incantation:

As I hold

In my hand

The vapor of magnetic love

So, more love

Returns to me

Drawn by the Divine above

With your eyes still closed, find the pouch with your free hand. Hold onto it as you focus your visualization on what love looks like to you. Imagine moments with the loved one you want to attract, but be careful not to focus too much on a single person.

Once the image is clear in your mind, open your eyes and slowly deposit all of the loose ingredients into the pouch. Tie the pouch shut and make sure you keep it near or on you at all times. This can include putting it under your pillow or on your nightstand, carrying it in your pocket, or wearing it on a necklace under your shirt.

This spell may have to be renewed every few lunar cycles to make sure it retains its potency. Like all energy, it wanes over time, and as it does, so its ability to attract love to the practitioner.

Real-World Action

- Remind yourself of this spell when you step outside. Use the reminder to loosen any tension you're carrying and make you more approachable.

- Try to interact with more people. Join a book club, take a cooking class, or go out with friends and meet other people they know.

- Put love out into the world. Volunteer or reach out to people you already know to show your affection. This will eventually return to you with even more love.

Clear Communication Spell

Components You Will Need

- A piece of paper folded like a fan
- Incense with a minty scent (optional)

Follow These Steps

Stand in the center of your circle and close your eyes. Visualize a general conversation between you and another person. Whenever one of you speaks, imagine is creates a trail through the air. Some parts of the trail are easy to see, and others are blurred as if covered in fog. If you choose to use incense, you can imagine the smoke of the incense, making these foggy sections more obvious.

Begin slowly waving the fan. With each wave, a little more of the fog will vanish from the lines of communication that run from one person to the other. Be sure and fan the fog *away* from you, so that it will leave the circle of your energy and no longer hover around your communication. As the fog begins to thin, repeat this incantation:

What once was lost

Can now be found

No longer hidden

Behind foggy sound

The way is clear

And we will be heard

To each other's ears

Our intended words

Continue fanning until all the smoke has cleared from the lines of communication in your visualization. Inhale the minty smell, if you used incense, and link the scent to the idea of communicating clearly. This way, the scent of mint will always bring this spell to mind and add a little more power to it.

Mint is generally considered a calming scent. And that is the reason it works well for this spell. It calms the energy around speaking and allows for clearer communication.

Once the spell is over, carry the fan in your bag or folded in a pocket. You might not use it again, but it will act as a talisman to remind you of the spell.

Real-World Action

- Always think before you speak, especially when you're angry. Use very specific words.

- Insist on having time to think about your response before you say it and offer the same courtesy to other people.

- Don't assume tone carries well over written communication. Unless it is a professional message, use emojis, actions tags, or tone markers like "(sarcasm, of course!)" to ensure your reader understands the tone you're using.

Sexual Confidence Spell

This spell is a bit unique in that it has no incantation. It is purely a visualization spell that channels the energy you summon into a candle. This candle is then used as a reminder for the witch to light and focus on when they need to feel sexy and confident.

Another unique aspect of this spell is where it takes place. The practitioner needs to be comfortable while also having access to a light switch without leaving the protective circle, as the lights will need to go off about halfway through the spell.

Components You Will Need

- Comfortable clothes that you feel good while wearing
- A large candle in your favorite color
- A light or match and something to strike it on

- A candle holder sized to the candle you chose

Follow These Steps

Dress in the outfit you selected. These clothes should make you feel attractive and comfortable. Try to avoid things that are too tight as this will cause discomfort, and that is the opposite of the spell's intention. Since there is no incantation, all of the spell's intent and energy will feed into your visualization. So, you'll want to avoid as much discomfort as possible

Once you are dressed, settle into a comfortable position. This spell may be the best cast while lying in bed or reclining on a couch if the protective circle can be cast around either one of these locations. There should also be a table nearby where you can set the candle down without creating a fire hazard.

Set the candle in the candle holder on the table, then pick up the candle. Do not light it yet. Instead, settle into as comfortable a position as possible and close your eyes. Visualize yourself in a situation that makes you feel sexy and confident. It does not have to be an erotic situation, just one that makes you feel sure of yourself and desirable. If you struggle with feeling this way, create an imaginary scenario in your head.

Slowly visualize the energy of the Goddess, the God, and the Watchtowers empowering the scene in your mind. Each new addition of energy makes it glow a little bit brighter and makes the feeling a little bit more intense. Then, as energy flows through your visualization, imagine it sinking into your skin, traveling down your hands, and flowing into the candle.

You can imagine as many or as few scenes as you'd like. Through them, all, hold onto the candle and channel the charged energy into the wax. This is called "charging," and it will fill the candle with this positive, sexy, confident energy.

When you feel the candle is fully charged, open your eyes, and put the candle in the candle holder. Strike the match and light the candle, then douse the match and set it aside. Turn out the lights and focus your attention on the candle flame. Watch it dance and flicker like a dancer, one powered by the confidence you charged the candle with.

Find the mirror and hold it up so that you can see your own face. Watch the way the candlelight plays across your features and try on a few smiles. Find an expression that matches the allure and confidence you felt in your visualization. Practice this face several times, each time remembering how you felt when you visualized yourself full of confidence.

When the expression feels natural, set the mirror aside. Gently blow out the candle. You can meditate in the dark if that feels like a good next step. Or you can begin cleaning up the spell.

Unlike most candle spells, you want to keep the candle from this one. It is charged with your energy. So, every time you burn it, you will feel that allure and confidence returning to you. You can light the candle when you've had a long day, before a day, when you're with a partner or any time you need a little boost to remember that you deserve to feel sexy and confident.

Real-World Action

- Take time to look at yourself naked in the mirror. Find at least one thing you really like about your own body. We are more critical of ourselves than other people will be, so if you can find one, your partner will find a lot more!

- Learn what you like for yourself. Explore without a partner so that you know what you want from your partner when you are with one.

- Practice speaking up for what you want in all situations. Some people have a very hard time with this for a variety of reasons. But if you can get comfortable speaking up at work or in a restaurant, it will be easier to speak up with a sexual partner.

Money and Prosperity

Prosperity spells are probably the most common across every magic-using culture. These spells can be modified to attract several different types of wealth. It all depends on what the practitioner needs. In this case, the spell below will attract a new job. The second spell is one that will protect assets already in the practitioner's possession.

Attracting a Job

It doesn't matter why you want to attract a job. Maybe you have one and need another. Maybe you want a better one. Or maybe you've been searching, and nothing you find will actually pay the bills. Whatever your reason this spell will help pull more opportunities into your orbit.

Components You Will Need

- A small piece of paper with your ideal job details on it
- A small magnet
- A drawstring pouch
- A small picture of you (optional)

Follow These Steps

This particular spell requires a little bit of preparation before you raise the protective circle. Prior to casting the spell, spend some time thinking about the type of job you want to attract. A general attraction spell might bring in job listings well outside your industry or in the wrong pay grade. Or, worse yet, it could find you the perfect job but on the other side of the country.

So, take a little time and write down exactly what you want. What sort of duties do you want to perform and which are you willing to perform? You can also write out duties you don't want to perform, but every job has things that you aren't going to like. You just have to set your priorities.

ou should also write down the hours you want to work and where you would like the job to be located. You can also write down things like "near to restaurants" or "paid lunch" if they're the sort of thing your preferred field is likely to offer. Just keep in mind that the more restrictions you put on it, the fewer job opportunities the spell is likely to generate.

Once you've written out the details, raise the circle and call the various energies per instructions. Take your list and place it into the pouch, then add the magnet and your picture, if you've chosen to use one. As you're putting everything into the pouch, recite the following incantation:

Oh, powers Above

And powers around

Seek out work

Let it abound

Cinch the pouch shut and close out the spell. You can leave the spell pouch on your altar or carry it in your bag as you go about your day. If you follow the action suggestions below and have a dedicated interview outfit, you can also hang the pouch on the outfit's hangar so that the two can feed off each other's energy.

Real-World Action

- Create several resume options if you are applying in a few separate but related fields. Adjust your job descriptions, focuses, and skills to match each one, so it's ready to go.
- Create your own cover letter template that you can easily adapt when applying for a job.
- Have one particular outfit for interviews. Make sure it is comfortable but professional. Only wear it for interviews so that it gets you in the frame of mind to go through an interview.

Protecting Your Assets

While most prosperity spells are focused on bringing new abundance into someone's life, this spell is focused on protecting what you already have. Your assets don't have to be monetary, either. It can be ideal for a book you want to write, the energy you've worked hard to extract from toxic situations or your own sense of well-being.

Components You Will Need

- Something to represent your assets. It can be anything from a game token to a printed picture, so long as it fits in the smaller box or jar
- A box with a secure lid
- A smaller box or jar that fits inside the lidded box
- A handful of sharp things like nails, staples, or screws.

Follow These Steps

Set all the spell ingredients out in front of you. Pick up the item that you've chosen to represent your assets. Hold it in your hand and close your eyes. Visualize the specific assets you want to protect. This spell works best if you limit it to one *type* of asset, whether that be property, money, energy, ideas, etc. If you want to protect multiple types of assets, you should cast this spell several times over several days. Just be sure you use a different representation each time.

As you visualize your assets, imagine a colorful protective light swirling around them. Once your assets are completely protected by this light, guide this image into the representation in your hand. Feel the heat of the energy as it flows down your arm and into the item you've chosen.

Open your eyes once your hand and the representation have cooled off again. Take the jar or smaller box and place the representation inside. Close the box or jar and hold it in both your hands. Imagine another swirling mass of protective light, this one even thicker and brighter than the previous.

This light will form a shield around the jar or box. Visualize it coating the container in your hands and seeping into the material. Imagine the energy acting as a sealant to prevent anything negative from entering the container and taking what is yours. You have now placed two layers of protection around your assets, but there are two more to be added.

Take the larger box and place the smaller container inside. Then take the collection of sharp things and sprinkle them around the smaller container. These will act as defensive barriers to any energy that gets into the larger box looking for access to your assets.

Hold your hands over the open larger box and close your eyes once more. Imagine a heavy layer of energy pouring out of your hands and over the box. As your energy washes over the box, repeat the incantation:

What is mine shall stay so

Until I choose to let it go

No other shall come and take what's mine

'This now protected by power Divine

Continue with the visualization into the wave of energy begins to thin. When it does, break off the connection and shake your hands to chase off any lingering sparks of energy. Find the lid to the larger box and press it securely into place.

After you close out the spell and clean everything up, take the nested boxes somewhere safe. Popular hiding places include under the practitioner's bed or in their closet, especially if their room is warded. Others bury their boxes, particularly if there is an active threat to their assets or if they do not need to access the spelled box any time soon.

If you choose to do multiple spell boxes, do not put all your representations into one box. It is best to keep them separate and spread out so that they are harder to get into. Should you need to break the spell for whatever reason, you need only open the box and fan the energy away. Since it is your energy and your assets, you can then easily take back the energy you invested and remove the spell. Just be sure to cleanse everything involved in the working once it has been disassembled.

Real-World Action

- Regularly change passwords on your accounts and do not share them with anyone

- Shred all mail with account information on it, then recycle the shredded paper

- Keep a budget and regularly check your bank account. This will keep you updated on how much money you're spending and where it's going.

Success and Opportunity

Everyone measures success differently. Financial stability is the most obvious variety, of course. But creative success and successful relationships are also vital for people who want to live balanced lives. This is why the spells in this section are a little more general than the other spells in this book.

Both the **Attracting Opportunity** and the **Promoting Creativity** spells are left intentionally vague. There is a lot of room for the spell caster to improvise without altering the structure of the spell. This was done so that, no matter what opportunity the practitioner wants or what form of creativity they seek, they can tailor the spell to their needs and still expect success.

Attracting Opportunity

This is another spell that beginning witches can tailor to their needs without changing the actual structure of the spell. It is written so that the practitioner can define their own idea of opportunity instead of a form that may not fit their desires.

Components You Will Need
- A small magnet
- A piece of paper
- A pen

- An envelope or pouch
- Something to write on

Follow These Steps

Settle yourself into whatever position is comfortable given what you've chosen to write on. Settle the pen and paper on the writing surface with the magnet and pouch or envelope a little bit off to the side.

Hold your hands over the pen and paper as you close your eyes. Imagine opportunity as tiny stars dancing all around you. Some of them are far away, and some of them are closer. Through visualization, draw them closer until they are covering your hands and arms. Then guide them down into the paper and pen until they're absorbed into the materials.

Open your eyes and pick up the pen. Write out exactly what kind of opportunities you're hoping for. Be as descriptive as you like. You can even use multiple sheets of paper, so long as they fit into the pouch or envelope at the end. The entire time you're writing, try and remember that the paper and ink you're using are both infused with the possibility of new and dazzling opportunities. That energy, as well as your own energy and the energy you've called into your circle, are all focused on the words you're writing.

After you've written everything down, set the pen off the side. Hold your hands over the pages and recite the following incantation:

My eyes and arms are open

To all I see

May opportunity find me

So, mote it be

I welcome the fire

Of chance and design

To take the gifts, I may be given

By nature and Divine

Blow gently on the page to ensure the ink is dry. When it is, place the magnet on top of your words. Fold up the paper or papers, careful to keep the magnet inside. Then put the entire bundle into the envelope or pouch. Hold the pouch in you both hands and close your eyes once more. Bring back the vision of star-like opportunities swirling all around you as you recite the final incantation.

I pray, opportunity

That you will be mine

Called into my life

By Divine and Design

You may now close out the spell. This pouch should be kept on you at all times, whether tied to your belt or carried in your bag. The magnet will amplify the spell's attractive properties, and the pouch itself will act as a reminder to keep your eyes open for new opportunities.

This spell can be repeated as many times as necessary for each new type of opportunity the witch wants to encourage. As with other repeat spells, however, you should always use new materials. And when you have been given the opportunities you asked for; you should release the energy from your spell.

To do this, simply open the envelope and unfold the papers. Rip them gently as you thank the Divine and the Watchtowers for lending you their strength. Put the paper into the recycling and set the magnet out to be cleansed under the next new moon.

Real-World Action

- Update any social media that is linked to the opportunity you want. Whether it's a professional profile or an account showcasing your art, keep everything current.

- Get involved with the world you want opportunities in. Attend seminars and workshops, particularly if they're free. Engage with bigger names on social media in a professional way. Consume media from the area you want to grow in. All of these feed the spell and create channels for the energy to flow through.

Promoting Creativity

There are as many kinds of creativity as there are people in the world. And, for this reason, this spell relies solely on visualization, a small incantation, and a small talisman that won't get in the way when the practitioner uses it. It doesn't matter if they create through dance, welding, or writing. This spell should help them overcome any ruts they're stuck in and achieve their creative goals.

Components You Will Need

- A small charm you can wear or tuck into a pocket
- A table to hold the charm while you work

Follow These Steps

Stand in the center of your circle and slowly shake the tension from your shoulders. Close your eyes and let your head droop down to your chest. As you relax into this position, imagine creativity as brightly colored butterflies or Fae fluttering around you. Gently raise your head, eyes still closed, and slowly raise your arms out to either side.

Hold this position as you imagine the brightly colored beings fluttering toward you. They will alight gently, hesitantly, the way some ideas arrive slowly in your mind. As each being lands on your outstretched arms and hands, they become shimmering waves of energy that attract ever-smaller fluttering shapes. Each one lands with a little more confidence in the same way good ideas build on one another until you're steaming along through a project. Try to stay in this position until your arms begin to feel tired. Then, still moving slowly so as not to shake off the creative energy coating your arms and hands, lower your hands until they hover above the charm you selected. Visualize the energy slowly rolling down your hands and fingers before the charm draws it in and captures it inside. Recite the incantation as you feed more and more energy into the charm:

Blocks are gone

Your presence is wrong

And my power will shine

My work shall abound

From the energy all around

Guided by the Divine

Repeat the incantation as necessary until the last of the energy has been channeled into the charm. Then you may lower your arms and shake off any lingering sparks. From here you may close out the spell.

Keep the charm on your person in an easily accessible place. Whenever you feel blocked or stifled, rub the charm between two fingers and remember how it felt every time a new being alighted on your arms. Try to feel their energy now contained in the charm, which is now tied to your creative endeavors.

The charm's power will fade over time. Before you renew it, be sure to cleanse it of the original energy and thank the Goddess and God for their aid. You can also thank the Muses for their gifts if it suits your practice. This spell is general enough to suit any creative endeavor, of course. And, depending on the size of the charms, practitioners can make several and wear them as part of a magical charm bracelet or set of bracelets. This will work best if each charm is unique enough that you can discern them from touch alone so that you do not have to interrupt whatever you are working on to find the specific charm for the medium at hand.

Real-World Action

- Spend at least 20 minutes a day with your chosen creative pursuit. You don't have to make progress. Just turn off all distractions and get used to working with your materials.

- Start working without a goal in mind. Free-writing and doodling are great ways to get your creativity going. They give your spell more energy to work with so it can guide you and keep you in motion.

- Don't share a project before it is finished. This puts pressure on you to finish by a certain deadline, and that may cut off creative energy.

Friendship Spells

As with love spells, friendship spells should never be used on specific people. And for much the same reason. The spells in this section should be cast in a general, instead, on the practitioner. They will either help the practitioner attract new friends, or they will allow the practitioner to clearly see false friends they may already have.

Attracting New Friends

Making friends is hard, and it only gets harder the older we get. Some people overcome this issue but spending all their free time in social settings. But, for some people, that is entirely too overwhelming. For those people, this spell can help attract new opportunities to meet like-minded people while increasing the chances people will click when they finally do meet.

Components You Will Need

- A piece of jewelry or clothing you can wear to social events.
- Incense whose scent you find very appealing
- A match and something to strike it on
- Something to fan the incense smoke with (an index card works well)

Follow These Steps

This spell is the best cast around your altar or a table that can serve as a temporary workspace. You need enough space to put the incense on the table and then situation the jewelry or clothing between you and incense burner without risking any ashes hitting the item in question.

Light the incense and wait until the smoke is rising consistently. Then shake out the match and set it aside. Pick up the fan and slowly begin waving the smoke towards you, so it wafts over the garment. This action will draw energy into the garment or jewelry, then into you. It mimics your desire to have new friendships to enter your life.

As you waft the smoke closer, recite the incantation:

Making friends can be a chore

But not with aid from the Divine

With their hands to guide

Companionship shall be mine

Continue wafting until about a quarter to a third of the incense has burned down. Set the fan aside and snuff out the incense before closing out the spell. You should be able to wash the garment or clean the jewelry without losing any of the energy you imbued it with, should the need arise.

You should wear your charged object to any social gathering. It doesn't matter if it's coffee with an old friend, a solo trip to the farmer's market, or a work party. Wearing the charged item will remind you of your desire to meet and connect with new people. The spell will sync with your natural energies, and two will support one another throughout your time at the event.

Real-World Action

- Attend one community event every month or every other month. This can be something like a Meetup, a farmer's market, or a presentation at your local library.

- Reach out to friends and family you already talk to. Strengthening those connections will lead to introductions to more people, opening more channels for your spell to use.

- Pursue your interests. You are likely to meet a kindred spirit if you attend free art exhibits, local writing groups, or fitness classes that match your interests.

Discerning False Friends

Nobody likes to talk about the damage false friends can do. Even the idea of trusting someone only to have them betray you is enough to make some people cry. And, unfortunately, it is not always easy to discern true friends from those that can be trusted. This spell should provide practitioners with a bit of a leg-up. As with other amulet spells, the practitioner will need to wear the charged item in order to receive the boost. But so long as the jewelry is against their skin, they will have a customized early warning system when someone is deceptive.

Components You Will Need

- A piece of jewelry you can wear close to your skin
- A candle of any color and shape.
- A match and something to strike it against

Follow These Steps

Strike the match and light the candle, then shake out the match and set it aside where it will not smolder. Make sure the flame is burning bright and strong, then hold the jewelry up above the flames. Make sure that the flame cannot harm the jewelry, then shift your focus to the flame.

Feel the flame's heat and focus on the energy it is putting out. Visualize that energy going up into the charm and settling there.

As you focus on this visualization, recite the incantation:

As Earth holds me steady

And wind stirs the leaves

I will see the truth

I will not be deceived

As the fire burns mist away

And water washes all clean

I will tell the truth

Deceivers shall be seen

Repeat the incantation three times, each time visualizing more heat and energy pouring into the jewelry in your hands. Once this is done, you can set the jewelry aside and close out the spell. Because the candle was only used as an energy source and not fed any sort of energy, it can be used for later purposes in both mundane and magical situations.

Keep the jewelry on your altar until you are around the person or people you believe might be lying. When you know, you'll be around them, put on the jewelry, and wear it under your clothes. It will grow noticeably warmer against your skin when someone nearby is telling a lie. When you get back home, take the amulet off and return it to your altar, careful not to leave it out where it may be cleansed in the light of the new moon.

If you do decide to cleanse the pendant, it may require more than one cleansing. It depends on how much energy was channeled into the pendant, how often it was used, and how aggressively it was asked to pick up on deception. Those sorts of actions will ingrain energy into an object. Conversely, repeatedly charging the object may cause a permanent reaction in the amulet though this usually takes years of consistent use and charging.

Be aware that the pendant will warm up the longer it rests against your skin until it reaches body temperature. Do not mistake this sensation for a proper warning. When the amulet detects deception, it will become noticeably hotter. When the person is done speaking or has walked away again, the amulet will return to your body temperature.

Real-World Action

- Listen closely when people speak. Make a note of who talks about others when they are not around. Most of what people say in these instances is either false or exaggerated. Your amulet should pick up on the deception in their words.

- Do not gossip. It is hurtful and attracts other people who will then gossip about you in turn.

- Listen more than you speak. This will allow you to understand better what people are saying while also noticing any dishonesty in their words.

Shielding and Protection

Wiccans do not believe in casting curses or hexes. They know it can be done, of course. But it is against the rules that govern their religion. And, ultimately, they believe that it will do the spell caster more harm than good. But that does not mean that Wiccans are defenseless.

When a Wiccan is threatened, either magically or physically, they prefer to use defensive measures. If they are in physical danger, they will resort to appropriate real-world responses, of course. But they support these with magical defenses. Two such defensive spells are listed below. The first is a general armor spell that relies on visualization while the second creates a representation of a "reflective shield" that simply sends negativity back to its source.

Protective Armor Spell

The most commonly used Wiccan protection spell is an armor spell. It relies solely on visualization. This means, however, that the image in the practitioner's mind must be clear, vivid, and highly personal. The practitioner should be sure their circle is cast somewhere that allows them a comfortable place to sit, as there are likely to be there for quite some time.

Components You Will Need

- Time to create a highly detailed and personal visual representation

Follow These Steps

Settle yourself in a comfortable sitting position. Close your eyes and ground yourself to the release any excess tension you have stored in your body. Once your shoulders are relaxed, and you're breathing is even, try to clear your mind. Thoughts will still run through your mind, but just let them go and focus your attention on the visual of an empty white field.

Once you can know you ignore thoughts when they try to interrupt you, imagine yourself standing in that field. And then, very slowly, begin to imagine protective energies swirling around you. They can be any and all colors. And they may appear as crackling lightning, soft mist, or small fluttering creatures. The only rule they must adhere to is that they make you feel calm, protected, and at peace.

Starting with your fingertips, imagine the energy wrapping itself around you. This energy will not merge with your energy but rather sit on top of it. It will create a layer of armor between you and any negative energy that others may turn your way.

Visualize the energy slowly wrapping itself around you from head to toe. It will feel comfortably warm, and your skin may tingle faintly. These are all good signs that you are wrapping yourself in a protective layer.

If you struggle to maintain the vision of swirling energy, you can try imagining a more mundane suit of armor. Imagine the energy tingling against your skin as it changes from pure energy to a visual representation you are more familiar with.

Once the energy coats you from head to toe, center yourself. This will lock the shield in around you. It will not affect you in any way, but anyone trying to do you harm will find it harder than normal to reach you. If you need to release your armor for any reason, you can do so by finding its anchor in your center and releasing the energy the same way you release energy from a circle. Thank it for protecting you and let it flow back into the universe.

Real-World Action

- Remember that you are shielded. Adjust your reactions to things accordingly.
- Do not become cocky. Every shield has a weak spot, and magical shields are not meant to protect from negative energy we

deliberately call on ourselves, only negative energy unnecessarily directed from others.

- Act as a shield to other people. Speak up when you see someone being put down. This feeds positive energy into your shield and overwhelms negative energy with positive energy.

Mirror Box Protection Spell

This is one of the most complex spells in the book and requires a bit of DIY handiwork. It is also one of the strongest. And, once the mirror box has been created, the spell can be refreshed over and over with a lot less effort.

Because this spell does have a crafty DIY component to it, the practitioner should make sure they raise their protective circle somewhere they will have access to a tabletop or other similar work surface.

Components You Will Need

- Mirrored tiles or sheets of mirrored plastic cut to size
- A small box
- Glue
- Paint or other decorative supplies (optional)
- A small cushion or pile of fabric scraps to go in the box

- A talisman to represent the person who needs protection
- A table on which to work

Follow These Steps

Spread your materials out on the work surface. If you are using sheets of mirrored plastic, this should have been cut down to the size of each of the box's exterior faces. This includes the lid, the lid's sides, and the bottom of the box. You should not mirror the box's interior, however, as they will have a very different effect.

The mirrors on the exterior of the box symbolize spiritual mirrors that will reflect any negative energy away from you and back to its source. If you were to put mirrors on the inside of the box, it would reflect all your own energy back to you. This isn't an inherently bad idea. But it won't serve as a protection spell the way this one will.

Begin the spell by raising the circle and calling the energy as you normally would. Then settle down at your work station and begin gluing the mirrors into place. Cover as much of the box's exterior as you ca, including the bottom and every side of the lid. If you are particularly crafty, you can paint or create collages on the inside of the box, but this isn't strictly necessary.

Once the mirrors are in place and interior is as decorated as you would like it to be, place the cushion or fabric into the bottom of the box. Then set the box aside for now and pick up the talisman. This is where the visualization comes in.

Imagine your own energy. Everyone assigns their energy a particular color. Usually, though not always, it's their favorite color. Try to imagine this color swirling around and through you, a part of you even when it wanders off to follow a path you created when you gave energy to someone or something.

Now imagine that same energy swirling through and around the talisman in your hands. Do not push your energy into it. Just imagine your energy connecting to it as the energy flows from your hands and over the talisman. When you feel firmly connected, recite this incantation:

As you put out

So it comes back

This is my defense

It is not an attack

Mirrors to protect me

Warded on every side

And among the peace within

I shall abide

Gently place the talisman inside of the box and close put the lid on. Although the talisman is closed inside the box, it is important to remember that you are not closed in the box. Instead, you are now protected by unseen mirrors that will deflect negativity.

Closeout the spell and clean everything up, then put the box somewhere nobody will go digging through it. It is also a good idea to ground and center after this particular spell so that all the energy currently extended beyond your shields will be drawn back inside.

If one of the mirrors cracks, you will have to redo the spell. Sometimes a mirror will crack for mundane reasons like the box falls off a shelf or something is dropped on top of it. But sometimes the shields take such a heavy beating that cracks appear in the mirrors on the box. It is for this reason that practitioners should regularly check the box, regardless of where it is kept.

Real-World Action

- Do not engage with people who bait you. That allows their energy past your shields.

- Remind yourself that negative energy returns to its source. Try to be a source of positive energy

- Disengage from things that cause stress whenever possible. If it is your job, take at least 20 minutes every day to listen to music and distract your thoughts from work. If it is a person you have to interact with, choose one day or an hour every day where you will try to avoid interacting with them. This gives your shield more time to grow between you and the source of negative energy.

Luck and Chance

Spells to attract luck or affect chance are, understandably, some of the most unpredictable. And while they won't get you banned in Vegas; some witches are wary of them because they feel that such spells try too hard to shift a person's natural balance of luck.

In the interest of not upending the balance too severely, both of the spells in this section are fairly mild. They will attract a small amount of good luck or dispel a little bad luck if cast correctly. But they won't help anyone suddenly win the lottery or anything else just as unlikely!

Attracting Good Luck

Everyone could use a little extra luck now and then. This spell is excellent for people with a big test or interview, people going on a trip or even people who are going thrift shopping and want to find something special. It also works up very quickly and aids anyone who holds the dice. So it can be a quick gift to give someone when you're at a party or heading out for a night on the town.

Components You Will Need

- A die that you think is pretty or cool. Gaming dice are good options
- A dish of sugar
- A small bowl

Follow These Steps

Once the circle has been raised, and the energy called, place the bowl in the center of the altar and put the die or dice inside. Take a moment to ground and center so that your energy does not interfere with the other energies you're calling. It is not your personal energy that will boost your good luck, particularly if you're suffering a string of bad luck at the moment.

When you're centered, close your eyes and hold your hands either up to the sky or out toward the representations of the God and Goddess on your altar. When you feel attuned to their presence, recite this incantation:

Oh God and Goddess

wise and great

Controllers of

Luck and fate

I ask of thee

This small request

Sweeten my luck

At my humble behest

Open your eyes and take a large pinch of sugar from the dish. Sprinkle it over the die while repeating the second half of the incantation twice more, for a total of three times. Then pick the dice up from the bowl, shake off the extra sugar, and put the dice in your pocket or purse.

If you're doing dice for more than one people, it is best to do them all at once. You need only scale up the amount of sugar accordingly. It is rarely a good idea to petition the gods for the same thing over and over again in a short period of time.

When you clean up the spell, be sure to compost the sugar. It did not come into contact with any negative energy, but it might have picked up some bad luck as it was shedding good luck onto the dice. Composting it allows that energy to break back down and revert to a more neutral state.

Real-World Action

- Consider all your choices when making a decision. Well-reasoned decisions are more likely to turn out well, thus inviting good luck.

- Put positive energy out into the world. Do good deeds for others and try to be a generally positive person. This will attract positive energy into your life and improve your luck.

- Value safety precautions. Always wear a helmet or seat belt where they're recommended, and always use your turn signals. Such small acts greatly reduce your risk of injury and misfortune.

Banishing Bad Luck

Just as everyone needs a little good luck, sometimes they have a little too much bad luck. After enough stubbed toes, missed buses, and dropped eggs, it's time to call in a little extra help. This spell won't erase all of a person's bad luck, but it will ease a little bit of pressure and make way for a little bit of good luck to sneak back in.

Components You Will Need

- A piece of paper folded into a fan

- A small token to represent the target of the spell
- Sandalwood incense
- A match and something to strike it on
- A table to work at

Follow These Steps

Situate yourself in front of the table and place the incense burner directly in front of you. Strike the match, then light the incense. Only put out the match when you're the sure incense is smoldering with a clear, consistent stream of smoke. When the incense is firmly smoking, shake out the match and set it aside.

Take the token that is intended to represent the person suffering from bad luck. Set it on the table so that the incense burner is between you and the token. Pick up your fan and point up towards the sky or toward the representations of the God and Goddess on your altar. When you feel attuned to Divine beings, recite this incantation:

To bear the burden

Of luck run afoul

Is a danger to all

I cannot allow

Begin to waft the incense smoke away from you so that it blows across the token. Sandalwood is an excellent incense for cleansing. And it's sweet scent will drive away the more foul energy of bad luck to make room for better energy.

As you're gently wafting the smoke over the token, finish the incantation:

I beseech of thee

Great and giving divine

Breathe sweeter fate into my path

Make way for luck finer

Repeat the second half of the incantation twice more. After the third recitation, set down your fan and gently snuff out the incense. Closeout the spell and put the token in among the things you carry with you every day.

You should rub the token every morning when you get up and every night when you go to bed while repeating the second half of the incantation. As your luck begins to turn around, remember to thank God and the Goddess. If the gods feel slighted, they may rescind their good favor and let the bad luck return.

When you are ready to release the luck token, simply cleanse it in among the rest of your tools and supplies during the new or dark moon.

Real-World Action

- Count to ten before you take a risk. This will give you time to evaluate if the risk is worth potential negative outcomes.

- Move a little slower. Many people experience bad luck by stubbing their toe or dropping things. Slowing down a little bit gives your brain more time to process your surroundings.

- Reach out to a support network. Having others to rely on when things do go wrong will reduce the overall damage bad luck can do.

Divination and Seeking the Truth

Most witches prefer specific divination tools when they want to suss out information. But, for some, spellwork provides a short-term method that they can use anywhere, even if their divination tools are at home. Their portability does affect the components of the spells, however. They require a few more pieces than most of the spells in this book. But they're also easily adaptable without risking their potency.

Yes/No Question Spell

This is another DIY spell, but the end result is something much smaller than a mirror box. For this spell, practitioners will create a small pendulum, which is a divination device used to answer simple questions and, after quite a bit of practice, even find lost things.

Components You Will Need

- A piece of string about a foot-long
- A metal washer or a large wooden bead with the hole at the very

top or through the center

Follow These Steps

Unlike the other DIY spells in this book, this one can be done just about anywhere. So long as you are comfortable, you're in a good spot to cast this spell. So raise your circle where seems most convenient and settle into a comfortable position.

In order for this spell to work, the bead or washer must evenly wait on all sides. Pendulums work by swinging freely and moving to indicate yes or no in response to a user's questions. If the washer or bead is weighted more heavily on one side of the other, the pendulum will not swing properly. Similarly, it is important that the knot is balanced either at the top of the pendant or directly in the middle. In any other location, it will throw off the pendulum's balance as surely as an oddly-weighted bead would.

When you are ready, tie your string to the pendant. Make sure the knot and bead are properly balanced. Then, with your arm held out in front of you and the loose end of the string in your fingers, let the pendant swing free.

Give it a moment to settle. When it stops swinging, focus all of your attention on it. Decide how you want the pendant to indicate yes and no. A popular option is to have it swing back and forth for yes and side to side for no. Spinning in a circle usually means that the answer is uncertain or ambiguous, though it could also mean that the question was too complex or too vague.

Settle on how you want your pendulum to communicate with you and give it the instructions you've chosen. You can either do this by speaking out loud or by extending your energy down your fingers and into the pendulum itself. If you choose to extend your energy into the pendulum, be prepared to pull it back and then center yourself once the spell is complete.

You are almost ready to begin asking your questions. First, however, you must recite the incantation:

Back and forth

Side to side

That is where

The answers lie

Without my aid

The pendulum swings

And with its flight

It sets truth to wing

As you recite the incantation, visualize all the energy you've called into the circle filling the space inside of it. Feel it pressing in around you, ready to guide the motion of the pendulum. Now you are ready to ask your questions.

Make sure you go slowly and only ask one question at a time. You should also stick to easy yes or no questions so as not to overwhelm what the pendulum can do. After several questions, you may find that the pendulum is slow to answer or that it begins to answer one way and then changes to the other. This is a sign that the energies around you are growing restless and wary. At this point – and if the pendulum swings in a circle on more than two questions in a row – it is time to release the energy.

Once the spell has been closed out, you can store your pendulum on your altar or among your other magical tools. Some practitioners prefer to keep their closer at hand, as they find it easier to use when they spend a lot of time around it.

Should you be on the go when you need your pendulum, they can work as tools to raise your protective circle as well. Simply hold the pendulum out at arm's length and spin in a circle to draw an energy line around you. Then visualize the rising of the protective barrier like you normally would. This "quick set" method allows you to call upon the pendulum's abilities even if you're in the middle of a busy day.

At some point, you may choose to upgrade your pendulum. Most metaphysical stores have a wide range for sale, and there are even more available online or at renaissance fairs. If you decide to purchase one, it is only right to let your homemade one rest. You can call a circle and gently disassemble it, then return the pieces to mundane use after they have been cleansed. It is better for the environment - and for the items – to be reused rather than simply thrown away.

Real-World Action

- If you have a lot of questions, keep them written down. It will help you track answers and find that the answers are coming to you.

- Think carefully before speaking in all things. This will reduce confusion when you interact with other people. Reduced confusion means you will have to do less searching through magical means.

- Maintain an ordered list of your top five priorities. It doesn't have to be a physical list. But knowing your top priorities will help you make decisions that benefit your priorities rather than work against them.

Lie Detecting Spell

There is, unfortunately, no magical equivalent of a lie detector. Spells that come close, like this one, tap into your own instincts and perceptions, then give you a gentle reminder when something is going on that you should be paying very close attention to. The practitioner will end up with another amulet or talisman that can be refreshed whenever they feel the need.

At first glance, this spell may seem very similar to the spell that susses out false friends. But the differences in the incantations make a world of difference. Rather than seeking out any sort of malicious intent from people claiming to be your friends, this amulet will respond only to deliberate untruths. It is much more focused and, therefore, much strong spell.

Components You Will Need

- Cord or chain for a necklace
- A nondescript charm to act as the amulet

- A candle
- A match and something to strike it on

Follow These Steps

Set the candle on the table. Then strike the match and light the candle while focusing your attention on the heat of the match as it moves into the wick. Make sure the candle is fully lit before you snuff out the match. Only then should you shake out the match and set it aside where it will not smolder. Wait until the flame is burning bright and strong, then hold the charm directly above the flame. Make sure that the flame cannot touch the charm, then focus your attention on the flame.

The flame's power is in the heat and focuses on the energy it gives off. Visualize all of that energy rising up into the charm and settling there like an ember at the heart of the charm. As you hold this visualization in your mind, recite the incantation:

I will see the truth

I will not be deceived

Lies will be uncovered

They shall not be believed

Fire I beg thee, light my way

Earth holds me steady, so I will not stray

Water carry knowledge that I may see true

Air brings new life, and my trust renew

Repeat the incantation three times, each time guiding even more heat and energy into your chosen charm. After the third recitation, gather up the cord and string the charm onto it. Tie it at the proper size for a necklace; then set aside. Closeout the spell and blow out the candle. Because you only used the candle as an energy source, it can be used for later purposes such as everyday tasks or other similar rituals and spells.

Keep the jewelry on your altar until you need to keep a close eye on potential liars. When this happens, put on the necklace. Be sure to wear it under your clothes. When someone lies, it will grow noticeably warmer. Unlike the normal way a pendant warms up when worn, your lie detector will flash very warm when it encounters untruths, then return to its normal temperature.

As soon as you're done with the amulet in any given day, return it to your altar so that it does not become accustomed to mundane daily wear.

If and when you decide to cleanse your pendant, you may have to do it more than once. It depends on how often you put the pendant to use and how many times you have refreshed the spell. After enough time, certain spells will simply etch themselves into a pendant and refuse to let go. And this is one such spell.

Real-World Action

- Listen carefully when others speak. Don't just hear them so you can reply, but really listen. It makes inconsistencies easier to spot.
- Avoid lies yourself. Honesty, largely, begets honesty in return.
- If someone has consistently lied in the past, take their words with a grain of salt and trust your instincts.

Herbal Spells

Wiccans love using herbs in their spells. They can be a little difficult to work with, however, which is why most of the spells in this book don't use them. Herbal spellwork is an important skill for all Wiccans, however. And this section is meant to give the beginning watch a small primer in the use of herbs.

Not all herbal spells are focused on a particular herb the way the next two are. But beginners will find it much easier to work with the energy and properties of an herb if they are only using one at a time. Of course, practitioners should skip these spells if they are allergic to either of the herbs involved.

avender Sleep Spell

It seems like nearly everyone is stressed and anxious. Both conditions make sleep harder to come by. And this, in turn, creates a vicious cycle. This spell can help. The soothing scent of lavender has long been associated with improved sleep. Now practitioners can create their own lavender sachets to help them nod off at night.

he sachet can be kept under the practitioner's pillow. Or, if that is uncomfortable, the sachet can be stored under the bed or between the mattress and the frame. So long as the sachet is somewhere in the practitioner's bed, it should have the desired effect. It is also a good idea to cast this spell at night since it is intended to help you sleep.

It is important to note that this spell is not for those with lavender allergies. Even minor exposure can cause negative side effects. So if this spell is intended for someone else, please ensure they are not allergic before you give them the sachet.

Components You Will Need

- A drawstring pouch
- A few sprigs of fresh lavender
- Soothing music (optional)

Follow These Steps

If you choose to play music, make sure you choose a piece of playlist that is longer than you think the ritual will take. Generally speaking, a "sleepy time" playlist is better since it will give you more time to work and will not put an uncomfortable time restriction on your spellwork.

Once the music is playing, the protective circle is in place, and you have raised the energy, gather the lavender in your hands. Raise it up toward the sky and recite this incantation while looking in the direction of the moon:

Oh great mother moon

Bright and shining in the sky above

Hear my plea

Extend your love

I year for sleep

And restful nights

But my eyes will not shut

Till I see dawn's light

Lull me, oh mother

To sleep beneath your light

May this herb in my hands

Sing me through your gentle night

Carefully fold and press the stems of lavender between your hands until you can clearly smell the flower's scent. Then, holding the petals and stems in one hand, pick up the pouch. Deposit as much of the lavender inside as you can and cinch the pouch shut. You can also rub the pouch along the palms of your hands to collect the lavender oil from your skin.

This spell is one that relies very heavily on real-world action. It is very much a catalyst, not an agent of change. It even works well for those who need sleep aide, since you do not ingest the lavender and there is no risk of a drug interaction. The sachet simply rests under your bed or pillow so that you can draw on its soothing effects whenever the need arises.

You should check your sachet about once a week to make sure no mold has begun to grow on the lavender. Generally speaking, it will simply dry out. But every now and then it may develop and a little bit of mold. In these cases, you should compost the lavender and wash the pouch in hot water to ensure no mold is left alive.

This spell works very well with the **Calming Mint Spell** directly below, as well as the **Hematite Grounding Spell** found under the *Crystal Spells* section.

Real-World Action

- Turn off all electronic screens at least 20 minutes before you lay down. Put a blue light filter on your phone, so you can set your alarm without exposure to blue light.

- Avoid caffeine and food for at least three hours before eating so your system can settle down for the night

- Try to go to bed at the same time every night. Regular patterns help our bodies know when they can expect rest.

Calming Mint Spell

Some spells call for specific herbs because of their magical properties. This spell, on the other hand, calls for mint because of its well-documented ability to soothe people. It does not lull people to sleep the way lavender does. But it can soothe frazzled nerves and help people slow down when things feel like they're moving too fast.

Like the Lavender Sleep Spell, the Calming Mint Spell creates a sachet. This can be carried around or placed in a pocket of the witch's bag to be drawn out when needed. Unlike the lavender sachet, however, this one should not be kept under the witch's pillow. There is no guarantee the safety pin will stay closed. And nobody should be woken up by a safety pin poking through their pillow.

Components You Will Need

- A handful of raw, fresh mint leaves
- A mint candle or mint incense
- A match and something to strike it against
- Several safety pins
- A small square of cloth in a soothing color

Follow These Steps

You can perform this spell on the floor or on the table, wherever is most comfortable. The important part is that you have space to ground and center before you make the sachet. As this is a calming spell, grounding will allow you to draw on the steadiness of the earth while centering keeps your energy focused where it needs to be.

After you've properly grounded and centered, spread out the square of cloth on the ground. Take your match and light it, then use it to light either the candle or the incense. Although fresh mint has a very strong smell, the flame or a candle and the smoke from incense are wonderful tools for focusing your attention. Their scent just enhances the overall effect of fresh mint.

Set the candle or incense far enough away that you cannot knock it over while you're working your spell. Take the mint leaves in your hand and turn to the north. Because the earth is the calmest of all the quarters, the incantation for this spell only invokes the Northern Watchtower:

Mighty Northern Quarter

Home of ever-steady Earth

I pray you now guide me

For respite I do search

My mind grows weary of wander

And my body grows weary of toil

Guide me to your foundation

The steady calm

Of Earth's nurturing soil

Gently squeeze the mint until you crush it just enough to release some of the mint oil. Then lay the leaves in the middle of the fabric square. You can also wipe your hand off on the square to transfer more oil from your skin, but this is optional.

Settle the leaves in the center of the cloth and carefully fold it into a packet. This is most easily done by folding the fabric up from the bottom to the midway line, then down from the top to the current bottom of the cloth. Fold in one side the then the other until you have a small square with the leaves in the center.

Safety pin at least two sides to prevent the fabric from unfolding. Once the sachet it secured, you can close out the spell and put the sachet in your bag. Like the lavender sachet, you should check on this one every few days to ensure the leaves dry properly and do not mold.

It is time to renew the spell when you can no longer smell the mint. You can reuse the same cloth and safety pins, though you should wash the cloth in between spells. If you choose to cast the spell again, make sure you sew a line around all four edges of the cloth. Without it, the cloth will fray and become much harder to work with.

Real-World Action

- Practice grounding and centering as a way to calm yourself.
- Create a soothing habit that you can use on the go. Tap your wrist three times, hum a happy song, or repeat movie line that makes you smile. Something small and easy to use when you're on the go.
- Focus on doing one thing at a time whenever possible. Multitasking is rarely as effective as focusing on a single task and often leads to feeling frazzled.

Candle Spells

Like herbs, candles appear in a great many Wiccan spells. They're versatile, affordable, and usually easy to find in a rainbow of colors and an array of sizes. Unlike most spells, however, these spells use candles as their focal point. Everything from the incantation to the spell's intent is centered around the witch's handling of the candle.

Knobbed Candle Banishing Spell

Of all the spells in this book, the Knobbed Candle Banishing Spell takes the longest. Practitioners must sit down with the candle every day for seven days in a row. Each time, they must visualize the negative energy vanishing from their lives while the candle burns through one knob.

It is a very time-consuming spell, and it requires a fair amount of focus. And, of course, it is the one spell in this book with a very particular piece of specialty equipment. But it is also one of the most potent banishing spells in Wicca. Some practitioners date the spell as going back to pre-Christian England, though the evidence is scarce. Regardless of its age, it is an almost foolproof way to remove unwanted influences from someone's life.

Components You Will Need

- A candle with seven knobs (usually available online through witch stores)
- A match and something to light it with
- Time to sit down with the spell every day for seven straight days
- A comfortable place to sit

Follow These Steps

This spell works best when you sit down at the same time every day for the seven days this spell requires. Each knob can take anywhere from twenty to ninety minutes to burn, depending on the candle you buy. If you're unsure of the exact time or if you can dedicate that much time, try and contact the seller to ask. Many candle makers know their products very well, particularly those that make candles for magical use. A candle's burn time is usually something they know very well.

Settle into a comfortable seat and bring to mind the thing you want to banish. Do not name it out loud, as that is likely to draw its attention. But keep your focus on it as you light your strike your match and light your candle. Once the candle is securely light, shake out the match and let it somewhere safe. Then get comfortable in your seat and place your hands on your legs or knees.

The incantation for this spell is not a poem, but rather a very straight and to-the-point statement.

lit the candle

To drive you out

I wish you gone

So mote it be

Some people find that yelling the statement at the candle is the most effective way to generate a lot of energy for the spell. Others find that this draws too much attention when all they want is a little bit of peace. Decide which method works best for you and speak the incantation. You can also repeat the incantation on and off throughout the time you're watching the knob burn. During this time, you should also be focusing on the thing you want to banish. You can imagine it leaving your circle of influence, or you can imagine what your day would be like without the toxic energy you are trying to remove.

When the knob has completely burned down, blow out the candle and close out the spell. If the knobs are very close together, it is better to burn a small distance into the next knob than to leave the current knob unburned.

The next day, preferably around the same time, return to the same spot and repeat this process. Like before, focus on the outcome you want and watch as the knob slowly burns down. You should also feel any anger you have towards the situation fading as the knobs burn down. This is because each successive knob on the candle removes some of the connection between you and the source of the toxic energy.

On the final day, burn the candle until it goes out on its own. Then close out the spell and throw the candle away. Which witch usually try to reduce their waste output and reuse as much as they can, this is one spell where that would be a bad idea. Deliberately keeping even a piece of the candle around will only invite the toxic energy back into your life. If you want a clean slate, you have to get rid of anything that remains of the candle.

Real-World Action

- When you start to think of the thing you want to be banished, immediately think of something else. Hum a catchy song, repeat a poem. Anything to get your mind on a different track.
- If you're banishing a bad habit, replace it with a better habit. This will give you something to do in place of the habit you're trying

to banish.

- For those banishing isolation or loneliness, try going somewhere new for at least 10-20 minutes every few days. Check out your local library, especially if they have a program. Drop into your local park and see if they have community days. You might not meet new people right away, but it gives the spell more ways to affect change.

Etched Candle Creativity Spell

This book already contains one creativity spell, true. But not all spells work well for all people. And while a small, portable charm is best for some creators, a solid and long-lasting generator for creative energy is a much better bet. This spell is a bit unique in that the candle it calls for needs to be very large. A heavy pillar candle is a good option. A three-wick candle with a broad base and lots of space to work with is even better.

Unlike the other creativity spell, this spell has no incantation. It is driven solely by the energy the practitioner pours into the candle as well as the intention they etch onto its surface. This spell is a fairly large one that requires a large deposit of energy into the candle. It is likely to leave practitioners exhausted, hungry, and thirsty afterward. They should be sure to plan accordingly.

Components You Will Need

- A very large unscented candle in a neutral color
- A dull etching tool, a pen without the ink well inside, or a tapestry

needle

- A match and something to light it with
- A candle holder matched to the size of your chosen candle.

Follow These Steps

Sit down in your circle, either on the floor or at a table. Shake out any tension in your shoulders. With one hand, hold the candle steady against the table. Use the other to begin scratching symbols and words into the surface of the candle.

There is no specific pattern as to what you should carve into the wax. You can write out your specific intentions. Or you can scratch in doodles that relate to the work you're trying to complete. Some practitioners choose to scratch in whole prayers so that, as the candle burns, it releases the energy they've channeled into it and activates the prayer etched on the outside.

No matter what you choose to carve, make sure that, it is somehow related to your desire for more creative energy. As you etch or carve, imagine your personal energy swirling around your hands and sinking into the wax. The more energy you put into the candle, the more it will return when the wick or wicks are lit.

You can also imagine the energy of the Watchtowers and the Divine circling around you and joining with your energy. This might alleviate some of the exhaustion that a large working will leave behind.

When you are finished carving, hold the candle in both hands and give one more large, deliberate push of your energy into the candle. Visualize it glowing with the signature color of your own energy, shot through with the bright colors of the energy from both Divine beings and all four Watchtowers.

You can keep this candle in your creative workspace for as long as you like. When you are ready to burn it, offer up a small prayer of thanks to the powers that aided you, then light the candle. After it has been lit, your entire focus should be on your creative endeavors. If you find your focus shifting, blow out the candle so that you can save its energy for your creative pursuits.

Real-World Action

- Sit in front of your medium, without distractions, for at least 20 minutes every day.

- Spend 20 minutes a day looking at a new form of media. Check out a new artist you whose work you don't know, read quotes from authors you're unfamiliar with, watch videos for a martial arts style you don't currently practice. New media might set off new ideas.

- Give a new media form a try. Spend an hour or so each week trying something new, whether it's a watercolor instead of oil crayons, poetry instead of prose, or a waltz instead of a tango. Switching things up makes our brain think in new ways.

Moon Spells

Moons spells, like herbal spells, are very common in the wider Wiccan community but very limited in this book. This was a deliberate choice so that practitioners could become comfortable with the practice of spell casting before they began working with timing restrictions. But, as with all things, a little practice goes a long way.

The most basic of moon spells are an attraction spell performed on the full moon and a banishment spell performed on the new moon. Both spells are written so that they can be fine-tuned for just about any situation. Practitioners need only remember that, in both cases, they should never cast these spells on specific people.

Waxing Moon Attraction Spell

It does not matter what you want to attract; the waxing moon is the time to do it. The moon is ripe with the promise of new beginnings. And Her energy will fuel this spell with more than enough juice to bring the practitioner solid results.

Like many other spells in this book, this one involves fanning incense smoke to symbolize the direction the practitioner wants energy to flow. But because the other spells are banishing spells, practitioners should not use the same object to direct energy, even if it has been cleansed. They should grab a new piece of card stock or create a new hand fan to use in attraction spells.

When storing their magical tools, witches should be sure they keep these tools separate, especially if they have not yet been cleansed.

Components You Will Need

- A small dish of honey
- Incense with a light scent that invigorates you, such as lemon
- A match and something to light it with
- Something to fan the smoke with

Follow These Steps

Set the incense on the table and light it with the match. When it is smoldering properly, shake out the match and set it aside. Keep the honey off to the side so that the incense smoke does not reach it.

Recite the incantation as you waft the smoke toward you:

As the moon grows in the sky

Attraction grows by and by

Now is the time

I pray thee come to me

As I desire

So mote it be!

Feel the energy of the moon mingle with the smoke as it washes over you. Whereas sunlight is hot, moonlight is just a little bit on the cool side. It tingles across the skin and leaves practitioners feeling a little bit lighter on their feet. It is the energy that makes us feel free to fly and explore, especially the light of the waxing moon. This is the energy that mingles with yours when you cast a spell tied to the waxing moon.

As you feel the moon's energy connect with yours, set aside the card and the incense. Make sure that the smoke will not waft over the honey as you're working with it, as you don't want smoke particles in the honey. Pick up the dish of honey and hold it up toward the moon, even if you're indoors, then recite the second incantation:

Touched by the moon

Blessed by her light

I call upon this sweetness

To bring forth delight

Set the honey back down and close out the spell.

Over the next few days, while the moon is still waxing, make sure you eat a little of the honey every day. Drizzle it over fruit or meat, have it in your tea, or use it in your baking. Each time you consume the honey, you will be bringing more of the moon's energy into yourself and increasing the draw for whatever it is you seek to gain.

This spell should leave practitioners feeling more energetic, rather than drained. It is a quick and easy spell that can help new practitioners get in sync with the phases of the moon. It pairs very well with the **Rose Quartz Self-Love Spell** a few sections down as well as the **Attracting Opportunity Spell** from a few sections back.

Real-World Action

- For those seeking connection with other people, repeat in your mind that you are likable and approachable. It will encourage you to use more inviting body language.

- For those inviting creative success, spend time in front of your medium. You don't have to work. Just sit with your medium for 20-30 minutes every day with absolutely nothing else going on. It will take some of the stress out of just sitting in front of your medium.

- For those inviting new career opportunities, look for free classes in your area that may relate to your chosen career. Many public libraries offer business classes, writing classes, and a variety of seminars. These offer chances to learn and network, which gives the spell more to work with.

New Moon Banishment Spell

This banishing spell works in a very similar way to cleansing. The spells require the vacuum-like nature of the new moon. And though it is more effective when performed openly under the new moon, that is not a requirement.

Components You Will Need

- Dragon's blood incense or another incense with a musky "heavy" smell
- A match and something to strike it on
- Something to fan the smoke with, such as an index card or paper fan
- Access to a window (optional)

Follow These Steps

This spell works best if you can fan the smoke out of an open window. If you do not have access to one, however, you can always use visualization to achieve a similar effect.

Once your circle is set, light the incense. Dragon's blood is a very heavy, cleansing scent and so is perfect for this spell. As the incense smolders, use a fan or card to waft the smoke away from you slowly. While you are wafting the smoke away, focus your mind on the thing you want to banish. Imagine it sailing up into the sky and vanishing into the dark space where the moon's light usually shines down. As with other banishing spells, it is best not to name the thing you are trying to banish.

For this particular spell, visualization is enough. Ever wave of your fan pushes more of the energy into the dark space of the moon where it will be captured and cleansed before it is released.

Real-World Action

- If you are trying to banish a source of toxic energy, do not voluntarily engage with the source.

- If you are trying to banish a bad habit, set reminders in your phone to use a replacement habit or to go do something if you're putting it off.

- If you're banishing an illness, please see the "Real-World Action" portion of **Banishing an Illness** in the *Wellness and Health* section of this chapter.

Crystal and Stone Spells

Witches love crystals and stones. There are exceptions, of course. But there is a reason that pop culture decorates every witch's home with large, glittering crystals. More advanced spells will often use stones to boost or guide the spell's intention. But, for now, practitioners can use the spells listed below to familiarize themselves with rose quartz and hematite. Both stones are among the most popular in spellwork and are usually easy to find either online or in a metaphysical shop.

Rose Quartz Self-Love Spell

While most love spells focus on attracting love from others, it is incredibly important that people also work to love themselves. Many people suffer from body image issues, among other things, that make it hard for them to appreciate the body that carries their soul through this world.

This spell will help people come to terms with the beauty of their own body. Appreciating oneself is a long journey with many steps, and this spell is only one. But it can make each step a little bit easier. And, as the practitioner becomes more comfortable, the spell can be repeated to encourage even more self-love and acceptance.

Components You Will Need

- A picture of yourself, the more recent, the better

- A piece of rose quartz

- A shallow bowl or deep saucer

- A small mirror

- Incense or a candle in your favorite scent

- Petals from your favorite flower (optional)

Follow These Steps

Place the shallow bowl on your altar and gently place your picture inside. As this is a spell to promise self-love, it is important that you treat yourself gently throughout the spell.

Next, gather the petals from your favorite flower. It is fine to buy them already plucked or to pluck them yourself. You may also set the entire bloom into the bowl with your picture as long as you can still see your image in the bowl. Take a moment to appreciate the beauty of the flower and remind yourself that you too have beauty and that you are just as beautiful as your favorite flower.

Light the incense and set it so smolder so that the smoke wafts down over your picture and the flower. Breathe in your favorite scent and see how it complements the beauty of both you and the flower.

Pick up the rose quartz in one hand and the mirror in the other. Look at yourself in the mirror and try to give a kind smile. If you struggle with your self-image, try to focus on one feature about your face that you like. As you repeat this spell over time, you may find that it is easier to find beauty in the whole image. For now, remember to be kind to yourself and just focus on the things you like.

Without looking away from the mirror, squeeze the rose quartz in your hand and recite the following incantation. It is not a poem, but rather a series of kind words to repeat to yourself.

I am a child of the moon and of the sun

I am a child of the stars and of the earth

Their beauty is my beauty

And my beauty is their beauty

As they deserve love, so I deserve love

As they deserve respect, so I deserve respect

As I love them, I shall learn to love myself

So mote it be

Gently set the mirror and the quartz back on the table. Closeout the spell and carry the bowl with the flowers and your photo to a table in your home. You can set it on your desk or your bedside table, or a side table in the living room. Wherever you set it, just make sure it catches your eye at least once a day. When it does, repeat whatever line of the incantation most easily comes to mind.

Many practitioners find that the incantation also works well as a daily reminder or a good intention for their day. They remind themselves of their connection to the glories of nature, and it helps calm their self-doubt.

Real-World Action

- Practice smiling at yourself. This might feel hard to do at first, but studies back up the importance of physically smiling at yourself to boost your mood.

- Say one good thing about yourself every morning. Even if it's "I rinsed off the breakfast dishes," it's something positive to counter any negative self-talk

- Set a small, achievable goal every day. Something like "push back my cuticles" or "drink a full 8 oz of water before I put my glass down". Small acts of self-care will change the way you think about yourself, and the spell will help that change grow.

Hematite Grounding Spell

Everyone has seen hematite, even if they didn't know it at the time. The shiny black beads that aren't quite metal but aren't quite stone are hematite. They are popular in shell necklaces and punk jewelry which is an interesting combination. But hematite is even more versatile than that.

It is considered a protective stone by most Wiccans. It can absorb or deflect negative energy, depending on how it is used. And, thanks to its ability to absorb and "ground" negative energy, it is perfect for spells that will "ground" frazzled witches.

Components You Will Need

- A few beads of hematite or a hematite stone that can fit in your palm
- A pouch

Follow These Steps

Hold the hematite in the palm of your hand and close your eyes. Imagine the beads humming or buzzing against your palm, then settling down as they align themselves to your energy. When they are perfectly calm, recite this incantation:

As hematite grew

Within the ground

So now I

Seek to be found

Among stone and root

Grounded deep to Earth

Lest fear overtake me

Here I know my worth

You may find that you want to repeat the incantation a few times. Each time you do, imagine threads of your energy winding in and out among the hematite beads, stringing them together and interlacing them with your own energy. When you feel fully connected to them, slowly deposit them in the pouch and close out the spell. Keep the pouch somewhere you can easily access throughout the day so you can hold onto the hematite if you need to feel more grounded.

Real-World Action

- Practice grounding and meditation
- Track when you feel frazzled and look for patterns
- If possible, get 15 more minutes of sleep a night. Fifteen minutes is the length of one REM cycle and will help you feel more refreshed.

Chapter 6: Where to Go From Here

These spells are only the beginning of what is sure to be a long and fulfilling journey. Wiccans understand that magic is not just something they do. It is part of who they are. Every day, in everything they do, they are connected to the Divine, to the Earth, and to all the living things that surround them.

Every spell teaches a witch something new, even if they have cast the same spell a hundred times before. Each time, the witch will record the act in their Book of Shadows, then make any notes about the outcome when it becomes apparent. It is through these notes that witches learn the path that is most comfortable for them. And, over time, it is through these notes that magical practices are handed down from one generation to the next.

Although this book covers a wide array of spells, many practitioners find that they work best when they rely on one of two core varieties. And this is because it allows them to explore the nuances of their chosen branch without worrying about stumbling off of that path and into another, closely related selection of spells.

Candle magic is an excellent example of the areas that magic paths overlap. Many branches of magic use candles. The act of lighting a candle carries a lot of symbolism, as does the act of letting one burn or snuffing one out. But only with the specific branch of candle magic do the candles take center stage.

Witches adept in candle magic know the properties, benefits, and downsides of every candle making material. They can tell the burn time of a candle from its base material and size. And many of them even go so far as to make their own candles, so they know exactly what they're using in their spells. These witches know everything about the candles they use in their spells. And those other witches may cross into candle magic while pursuing their own paths; they are not Candle Magic Witches.

The only way a practitioner will know the past that best suits them is if they explore each path in turn. Some avenues will immediately stand out is difficult to work with. Stones are notoriously picky and herbal magic requires a great deal of research, particularly if anyone plans to ingest the herbs from their spells. Many witches find themselves shying away from these paths and moving to other more broad types of magic.

No matter which paths speak to a witch, they must always follow the Wiccan Rede. And, at its core, that means they can do no harm. This law governs all Wiccan magic without exception. And while not all magic is performed by Wiccans, anyone who follows a Wiccan path knows the boundary line and will not cross it.

All of this might be overwhelming for some. But the longer practitioners sit with their magic, and the more time they take to understand the fundamentals of the practice, the more powerful they will ultimately become. Wicca is a religion that favors learning, and that is plainly evident in the approach that Wiccans take to magic.

So now that this book is done, its readers must find the next step on their path. This will mean more reading, more research, and more magic. It will mean exploring themselves and the world around them to see how the two interconnect. And it will mean learning the paths that their energy travels most readily.

If practitioners found that Divination spells spoke to them, they may want to explore various divination practices. Those that found moon spells easy and fulfilling may find a home among the astrologers and astronomers. Herbal spells often lead to holistic healing practices. And wellness spells are often the first steps on the path to becoming healers of all sorts.

And if a practitioner gets further down a path only to find that it is not for them, there is no rule saying they can't turn back and start over again. Magic is about exploring the self and the world and the universe. It is about supporting humans and their connection to the Divine, which is present in nature all around. It is about learning. So don't be afraid to go out and learn.

Conclusion

You have reached the end of this book, Wicca Book of Spells. We hope this book has giving you the opportunity to begin your studies in the magic and enlightenment of Wicca and we look forward to hearing from you if you enjoyed your time reading it. This book is just the beginning of what all you can discover out there in the world and what the religion of Wicca is all about. We encourage you to reach out to other Wiccans in your area to get their tips and insights into how to be a Wiccan and where you should start in your journey.

Always remember that the true meaning of being a Wiccan is to become more connected with the earth and living in peace with the energies of the nature around you. Once you have gotten to this harmony you should see that you are in the right frame of mind to begin your incantations and ritual casting.

Let's hope it was informative and able to provide you with all of the tools you need to achieve your goals whatever they may be.

Finally, if you found this book useful in any way, a review on Amazon is always appreciated!

Wicca Candle Magic

The Ultimate Guide to Candle Spells, Wiccan Candle Magic and Rituals. A Book of Shadows for Wiccans, Witches, Pagans, Witchcraft practitioners and beginners.

ESTHER ARIN SPELLS

INTRODUCTION

Congratulations on choosing Book title here and thank you for doing so.

Fire has been a source of comfort for many people since the dawn of time. In more modern times that comfort has been converted into a more compact and portable version, candles. There are few things more calming or peaceful than lighting a candle after tidying up your house or sitting by a fire pit wrapped in a blanket on a chilly fall night. This book is meant to only expand that comfort and overall pleasant atmosphere into a deeper and more ritualistic place.

In this book you will learn all of the basics of Wicca candle magic and how to use it. After reading this book you will have obtained an overall general knowledge of the origins of candle magic in the Wiccan religion as well as the importance of candles in Wicca rituals. You'll obtain a basic knowledge of candle colors, flame meanings, anointing, sigils, and a few beginner spells to try for yourself.

Candle magic can be used for a wide variety of spells and rituals that you will be able to explore after mastering a few of the ones in this book. After learning the basics of candle magic you will be able to dive into Wicca and expand your abilities to other areas of Wicca magic that we will touch on such as crystals, oils, and herbs.

If you are ready to expand your understanding of Wicca culture and rituals as well as try a few things out for yourself along the way this book is the place to start. There are things you need to know before you start performing candle magic. In Wicca tradition, fire take center stage, it can either be in the ritual bonfire or tall candles that are a sign of honoring their god as well as the goddess.

There are also small tea lights that mark the sacred circle boundaries. Candle magic is a delightful way to work with the fire element. They work with a mesmerizing flame that is from a simple, elegant as well as a highly symbolic candle.

It is a way of bringing together the unseen universe energy to work and change the physical world. There can be a tangible or intangible change that will bring hope to a situation that has a negative outlook.

As a beginner, candle magic will be comfortable as well as simple for you to learn. For you to start practicing witchcraft, this is the easiest way to start that. No matter the culture that you come from, you will find something interesting to learn about candle magic. For you to get the result you desire, you need to combine both fire and color. You need to know how the magic works so that you do not mess up along the way. You have to light a candle and say some words loudly when you are performing the spell.

Candle magic will help you shape your life, and you require having patience.

CHAPTER 1: Origin of Wicca Beliefs and the Importance Fire

Wicca originated in the early 20th century as a religious practice of witchcraft, but has become more popular in recent years. It has since blossomed into a more modern idea of natural magic and although it can be a religion for some people it is not necessarily a religious practice in all cases.

Although the Wicca religion originated in the 20th century, many claims that its roots date back to pre-Christianity with its obvious influence from ancient folklore and ritualistic magic. Some even claim that Wicca is a derivative of ancient religions as far back as the Paleolithic era.

Their foundation for this belief is the fact that there have been archeological discoveries dating back to the Paleolithic period that may indicate the worship of gods and goddesses similar to those of the Wiccan religion. Paganism or witchcraft in history was sometimes referred to as the "Craft of the Wise".

This was because many of the people who practiced witchcraft were skilled in herbs and simple medicinal properties. This made them a great asset to their communities because they had the power of healing. In certain cultures, people who performed witchcraft were revered and welcomed as the leaders of their communities. These basic principles of herbs and medicines have filtered down into Wicca culture and that part of the reason why many Wiccans believe their religion is based on one of earth's oldest set of beliefs. Many Wiccans would say that their "founding father" so to speak was Gerald Brosseau Gardner.

Who was initiated into a coven of witches in the late 1930s. He wrote a few books on topics of Wicca such as *Witchcraft Today* and *The Meaning of Witchcraft* which were both written in the 1950s. His greatest success was the 'Book of Shadows' which is a number of spells and rituals that he gathered together into one place for easy access.

This book is thought to be a major source of influence for a large number of witches and Wicca culture as a whole. It combined with the other two books created a visitation of Wicca ideas across the globe.

As in most other religions, there is a wide variety of beliefs about specific scenarios and topics within the Wiccan religion. However, there are a few fundamental things that the Wicca community generally agree on and build their beliefs off of.

The Wiccan religion consists of a series of beliefs that include a variety of gods, goddesses, and various other deities. They believe in the divinity of nature and combine both pantheistic and polytheistic ideologies into one complex set of beliefs. Pantheism is the idea that the universe and everything in it is a divine manifestation of an all-inclusive god and Polytheism is the belief that there are many gods and goddesses.

Wiccans believe in 5 fundamental elements that they believe the universe is made up of; earth, wind, fire, water, and spirit. So Wiccans combine these two beliefs by believing in god and goddesses while also believing that everything in the universe has a spirit, including the first four elements and that spirit is a segment of their all-encompassing god. Wiccans also have an ethical code that most of them live by which, "If it harms none, do what you will." They believe in rituals of purification and meditation. They celebrate many yearly occurrences found in nature such as the summer solstice, different phases of the moon, eclipses, and Samhain (Halloween).

They practice magic as well as invoke deities and spirits will doing their various rituals and spells. Wiccans go by the term witches despite the western world's negative connotations associated with the term. Wiccans are often associated with Satanism because they refer to themselves as witches, but they deny any and all ties to the Satanic religions.

Gardner's Wicca coven was succeeded by other independent groups that also identified as Wiccan, but with a few different beliefs. For example, Dianic Wiccans believed most of the same ideals as Gardner, but they forswore the term witch as their identification and believe that Wicca was a women's religion. Following Gardner's original teachings Wiccans were expected to do all of their worship in the nude. With this being their main issue, another sect of the Wiccans broke off in the mid to late 1900s. They rebuked the idea of nude worship and instead opted to wear robes for their rituals and worshipping. They called themselves the Traditionalists which derived from the idea that wearing robes originated from a set of pagan beliefs far before Gardner's time. Currently there are six core distinct systems of Wicca, although there are many other branches.

The first is Gardnerian Wicca which we already discussed above. They are led by a high priestess and their coven is looked at as a household with a distinct lineage and a large number of descendants. They are stricter about following their traditions than other Wiccans. They do at times come up with new ideas to add to their rituals and spells which is accepted as long as they are not completely disregarding their original beliefs. The next is called Alexandrian Wicca which is the most similar to Gardnerianism, but has a few key differences. They also believe in having one singular high priestess to rule over them, but are more wide-ranging and lenient than Gardnerianism.

For example, unlike in Gardnerian Wicca, nudity is optional for any ritualistic occasions and they include things like wands and daggers in their rituals and spells. The women-only Dianic sect of Wiccans that we mentioned briefly before focused solely on goddesses and most of them consisted of women-only covens. These covens tend to be more democratic in their leadership than having one sole high priestess.

Many of these groups are very avid feminist, politically minded, and have a large lesbian occupancy. However, they do not contradistinguish any women based on their sexual preferences. Another faction is called Celtic Wicca. This certain brand of Wicca offers correspondence courses for their rituals and ideals. This basically means that they will teach their beliefs over vast distances whether that be through mail, email, phone calls, etc. They are known to be much more public with their beliefs and traditions which has brought on some scrutiny from other more secretive sects. Georgian Wicca is really a larger stem off from Alexandrian.

It was started by George Patterson and largely uses Alexandrian rituals and doctrines as their base of beliefs.

However, they are very eclectic and accepting of all ideas and thoughts from a variety of opinions. Patterson was not one to expect people to follow his ideas blindly. He wanted and even encouraged his group to question and explore all of the possibilities.

Lastly is Discordianism or Erisian Wicca, which is a very chaotic form of Wiccan and by far the most erratic of the six major groups. Gregory Hill, most often referred to as Malaclypse the Younger was the main source of inspiration for this movement. He wrote the *Principia Discordia* alongside Kerry Thornley, a strange book filled with odd humor and literal contradictions that is used as the sole inspiration for this sect of Wicca. In modern times there are a variety of ways that people look at Wicca.

Some people simply want to dabble in Wicca culture. They want to learn a few spells and practice a few rituals, so that they can use Wicca to reach a more spiritual place within themselves.

They may not classify themselves as Wiccans or witches; they just simply agree with some of the teaching and identify independent of the Wiccans. There are others who may feel that they truly believe in the craft and that they want to dedicate their lives to living by the Wicca principles. This in and of itself can have two paths. Some people may want to live their lives worshipping by themselves in their own personal way. While others may want to practice their beliefs with others of like mind. These people typically opt to joining a coven.

Joining a coven requires you to have an initiation. This initiation is not what many outsiders would presume it is. It is not typically just a one-time ceremony. Most covens will not share the furtive process of their initiation sacraments. However, there are a few common denominators that most covens share when it comes to initiation.

The first of those common denominators is spending a significant amount of time with the coven. It is important that the initiate feels comfortable with their new coven and that the coven feels the soon to be fellow witch will be a good fit and supportive asset to their community.

The next step is very similar to an apprenticeship of sorts and eventually there is an initiation ritual at the end. When being initiated into a coven the initiate spends a non-specific amount of time with an experienced witch in the coven. They shadow this member of the coven and learn everything that they can from them about the coven, the craft, rituals, and traditions. Once the mentor and the initiate feel that they are ready to devote themselves to the camaraderie of the coven and dedicate themselves to the craft then they will become an official witch and member of the coven. Joining a coven is a very serious decision and is not to be taken lightly. Many witches have compared joining a coven to being married. You make a solemn vow to commit your life to the coven and to the Wicca beliefs.

Once you are in a coven you are expected to take vows of secrecy, attending any meeting or rituals that the coven may be having, and to become a part of the moral support group that is the coven. Most covens will not share the furtive process of their initiation sacraments. However, there are a few common denominators that most covens share when it comes to initiation.

The first of those common denominators is spending a significant amount of time with the coven. It is important that the initiate feels comfortable with their new coven and that the coven feels the soon to be fellow witch will be a good fit and supportive asset to their community. For those who choose to seek a companionless pursuit of Wiccan there is typically what they call a "self-dedication" instead of an initiation ritual. This self- dedication is up for much more interpretation than a formal initiation into a coven. For a self-dedication the witch can pretty much choose to establish their allegiance any way they want to.

There are no other witches or individual to take into consideration, so the witch is able to commit themselves to Wicca in whatever way they see fit. It is not a commitment to anyone but yourself and the deities or spirits that you choose to involve. However, it is typically suggested the you spend "a year and a day" practicing Wicca before you make this dedication, but you can take as long as you would like. This is just a suggestion to make sure that you are certain of your decision to pursue Wicca before you make such a big commitment. Many people who choose to follow a solo path will spend a large majority of their time learning their craft through a combination of reading, trial and error.

Fire is one of the key elements of survival and has been since the dawn of time. Although there was a small-time period of survival without fire in the early years of humanity, there was a boom in population and flourishing once fire was discovered. Fire allowed humans to survive in colder climates, cook their food which killed bacteria thus increasing survival rates, defend themselves against predators, and see in the dark. Fire has always been an essential element for humans and this importance transfers into Wicca as well. While all the five elements are essential in Wicca because they are the elements that make up the universe, fire is essential when discussing candle magic specifically because without the fire to light the candle one cannot perform any candle spells or rituals.

Fire is a key component when doing candle magic and a highly revered element in Wicca culture. It is a greatly important component for not only candle magic, but other rituals and spells. Many people will use fire and candles to create a better environment or spiritual setting for their rituals or spells without necessarily using them directly for the spell itself.

When doing candle magic, one must pay attention to not only which candles to use for which spells, but also how the flame of the candle is burning. There are a variety of things that your candle flame may be telling you, you just need to be receptive to its actions. I will list some of the possible things that your candle flame may be trying to tell you.

If your candle flame is burning **normal or even** that is a good sign. This means that your spell is going as planned and that you will hopefully see good results from your candle spell, although it may not be immediate. Although the results will not happen as quickly as they would if your flame was stronger, they will still come in time and it is important to focus on the good outcomes when you are practicing spell work.

If your candle flame is burning **very strong or tall** that is an even better sign. This means that your spell is going even better than expected. Your requests are likely being heard and even propelled forward by the immense energy behind your spell. This means that you will likely see great results in a very timely manner.

If your candle flame is burning **small and steady** is not necessarily a bad sign, but probably not the flame you are wanting. This means that your spell is working, but there is not much energy flowing through you spell. You may have to show some patience while waiting for your results but keep a diligent and persistent mindset and you will likely get the results you desire.

If your candle flame is not only **small**, but also **bending and flickering** this is not what you want. This likely means that your spell is not working. This could be because of pouring timing or just an overall unlikely result of your desired outcome. If this flame is overcome by the melting wax and completely goes out that is a pretty definite indication that your request is not going to be granted at that time.

If your candle flame is **strong and dancing** this can be a good indication that your spell will probably be successful, but there may be some unexpected obstacles that you may have to overcome. You should try to focus on your goal and try your best to resolve any complications that may be in the way of your spell being a success.

If your candle is **flickering on and off** repeatedly this may indicate that there are spirits present. This could be a good thing or a bad thing. If your candle begins to do this while trying to invoke a spirit or doing reverential work for gods, angels, spirit guides that is a great sign. It means that your ritual is fruitful and that your appeals are being understood.

If your flame is ***crackling or popping*** like a sparkler suggests either transmission with or obstruction by outside forces. If your flame is uneven while this is occurring is most likely someone or something trying to interfere with your spell. If your flame is just being noisy in general while also being steady and strong this could be an indication of a spirit or ancestor trying to communicate with you. It is your job to try to decipher what is occurring through your own intuition and feelings.

If your candle ***will not light*** this means that the spell you are trying will not have the outcome that you desire. It may not be the right time to perform this spell or it could be that the thing you are trying to influence is just not in your realm of control. You may also just not be ready for the spell yourself. You could try a cleansing or series of meditational episodes to try to prepare yourself. Once you are feeling that you are in a better head space you can try the spell again.

If your candle flame completely ***extinguishes*** that means that what you are requesting will most likely not manifest itself. It could be a result of outside forces working against you or it could just mean that it is just not in your best interest for this spell to succeed. You must acquaint yourself with the reality that your desires may not be what is best at the time and try to move forward.

If you candle becomes ***inextinguishable*** and you cannot snuff it out this most likely means that your spell is not quite resolved. This could indicate that you may have missed a critical phase in your spell or a memorandum may have gone unnoticed. The best thing for you to do in this scenario is to reexamine your steps that you took and make sure that you did not miss anything. If you find an area that you think could be the issue, try your best to resolve it. Once you feel that the matter has come to rest you should then try to extinguish the flame again.

If you candle is emitting a ***lot of smoke*** this could be an inkling that the element of air is present in your ritual or spell. The air element is typically a sign of communication and examination. This is traditionally neither a good or bad sign. It is mostly just an indication that you need to focus on the smoke and try to understand what the shapes and movement are trying to portray to you.

If your candle is exuding ***white smoke*** this signifies good omens. It is often associated with magnanimous spirits and satisfaction. It is essentially a sign of a blessing from the spirits and means that your intentions have been acknowledged and will be granted.

If your candle begins to emanate ***black smoke*** that is not a good sign. It displays a presence of detrimental energy. It could symbolize disharmony, bad omens, or a contradicting force. It is important that you do not continue your spell if there is a presence of black smoke. You should stop your spell immediately and do a series of cleansing and meditation before continuing at a later time.

If the smoke begins to ***blow away from you*** intakes that your energy is withdrawing from you and heading elsewhere. This is usually an indicator that your spell will not be successful unless it is in regard to a spell that is being directed towards another being. For example, if you are trying a healing spell towards another individual or trying a spell of manipulation or persuasion then this could be a good omen in that case. This could suggest that your energy is flowing towards the other individual and that your spell is going as planned.

If the smoke begins to ***flow towards you*** it suggests that you are captivating what you desire. For example, if you are trying to invoke love into your life then smoke flowing towards you would be a good omen. However, the reverse would be if you are working on a curse or hex because if the smoke starts flowing towards you in this case it would indicate that bad things will come to you as well.

If your candle starts to emit a **blue flame** this is a good omen. Blue flames generally suggest that a higher spiritual being has taken an interest in your magic. It shows that a powerful, even angelic energy is fueling your flame.

If you candle begins to form a **crater in the wax** does not imply that your spell is going as planned. It tends to point to a lack of energy or effectiveness of the smell.

If your candle **burns very quickly** it is typically a good thing. It means that your spell has been filled with lots of passion and energy. Once the wax has melted and begun to hard you may be able to see hidden shapes and messages in the wax that could leave you to a revelation in your spell or ritual.

If your candle burns with **no wax drips** this is also typically a good sign. It means that your spell went according to plan and that you executed it correctly. The results of your spell will go exactly how you projected.

If you notice that your candle wax is **favoring one side** when it is dripping this is an implication that something is unstable or off balance. Usually it indicates something inside of yourself being a little off; whether that be physically, mentally, or emotionally.

If you notice that you candle wax is emitting lots of **black candle crud** into the wax this could denote unforeseen consequences. It is usually not so serious as to cause any significant harm, but it can indicate hassles, bad karma, or guilt in your future.

Candle soot can mean different things depending on the color. **Black soot** is an indicator of bad or negative energy. If this soot is only present at the top of the candle, then you can most likely assume that the bad energy was overcome. However, if the soot remains consistent and covers the entirety of the jars surface then it could mean that your spell did not work and may need to be redone. If **white soot** is present it tells that you had spiritual assistance in your spell, but it is a very rare manifestation. If while you are performing your ritual or spell a ***striking mishap*** occurs such as a candle breaking, exploding, or falling off of a table this means that your magic has been rejected by a preeminent power.

Chapter 2: Candle Colors and Their Meanings

You probably have performed a form of candle magic already without even realizing it. Candles are put on virtually every birthday cake on the planet.

Your cake is brought out with your candles on it and what happens next?

Your friends and family start singing happy birthday to you and then you make a wish.

You focus all of your energy on that wish and then you blow out your candles. The idea is pretty similar with Wicca candle magic.

You light a candle or two and then you make a 'wish' or state your intent. The only difference is you don't blow out the candle. Candle magic is a great place to start if you are coming into this completely clueless. It is fairly easy to understand, and you can do simple spells with little supplies.

The fact that most candles are also fairly inexpensive to purchase makes it even more appealing for beginners. It is likely that if you are just trying to dabble and find out if Wicca is something you are interested in then you are not going to want to spend a fortune just to test it out. However, if you do find yourself enjoying Wicca then candle magic is a great stepping stone for other, more complex forms of magic. Starting with candle spells will help you learn how to focus your energy and concentrate on what you are trying to obtain.

The idea behind candle spells is to harness the energy from the fire and being about change. Having a candle as the focal point really helps with your focus as a whole. Candles in and of themselves are mesmerizing. Often people will find themselves getting lost in the small flames rising from the candle's wick as they stare into them. This ability that candles have to capture our attention is a great asset for candle magic.

It makes staying focused much easier and helps you feel the energy arising from the candles. Candle magic is referred to as a form of sympathetic magic. Sympathetic magic is based on the idea that one can perform magic on an object that represents a person or thing and the person or thing that is representing will be affected by it. It has been summarized as "like produces like" by Sir George Frazer.

Frazer also stated this about sympathetic magic, "From the first of these principles, namely the Law of Similarity, the magician infers that he can produce any effect he desires merely by imitating it: from the second he infers that whatever he does to a material object will affect equally the person with whom the object was once in contact, whether it formed part of his body or not."

This idea has transcended into another more modern tradition that is called correspondence. Correspondence is the idea that specific items or things represent a magical conception. For example, specific colors representing certain magical concepts; like red meaning passion or green meaning growth.

This correspondence has been made with specific herbs and quartz as well; such as rose quartz exhibiting love or sage depicting wisdom. Another example of correspondence would be the use of a voodoo doll. The doll is the correspondence and the act of practicing magic on this doll would be considered sympathetic magic.

The thought process behind using candles for spells is that they are essentially a conduit for your intentions to the celestial realm. As you perform your spells your intentions are transferred into the candle through your energy and your focus.

As the candle melts its physical form is deteriorating and transferring itself into a non-physical plane of spirituality. As the candle does this it takes your intent with it, thus creating a better connection between you and the spiritual plane. Each part of the candle represents one of the fundamental elements that we have discussed previously.

The wick of the candle is the representation of the earth element and it is essential to ensure that your candle stays ignited. The wax of the candle represents the water element. This is based on the idea that wax, like water, changes between its three forms of solid, liquid, and gas. The air element is obviously present in that oxygen is required to keep the flame lit. The fire element is also quite obviously present in the actual flame itself. Then the spirit element which is also referred to as Akasha is represented by the focus that you show to the candle and the energy that you transfer to it.

When you are performing candle magic or any kind of magic it is important to examine your motives before you go through with anything. You need to evaluate what your intent is and make sure that it follows the Wicca rede of "Harm None." It is important that you follow this rule. Do not cause any harm to others including more innocent sides like manipulation even if you think you are justified in your intent. Although you should not aspire to cause any harm in the first place. If you get to that point you must realize that anything that you cast will come back to you threefold as previously stated.

Before starting any type of candle magic you need to understand how serious it is. It is often said that any magic done whether it be positive or negative will come back to you threefold. You should always keep that in mind when you are practicing any magic spells or rituals. It is also important that you are as precise as possible with your words when casting spells. Any slip up in your spell could result in unforeseen consequences. Choose your words wisely and carefully when practicing candle magic and always be aware that your magic will affect the world around you in some way. It is also important to be aware of your surroundings when you are preparing to do candle magic.

Most spells require that the cuddle burn completely through, and this can take several hours or days depending on the candle; so, it is important to pick a location that will not be disrupted. In other words, if you have pets or small children it is probably a good idea to place the candles in a room shut off from them or in an area that they cannot reach. You should not leave any candles unattended because they are obviously a major fire hazard.

However, if you absolutely must leave the house, it is probably a good idea to place the candle in an area that is not flammable. Some people will opt for putting their candles in the bathroom sink or tub. This is not only to ensure that your spell goes properly, but also to ensure the safety of yourself and those around you.

The first step for your candle magic process is to find or make an altar. You can use virtually anything with a flat top, but if you want to be creative and have a specific place to always do your candle spells then you can make your own altar out of whatever you see fit. Another thing to consider is what time of covering or tablecloth are you going to use on your altar.

You can virtually use any color that you would like, but you may have to have a specific color for certain spells, so keep that in mind. Many people will just use white because it is a good multipurpose color to choose. Others will simply pick whatever color that they like the most because it is not necessarily of any importance unless otherwise suggested in the specific spell you are trying to perform. Another thing that some people like to do is to have something on their altars to represent each of the five fundamental elements of Wicca. Depending on what sect of Wicca they are from these items may differ.

A few options for someone starting out would include a candle, athame, or the sun for fire; a bowl of water, shell, or some other seafaring creature for water; crystals, flowers, or herbs for earth; and an angel, star, or the number five to represent spirit. Once you have set up your altar you need to bless it before beginning any spells. There are several specific rituals that you can do to bless your altar. Another option is just to make up your own blessing focused around what exactly you want to use your altar for. It is all up for interpretation and you can do whatever you feel the spirits are leading you to do. Some people also like to use incense when they are doing candle magic.

This is not true for everyone nor is it required. It is also another way to represent one of your five basic elements, air. Some spells may require you to use specific incense, but most of them do not. It is said to help add a little power or energy to your spell if you do use incense while working, but it is again entirely up to you unless specifically stated in the spell. The incense is also supposed to help ferry your thoughts and prayers into the universe.

Lastly you want to make sure that you cleanse, consecrate, and inscribe your candles properly; but we will discuss that with more detail in a later chapter.

The type of candles you use are not of particular importance. It is believed that candles made from things like beeswax or soy are more powerful than others because they are derived from nature. With that being said paraffin candles will work as well and they are typically a less expensive alternative.

Another option for your candles would be to make your own. Some believe that making your own candles is the best route because your energy is being transferred into the candle as you make. While making the candles you would want to focus on what you specifically you are making the candle for whether it be a specific spell or ritual.

This will help transfer your energy into the candle and help ensure a good result when performing your spell or ritual. One thing to consider when choosing your candles is the length of time that it will take your candle to burn.

You don't want to buy huge candles because you cannot reuse them for a separate spell. However, you also do not want to buy a candle that will go out too quickly because it needs to last for at least as long as your spell will take. Another thing to consider is whether you want to use scented candles or not.

This also does not particularly matter, but most people who practice candle magic opt for non-scented candles. This is partially due to the fact that you may need several different candles for one spell and not all scents mesh well together. Another reason is that if you do use a scented candle you need to make sure that scent coincides with the spell that you are going to be performing. You wouldn't want a scent associated with negative connotations to be swirling around your spell for prosperity, so just keep that in mind. It may just be the safest bet to use candles that are not scented when you are starting out.

Some of the types of candles used for Wicca include taper candles, votive candles, chime candles, pillar candles and jar candles. Taper candles are long and tall and typically you can guess how long these candles will burn by how long the candle itself actually is.

For example, a 12 in taper candle will burn 12 hours and a 10" taper candle would burn for about 10 hours. Votive candles are short stubby candles that are typically white. These candles will burn for about 3-4 hours and are usually used for spells that are to be performed more than once. Chime candles are similar to taper candles, but they are much shorter. They will typically burn for around 2-4 hours.

The largest and longest lasting candles are jar and pillar candles. Pillar candles will burn between 30 -90 hours depending on how tall they are. Jar candles are on a similar plane, depending on the size of your jar candle it can burn anywhere between 2-7 days. Jar candles are used in magic that is in the realm of hoodoo. These are not used very often unless it is for a big spell. If you do use a jar or pillar candle in a spell you will likely need to make sure that it is still lit every day and send up a prayer or statement of intent each day as well.

Another option that you can look into is trying 'ritually charge candles. These candles will help add a little more energy behind your spells. They add this energy because they are made are hand crafted by artisans for a specific purpose.

These are said to be good for beginners because it will help give your spiritual energy towards the candle a bit of a boost. This will help ensure that your intent is heard and you spell will go according to plan. You do not have to use colored candles when performing candle magic. It is completely up to your preference.

Candles were used in spiritual rituals and magic long before colored candles were ever created, so it is not a requirement. However, the candle colors are supposed to represent certain things and add that specific desire to your spell work. There are a variety of different colored candles. Each color means something different and it is important that you memorize each of their meanings.

This will help you better understand the spells you are casting and their meanings. It will also help you more easily pick what supplies you need for your spells and rituals.

White is the most multipurpose candle color. It is used for a variety of things and has a large pool of meanings. White candles can represent harmony, innocence, chastity, peace, rain, healing, balance, incorporeality, honesty, and consecration. It is used for magic that includes small children because it represents their innocence and purity. It is also used to help balance your aura.

Black candles represent intelligence, grounding, guardianship, safety, and pride. It is also a simple of reversing. It is often used in spells that intend to do this such as un-hexing, banishing negativity, and uncrossing. It is used to depict scrying, defense, and even shapeshifting.

Blue is used to illustrate forgiveness, will power, sincerity, truth, focus, communication, and good fortune. It is also used to help with things like weight loss, organization, domestic harmony, and removing bad vibes. It is used for astral projection and to represent the water element.

Gray represents compilation and loneliness. It is also often used for removing negative influences and glamour spells.

Brown candles portray concentration, stability, and the earth element. Brown candles are used for lots of magic that include goods and material things. It is used for house blessing, real estate, construction, food, or financial crisis. It is also used to represent all earth and animal magic. It is often used to help locate lost objects as well.

Green candles are a symbol of prosperity, acceptance, good luck, and abundance. They are used for spells including money, growth, and healing both physical and emotion. It is also used for all plant and tree magic for obvious reasons as well as to help with weather spells. They are also used to help counteract bad traits such as greed, envy, and jealousy.

Copper is used to display things related to business and money. It is used for spells that indicate success in business, money, and growth in career aspects. It is also a symbol for passion and fertility.

Gold, as you can probably guess, is used to illustrate abundance, luxury, great fortune, and prosperity. It is good to use for luck that is needed as quickly as possible. It is also used to represent masculinity both in divinity and energy. It is a representation of the sun and solar energy because of its resemblance to sunlight. It is good for showing understanding, health, positive attitude, attraction, and justice.

Silver is the opposite of gold in that it represents feminine energy and divinity. It increases psychic awareness, communication, dreams, and meditation. It indicates stability, victory, and intuition. It is a great color to use for gambling luck, and is used for all moon magic as its color resembles that of the moon.

Light Blue is used to mirror peace, spirituality, and tranquility as well as protection.

Lavender represents knowledge and intuition.

Indigo is used to help overcome depression and help encourage meditation. It is used to invoke spiritual guidance and divination. It creates an aura of ambition and dignity while increasing psychic ability. It is also used to help stop lies and gossip.

Purple represents influence, wisdom, independence, and government. It is a great source of spiritual power and is often used to contact spirit or drive away evil. It can also be used to break a habit or change one's luck.

Violet represents goddess, clarity, insight, and spirituality. It is also used to show tension or to connect to a higher self.

Pink is used to reflect femininity, romance, love, compassion, and partnership. It shows nurturing and protection of children. It is also used to show case maturity, self-betterment, and healing both spiritually and emotionally.

Orange is used as a symbol of self-expression, ambition, and creativity. It is used in intellectual, legal, investments, and business matters. It is used to help overcome addiction and mirrors joy. It is also used to showcase fun, opportunity, celebration, vitality and action.

Red is used to display vitality, fertility, passion, and sexual potency. It is also used to imply things such as courage, strength, survival, assertiveness and independence. It also represents darker things such as war, danger, and conflict. It is used to represent the fire element as well as display the heat competitions and sports.

Yellow is a symbol of success, happiness, inspiration, and pleasure. It represents learning, concentration, confidence, and persuasion. It displays imagination, charm, memory, and flexibility. It represents solar magic and the air element.

Chapter 3: Selecting the Proper Candles, Preparing Yourself, and Preparing Your Sacred Space

Regardless of the path you want to follow, the art of preparing a ritual place is essential. You don't have to have a lot of items to make a place look sacred. However, with a few candles as well as a few flowers here and there, you can transform a room to be one of the most sacred ever. Scholars have identified that a lot of spiritual people doesn't necessarily need a lot of items to transform a room into a ritual place.

However, some select a few candles and use them to light the room. With fervent prayers and silence, the room is made the place of worship. It is worth noting that you don't have to do what other people does to be useful. In other words, you can be unique in your way and select a few candles with different colors.

The art is linked to the fact that different colors display an elegant image. Also, different colors have a different meaning in ritual places. Depending on what you believe or rather your way of worship, the colors of the candle may reflect various issues. For instance, in most cases, when the ritual sacrifice is more of asking for forgiveness, a red candle may be selected.

On the other hand, a white candle may be used when the ritual sacrifice is more of seeking and praying for peace in the nation. What matter in a ritual sacrifice is the art of cleaning less; In other words, you have to clean the place and select your colors wisely. In other words, to light a room, you need to ensure that it is clean and everything is in order.

Before placing the candles, you have selected, the art of having a decent place is critical. It makes the room looks more unique and ready for a ritual sacrifice. So, you know all of your basic candle colors, sizes, and types. The next step is to figure out which candle you need to use for each specific spell. While some spells will tell you exactly what supplies you will need for it, others may not. Even if it does give you a list, it may not go into the details that you need to know.

For example, it may say you need a red candle, but not what type or size. It may just say you need a candle but not what specific colors, so you need to be able to deduce what to use on your own. It may also be that you want to do a spell that you are writing yourself.

In that case it is imperative that you choose the proper tools to help portray your intent to the spirits.

This chapter will help you do just that. The first step is to identify your intent. What is the base idea behind your spell? Is it growth, romance, healing, etc. Once your specific intent has been determined then you can start decided which candles to involve in your spell. Below is a chart of common intents associated with spell casting and a few suggestions for what candles you can use.

There of course are other intents and candle colors, but these are just a few of the most common ones.

If you are working on a spell with an intent that is not listed, just refer back to the last chapter to see which candle colors are associated with what.

Spells Intent or Focus:	Color Candles to Use:
Love/Passion	Pink, Red, White,
Healing/Health	Gold, White
Protection/Safety	Black, White, Pink. Light Blue
Success/Prosperity	Copper, Gold, White, Green, Yellow
Spirituality/Meditation	Violet, White, Light Blue, Indigo, Purple, Silver
Learning/Intellect	Lavender, Orange, White, Yellow, Black
Cleansing/Drive Away Negativity	White, Purple, Black, Gray
Serenity/Peace	White, Blue, Light Blue
Money	Green, Copper, White
Fertility	Copper, Red, White
Self-Improvement	Pink, Orange, White
Strength/Energy	Red, White, Gold
Overcoming Obstacles	Orange, Indigo, White
Confidence/Assertiveness	Red, Yellow, White
Inspiration/Creativity	Orange, Yellow, White
Luck	Green, Silver, White, Purple

Find Lost Object	Brown, White
Communicate with Spirits	Purple, White, Silver, Violet
Astral Projection	Blue, White
Sun/Solar Magic	Gold, Yellow
Earth/Animal Magic	Brown
Moon Magic	Silver
Tree/Plant Magic	Green
Contact Masculine Divinity	Gold, White
Contact Feminine Divinity	Silver, Violet, White

As you can see there are several color candles that you can use for certain intents. This means that you can either choose one of the colors or you can get one of each of the colors. If you do one candle of each of the colors that align with your spells intent this could help you harness more energy and thus could create a more successful outcome.

The more energy that is put into your spell from all angles, the more likely you are to have a great outcome. So, with that in mind if you have one spell that is particularly important then you should pull out all the stops.

You should have multiple candles and you should do a number of things that you will learn more about in the later chapters of the books.

You should inscribe you candles, anoint them, and leave them in to the moonlight to charge.

You should burn incense that aligns with your intent.

You should even try to align your spell work with the proper moon phase and pick the best day of the week for your intent as well.

You will learn more about all of those things in the chapter to come, but one thing you should always do before or during your spell work is practice meditation.

Once you have found the proper candles for your spell or ritual the next step is to prepare yourself.

You want to make sure that you are in the right headspace before performing any spells or rituals. It is important that you do not have any internal wars going on because it can affect the outcome of your spells. If your heart and mind are not in the right place it can even, make it difficult for you to perform the spell at all. If the spirits feel the imbalance in your spirit, then they may not be as receptive to your requests.

One of the ways to make sure that you are in the right mindset for your spell work is to try some meditation. **_Meditation_** will help you reduce stress, enhance self-awareness, and control anxiety. These are all things that can throw your inner self out of balance and can cause issues with your spell work. There are several meditation techniques that you can try to help alleviate any inner malaise that you may be feeling.

The majority of your bodily functions are involuntary or compulsory meaning that you do them without even thinking about them. Blinking, breathing, and heartbeat are just a few examples of involuntary actions your body performs all the time without you really noticing. One of the key components of meditation is to take yourself out of autopilot and focus on trying to control the involuntary actions that you can.

There are several types of meditation techniques, but two of the most popularly used ones are mindful meditation and concentration meditation. Concentration meditation is centered around the idea of focusing on one particular thing.

This particular thing could be your breathing, your heartbeat, a candles flame, etc. What you focus on is not very important. The main thing is that you are focusing all of your thoughts on that one specific thing. If your mind begins to wander you want to refocus yourself on that thing. Keep doing this over and over again and it will help calm you and increase your ability to concentrate. It may be hard to do it for very long when you first begin, but like most things it becomes easier with practice.

Mindful meditation is centered around the idea of focusing on where your mind wanders when you are left alone with your thoughts. To practice mindful meditation, it may be easier to start off focusing on something like your breathing. However, unlike in concentration meditation, once your mind begins to wander let it. Focus on what kind of thoughts your mind gravitates to when you are just trying to relax. Are your thoughts centered around negative thoughts or stressful scenarios or are your thoughts gravitating towards positivity and happy thoughts?

If it is the negative thoughts that your mind is gravitating towards it may not be the best time to perform any spell work. You should maybe take some time to reflect on your meditation and try to discover the root of the negativity that it is stemming from.

However, if you feel that your thoughts tended to go towards a more positive vibe then that is probably a good indication that you are in the right mindset to perform spell work. A lot of meditation is done while staying completely still. Here are a few step by step instructions on sedentary meditation. The first thing you want to do is find a quiet and peaceful place to practice your meditation. It is hard enough to focus your mind without outside distractions.

Trying to do so with noises and other people around makes it nearly impossible, so find a nice solitary location that has a pleasant atmosphere to it. The keep to meditation is that you want to uplift yourself mentally, physically, and emotionally. If you try to practice meditation in a place that makes you feel gloomy or negative this will most likely result in an unsuccessful meditation session.

You want to feel better after practicing meditation, not worse. After you have found a nice quiet place, settle into whatever position is most comforting for you. Some people like to sit, others like to lay down, or some may even pick a specific yoga pose that they find most comfortable. This will help relax your body and make focusing on your meditation much easier. Some people even have furniture specifically for their meditation. There are meditation chairs or cushions that you can buy online, or you could just find something like a nice comfy bean bag chair.

Once you have picked your location and your position that is most calming for you, close your eyes and try to relax your breathing. Some people like to use eye masks to cover their eyes to help them focus and to disregard distractions. You can use just a normal sleeping eye mask, or you could try one of those cooling spa masking that you store in the refrigerator if you think that would be more soothing for you.

Focus intently on your breathing and try to keep it at a regular pace.

Some people suggest breathing in intervals, in for three to five seconds and out for the same amount of time.

Others say not to try to regulate your breathing, but just to breathe naturally. You can choose whichever you prefer. If you find that it is difficult for you to keep a steady calm breathing routine, then it may be helpful to try counting the seconds in and out. Focus on how your breath affects your body. Feel your rib cage expand and contract as your lungs breathe in and out. Focus on your shoulders lifting and falling as you inhale and exhale.

Try to pay attention to all of the things that your body is doing that you usually do not notice. There are also forms of meditation that are considered moving meditation techniques. Qigong, tai chi, and walking meditations are all examples of moving meditation techniques. Qigong is an ancient Chinese technique that combines meditation and exercise.

In Qigong you go through a series of slow movements that you repeat over and over. This creates a great environment for meditation. The repetition of the movement combined with the deep steady breaths helps to keep your mind focused and calm. Tai chi like Qigong is an ancient Chinese technique that consists of a series of movements and positions mixed together to create a fluid technique. It was originally created to help with self-defense but has since turned into a great source for meditation as well.

Walking meditation or kin hin is essentially just like sedentary meditation, but you do it while you are walking. Many people will choose to walk in a calming peaceful place away from distractions and loud noises.

Forests and walking trails are good options for a place to practice walking meditation. Another option, if you live close to the ocean, would be to walk along the beach at calm time of day like early in the morning or close to sunset. Just remember that no matter where you choose to practice your meditation it is important that it is in a positive and uplifting environment.

Once you feel that you have the proper mentality to perform spell work then you can move onto the next of preparing yourself. This, like most things in Wicca, is not a requirement but simply a suggestion. Some people like to do a formal spiritual cleansing of themselves before performing any spell work. You can cleanse yourself by following these steps.

The first thing you will need to do is gather the necessary supplies for a ***spiritual cleansing***. You will need a white candle, sage or frankincense incense, a bathtub, cedar oil, hyssop oil, and sandalwood oil. Your first step in the cleansing process is to prepare your candle and run your bath water. You will want to anoint your candle with hyssop oil first and then light it. You will also want to light whichever incense you chose to use.

Once you have done that and your bath water has been run you will want to add a few drops of each of your three oils (cedar, hyssop, and sandalwood) to your bath water. Submerge yourself into the bath water and wash yourself as normal. As you are cleansing yourself be mindful of your work. Focus on what it is you are doing and what it represents.

Once you have full washed and dried off you will then want to anoint yourself with sandalwood oil. Just put a few dabs of oil on your heart, wrists, forehead, feet, knees, and lower stomach. If you only have a shower, not a bathtub that is okay. Just follow the same instruction, but you can use a bowl or sink instead of a tub. Use a washcloth to cleanse yourself as usual.

Another thing that some people choose to do when preparing for a spell is change their eating schedule or they will have their favorite meal the day before. This is to help make sure that the individual is in a pleasant state of mind for their spell work. It is recommended that you get at least a full eight hours of sleep the night before you plan to do a spell and that you meditate on your spell the day before. Go over the spells steps and words and envision yourself obtaining what it is that you desire.

The more time and energy you put into your spell before you do it, the more likely you are to have a fruitful outcome. Some suggest that if you do not live alone to ask your roommates or family to not disturb you so that you can focus on your intended goal.

If you are doing spell work with others it is important to align your energies with each other. Some people suggest doing something harmonizing before doing any spell work as a group. You can meditate together, sing or chant a song, or do a group anointing with the same oil. All of these activities will help to bring the group together and enhance your joint energy. When it is finally time to do your spell work you want to ensure that you have the right atmosphere.

Whether you are working alone or with a group you need to make sure that your environment is an inviting one and that there is no negative energy present. If you are a part of a group endeavor and you find that one particular person is throwing off the groups energy it is very important to stop while you're ahead.

Try to identify who is carrying the negative energy and help them through it if possible. If the person is not able to let go of the negative energy that they are harboring you should either ask them to leave if they are not imperative to the spell or try to plan for a different day. Try enriching your atmosphere with things that bring positive vibes into the scenario. Some people like to play music in the background or perform their spells in a favorite location in their house.

Some people will burn incense or extra candles around the room just to help facilitate the spell work. Incense all have various uses which I will list in the chart below. Use this chart to help determine what incense would work best for your intended purposes.

Surround your space with whatever brings you joy and that will in turn create a good environment to perform you spells and rituals in.

WICCA

Incense:	Purpose:
Acacia	help spark or encourage psychic abilities
African Violet	for protection and spirituality
Allspice	used to promote good luck and financial gain
Aloe	used for spirituality, good omens, strength, and love
Althea	for psychic powers and protection
Amber	used for happiness, love, healing, and comfort
Ambergris	an aphrodisiac and used for dreams
Angelica	used to promote harmony, insight, meditation, understanding, stability, integration, and protection
Anise Seed	used to help with emotional balance
Apple Blossom	friendship, love, and happiness
Basil	wealth, confidence, assertiveness, concentration, luck, and sympathy
Bay	Helps induce prophetic dreams and psychic powers
Bayberry	used to attract money, prosperity, happiness, control, and protection
Benzoin	helps with depression, grief, anger, and anxiety
Bergamot	concentration, confidence, motivation, courage, prosperity, and money
Bistort	usually used with frankincense to help with divination
Blue Berry	to ward off unwanted spirits and influences
Bracken	produces rain

Cardamom	used for motivation, concentration, and clarity
Carnation	Used for love, lust, protection, and healing
Cedar	Insight, wisdom, prevent nightmares, purification, balance, money, and healing
Cedarwood	Money, balance, purification, healing, and protection
Chamomile	Used to enhance peace, harmony, and calm
Cherry	attraction and love
Cinnamon	to gain success and wealth, strengthen psychic gifts, aid in healing, lust, strength
Citron	aids in healing and strengthen psychic gifts
Citronella	healing, cleansing, and warding off
Clove	used in divination and exorcisms, for protection, pain relief, and to ease fear, helps improve focus and memorization
Coconut	for purification and protection
Copal	attract love, spirituality and protection, used for purification and to uplift spirits
Cypress	Used for will power and concentration, helpful in healing and self-assurance, good to alleviate anxiety and stress, comfort and strength
Damiana	helps facilitate visions of psychic proportions
Dittany of Crete	divination and aids in astral projection
Dragon's Blood	attracts love, enhance psychic awareness, courage, purification, protection, and ward off negativity
Elecampane	strengthen clairvoyance and scrying
Eucalyptus	Protection, Purification, and Healing
Fern	Produces rain, and help exorcise evil entities

Frankincense	Induce psychic visions, good luck, consecration, astral strength, and spirituality
Frangipani	brings in love and friendship
Fumitory	exorcises poltergeists, demons, and evil entities
Galangal	breaks curses by sorcerers
Gardenia	encourages healing, love, and peace
Ginger	Produces love, lust, and wealth
Ginseng Root	protects against all forms of evil
Gotu Kola	aids in meditation
Heather	produces rain, conjuring friendly spirits
Hibiscus	attracts love, lust, and used for divination
Honeysuckle	used to promote good health, healing, luck, money, happiness, friendship, and psychic powers
Hyacinth	protection and happiness
Jasmine	used for luck, love, dreams, money, purification, wisdom, skills, astral projections, and calming
Juniper	protection, healing, calming, break evil hexes and curses
Lavender	relaxation, love, happiness, healing, cleansing, and to induce sleep
Lemon	purification, love, and healing
Lemongrass	clarity
Lilac	attract harmony, soothes, and increase psychic power
Lotus	protection, mood elevation, healing, spirituality, aid meditation, and open the mind's eye

Mace	increase and stimulate psychic gifts
Mastic	intensify sexual desires, stimulate psychic gifts, summon friendly spirits
Mesquite	add to other healing incenses to ramp up the effect
Mint	attracts money and increases sexual desire
Musk	prosperity, courage, aphrodisiac, aids sensual atmosphere and passion
Myrrh	meditation, healing, purification, spirituality and consecration.
Nutmeg	aids meditation increase psychic powers, aids prosperity
Oakmoss	attracts money
Orange	money, love, luck, and divination
Patchouli	promotes fertility, money, love, mastery, growth, and sensuality
Passionflower	aids in sleep, soothes troubles, aids in peace of mind
Peppermint	healing, energy, and mental stimulation
Pine	attract money, cleansing, strength, and grounding
Poppy Seeds	money, good luck, female fertility, and attracts love
Rose	calm energy, increase courage, house blessings, love, prophetic dreams, and fertility
Rose Geranium	used for protection and courage
Rosemary	dispel depression, preserve youthfulness, aid in healing, memory, energy, and remembrance
Rue	restore health
Sage	purify sacred tools and spaces, protection

WICCA

	against evil, clarity, wisdom, money, healing your body soul, and mind
Sagebrush	banish evil negative entities, aids healing
Sandalwood	purification, haling, spirituality, protection, and astral projection
Solomons Seal	used as offering to ancient deities
Star Anise Seeds	increase psychic powers
Strawberry	friendship, luck, and love
Sweetgrass	conjure helpful spirits
Sweet Pea	courage, friendship, and love
Thyme	purify your sacred space, good health, and aid healing
Tangerine	attract prosperity
Vanilla	enhance memory, lust, mental alertness
Vervain	exorcise evil entities
Vetivert	love, peace, and money
Violet	used for protection, healing, love, wisdom, and luck
Willow	promotes healing, avert evil, and attract love, used as an offering to the sacred deities
Wisteria	protection against evil in all forms
Wormwood	increase psychic powers, conjure spirits from their graves
Yarrow	courage
Ylang-Ylang	euphoria, love, and harmony

Some people like to cultivate their ritual environment or space by doing a dedication ritual. You can dedicate your space however you feel is appropriate, but one of the most common ways is to follow this simple **dedication ritual.** For this ritual you will need a white candle, myrrh oil, and frankincense oil. The first step is to anoint your candle with the two oils. You can read about how to properly anoint your candles in the next chapter. Once you anoint your candle you want to hold it in your hands and walk around your ritual space in a clockwise wise direction. After you have walked around your space a few times you will need to place your candle in the center of ritual space and let it burn until it burns out.

There are some other techniques that can be used to help dedicate your sacred space. Some people like to use their myrrh and frankincense oil to anoint the four corners of their sacred space. Others will use their favorite crystals and place them at North, South, East and West around their sacred space. Some people also like to place figurines or portraits of whatever deity they have chosen to dedicate their sacred space. Another thing to consider is making sure that your sacred is protected from negative energies and forces. Some people like to include mirrors in their sacred space because it is believed to reflect negative and positive energies. Other will display pentagrams or the Algiz Rune for protection. Sea salt or dried basil are two more great options to ward off evil spirits and negative energies. Just sprinkle salt around your sacred place or hang some dried basil to keep the intrusive energies out. Some people will also opt for protective stones and crystals. Amethyst, Agate, Jasper, Onyx, Emeralds, Rubies, and Sapphires are just a few examples of protective stones you can use for your sacred space.

Chapter 4: Preparing Your Ritual Candles

There are several ways to prepare you candles before performing your spells of rituals. These ways of empowering or charge your candle include cleaning, anointing, carving your candle, and other methods. All of these methods help to ensure that your candles are in prime condition for your spell. Charging your candle will make it more powerful and thus create a more powerful, successful spell. The idea behind ***cleansing*** your candle is to remove any negative energy that is surrounding it.

Negative energy can be transferred in many ways. It is important to make sure that your candle does not have any of these unfavorably energies, so that it will not affect your spell or ritual in a negative manor. There are a few ways to perform a cleansing. The first is to leave your candle outside overnight. The idea behind this form of cleansing is that your candle will absorb the moonlight's energy and that will dissolve any adverse spirits attached to the candle. Another is to douse the candle in incense or sage smoke. Sage is used for healing. Its scientific name, *Salvia Officinalis,* even indicates its restorative properties. Salvia derives from the word salve in Latin which means to heal or to soothe, so it is obvious why it is the preferred herb to use for cleansing.

Another way to cleanse your candle is to entomb it with sea salt and leave it for the night. Salt has been used in a variety of other religions and cultures such as Buddhism or Shintoism as well over the years as a source of purification or to repel evil.

The last way is to cleanse your candle is actually a pretty common way that people clean candles for just general home cleaning. This method is simply wiping the candle down with rubbing alcohol from bottom to top. If you are using a jar candle you would want to wipe the entire outside of the jar as well as any bit of candle that is exposed as well. While you are cleaning you candle it is important that you focus on your work as you do it. Try meditating on the removal of the negative energy and asking for blessings while you work. Charging your candle can also be done by ***dressing or anointing it***.

The process is done by rubbing a specific oil over the candle. There are different opinions on how exactly to apply the oil. Some people will start in the middle of the candle applying the oil and work their way down. Others will start at the bottom of the candle and work their way up to the middle. Some suggest that if you are asking for something you would want to rub the oil from the top to the bottom; and if you are trying to rid yourself of something you would want to rub the oil from the bottom to the top. The directional application is supposed to be another way to signify your intent. However, this is really not a crucial consideration as long as you have the right intentions while anointing your candle. You want to try to envision yourself with whatever it is that you are seeking. For example, if you are working a love spell you would want to envision yourself with your perfect match. Here is a basic chart of some commonly used oils and their purposes in Wicca.

Oil:	Purpose:	Oil:	Purpose:
Purification	Myrrh, Frankincense	**Healing**	Carnation, Eucalyptus, Lotus, Myrrh, Narcissus, Rosemary, Sandalwood
Concentration	Honeysuckle, Lilac, Rosemary	**Meditation**	Jasmine, Acacia, Hyacinth, Myrrh, Magnolia, Nutmeg
Protection	Cypress, Myrrh, Rose, Rue, Rosemary, Violet, Geranium, Patchouli	**Peace**	Gardenia, Magnolia, Benzoin, Rose, Tuberose
Money	Vervain, Honeysuckle, Mint, Bayberry, Bergamot, Almond	**Fertility**	Musk, Vervain
Power	Carnation, Rosemary, Vanilla	**Courage**	Musk, Iris, Rose Geranium
Harmony	Basis, Lilac, Narcissus, Gardenia	**New Beginnings**	New-mown Hay
Psychic Powers	Anise, Acacia, Cassia, Lilac, Mimosa, Heliotrope, Tuberose	**Passion**	Cinnamon, Cassia, Clove, Lavender, Musk, Neroli, Patchouli, Stephanotis, Vanilla, Violet

Some people will also add herbs to their oils to generate even more power.

Different types of oils are associated with different things just like candle colors. Here is a basic chart of what some basic herbs are used for.

WICCA

Herb:	Purpose:	Herb:	Purpose:
Basil	romance, love, initiation	*Aconite*	create illusions, diminishing, magical prowess, returning
Ivy	prevent drunkenness	*Bay Laurel*	Prophecy, visions, honor
Mandrake	protection, magical endeavors, sight	*Lavender*	Love, honesty, calming
Mug wort	astral projection, sleep and dreams	*Rue*	Dismiss evil
Sage	wisdom, insight, prolongs life, rebuke evil	*Tansy*	meditation, reveal secrets
Elder	divination, protection from lightning, and summoning Mother Goddess	*Clover*	Consecration, Luck, Healing
Fennel	Strength, Fertility, and Virility	*Yarrow*	divination, and tarot work
Pennyroyal	Consecration, contact with the dead	*Juniper*	Tree magic, justice, and invoke spirits

WICCA

Benzoin	Mental and emotional strength, visions	*Anise*	good sleep, safety, and preserve youth
Eyebright	Visions, clairvoyance, and psychic balance	*Ferns*	Invisibility
Blessed Thistle	sexuality, removes curses	*Angelica*	protection from evil
Agrimony	deep dreaming, and invokes sleep	*Hops*	Sleep, dreams
Hyssop	spiritual cleansing and protection	*Cinnamon*	purification, strength, awareness, and energy
Foxglove	elemental spirit communication	*Cinquefoil*	enhance all spell work, and flying ointment
Mistletoe	Fertility, prophecy, and immortality	*Pomegranate*	cycles, mysteries
Rosemary	eternal youth, protection of house, increase memory	*St. John's Wort*	Attainment, power, and success
Comfrey	assures safe journeys	*Horehound*	inspiration

The next way to charge your candle is by inscribing or carving your candle. This is basically a process of carving things like symbols, names, or initials into your candles that help represent your intent.

For example, if you were working a love spell then maybe you would carve the names of the two people involved in the spell. If you were working a healing spell, then you could choose a symbol that means healing. These source of the symbols does not matter as long as your intent is clear. You can use common Wicca symbols, symbols derived from a variety of cultures, or you can make up your own if you would like.

As long as you know what your symbols stand for and your intent is clear you can inscribe whatever you would like onto your candles. There are specific tools that you can buy for inscribing your candles, but generally you can use anything that has a fine tip. Some people will you something small like a pin, toothpick, or those little sticks you would find in a martini glass.

The important thing is that you focus, again, on your intent and how these inscriptions are supposed to help your spell. Some people would suggest inscribing your candles before you anoint them as to not make too much of a mess. Here are a few popular symbols derived from various sources that you may want to try out for your inscriptions.

WICCA

Air	Earth	Water
Fire	Spirit	Yin/Yang (Harmony)
Sun or Gold	Goddess	God
Love	Purification	Peace

WICCA

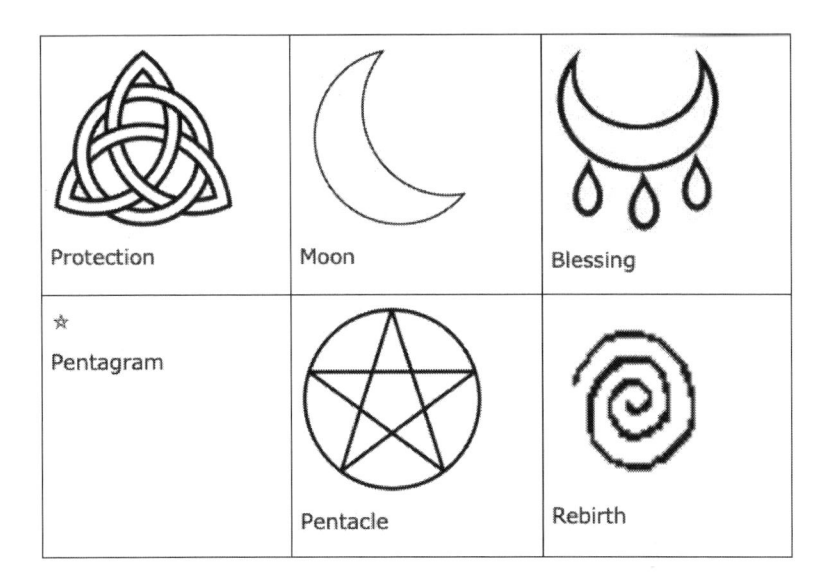

Protection	Moon	Blessing
☆ Pentagram	Pentacle	Rebirth

Another step that some people will choose to do is to encircle your candle with sachet powders, witchcraft dusts, etc. Sachet powders are a variety of perfumed powders used to aid your spell work as well. There are a variety of powders and dust, all of them have various uses like oils and herbs. The idea is that by creating a circle around your candle you are protecting yourself as well as helping charge the candle with even more energy.

Abramelin powder is derived from an old Jewish formula and is often used for consecrating tools and for protection. Some people will place it in their window seals and doorways when performing a seal of protection around a house.

Salt is often used for purification purposes and protection. Some people insist on using only kosher salt because they believe that it is more potent of powerful than plain old table salt.

Witches' Salt or Black Salt is used to drive away enemies and evil in general. This salt can be a combination of several things. Some witches' salts are made of charcoal and salt, iron and salt, or black pepper and salt.

Saltpepper is used to help remove negative influence or spiritual cleansing and is often used with mixing other powders. Sulphur Powder is used to help clean out negative energy and is often mixed with salt. Crown of Success is a sachet powder that is used in aiding success and achievement in all facets of life.

Banishing Powder is most often used to help fix mistakes that are brought upon ourselves. Despite the countless warnings that are given about working spells that can bring negative energy or spirits people still get themselves into scenarios that they need to get out of.

Banishing powder is a great tool to help remove unwanted energy or people without being too destructive.

Kiss Me Now! is a sachet powder used to increase sexual encounters. It is often used by people who feel the need to increase their sex drive in their marriage or by people who just want to have a little fun.

Bewitching Powder is a sachet powder is often used in love spells. It helps add a bit of sexual allure and mystery to the equation.

Look Me Over is a sachet powder used in attraction spells and glamouring spells. It adds a bit of attractive appeal without being manipulative. Some people suggest using is on a daily basis to help increase your overall magnetism.

Crucible of Courage is used to help increase courage, persistence, and boldness. It is used often when working against powers or forces that are perpetually stronger or more negative than your own.

Tranquility Powder is a soothing powder used for calming scenarios and gently reinstating peace.

Planetary Sachet Powders are associated with certain gods and goddess. Each of these gods have certain characteristics, so you could use the powder that coincides with a certain god or goddess if you wish to invoke them or if you wish to portray something that they are associated with.

Type of Sachet Powder	God/Goddess Associated	God/Goddess Of What?
Sun Sachet Powder	Apollo	music, poetry, sun, light, archery, plague, knowledge, medicine, and oracles
Mercury Sachet Powder	Hermes	shepherds, land travel, and literature
Venus Sachet Powder	Freya	love, sex, lust, beauty, sorcery, fertility, gold, war, and death
Terra Sachet Powder	Gaia	mother of all life
Moon Sachet Powder	Artemis	hunting, wilderness, and wild animals
Mars Sachet Powder	Mars	war and agriculture
Jupiter Sachet Powder	Zeus and Thor	sky, lightning, and thunder
Saturn Sachet Powder	Kronos	time
Uranus Sachet Powder	Ourania (Urania)	music, song, dance, astronomical writings, and astronomy
Neptune Sachet Powder	Poseidon and Neptune	sea, horses, and earthquakes
Pluto Sachet Powder	Hades or Pluto	underworld and wealth

Zodiac Sachet Powders like the planetary powders are used to symbolize characteristics or element associated with each zodiac sign.

Type of Zodiac Powder	Element Associated	Characteristics Associated
Aries (Ram)	Fire	fiery, independent, energetic, turbulent
Taurus (Bull)	Earth	determined, ambitious, materialistic, beauty, artistry
Gemini (Twins)	Air	adaptable, outgoing, impulsive, unreliable, intelligent
Cancer (Crab)	Water	loyalty, emotional, intuitive, compassionate, and deep
Leo (Lion)	Fire	protective, vivacious, leader, spoiled, honest, impatient
Virgo (Virgin)	Earth	modest, down to earth, selfless, analytical
Libra (Balance)	Air	partnership, fairness, balanced, charming, genuine
Scorpio (Scorpion)	Water	intuitive, clairvoyance, intense, trustworthy, mysterious
Sagittarius (Archer)	Fire	knowledgeable, adventurous, straight forward, careless, inconsistent
Capricorn (Sea goat)	Earth	persistent, sensitive, ambitious, disciplines, realistic
Aquarius (Water bearer)	Air	friendly, inventive, loyal, unpredictable, stubborn, extremist
Pisces (Fishes)	Water	kind, imaginative, intuitive, sensitive, selfless, escapist, pessimistic

All of these ways to charge your candles are just suggestions. You can do any of these things or any combination of these things. You don't have to charge your candles before working any spells, but it is highly recommended.

However, in the end it is completely your call. One thing that you need to be aware of when doing candle magic is how to properly dispose of your spell remains.

The first thing that you want to do is to release of your energy and spell work from objects that are not biodegradable. You can do this by praying over these objects. You will want to say something along the lines of, "Release all of my energy and will from this object (jar, plastic, wax, etc) and let no magic be left in it".

Throw away any non-recyclable items. If there are recyclable items you will want to clean these items with sage or florida water. You will then want to burn any biodegradable items. If this spell is something positive you should bury it close to your home.

However, if you are dabbling in magic that involves the dark or negative energy you will want to bury your spell remains far away from where you rest your head. If you do not want to bury your biodegradable, you can either throw them into running water if it is safe for the environment or burn them if it is safe to do so.

Another thing you need to consider before you do your spell work is to decide when you need to do it. You can do your spells or rituals whenever you please or need, but there are some people who like to plan their rituals ahead of time and decide on a day that will also help energize the spell. Some people will choose a certain day of the week based on what is associated with that day, and others will make their decisions based on where the moon is in

WICCA

its cycle.

Every day of the week is associated with a planet, colors, certain deities, and intents. This chart will help you figure out which day of the week is best suited for your spell and will make a great reference for your future spell working.

Day of the Week:	Intents Associated:	Deities Associated:	Colors Associated:	Planets Associated:
Monday	-Peace -Wisdom -Travel -Emotions -Beauty -Sleep -Glamour -Fertility -Insight -Illusions -Dreams -Prophecy	-Luna -Artemis -Selene -Diana	-Silver -White -Blue	Moon
Tuesday	-Success -Courage -Victory -Rebellion -Protection -Conviction -Wards -Defense -Strength	-Ares -Tiwaz -Mars	-Red -Black -Orange	Mars
Wednesday	-Arts	-Mercury	-Purple	Mercury

WICCA

	-Luck -Gambling -Creativity -Chance -Transport -Change -Fortune -Communing	-Hermes -Woden	-Orange	
Thursday	-Strength -Wealth -Healing -Prosperity -Abundance -Protection	-Juno -Thor -Jupiter	-Blue -Purple -Green	Jupiter
Friday	-Birth -Love -Friendship -Pregnancy -Passion -Romance -Gentleness -Fertility	-Venus -Freya -Aphrodite	-Aqua -Pink	Venus
Saturday	-Cleansing -Wisdom -Protection -Spirituality -Banishing	-Saturn -Hecate	-Purple -Black	Saturn
Sunday	-Fame -Prosperity -Wealth -Promotion -Success	-Apollo -Brigid -Helios	-Yellow -Gold	Sun

So for example, if you were wanting to do a fertility spell it would probably be best to do it on a Monday or Friday because those two days are associated with fertility. If you were doing a spell for courage you would probably need to do it on a Tuesday for it to have the most potency, so on and so forth. Use the above chart if you want to ensure that you are doing everything you possibly can to ensure that your spell work is as successful as possible.

Another thing that people bring into consideration is the phases of the moon. The moon is known to let off a lot of magical energy and some find it very important to make sure that you are harnessing the proper energy from the moon when you are doing you spell work. Each phase of the moon is best used for certain types of spells.

A waxing moon phase would be the best time to perform spells that are trying to bring things into your life. As the moon is in the process of reaching its brightest and most powerful state, the full moon, it is bringing in new light each night. The idea is that you follow the moon's example and use this time to cast spells that are asking for something. For example, if you were using a spell to ask for courage, money, wisdom, etc. this would be a good time to do so. A waning moon phase would be the best time to rid yourself of something or banish anything that is unwanted. As the moon is waning it is slowly losing its light. The same idea as the waxing moon, just the opposite. As the moon is losing its brightness you too can lose things that you need to. For example, if you are wanting to do a spell to help rid you of a depressive episode or an illness this would be a good time to do it.

A new moon is the beginning of a new lunar cycle. This is a great opportunity to bring about new changes in your life. You would want to use this time for magic that is going to be initiating something new. For example, if you just got a new job you might want to do a spell for prosperity in your new job during the new moon.

A full moon is by far the most powerful of all the moon's phases. Many people will choose to save the lunar cycle's full moon for very important spells. For example, say you and your spouse had been trying for a baby for years. You have tried everything that you can possibly imagine and nothing has worked.

You want to do a fertility spell as a last resort. It would probably be a good idea to do that spell on a full moon to ensure it harness the moon's most powerful energy of all. A dark moon phase is the least favorable time to do magic because the moon is letting off little to know energy.

During this time many spell workers will choose to avoid working during this time. They will instead use this time to reflect and recharge themselves for the new lunar cycle to come. These phases are just general ideas that some people choose to follow. It is not a rule and if you feel that you need to perform a spell outside of what these phases suggest then you are completely in your right to do so. Do whatever you feel is necessary to ensure that your spell work is done at the right time for you and your life.

Chapter 5: Single Color Candle Spells

Red Candle Spells

Spell to Stop Procrastination

As the title of the spell indicates, this spell is to help you stop procrastinating. So, if you are a notorious procrastinator this spell is for you!

Materials you will need:

One red candle

Almond and lemon oil

A waxing, new, or full moon

To start this spell, go outside. You will need to do this spell outside in the direct moonlight.

Mix the almond oil and lemon oil together. Anoint your candle with the combined oils as well as yourself. Place the oil on your wrist and forehead.

Inhale the scent of oils and concentrate on the sense of energy that it gives off.

Place your candle in a safe and secure place on the ground where there is not fear of catching anything shrubbery or grass on fire.

Light your candle.

Say your incantation. You can write your own or say something along the lines of, "Candle red, blazing flame, help me learn how to refrain;

from being so slow and lazy too for this is not something that I should do. Glowing moon up in the sky give me the spirit to change my ways. For those who wait until the last day often times do not get any praise."

Meditate on your procrastination and why it is that you struggle so much with getting things done early. Try to find the root cause of your procrastination and ask the moon to rid you of it.

For example, if the reason that you procrastinate is because you have anxiety ask the moon to rid you of this negative feeling in your life.

If you are currently procrastinating in regard to something then take a moment to meditate on the idea of completely that task. Imagine the relief that you will feel when it is complete and focus on that. Try to harness that feeling of relief and use it to inspire yourself to finish the task as soon as possible.

Imagine that the flame of the candle is your procrastination and extinguish it.

Passionate Candle Spell

This spell is good if you know exactly what you need and want out of a relationship. Do not go into this spell with no idea of the type of relationship you are looking for. A relationship takes two people and you need to make sure that you are ready to put in your fifty percent. If you feel that you are in a position in which you have a healthy self-worth and feel that you can contribute to a healthy passionate relationship but are having a little trouble finding your other half then this may be a good spell for you to try.

Materials you will need include:

One red spell candle

Red writing utensil

Piece of paper

Cinnamon, jasmine, or rose oil

A carving tool

Steps to follow:

Try lighting some incense or putting on some light romantic music to set the proper atmosphere for your spell work.

The first thing you want to do is prep your candle. Try some of the techniques that we have previous discussed. Carve a heart to symbolize love or another symbol of your choice that signifies what you are looking for in your partner.

Light your candle and begin your spell work.

The next thing you need to do is take out the piece of paper and red writing utensil. Write a list of some of the things you find most important for your partner to possess.

On the other side of the paper list the characteristics that you think you need to improve upon to ensure you are the best partner you can be.

Place this sheet of paper next to your candle and anoint the sheet of paper with one or all of the three oils listed above.

While you are anointing the sheet focus on the characteristics that you are searching for most as well as the characteristics you aspire to develop in yourself. Chant or read off the characteristics as you go through them.

Once you have listed all of the characteristics say something to finish off your spell. You can come up with your own finishing line or you can say something along the lines of, "Passion of mine, passion be thine, passionate hearts make passionate minds. Passionate love makes our souls entwine."

Allow the candle to burn out on its own.

Reignite the Flame Spell

Sometimes after being in a relationship for an extended period of time you have lulls of passion. This spell is designed to help rekindle the flame that you had in the beginning of this relationship. It is to help give you back the fireworks that you experienced in the beginning of your relationship.

Materials you will need:

Two red candles

Jasmine oil

Rosemary

Steps to follow:

Start by setting the mood for your spells work like in the previous spell. Try lighting some incense or dimming the lights in your sacred space.

Carve your initials into one of the candles and your partner's initials into the other.

Anoint your candles with the jasmine oil.

Place your two red candles very close to each other and light them simultaneously. Make sure that your candles are close enough that the two candles waxes will melt together into one.

Create a circle of rosemary your two candles.

Say your spell at this time. You can create your own or say something like, "As these two melts into one, let our hearts do the same. Bring us close together and reignite our flame."

Let the two candles burn out completely.

You can try reading the wax after it has melted and see if it gives you any indication on how to add value to your relationship.

Pink Candle Spell

Moonlight Charged Attraction Spell

This spell is to be used to help you attract a potential partner. It is supposed to help you produce a more appealing aura.

Materials you will need:

One pink candle

Carving tool

Perfume or cologne

Cinnamon, jasmine, or lavender incense

Steps to follow:

Set the scene for your spell work as usual.

Light whichever incense you chose from the three listed above.

Use the carving tool carve a heart or other symbol for love into your candle.

Place the candle in the moonlight that shines through your window. With the bottle of perfume or cologne next to it.

Light the candle as you visualize yourself attracting a partner.

Say your incantation. You can create your own or you can say something like, "Moonlight shine bright, help me to shine in my own right as bright as you do in the night."

Allow your candle to burn all the way out.

Wear the perfume or cologne out to help you attract your new love.

Green Candle Spells

Quick Money Spell

This spell is a great starter spell. It is simple and it will hopefully bring you a little bit of money along the way. You will probably not win the lottery with this spell, but you might find a twenty-dollar bill on the street.

Material you will need:

One green candle

A handful of pocket change (dimes, pennies, nickels, quarters)

Carving tool

Mint or Vervain oil(optional)

Steps to follow:

Start as usual by setting your atmosphere. You can play some music or light some incense.

Start by carving a symbol for money into your candles. You can use a standard dollar sign or any other symbol associated with money.

At this time, you can anoint your candles with one of the two oils listed above if you wish. This is not required, but it can add a little umph to your spell if you do use it.

Take the handful of pocket change into your hands and start to imagine more money coming into your life. Meditate with the pocket change in your hands and focus on your intent.

Once you have done that take the pocket change and create a circle around your green candle with the change.

Select a specific coin of your choice out of the handful and place it by itself under the candle.

Light the candle and say your spell. This can be a spell of your own making or you can say something like, "Green candle, green money, silver coins, silver lining. As like attracts like, let this do the same."

Let the candle burn completely out.

Take whatever coin you placed under your candle and put it on your person. Place it in your wallet or purse and carry it around with you. This will help you carry the good fortune around with you and hopefully you will come across some money.

Attract More Cash Spell

This spell is used almost like a charm spell. It charges actual cash with fortunate energy so that it will attract more money to you.

Materials you will need:

One green candle

Patchouli oil

A bill of your choice (5, 10, 20, etc.)

A green rubber band

Carving tool (optional)

Cedarwood, Cinnamon, or Jasmine incense

Steps to follow:

Start by setting the atmosphere for your spell work up with lighting a bit of incense that is associated with money. Choose one of the three incenses listed above or another incense that has the same purpose. The three listed above are really just suggestions.

Start by anointing your candle with patchouli oil. You can also carve a symbol for money into you candles as well if you would like, but do that before you anoint your candle if you choose to do so.

Take whatever bill you chose and fold it in half. Wrap the bill around the candle and secure it with the rubber band. Place the bill close to the bottom of the candle so that the flame will not light the money on fire.

Hold the candle between your hands with the money wrapped around it. Now meditate on the idea of having being financially comfortable or even excessively wealthy if you want. The more imagination you have, the more energy you will be putting into your candle.

Imagine the feeling that you would have if you were to be walking down the street and found a hundred-dollar bill on the ground. Harness that feeling and focus on it.

Once you feel that you are consumed with that feeling of joy start to say your incantation. You can say, "As this money stays at my side, let it be my solemn guide. To more money shall it lead me, then more joyous shall I be", or you can write your own words if you prefer.

Light the candle and allow it to burn until it gets close to the dollar. Once it gets close to the dollar snuff out the candle and let the wax cool.

Once the wax has cooled unwrap the bill and place it in your wallet. Make sure that you put it in a separate place from where you usually keep your spending money. You do not want to accidentally spend your good luck charm.

Keep the money on you as long as you feel necessary and it will bring you good fortune.

Good Luck 7 Day Spell

This spell is to be used to help harness the luck associated with the color green. It will also help you practice being thankful and positive about all of the things that you are fortunate enough to have come into your life.

Materials you will need:

Seven green candles

A green writing utensil

Seven small pieces of paper

A small bowl

Frankincense (optional)

Steps to follow:

Begin by lighting a bit of frankincense incense the night before you plan to work your spell if you would like to help create an aura of attracting good luck. Let this incense burn completely out.

Write a positive affirmation on each of the seven pieces of paper with your green writing utensil. These are just things to encourage you. You can write things like, "I live a blessed life", "I am a powerful and loving being", "I can do anything I set my mind to." Any affirmation that makes you feel good about yourself and creates a positive energy within yourself.

Put all of your affirmations in the bowl after you fold them up.

Place the seven green candles in a row in your sacred space.

This spell will take place over the course of seven days.

When you wake up in the morning after you have burned your incense light one of the green candles. Pick one of the affirmations at random. Read it out loud and then slide it under the candle that is lit. After about 20 minutes, or when you leave the house to start your day extinguish the candle.

The second day light two candles, the first candle again and add a second. Read the affirmation from the first day again and then pick another from the bowl at random. Read the new affirmation aloud as well and place both of the affirmations under their corresponding candles. Let the candles burn for the same amount as the first day.

Keep repeating this process every day for seven days. Each day add a new candle and draw a new affirmation.

You will find that your luck is increasing more and more as each day passes and more candles are added.

Fertility Spell

This spell is used to help create the proper atmosphere best suited to help aid in conception. Many women struggle with fertility issues and need try endless amounts of medicines and treatment to help with this. However, this can all cause a lot of stress and anxiety for the women which makes it even harder for them to conceive. This spell will help alleviate that anxiety and create a more calming environment to help with the difficulties that come with a struggle to conceive.

Materials you will need:

One green pillar candle

Clary sage, geranium, and geranium oil

Carving tool

Poppy seed incense

Steps to follow:

Before you begin light the poppy seed incense and carry it around your sacred space in a clockwise motion. Make three trips around your sacred space with the incense in your hand, wafting out the smoke with your other hand.

Place the incense down in your sacred space.

Play some peaceful, relaxing, or romantic music to help set up the best atmosphere.

Sit in front of the candle and try to practice some meditation. Place your hands on your belly and image your belly growing from a pea, to an apple, a football, to a watermelon. Imagine the immense happiness that you will feel when you succeed in getting pregnant. Focus on transferring that joy and happiness into the candle with your mind. Hold the candle if you think that this will help you transfer your energy.

With your carving utensil carve a fertile symbol that resonates with you into the candle. While you are carving visualize yourself pregnant and unequivocally happy.

Anoint your candle oil with one or all of the three oils listed above and place your candle on your headboard or bedside table where you and your partner sleep.

Whenever you unite with your mate light the candle and place it close to you. Afterwards snuff out your candle. Relight the candle every time that the two of you join together.

If your candle burns out completely before you successfully conceive repeat the spell and try to add even more energy into your candle.

Blue Candle Spells

Healing Spell for Self

This is to be used for simple illnesses like a scraped knee or flu. It can also be used for chronic issues that are fairly simple in nature like migraines or arthritis. This spell is not a cure all. It is simply desired to help the body repair what it is already repairing in a faster and more efficient manner.

Materials you will need:

One blue candle

Eucalyptus oil (optional)

A bit of dried clover

Carving tool (optional)

Before you get started you have the option to inscribe and anoint your candle. This is not required, but it may help increase the energy in your spell. If you wish to do so take your carving tool and carve a symbol for good health into you candle. Once you have carved your symbol anoint the candle with eucalyptus oil.

Sprinkle a bit of dried clover over your candle and light it.

As your candle is burning try closing your eyes and meditating on your healing process. For example, if you have a bronchitis focus on your lungs contracting and expanding. Try to visualize your lungs growing stronger and expanding with ease.

Expand this meditation outward until you are visualizing a radiant light of wellness coming from your entire being. Take deep breaths in and out and envision yourself feeling better. Envision yourself when you feel your best.

Once you have meditated on that for a few moments open your eyes and sprinkle a little more of the clover into the flame of the candle.

Close out your spell with an incantation as usual. You can say your own or use the one that is provided as a sample. "Candle of blue and clover of green. Clear me of these ailments both seen and unseen."

Let the candle burn for at least 15 minutes after your spell is complete. Preferably let it burn until it is completely out.

Home Protection Spell

This protection spell is used to keep out negative energies and spirits. It also helps promote positive energy and healing within your home and among your family and friends when they are in your home.

Materials you will need:

Blue votives or tea lights (enough for every window and door on the perimeter of your house)

Eucalyptus and ginseng root incense

Steps to follow:

Before performing any spell work you need to clean your entire house so that the positive energies have a place to feel welcome.

Light the eucalyptus and place it on the right side of your front door to promote protection within your home.

Light the ginseng root and place it on the left side of the front door to ward off evil spirits and negative energy.

It is important to be very careful when performing this spell because you will be leaving candles unattended for a few moments at a time. Put any pets away that make knock them over and make sure that there aren't any kids that are too young in the house.

Place and light one of the blue candles on the floor in the center of the front door.

Work clockwise through your home placing a candle in each window and door to the outside and lighting it. If you have a chimney as well, place one in front of that as well.

Once you are back at the front door you can say your spell. You can write your own or you can say, "Let this house be filled with only happy, healthy, and positive energy for the good of all, bout in it and not."

Leave all of the candles burning simultaneously for at least five minutes.

Extinguish the candles in the same order that you lit them in; starting with the front door and continuing clockwise.

If you ever feel an uneasiness or general negative energy arrive into your house you can reuse the candles from this ritual. Simply light one and place it in the center of your house. Let it burn until it burns out.

Increase Patience Spell

In this spell you will create a talisman to help you with your patience and remind you of how to properly respond to stressful situations.

Materials you will need:

One blue candle

Writing paper

A blue stone or piece of jewelry

Lavender, vetiver, bergamot, or palmarosa oil

Steps to follow:

Begin by anointing your candle with one or all of the oils listed above.

Take out the writing paper and begin to write about whatever stress inducing issue has caused you to work this spell.

If while you are writing you feel yourself getting irritated by the situation again stop yourself and try to analyze where those feelings are coming from. Try to figure out why you are having trouble being patient in this specific scenario and try to address it.

Write anything that you want for 10 to 20 minutes.

When you feel that you have realized what has been triggering your irritation and that you can let go of it pick up your stone or piece of jewelry. Try to envision a blue light that starts in the rock or jewelry and expands outward until it encompasses your whole body.

Once you feel that the light is surrounding your body and say these words or words of your own, "Peace with patience, easy as they flow. Let these stressors be let go."

Place the talisman in front of the candle and leave it there until the candle burns down completely.

Carry or wear the talisman on your person and hold it whenever you feel something starting to trigger your impatience.

White Candle Spell

Healing Spell for Others

This spell is to be used to help carry along the healing process of those you love. This should not be done without first consulting with the sick party. You need to make sure that they are okay with you working a spell or "praying" for them before you carry on with your spell work. It is also important that your mind is not clouded with worry while you are working the spell because it can cause unnecessary issues in your spell work.

Materials you will need:

One white candle

Eucalyptus or Lavender oil

Carving tool

Picture of the friend (optional)

The first thing you want to do is carve the name of the person who is sick into your candle.

The next step is to anoint your candle with either the eucalyptus or lavender oil.

As you are preparing your candle reflect on past times that you have had with the friend or loved one. Pick out your favorite memory with them where you were most happy and try to put that positive energy into the candle as you work.

Once you have prepared the candle you can sit a photo of your friend or loved one next to the candle if you would like.

Light the candle and begin your incantation. You can say what you would like, or you can use the words provided. "Healing light, shine bright, make (person's name) well tonight"

Let the candle burn all the way down.

Indigo Candle Spells

Get in the Zone Meditation Spell

Many people find it hard when they are first beginning to do spell work to calm and quiet their mind. This is one of the most key elements of spell work because it is important that your internal emotions and anxieties do not cause issues within your spell work.

This spell will help you "get in the zone" for your spell work. It will help you calm your spirit and ready yourself. Performing this spell would be a really good idea if you are going to be working a big spell that could be kind of stressful for you. A good example of an emotionally stressful spell would be if you are planning to do a fertility spell or a healing spell for a loved one. Spells like these can be very emotionally hard for people. However, it is very important that you keep a positive energy about yourself when working these spells because the negative feels can affect the end results. Working this meditation spell will help you get back into a positive mindset and will make it much easier to focus on your positive energy for your spell work.

Materials you will need:

One indigo pillar candle

Meditation music

Angelica and cypress incense

timer (optional)

Steps to follow:

Begin turning on some music to help you meditate. Choose something that is calming and not too complex. Music with lyrics typically can be distracting so opt for something a little more instrumental.

You do not have to listen to actual music. You can listen to nature records as well. Some people find that listening to running water or a thunderstorm is more calming for them.

This is completely your choice. Just choose whatever makes you feel most relaxed.

Light the angelica incense for meditation and the cypress incense for concentration.

Find a comfy position that you can relax in.

Light the indigo pillar candle and spend a few moments focusing on the candle's flame. This will help you get into the mindset of focusing your energy on one specific thing. Once you feel relaxed and focused you can begin your meditation.

Slowly let your eyes close and begin to take deep breaths. In through your nose and out through your mouth. Follow the deep breaths that we discussed before feeling your abdomen expand and your lungs inflate. Focus on these deep breaths for about three minutes.

After those three minutes you can return to your normal breathing rhythm.

If when you return to your normal breathing, you find that your mind begins to wander try to focus on your breath again. If you still cannot focus you can return back to your deep breathing. This often helps you focus because you have to consciously tell yourself to take a deep breath.

Feel the calming energy that radiates from the indigo candle. Let that energy pour over you the way that a shower does after a hard day's work. Let your mind relax.

Try to continue this for at least five minutes; you can do it for longer if you would like. If you find that it is hard for you to focus any longer than the five minutes, it is okay. It is often hard to meditate when you are just beginning, but it will get easier. If you want to use the timer and set it for a specific amount of time that is fine as well.

Once you feel that you have meditated to your fullest extent or your timer goes off take a final deep, calming breath. Open your eyes and extinguish your candle.

Keep the candle for another time when you want to repeat this spell.

Each time that you do repeat this spell try to do it for a little bit longer. The more you practice your meditation the better you will become at it.

Indigo Clarity Spell

This spell is used to help you find clarity in a situation that you are finding difficult to navigate. There are many instances that can make it difficult to find clarity. As humans we often over think things and dwell on them for too long. This spell will help you figure out what to do in a situation that you are having trouble with. It is often hard to find a solution to a problem with your mind is so consumed with the issue that you cannot see it from any other angle. This spell will help you let go of the issue and allow you to see it from another perspective. This may help give you clarity about what you need to do.

Materials you will need:

One indigo votive candle

Journal

timer (optional)

Steps to follow:

First thing you want to do is write down whatever situation you are having trouble with in the journal.

Light your candle.

Read whatever you wrote down in your journal out loud into the candle's flame. Imagine the flame burning away the murkiness that you are struggling to sift through in your situation.

Watch the flame for a few moments and take a few deep breaths to try to open your mind to what the Universe may try to tell you.

Close your eyes and try to reach a state of meditation. Do not focus on the issue that you are having. Try to let it go and instead just focus on yourself. Keep your mind's eye open for anything that the Universe may try to tell you during this time of meditation.

Try to continue this meditation and reflection for about five to seven minutes. If you find yourself getting lost in your meditation or feel that you are finding a sense a clarity and do not wish to stop, you are of course allowed to go as long as you would like.

Once you have completed that part open your eyes and write down anything that you found particularly helpful that was realized during your meditative state.

You will most likely not receive a direct answer about how to fix the issue immediately. It may take a few days for the messages you received during your meditation to marinate in your subconscious. Be patient and mindful of your thoughts. Don't let yourself continue to dwell on the situation. You will have your answer in time.

Black Candle Spell

Reverse Psychic Attack Spell

This spell can be used if someone is purposely using magic to attack you and it can also be used to combat negative thoughts from others that are attacking your psyche even if they are not intentionally doing it. Most people are not going to be experiencing an actual magical attack because odds are if you do Wicca magic you may be the only person that you know of that does. However, there are many ways for people to attack your psyche without magic and these attacks can either be intentional or unintentional on the attacker's part. For example, manipulation is a great example of an attack on your psyche. This spell can help you rid yourself of that manipulation.

Materials you will need:

One black candle

Honey

Five garlic cloves

Sagebrush incense

Sea salt

Begin by lighting your sagebrush incense. This incense is a good choice for this spell because it banished negative energies, but it also aids in healing. There is a degree of healing that needs to be done for your psyche as well and this incense does a good job of accomplishing both things at once.

Create a circle of salt on the ground that is big enough for you to sit in with your candle in front of you.

f you would like you can do this spell outside during the waning moon phase. This is not a requirement. It is merely a suggestion, but it would be a good idea if the person who is attacking you has a particularly strong hold on you. Like if the attacker is a significant other that manipulates and controls you. The moon's power will help rid yourself of the negative affects the psychic attack or attacks have had on your mind.

Step into your salt circle and have a seat.

Place the garlic cloves in the form of a pentagram with the black candle placed in the middle. Light the candle.

Take a moment to meditate and focus on letting go of the negative energy that has been forced onto you by your attacker. Take a few deep breaths, slow and steady. Release the hold that your attack has on you. Let yourself be free of their grasp and feel yourself come back to a balanced state. Envision the garlic soaking up all of the negative energy as it flows out of your body.

When you have felt the negative energy leave your body say something like, "I am free of (say your attacker's name if you know it or say their) grasp. They will hold me back no longer with their negative thoughts or energy. I am protected from their harmful words and actions. I will rid myself of them and their hatred. The wounds that they have given me are healed and they will no longer have control over my psyche."

Eat a teaspoon of honey to symbolize the goodness that you will replace the negative thoughts with.

Bring your candle inside and let it sit on your window sill in the moonlight until it burns down completely.

Bury the garlic cloves far away from you house. They absorbed the negativity that had been placed inside of you, so it is important that you do not keep them close.

Orange Candle Spell

Increase Courage Spell

This spell is to help you work up the nerve when something is coming in your life that may cause you to have a bit of fear. This could be for an interview, starting a new job, an audition, procedure, or anything that is causing you to be nervous. Tuesday is thought to be the best day to perform this spell because it is associated with the planet Mars which is a symbol of courage. However, you can do this spell whenever you would like.

Materials you will need:

Four orange candles

Clove oil

One small object to charm (crystal, pendant, necklace, etc)

Carving tool

Piece of Paper (optional)

Steps to follow:

First start by inscribing something that represents courage to you in your candles. You can do a lion, superhero, the symbol for mars, or anything that you want.

Then you need to anoint your candles with the clove oil.

Once you have anointing your candles you want to set them out so that they make a square.

Place your small object that you want to charm in the middle of the square of candles.

Then meditate on a time that you felt really brave. Think about the memory that stands out most to you in your past where you felt like you were filled with courage. Focus on this memory and try to visual yourself feeling that way again in this current scenario that scares you. If you would like you can write down this memory on a piece of paper and place it into the square of candles as well.

Once you have a solid idea of that moment of courage try to transfer that courageous energy into your small object. You can hold the object in your hand for this portion if it helps you better visualize the transfer of energy. Once you feel that you have successfully transferred your courageous energy place the object back in the square of candles.

Light the candles are start saying your spell. You can use your own or the one that we have provided for you. "Cowardly lion be no more, instead have courage like fire that comes from the core."

Allow the four candles to burn completely down.

Take your charm with you whenever you do eventually have to be in the scenario that is making you anxious. It will help remind you of the time that you were most courageous, and it will transfer that courageous energy back to you.

Chapter 6: Multiple Color Candle Spells

Successful Employment Spell

This is a good spell to use if you are applying for a new job that you really desire, but you are not feeling super confident that you will get it. You want to make sure that the way you frame your spell is centered around the idea of you getting the job being for the good of all. You do not want to center your spell around the idea of winning over others and bringing disappointment to those who also applied for the job. Always remember the Wicca rule that whatever you put out you will get back three-fold.

Materials you will need:

One green candle

One orange candle

A carving tool

New-mown Hay oil

Steps to follow:

On the orange candle carve a symbol that will symbolize your success. This can be a simple "S" for success or a "V" for victory. You could also carve a symbol that represents the job you are wanting to get. If you are applying to work in an office job you could draw a phone or computer. If you are applying for a job in construction you could draw a hammer. It is completely up to your imagination.

On the green candle you want to draw a symbol that stands for your good fortune. You can represent this with an "F" for fortune or a symbol that you choose yourself.

Place the two candles next to each other in your sacred place and light them. Light your orange candle first and then your green. This is to represent the success of obtaining the job first and then the good fortune you hope to have once you have started the position.

Once you have lit your candles you can say an incantation of your choice or you can use the one provided. "Orange like fire, Green with desire. My need is dyer, help me get hired."

Let the candles burn completely out.

Bills Stability Spell

A large percentage of people live from paycheck to paycheck. They make just enough to cover the bills with little to no money left over. This spell is used to help bring you peace of mind about your bills it times when you feel like you are drowning in worry about how you are going to pay for something.

Materials you will need:

A piece of paper

A bit of basil

Patchouli, Bergamot, or Almond oil

A large jar candle that is either gold, gray, brown, or orange

A metal plate or pan

Steps to follow:

Start by anointing your candle with one of the three oils listed above.

Try to focus on being at ease. Meditate on the idea that everything will work itself out.

Light your candle and say an incantation. You can use the one provided or you can write your own. "All good things come in this time of need. All the things needed to help me succeed. With harm to none, and good fortune for all. So let it be until this week is done.

Take your piece of paper and write down some positive words. Write as if the spell has already been successful and you have made it through the slump. Write things like, "We had enough money", "We made it through this month", "The bills are paid and all is well", etc. Write whatever words are affirmations for you in this time of hardship.

Once you have written down your affirmations fold it in half and place it into the candles flame and let it catch fire. This will help send those affirmations into the spirit realm and make them come to pass. Be careful while doing this because it is fire and it is dangerous.

Once you have lit the piece of paper, place it on the metal pan or plate and let it turn to ash.

Let the candle burn until it completely burns out. This could take 5 to 7 days.

Once you have completely the spell work take the ashes from the piece of paper and bury them in your backyard. This will help keep your affirmations close and bring them into fruition.

Job Search Spell

This is good for helping increase your luck in finding the perfect job for you when you are searching for a new career path. It is recommended that you do this spell on a Sunday because it is associated as the day of rest from work.

Materials you will need:

One gold or yellow candle

Clover oil

Carving tool

Inscribe your candle with a symbol for luck. This can be a four-leaf clover, a horse shoe, the number seven, or anything else that you want to choose as your lucky symbol. If you yourself have a personal lucky number or object, then you should inscribe whatever it is. This will help to add your own personal lucky energy to your candle.

Anoint your candle with the clover oil for luck.

Light your candle as you say your spell. You can write your own spell, or you can use the one provided. "Spirits of luck, spirits of gain, help me attain a job for which I fain."

Take a few moments to meditation of the joy that comes from getting a job that you really are excited about. Imagine yourself in the perfect position.

Let the candle burn for at least 8 minutes while you meditate on your future endeavors. You can let it burn longer if you would like.

This spell is repeatable, so you can do it every Sunday until the candle burns down completely, or until you find your perfect job.

Spell to Banish Depression

This spell is designed to help get rid of a depressive episode. It will not cure the condition, but as many people with depression know it often comes in waves. Sometimes you may be fairly okay, but other times it feels like you are drowning in a sea of darkness with no way out. This spell is to help get you out of those depressive ruts when they occur. It is important to make sure that you are in the best state of mind possible before working any spell magic. Although depression creates a very dark and negative feeling you need to try to meditate as best as you can before you perform any spell work.

Materials you will need:

One smaller black candle

Three normal sized white candles

One small black object (rock, pendant, etc.)

One small white object (rock, feather, etc.)

A small black cloth

Steps to follow:

Place the three white candles in a triangle shape with the small black candle in the middle.

Pick up whatever small black object you chose and hold it in your hands.

Meditate with the object in your hand and focus one directing all of the negative energy that you are feeling inside into that object.

When you feel that you have released all of that negative energy into your object place the stone next to the black candle in the middle of the three white candles.

Light the black candle.

Say an incantation of your choice or use the one provided. "I release these negative thoughts and feelings. I watch them float away as I pursue my inner healing."

Then pick up your small white object and hold it in your hands, the same as the black. However, this time focus on pulling in positive healing energy from the object. Focus on things that bring you joy and happiness.

Once you feel yourself being filled with positive energy place that white object on the outside of the point of the triangle of white candle that is closest to you.

Light the three white candles and say something along the lines of, "I welcome this positive and loving energy into my soul and thank the Universe for its blessings."

Once the black candle has completely burned out clean up the wax and disregard it as needed. Make sure to clean the candle holder before storing so that you remove any negative energy that has been transferred to it.

Pick up the black object with the black cloth. You want to do this with the cloth so that you can avoid physical contact with the object. You have transferred your negative feelings into this object and you don't want them slipping back in.

If you live near a river, stream, or any body of water it is recommended that you throw the black object into if it is safe for the environment. The moving water will help wash away all of the negative energy. If you cannot throw it in a river bury it in a place that is far away from where you rest your head.

Keep the small white object near you at all times. It will stand as a reminder and bring you comfort when you are feeling less than a hundred percent.

You can let the white candles burn out or you can snuff them out and relight them when you feel a depressive episode creeping back in.

Lucky Spell

This spell is used to help boost your good luck. It will help create an environment in which you attract omens of good luck and not bad.

Materials you will need:

One white candle

One black candle

One green candle

A bit of chamomile

A pinch of star anise

Steps to follow:

Arrange the candles in a line in this order: black, white, green.

Sprinkle the chamomile and star anise around the candles to form a circle.

Light the black candle and say something like, "All bad luck, away you shall veer."

Light the green candle and say something like, "All good luck, please stay near."

Light the white candle and say something like, "Let goodwill and fortune ring clear."

Meditate on all of the things that go right in your life and thank the Universe for its blessings. Make a vow to try to be more aware of the good in the day to day, and to focus less on the small insignificant bad things.

Let the candles burn all the way down.

Over the next few weeks try to write down all of the good things that happen to you no matter how trivial they may seem. This will help you to learn to focus more on the "good luck" than the bad.

You can repeat the spell as many times as you would like throughout the course of those weeks.

Answers Spells

If you have a question that you are dying to know the answer to, but not matter what you do you cannot seem to figure it out this may be a good spell to try. Odds are the Universe is not going to plaster a billboard next to your house with the answer, although it might. So, with that in mind you need to be aware that this spell is more about helping you notice things that you may not have noticed before that could clue you into the answer of the question that you are dying to know.

Materials you will need:

One yellow candle or gold

One strip of paper

A carving tool

Steps to follow:

Write the question that you have down on the strip of paper in as concise a manner as possible.

Carve something into the candle to represent your question. It can be a symbol or just a few words to summarize the question.

Light your candle and then stick your strip of paper into the flame and let it burn.

Allow the candle to burn down completely.

You should receive some clues or an answer within seven days.

Blossoms of Spring Spell

This spell is created to bring in an abundance of positive energy, joy, and happiness into your life. Spring time is filled with the concepts of blossoming, new beginnings, and growing into something beautiful. This spell takes that spring time energy and harnesses it in a way that can bring that growth and prosperity into your daily life.

Materials you will need:

One green, pink, and white small tea light candles

½ cup of flower petals

Clove or tangerine incense

Steps to follow:

Gather your choice of flower petals the day before you plan to do the spell. Place the petals in a bowl and live them outside in the moonlight overnight to absorb the moon's energy. Try to do this during a full moon or a waxing moon to ensure you get the most energy transferred to your flower petals as possible.

Light your clove or tangerine incense. You can burn both if you would like.

The next day, place your three candles in a triangular formation on your altar, table, or on the ground in your sacred space.

Then use the flower petals to create a circle around the candles.

Light the three candles in no particular order.

Take a moment and meditate on the wonders of spring and the new life that it creates. Think about the good things in your life that you would like to see grow and take root.

After a few moments you can say an incantation of your choice or you can use the one we provide. "Thankful for the presence of Spring, oh how the flowers grow, and the birds love to sing. Let this growth and joy show in my life, the same as they do in this wildlife."

Let the candles to burn out on their own.

Once the candles have completely burned out take the petals and spread them outside, in your backyard if at all possible.

Marathon of Work Spell

This spell is perfect for an intense final exam week or a big project that you are having to conquer at work this is a great spell to try. It will increase your confidence and help you focus on the task at hand.

Materials you will need:

One orange or yellow candle

One amethyst or quartz crystal

Lemon or rosemary oil

A ¼ cup of flower petals

Begin by scattering the flower petals on your altar or workspace.

Anoint your candle with the lemon or rosemary oil and then roll the candle in the flower petals so that they stick to the candles surface.

Set the candle upright and place your crystal next to it.

Meditate on the idea of being done with your project, homework, exams, or whatever you are doing this spell in regard to. Try to focus on how happy you will be when you are finished and harness that positive energy.

Light the candle and say something along the lines of, "Give me focus and energy in this overworked time. Help me be patient until these virtues are mine."

Place your crystal in your work space or on your desk to help remind you to keep up the good work and to focus.

If you ever begin to feel sluggish or run down hold the stone in your hands and take a few moments to meditate and draw out some of the crystal's energy leftover from the spell.

Binding a Trouble Maker Spell

Wicca magic is not to be used to harm others. However, it can be used to shield yourself from people who are trying to create turmoil in your life. Some people will try to tear you down and destroy your life no matter how much you try to do to show them that you are not an enemy. If they feel that you are a threat to them some people will stop at nothing to try to bring your life into a state of destruction. Talking it out does not always work with people who are like this and sometimes you may have to have a little magical intervention. The idea behind this spell is to capture whatever negative feels a specific person has towards you and trying to neutralize that energy. You need to make sure that you do not wish any harm upon this person. This spell is only to neutralize the threat of this person causing harm in your life. It is not to perform your own personal karmic justice.

Materials you will need:

8-12 inches of string or yarn

One black or white candle

Steps to follow:

Begin by lighting your candle and laying your piece of string or yarn in front of it.

Take a few moments to gather your thoughts. Do not dwell on the negative energy that exists between you and the other person. Instead try to focus on the feeling of being at peace. What you want is to have peace and that positive energy is what you need to focus on.

Once you find that you are feeling at peace you can pick up your string or yarn and tie a knot towards the left end of the string. As you tie this knot say "I bind the (anger) and (negativity) that (name of the individual) has directed towards me." You can replace the things in the parentheses with whatever you think best suits your personal scenario.

Begin to tie another knot close to the center of the piece of string or yarn. As you tie this knot say, "I bind all of the ongoing and unnecessary conflict that this person has brought upon my life"

Tie one last knot on the right end of the string. As you tie this final knot say, "I bind these things with all of my power for the greater good."

Next you will take the string or yarn and bury it. Do not bury it close to your home because it is carrying negative energy. As you bury it visualize it decomposing into the ground. The ground will eventually neutralize the negativity that is on the rope, but you do not want it close to home while it is still harboring those bad energies.

Pets Protection Spell

This spell is to be used to help keep your animals safe and sound. It will protect them from evil and help them live a long and healthy life.

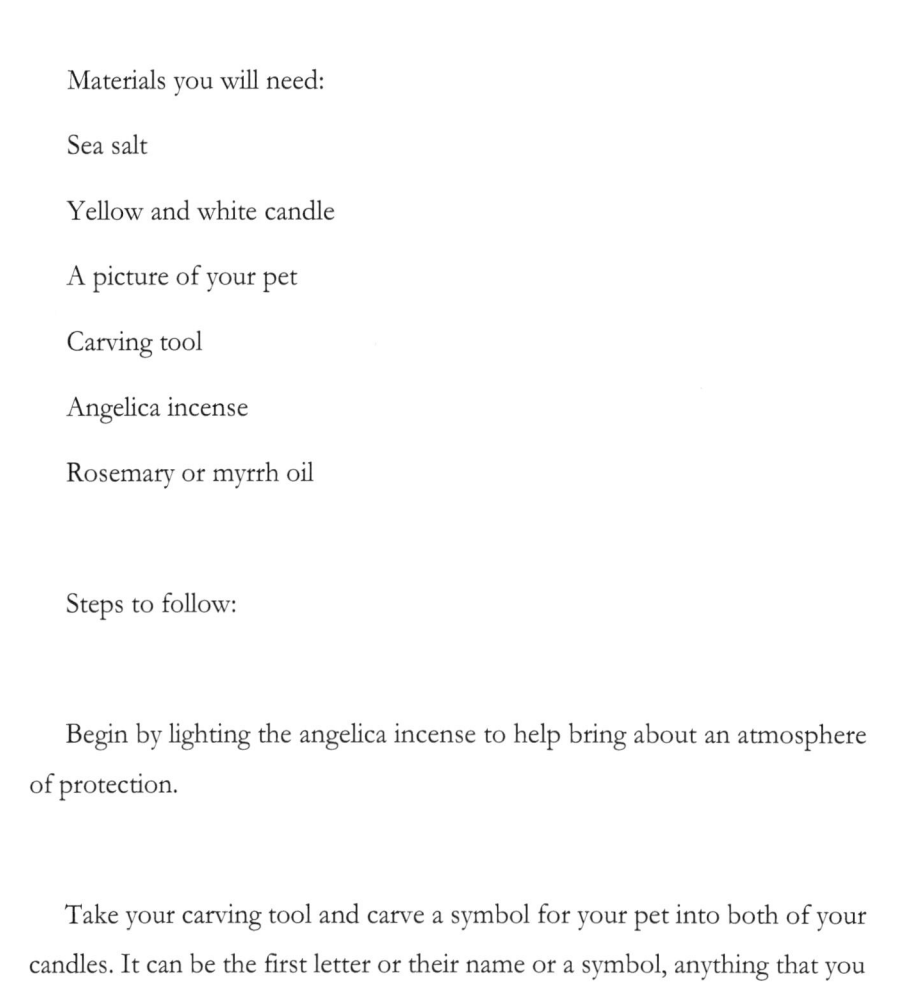

Materials you will need:

Sea salt

Yellow and white candle

A picture of your pet

Carving tool

Angelica incense

Rosemary or myrrh oil

Steps to follow:

Begin by lighting the angelica incense to help bring about an atmosphere of protection.

Take your carving tool and carve a symbol for your pet into both of your candles. It can be the first letter or their name or a symbol, anything that you want to put that you think represents your pet.

Then take your two candles and anoint them with the myrrh or rosemary oil.

Place the two candles on your alter or work space with the photo of your pet in the middle of them.

Create a ring of salt around the two candles and the photo.

Light your two candles and take a moment to meditate on your how much you love and appreciate your pet. Focus on all of their wonderful personality traits and how happy they make you. Think of a favorite memory with them and take a moment to be thankful for the joy that your pet has brought into your life.

Say a little prayer to the Universe asking for them to keep your pet healthy, happy, and safe always. You can say anything that you would like, but if you struggle to find the words here is a sample:

"Spirits of the Universe hold (name) close in your arm. Keep them safe always and meet every need that I may not see. Keep them warm, keep them fed, and always keep them by my side. Let me not forsake their needs as you have not forsaken mine. Let them always feel loved and wanted. Let them never be forgotten. Bless (name) for all their days as they have blessed my life in so many ways."

Let the candles burn down completely.

Clean up the salt and put away your picture.

Spend some extra time loving and cuddling with your pet to help seal the deal.

Happy News Spell

This is a good spell to start with. It is low stakes and does not take a lot of practice. It also has very little materials that you will need to complete the spell. You simply follow the steps with a general idea and you will find that it is quite successful with very little effort.

Materials you will need:

One gold, green, yellow, or orange candle

Patchouli, cinnamon, or bergamot oil

Steps to follow:

Begin by anointing whichever color candle you chose with one of the three oils listed above.

Meditate and think of a time when you received really good news that filled you with so much joy that you could not contain it. Like being accepted into your dream college, getting engaged, finding out you were pregnant, etc. Whatever your memory is, try to focus on it and harness that feeling of utter joy that you were feeling at that moment.

Once you have that feeling locked into your mind say these words, "In three days' time happiness will arise, whether it be blue skies or apple pie, I know that it will make me smize."

Light your candle and say, "let it be so."

Let your candle burn completely out.

Be on the lookout for happy surprises to come your way.

Beauty Spell

This spell is used to renew your body in both a physical manner and a mental one. You will be using a few strange ingredients that you may not expect, but just go with it.

Materials you will need:

Five to Seven Pink Candles

A knife

A spoon

Fresh flowers

An avocado

ylang-ylang incense

Steps to follow:

Begin your work by lighting your ylang-ylang incense to help fill your space with harmony and euphoria.

Next pick up the avocado and hold it in your hands. Close your eyes and take some deep breaths while calming yourself and trying to relax your brain.

Slice the avocado in half with the knife. Scoop out the avocado's pit and rinse it off with water.

You are going to eat your avocado, so if you would like salt on it you can add that at this time.

Make a circle large enough for you to sit in with the fresh flowers being mindful and thankful to the Universe for supplying you with nature's materials.

Place the candles on the outside of the circle of flowers making an even bigger circle consisting of pink candles to help create an aura of self-love.

Sit inside the circle with your avocado and eat it out of the skin with your spoon. Take your time eating it and savor its nutrients.

After you finish eating the avocado close your eyes and say, "Thank you Universe for supplying me with these supplements to make my beauty as bright as yours."

Take the avocado pit, wrap it in a paper towel, and carry it around with you for a few days to help resonate the feeling of beauty.

If you live in an area where avocados can thrive plant it and watch it grow into a beautiful tree as you grow into a more beautiful version of yourself.

New Year Blessings Spell

This spell is to be done at the beginning of the new year to help you manifest a few things that you want in your life in the coming year. It centers around the cardinal directions of North, South, East, and West. Each cardinal direction is associated with one of the four basic elements of life (water, fire, earth, air). There will be a chart below this paragraph that explains what manifestations can be created from which direction/element. Choose one goal for each of the four directions that you would like to manifest in the coming year. The four goals can correspond with each other to go towards one major objective, or they can be completely separate thoughts.

Cardinal Direction	Element	Manifestations
North	Earth	Physical possessions, opulence, practical concerns, family affairs
South	Fire	adoration, energy, courage, eagerness, passion
East	Air	artistry, transitions, motivation, new conceptions, certainty of perspective
West	Water	psychic awareness, emotional issues, restoration, cleansing, intuition

Materials you will need:

A color pillar candle of your choice

Journal

Writing utensil

Steps to follow:

First pick the four manifestations that you would like to focus on for the new year.

Take your journal and write down what manifestation that you have chosen for each of the four directions. Under each choice write a short synopsis of how you plan to pursue this goal and what you can do to ensure that you reach it.

Once you have decided on your manifestation for each direction, start your ritual by facing your body in the direction of North. Keep good posture with your back straight and chin slightly tilted upward. Keep your elbows at your sides and palms facing upward to symbolize your openness to new blessings.

Say, "Spirits of the North hear my call and aid me in the new coming year by supplying my life with (North goal)."

Then turn your body to the East.

Holding the same position as before, say, "Spirits of the East hear my call and aid me in the new coming year by supplying my life with (East goal)."

Face the South.

Still holding that position, say, "Spirits of the South hear my call and aid me in the new coming year by supplying my life with (South goal)."

Turn to the West.

Say, "Spirits of the West hear my call and aid me in the new coming year by supplying my life with (West goal)."

Light the candle that you chose. Make sure that the color of the candle either corresponds with your new year manifestations, best represents you, or has a great deal of personal meaning for you.

Pick up your candle and hold it with two hands.

Face North again, but this time try to harness all of the joy and positivity that possessing your goal for North would give you.

Once you have harnessed that feeling marinate on it and take three deep breaths, in through the nose and out through the mouth. Be careful not to accidentally blow out the candle.

Follow this same process for each of the four directions.

Put your candle back in your workspace or on your altar.

Face North again and make a positive statement about the year to come. For example, you could say, "This year I will prosper and thrive."

Again, follow that step for each of the four directions. You can say the same positive statement for all of the directions, or you can say a different positive statement for each direction. It is completely up to you.

Say one last prayer of thanks to the Universe for listening to your desires and helping you reach your goals.

Extinguish your candle.

In the coming year whenever you are feeling discouraged about reaching your goals relight the candle and take a few moments to practice a bit of meditation. Take out the journal that you wrote down your manifestations in and read through them again. Take a moment to focus on those goals again. Think about what you have done so far to help make those goals a reality and write the steps that you have taken so far down. This will help you stay focused on your goals and reassure you that you are making progress. You just have to remember that patience is key and every step you make is getting you closer to your goal. Stay positive and keep going.

Conclusion

Thank you for making it through to the end of this book. We hope that you found it informative and enjoyed everything that you learned. This book is not only a good one time read, but also a great reference for yourself when you are trying spell work in the future.

With the help of this book you should be able to conquer any spell in your wake. You can even come up with your own spells to try out. Referring back to this book in the future will help you decide what colors to use in your rituals and how to execute them properly. If you have a question about what kind of oil would be good for a healing spell or what kind of symbol you should inscribe into your candles this book will always be there to help.

With its breakdowns of colors and their meanings and charts filled with endless information on herbs, symbols, and oils; this book really is one to stand the test of time. We hope that you have found this book informative and we can't wait to see what you are able to accomplish with the tools that you have been given.

Always remember that what you put out is returned back to you threefold. Keep this in mind as you continue your own spiritual journey into the art of wicca. Fill yourself with positive energy and you are sure to prosper in this environment of magic.

Finally, if you found this book useful in any way, a review on Amazon is always appreciated!

Wicca Moon Magic

The Ultimate Guide to Lunar Spells, Wiccan Moon Magic and Rituals. A Book of Shadows for Wiccans, Witches, Pagans & Witchcraft practitioners and beginners.

ESTHER ARIN SPELLS

INTRODUCTION

Congratulations on downloading Wicca Moon Magic and thank you for doing so. You have taken the important first step in discovering the art of Wicca Moon Magic and what it takes for you to become a Wiccan yourself.

The word Wicca originates from the Old English and means simply, "witch." Older Germanic languages attribute additional meanings such as foretell, speak, and divine (as in divination).

The birth of Wicca as a modern religion can be traced back to the writings of a retired British civil servant, Gerald Gardner—in fact; there is an entire branch of Wiccan practice devoted to him called Gardnerian Wicca. He published his definitive book on the subject, Witchcraft Today back in 1954. Gardner also founded a coven—essentially a prayer/workgroup for witches, numbering anywhere from four to 40 members or more—and several members of his coven went on to publish books on the subject of witchcraft and magical living.

In Gardnerian and other traditional practices, a coven is led by a priest and priestess, who oversee the ceremonial Sabbath rituals and often represent the god and goddess during these rituals.

Wicca moon magic has had its ups and downs in the magical community, booming in popularity shortly after its beginning, and today in full force as magic and other nature-focused practices enter the popular culture once again

CHAPTER 1: Why the moon is magic

Magic and the Phases of the Moon

The great part of following the Moon for your magical work is that you get a chance each month to manifest what you truly need. New moons are a perfect time for beginnings, though they require a certain degree of courage and faith for you to move forward. Think deeply about your desires and plan ahead—imagine your future success.

Magic involving purification, initiation, beginning a project or new union, are all excellent workings to be undertaken beneath the new moon. The new moon is pristine, pure in spirit—if you are planning to detox, discard a negative habit or begin a new diet or fitness routine, the new moon is also suitable for affirmations concerning these things.

Waxing moons are when the new moon is growing towards the full moon, and are wonderful times to do magical work concerning abundance, growth, strength, physical and mental health, and striving towards a long-awaited goal.

Magic regarding career and finances are best undertaken beneath waxing moons; however, there is a time when an emergency dictates the action. Just understand that the Moon's energy, combined with your spellcraft, will yield a result of a particular kind. Magic to aid in the search for a new job may find you opportunities during the waxing moon; the same magic may cause you sudden, unexpected job loss during the waning moon—but such upheaval might also reveal an opportunity you would have never seen were you to be at the office that day.

Full moons are the culmination; the moon is at its strongest now, and psychic abilities are at their most sharp. A spell you begin several days or a week before the full moon can now be realized fully. Full moons can be time for celebration, concentration, and manifesting your dreams.

Waning moons are times of recovery, rest, and cleansing. Spell work undertaken beneath a waning moon will be about getting rid of what is not necessary for your life or shaking off whatever's holding you back from realizing your goals. Banishing or protection spells can be useful at this time as well.

Dark moons are the best times for spells of reflection, regarding personal growth. Do you crave to rise like the phoenix and shake off the binds of old habits and ways? A spell for renewal and personal insight during the dark moon can help lead the way.

Days of the Week

Sunday is a perfect day to do magical work regarding health, finances, fortune, and abundance—anything that you can imagine growing bigger with the Sun's light can be done on this day. Sunday's colors are orange, yellow, white, and blue. On this day, mother goddesses and sun gods can be called upon to aid you in your work.

Monday is a tricky day for magic, but it is a good time for beginnings. It's the day of the Moon—and by the Moon's light, we don't always see things accurately with our eyes, but we can often intuit them with our heart. Monday's colors are blue, red, and black—the Nigerian god Papa Legba—an African version of Mercury—is honored this day. Give him an apple, some coffee or cola, and some candy, and ask for his guidance or to help with an endeavor.

Tuesday is a day of battle and strength. Today is best for spells of protection or strength. Tuesday's colors are red and gold, but it is best not to wear red on your person this day.

Wednesday is a day of communication and being bold. Wear red somewhere on you to attract good fortune and luck. Magic involving trade, the arts, making beneficial connections, and receiving good news can be performed on this day.

Thursday is a day blessed by lucky Jupiter. The wheel of fortune tarot card favors this day. It is an excellent day for magic involving self-love, rejuvenation, manifesting wishes, and luck in business.

Friday is a day of love, but can also be a day of justice. It is ruled by Venus but is also a day thought to be sacred to Oshun and Oya. Magic involving trust and fidelity, healing, love and friendship, and justice for the innocent can be handled on this day.

Saturday is ruled by Saturn, and can be a heavy day to work with—but it is the best day for spells of protection. Keep in mind that in some practices it is also a day of love goddesses, which goes to show that magic involving romance must be utilized with great precaution.

What is it about the Moon that evokes curiosity, awe, and even a twinge of dread? Why is it that the specter of wolves or wild dogs baying at the Moon sends chills down people's backs? And what happens to the minds of unstable people at the Full Moon to have made the word lunatic associated with insanity?

How did a lunar mystique evolve that can be seen in the mythology of all eras and on all continents, including among the Greek, Roman, and a variety of native cultures? Lunar images appear as a powerful symbol of human consciousness throughout world literature from ancient to modern times.

Few people can fail to be moved by the beauty of the Full Moon and intrigued by the cycle of changes the Moon undergoes in a month. Today we pride ourselves on being scientific and rational, so we tend to ridicule what our "primitive" ancestors believed about the Moon. Yet, if the Moon has no power, how do we explain the almost universal preoccupation and fascination with it? As it turns out, there does seem to be some basis for the common belief that the Moon affects our lives. Scientific studies over the past several decades have begun to validate connections between the Moon and human, plant, and animal life.

We'll explore the beliefs of our ancestors about the Moon, the suppression of such beliefs by the knockout team of the Church and science, and the natural principles scientists are now rediscovering. We'll look at some controversial research findings and some ways that modern life may have masked or altered our natural rhythms, causing tension and stress. In doing so, we'll draw on the work of two painstaking and pioneering researchers into the Moon's history and the scientific evidence for its power.

The Moon was once an object of worship for people the world over. As explorers from the West traveled throughout the earth's islands and continents, they found people everywhere sharing a fascination and reverence for the Moon and even many identical beliefs about it. There was a linkage of the Moon with fertility and childbirth, and some connection was made between women's menstrual cycles and the cycle of the Moon. Was the universal reverence for the Moon an example of primitive superstition by ignorant people, or did it reflect centuries of observation of the powerful effect the Moon had?

Before Christianity became the dominant religion in Western civilization, there were many gods. Among the most commonly worshipped was the Moon goddess, who was known by many names, including Diana, Artemis, and Hecate. People looked to her to insure fertility, safe childbirth, good crops, and success in hunting. In those days, there was a high rate of infant mortality and death in childbirth, so her temples were popular ones. No woman who wanted a child and wanted to live through her pregnancy would neglect Diana.

Throughout Europe, in the millennia before Christianity, the Moon religion was the dominant one. Rituals, ceremonies, and revels were held routinely at the Full Moon. Certain Full Moons were considered especially powerful and holy; perhaps these so-called primitives were attuned to the fluctuations in the energy and power of the Moon, which we will become familiar with as we work with the processes in this book. The Full Moon revels may have constituted a safe and possibly even healthy outlet for the emotions that build up throughout the monthly cycle and tend to need release around the Full Moon. Halloween and Easter are actually holdovers from celebrations of that era that were shrewdly preempted by the Church fathers.

Now known by the names of Wicca, paganism, or witchcraft, the Old Religion was not a matter of witches and goblins and was certainly not a matter of devil worship or Satanism. Instead, it was a spiritual practice based on centuries of observation of how the Moon and other natural forces interacted with plants, animals, and human beings.

The old Angle-Saxon word **Wicca** simply means knowledge, and it embodied knowledge of when to plant, hunt, and fish, and of how to heal using plants, herbs, and other natural means. Even now good farmers know to watch the Moon for planting and harvesting. They find, as the ancients did, that seeds sprout far better just after the New Moon, especially the New Moon in Taurus, which falls in late April or early May? Likewise, avid fishermen buy Moon calendars telling them the times when fishing is best.

The Moon corresponds to the more feminine side of people, whether male or female, and the Old Religion itself was a celebration of the feminine aspect of nature, with a goddess and with priestesses rather than priests. As Christianity grew more powerful, the Moon religion came to be regarded as dangerous and wicked, along with the corresponding, more feminine side of us that is in touch with the Moon and with emotions, natural rhythms, and instincts. The decline of the Old Religion paralleled a period in history when society became strongly patriarchal and women were put in an inferior and powerless position.

The Old Religion was suppressed by religious persecution, by forceful conversions, by witch-hunts and witch burnings, but it was once the religion of the people. Perhaps you've seen statues of Mary with a crescent Moon under her foot. This symbolizes the stamping out of the Old Religion. And yet, in places where the Old Religion was strong, Christianity won out only by establishing the worship of Mary, in which the cult of Diana persisted, thinly disguised. In forcibly suppressing Wicca, we unfortunately also suppressed much of the knowledge of healing and natural rhythms that accompanied it.

I'm not for a moment suggesting we go back to worshipping the Moon, but at least we can stop ignoring it and start paying attention to the rhythms and cycles it represents. As we'll find out in the course of this book, there is a cost to ignoring this part of ourselves, in terms of stress, fatigue, frayed nerves, and exploding tempers. This ignorance leaves us feeling deprived, as well as out of touch with ourselves and our needs. We can relieve stress by not working against the grain. We can come to know the periods when our bodies, minds, and spirits need rest, as well as the periods most productive for work. In order to do that more consciously, you'll find information here about the best uses of the Moon's signs and cycles, as well as tables to help you keep track of the Moon's daily and monthly course.

The Lunar Calendar

In ancient cultures and in many modern ones until recently, the Moon's cycles were the way we marked the passage of time, a natural, easily visible calendar. The Full or New Moon against the backdrop of the constellations was a sign that particular time of year had arrived, with its own set of activities and conditions. The word month it derives from the word Moon. A month lasted from one New Moon until the next, and each quarter was one week long. There were thirteen Moon cycles in a typical year. Each period was named for its characteristic quality or events. We still call autumn dances the Harvest Moon Ball, but we've forgotten that in earlier times the harvest was celebrated by a huge feast and merrymaking.

Many Moons ago, Native Americans kept track of their months the same way, naming them for happenings during that particular Moon. January was the Wolf Moon, since packs of wolves would roam the empty countryside, looking for food. April was called the Pink Moon, for the flowers that suddenly burst into bloom that month. July's rainstorms earned it the name Thunder Moon, and the heat of August was given the name Red Moon. The Hunter's Moon was in October, showing both the opportunity and the preoccupation of that month. The Hawaiians also had a lunar calendar, and for them, July was the Wet, Sticky Moon. The Jewish calendar, which is dated differently from our own, still has a lunar basis.

If we were ever to revert to a lunar calendar, perhaps for synchronizing our rhythms with natures once more, we'd have to give the months modern names. February would be the Gray and Dreary Moon. April would be the Moon of the IRS. June would be the Many Wedding Moon. August would be the Shrinks' Vacation Moon. September would be the Back-to-School Moon. December would be the Bottomless Wallet Moon.

Why Are Mondays Blue?

Just as the calendar was once based on the Moon, the Moon also had its own special day of the week—Monday, or Monday. Each of the seven major heavenly bodies visible to the naked eye was assigned a day of the week: Sunday was the Sun's day; Monday was the Moon's; Tuesday was Mars's day; Wednesday was assigned to Mercury; Thursday was Jupiter's day; Friday belonged to Venus; and Saturday was for Saturn. The nature and concerns of the day in question seemed to the ancients related to the concerns of that planet. This belief and the planet assigned to a particular day of the week remained the same in all the European cultures. Perhaps this practice was, again, related to centuries of observation, and perhaps we would find some validity to it if we looked into it.

So, what kind of a day was Monday, that it was assigned to the Moon? We're going to find out, when we get into the astrological sections, that the Moon has much to do with the home, food, family feeling, and attachment to one's roots. Thus, it may primarily have been a day to stay close to the nest and take care of the family and roots. I can remember, back in the 1950s and earlier, when it was still rare for women to work outside the home that almost all housewives washed on Monday. In fact, when this connection was established, centuries ago, not only women but men and children all worked at home, for it was prior to industrialization.

Monday is no longer a primary time for those old-fashioned home-related tasks like washing, gathering food, or making clothing. Instead, Monday is associated with leaving home behind and returning to the stressful world of work. Not too coincidentally, vast numbers of people dread its arrival, and it has been labeled Blue Monday. Perhaps Mondays weren't always blue; maybe at one time, when we were closer to the lunar parts of our nature, people looked forward to Monday's renewal of the home fires and felt nurtured by it.

The Ancient Connection between the Moon and Women's Cycles

As noted earlier, the ancients prayed to Diana, the goddess of fertility, for safe childbirth—not something to take for granted in those days. Among many different peoples the world over, there was a common belief that the Moon had her own menstrual cycle. Even those not involved with Moon worship spoke of the Moon as having her period when the Moon was dark.

Many different tribes, ignorant of the facts of life, believed that women were impregnated by the Full Moon. Where did such beliefs originate? Were these beliefs the products of confused, primitive thinking, or was there in those times a close, readily-observed connection between the Moon and women's cycles that would cause them to leap to that conclusion?

Research seems to indicate an actual connection. As long ago as 1898, the Nobel prize-winning scientist Svante Arrhenius made careful studies of the menstrual cycles of twelve thousand female patients of a Swedish maternity hospital and found that the Moon did have a special effect on their cycles. In 1936, ten thousand German women were charted by Guthmann and Oswald, and more of them were found to have their periods at the New and Full Moon than at any other time. A study of over seven thousand women in 1962 by the Czech scientist Dr. Jeri Malek showed that the onset of bleeding occurred at the Full Moon more often than any other phase.

Folk wisdom also held that there were more births at the Full Moon. So did hardworking nurses in maternity wards. Doctors began to be fascinated with the question and to compile statistics. The foremost French medical journal, La Presse Médical, reported that the birth rate doubled just after the Full Moon.

A German physician, Dr. H. Gunther, reported increases in birth rates in Cologne around the Full and New Moon in 1938. Studies continued, and in Roanoke, Virginia, and Tallahassee, Florida, reviews of several hundred births found peaks of deliveries at the Full Moon and New Moon. Some researchers felt that the prevalent practice of induced labor, to avoid weekend deliveries cutting into gynecologists' free time, might be distorting the natural pattern of births. Thus they eliminated induced births from their study.

After reviewing a number of older and smaller studies that seemed to support a lunar effect on births, Dr. Walter Menaker decided to take a very large sample. He reviewed the records of over half a million live births in New York City from 1948 to 1957 and found that the highest frequency of births occurred at the Full Moon. A second study by Dr. Menaker of another half-million New York City births from 1961 to 1963 again pinpointed the peak rate of births around the Full Moon. It was speculated that perhaps the pull of gravity on the amniotic fluid increased with these lunar phases.

Research such as this inspired a woman named Louise Lacey to speculate that in ancient times, most of the women in the tribe were fertile at the Full Moon and that their menstrual cycles were synchronized with one another.

It has been seen that women who live together tend to adjust their menstrual cycles to one another. Biologists postulate some sort of subliminal olfactory perception of the released hormones as an explanation. Imagine living in an encampment or tribe where most of the women were ovulating at the same time and at their most responsive sexually, while overhead the Moon was full, and emotions were at their peak. The connection between the Moon and fertility would be strong, in this worldview, and so would the link with childbirth, since nine lunar months later, also at the Full Moon, children would be born.

Best Days for Casting Spells

In a lot of Wiccan and Pagan traditions, the days of the week greatly matter when it comes to casting spells. This is why if you are planning to cast a certain type of spell, you have to make sure that you do it on the right day. Otherwise, you may not be able to get your desired results or worse, get the opposite of what you want.

Each day of the week is associated with a specific planet. The days of the week are also associated with specific colors, deities, and elements. While it is true that you are free to cast a spell anytime and any day you want, you can have a higher chance of being successful with it if you cast it on the right day.

On Sundays, for instance, you should choose to cast truth spells and spells that generate warmth in your heart. This day is represented by the Sun and the deities Ra, Brighid, and Helios. If you are feeling frigid and resentful, you should use the energy of the sun to take away the anger and resentment that dwell in your heart.

Sunday is also a day that is represented by gold, diamond, quartz crystal, amber, and carnelian, as well as marigold, cinnamon, and sunflower. It is also associated with beauty, agriculture, hope, creativity, victory, and self-expression.

On Mondays, you should choose to cast spells that are powered by emotions. Monday is the most ideal day to cast spells for improving intuition and increasing confidence. It is also most ideal for casting spells for protection and clairvoyance. This day is associated with the colors white, silver, and light blue.

Monday is ruled by the moon. It is also a day that is represented by the deities Thoth and Selene. Moreover, it is represented by silver, pearl, moonstone, and opal, as well as catnip, sage, chamomile, comfrey, wintergreen, and other mints. This day is also associated with childbearing, family life, purity, virginity, wisdom, healing, and intuition.

On Tuesdays, you should choose to cast spells that inspire energy and passion. You should also choose to cast spells that increase your confidence. You should also choose to cast spells that can help you win a spiritual battle. This day is also ideal for casting protection spells.

Tuesday is ruled by the planet Mars. This day is represented by the deities Mars, Lilith, and Aries. This day is also represented by the colors orange and red, as well as holly, cactus, coneflower, and thistles. Tuesday is associated with iron, garnet, and ruby, as well as linked to conflict and war, enemies, protection, initiation, and marriage.

On Wednesdays, you should choose to cast spells that involve communication and granting of information. This day is governed by the planet Mercury and represented by the deities Athena, Mercury, Hermes, Lugh, and Odin. This day is also represented by the color purple, the metal mercury, and the gemstones agate and adventurine. It is also associated with aspen trees, ferns, lavenders, and lilies. Moreover, it is linked to traveling, journeys, loss and debt, and issues that are related to jobs and businesses.

On Thursdays, you should choose to cast spells for prosperity, success, and luck. Your spells are more likely to be more effective if you cast them during the waxing moon. Thursday is a really good day for spellcasting because it is ruled by the planet Jupiter, which is generous and benevolent.

Thursday is represented by the deities Juno, Jupiter, Zeus, and Thor. It is linked to green and royal blue colors. In addition, it is associated with tin, turquoise, lapis lazuli, and amethyst. Oak trees, honeysuckle, and cinquefoil are highly recommended to be used for spells during this day. Moreover,

Thursday is associated with family loyalty, honor, clothing and riches, and harvests.

On Fridays, you should choose to cast love spells as well as give offerings to your favorite gods and goddesses. This day is governed by the planet Venus and the deities Freya, Aphrodite, and Venus. It is represented by the elements copper, coral, rose quartz, and emerald. Furthermore, it is represented by the colors pink and aqua.

Friday is also the day when feverfew, apple blossoms, and strawberries are best incorporated into spells. Since this day is also associated with family life, fertility, sexuality, friendship, harmony, and growth, you may want to perform spells that revolve around these subjects.

On Saturdays, you should choose to cast banishing spells so that you can get rid of old and negative energies. If you have to do a binding spell, you should do it on a Saturday because this day is most ideal for getting rid of unwanted energies. It is also the most ideal day to cast spells that can help you develop or increase your patience.

Saturday is ruled by the planet Saturn. It is represented by the deities Saturn and Hecate. It is also represented by the colors black and dark purple, as well as the elements lead, apache tear, hematite, and obsidian. In addition, it is associated with thyme, cypress, and mullein. It is also associated with creativity, hope, fortune, protection, agriculture, and banishment of negativity.

Casting Spells on Sundays

Sunday is the ideal day to cast truth spells. These spells are done to help you seek for answers. They are ideal to be done if you want to get answers from people regarding something they did or said. You can cast a truth spell to find out the things that certain people refuse to tell you. Likewise, you can cast a truth spell to find out the truth behind lies. For your truth spell, you can use a variety of ingredients and tools, depending on what the spell calls for.

The following is an example of a truth spell:

This spell requires the use of a white candle, a blue candle, a needle, five senses oil, and compelling out.

To cast the spell, you have to use the needle to carve the name of the person from whom you want to get an answer from. When you are done carving his or her name, you have to use the five senses oil to coat the white candle. Then, you have to use the compelling oil to coat the blue candle. When you are done with that step, you have to light the two candles and place them on a table. See to it that the two candles are a few inches apart.

You have to focus your attention and energy on the blue candle while you recite the chant you created to find out the truth and get your answer. You can use any words that rhyme or whatever has a significant meaning for you. Then, you have to focus your attention and energy on the white candle while you recite the name of the person from whom you want to get the answer from.

You have to bring the candles closer to each other as you recite a spell that makes your intentions clearer. You have to use this spell to help you know the truth. Make sure that you let the candles burn. Wait for the flames of the candles to die out completely. When that is done, you can finally get the truth that you are searching for.

How about if you are speaking with a liar? If you think that the person you are talking to is lying, you can cast a truth spell to find out the truth.

Here is an example of a truth spell that you can use for this purpose:

You need to prepare dried yellow roses, dried mint, nutmeg, olive oil, and a yellow candle.

To cast a spell, you have to use the olive oil to coat the yellow candle. Then, you have to combine the yellow roses, dried mint, and nutmeg together in a container.

When everything is ready, you have to get the candle and roll it into the mixture of herbs. As you do this process, you have to think of your desire to gain clarity and receive the truth.

Light the candle and recite the truth spell. When you cast a truth spell, you must always keep in mind that you become bound to tell the truth. Thus, if you are the one lying, the spell will not work.

Casting Spells on Mondays

Monday is the ideal day to cast spells that can help you boost your confidence level. When you cast a spell like this, you can use a variety of ingredients such as wild crystals, tree barks, wild herbs, and wild flowers. You can also use crystals such as amber, jet, azurite, and citrine. In addition, you can use wild herbs and flowers such as thyme, lavender, and bay laurel. You can also add some fragrance oils, candles, and water that has been blessed. Every element you use can help you boost your confidence as well as interact with other people much better.

Here is an example of a confidence spell you can cast on a Monday morning:

This spell requires the use of sandalwood incense and a red candle. Sandalwood incense has an earthly scent while red candles represent strength and power. Ideally, this spell has to be done before taking a shower. Make sure that you speak slowly and loudly as you chant the spell. Refrain from whispering the words so that you can make a much greater impact.

To cast the spell, you have to stand before a full length mirror and light the red candle. Concentrate on the flame as you work up your energy. You must feel the positive energy starting to flow throughout your body. You have to be careful not to rush the process. It may take a while before you can finally work up some energy and this is alright. When you have worked up the energy, you have to look at your reflection on the mirror. Stare into your eyes and recite the chant.

You have to tell yourself that you are intelligent. You have to tell yourself that you can succeed in whatever you want to do. You have to tell yourself that you can speak clearly and calmly. You have to tell yourself that you can focus on the positive side of things. Moreover, you have to tell yourself that you should not allow yourself to be shaken. Tell yourself that you are intelligent and capable of achieving success one more time.

Then, you have to visualize yourself beaming with self-confidence. Imagine yourself finally getting over self-doubts. Light your incense and let it burn as you prepare for the day ahead.

Here is another confidence spell that you can cast to serve your intentions:

Ideally, you have to cast this confidence spell during the waxing moon or new moon. During this time, the energies that bring about confidence are high. The spell requires the use of a tiger's eye. However, if you cannot get a tiger's eye, you can simply use whatever gemstone you have. The spell also requires a yellow candle, three white candles, and a rope or wire that you can use to turn the gemstone into a necklace.

To cast this confidence spell, you have to get out of the house and stand under the moon. You also have to arrange your white candles into a triangle position. Then, you have to put the yellow candle in the middle. As you hold the tiger's eye, you have to meditate and work up your energies. See to it that you focus all your energies into the tiger's eye. Once you feel that you have already composed yourself, you have to light the white candle and recite the chant.

The chant can be anything. You are free to create whatever chat you want. Nevertheless, a chant that rhymes works much better. You also have to request for the energies of the universe to grant you the gifts of strength and courage. Afterwards, you have to light another white candle and recite the chant once more. Finally, you have to light the last candle and recite the chant once again before you light the yellow candle. As you light this candle, you have to hold the tiger's eye over its flame.

As you hold onto the tiger's eye, you have to recite the chant. By the power of three, you have to ask the energies of the universe to grant you strength and courage. Look at the flame. Focus on it. Meditate. Visualize yourself receiving the energies and imagine how you will feel when that happens. Imagine your confidence levels rising. Visualize yourself getting calmer. Take your time to envision the scenario. Allow yourself to send out the energies towards the gemstone.

Recite the final chant, which has to be about charging your gemstone with love, light, confidence, and strength. By the power of three and the energies of the universe, you have to ask for confidence and strength to be given to you. Once you are done reciting the chant, you can turn the gemstone into a necklace and wear it. You can use the rope or wire to turn it into a necklace. However, if you are not fond of jewelry, you can keep it as a token. Feel free to charge it again whenever necessary.

Casting Spells on Tuesdays

Tuesday is the ideal day to cast spells for protection. These spells are effective in protecting you against evil and keeping you safe.

The following spell is an example of a protection spell that you can cast on a Tuesday. It requires the use of blue or silver glitter and a wand or staff. For your wand, you have to choose blue, silver, or white color. The spell also becomes more effective when done outdoors. However, if the circumstance does not permit you to cast the spell outdoors, you can do it inside your home.

To do this spell, you can proceed with the steps of spellcasting as usual. However, rather than begin with the North, you have to begin with the West and then move clockwise from there. You have to use your wand to tap the ground while you recite your chant. You also have to call upon to whoever guards the watchtowers of whichever direction you go to. Make sure that you ask that you may be guided through the darkness and be safe at all times.

Once you are finished with the four corners, you have to stand in the center and recite your chant. Your chant has to be about banishing negative energies and never letting them come near you again. As you recite the last lines of your chant, you have to scatter the glitter around you and close the circle to end the ritual.

Casting Spells on Wednesdays

Wednesday is the ideal day to cast spells for better and more effective communication. So, if you are experiencing problems or difficulty with communication, you can cast a spell for it. A communication spell can help you strengthen weak lines of communication.

You can use herbs, such as chamomile to encourage understanding and improve communication. When you write down your spell, it is recommended that you use a pen with yellow ink since yellow is a color that is often associated with the element of air.

Likewise, you have to write the name of the person you wish to communicate with on a white candle, preferably using a pen with yellow ink. Take a few minutes to compose yourself and have an imaginary conversation with the person you wish to communicate with. You also have to think of how you want your conversation to flow so that you can send out vibrations and energies.

When you are ready for the spell to take effect, you can recite your chant or spell. Ideally, you should ask the powers of the air to help you send your messages to the person you want to communicate with.

Casting Spells on Thursdays

Thursday is the ideal day to cast a money spell. A spell like this can help you increase your financial stability. So, if you are experiencing financial problems or you wish to have more money, you must cast a money spell on a Thursday. However, you have to keep in mind that casting this spell still does not guarantee financial success. If you want to be a multi-millionaire, you still have to put in effort and do work.

You have to take note that casting a spell like this will only help you increase your chances of obtaining wealth. It will not actually make you rich, unless you do not make an effort to earn money. Money spells are not get rich quick schemes. They will not make you rich in an instant.

The following spell is a money spell that you can do in a few seconds. It is very simple and does not involve a lot of elements. This spell requires the use of lavender, a bag, and seven different forms of money.

You have to get the bag and put money in it. You can use whatever form of money fits you. For instance, you can put in a nickel, a penny, a dime, a quarter, a dollar, and so on, inside the bag. Then, you have to sprinkle lavender on your money and carry your bag with you for seven days.

Casting Spells on Fridays

Friday is an ideal day to cast love spells. So, whether you are trying to repair a broken relationship or attract love into your life, you can use a love spell to help you.

The following is an example of a simple love spell that you can do on a Friday. It is short, simple, and easy to do. It requires the use of vanilla extract. Make sure that the vanilla extract you use is genuine and not merely an imitation.

To start casting this love spell, you have to remove the lid of the bottle of vanilla extract. Imagine that a bright red light is coming from your eyes and turning the color of the vanilla extract to red. As you visualize this, you have to recite your chant.

Your chant has to be about love. It can be about bringing love into your life, fixing a relationship, strengthening a relationship, or anything that you want to happen with regard to your love life.

When you are done with this part, you have to sprinkle a drop or two of the vanilla extract in the four corners of your bedroom. Then, you have to put back the lid on the bottle and keep it under your bed.

Casting Spells on Saturdays

Saturday is an ideal spell to cast a binding spell. Binding spells are generally used to prevent something or someone from causing harm. Unlike curses, however, they do not inflict harm on the person. They are more like protection spells, except that they aim to get rid of the negative element instead of simply wanting to be protected from it.

The following is a generic binding spell that you can cast on a Saturday. It requires the use of a cardboard, a black yarn, a cauldron, and writing tools.

First, you have to get the cardboard and write words or draw images that represent the negativity that you wish to bind onto it. Next, you have to crumple the cardboard into a ball. When you are done with that, you have to wrap it with the black yarn.

See to it that you wrap the yarn twenty-one times around the crumpled cardboard while you chant your spell. Then, you have to tie the ends of the yarn into three sturdy knots. Lastly, you have to burn your cardboard wrapped in yarn inside your cauldron while you chant your final spell about getting rid of the negativity completely.

When the words or images that represent negativity are burning, you have to visualize things that represent positivity. You must feel the positive energy within you.

Chapter 2: The Wiccan Moon

The Horned God / The Sun God

The masculine god is often seen or referred to as the horned god. Horns are a traditional symbol of masculinity, representing qualities such as strength, sex drive, and energy.

During the Wiccan year, the horned god will adopt different personalities. For half of the year he can be referred to as the Oak King and for the other half, the Holly King. He is also referred to as the Sun God who is worshipped on the Sabbat of Lughnasadh. Some Wiccans believe that these are all different gods and will worship each of them separately and other Wiccans have them all fall under the God.

The Goddess / The Triple Goddess

The Goddess is the Feminine deity. Like the horns represent the masculine god, the Goddess is represented by three phases of the moon. This is why she is also called the Triple Goddess. Each phase of the moon represents a different form of the Goddess. The waxing moon represents creation and inspiration, the full moon represents sustenance and the waning moon represents fulfillment. The three forms of the Goddess are as follows:

The Maiden - The maiden is young, full of beauty and innocence. Her future is promising and filled with potential. She is associated with beginnings and the new moon.

The Mother - The mother is experienced and mature. She is protective, nurturing and selfless.

The Crone - The crone is full of wisdom, a leader and respected. She reminds us of our mortality and that our bodies will one day return to the earth. Despite this, she does not have a negative connotation. In fact, she is seen as a guide and her wisdom can help us through difficult times.

The Wheel of the Year

Yule
20-23 December

Samhain
1 November

Imbolc
2 February

Mabon
21-24 September

Ostara
19-22 March

Lughnasadh
1 August

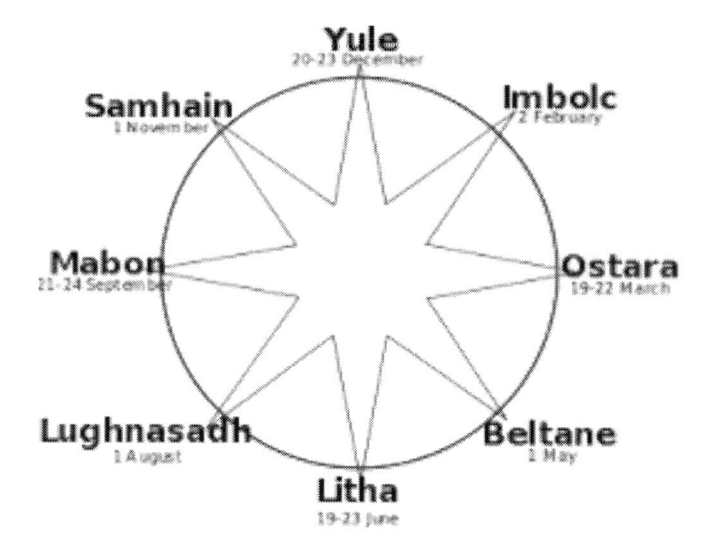

Beltane
1 May

Litha
19-23 June

The Wheel of the Year is the Wiccan calendar if you will. It represents the annual cycle of the Earth and is derived from the seasons. Wiccans believe that time is cyclical, a continuous cycle. This is why the festivals (or Sabbats) are represented by a wheel.

The wheel also represents the progression of life. We are born, we grow, we live, we decline and then we die.

This period of birth, life, and death is represented by the life of the Horned God during different seasons. The cycle of fertility (virginity, pregnancy, and birth) is represented in different seasons by the Triple Goddess.

The Sabbats

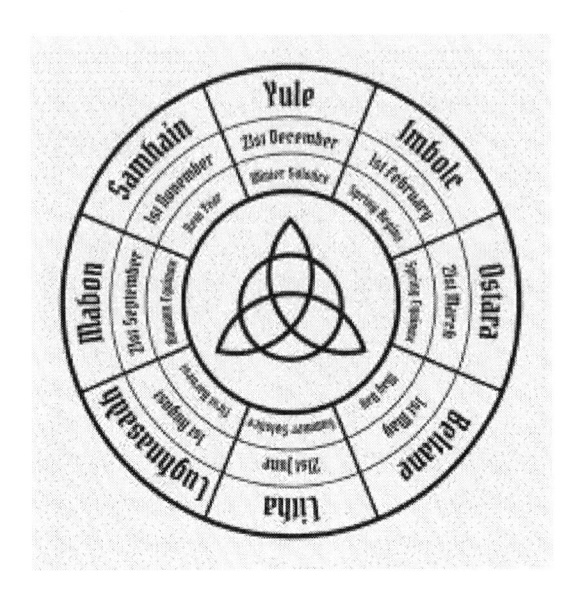

Yule: December 20-23. Yule is the winter solstice. The Goddess (in the form of the mother) gives birth to the sun god.

Imbolc: February 2. Candles are used to celebrate this Sabbat. They are to encourage the sun to shine brighter. The sun god at this stage is an infant and feeds from the breast of his mother, the Goddess. This also represents the end of winter because the earth is starting to feel the warmth of the infant sun.

Ostara: March 20-23. The spring equinox. The God is now a child, and the Goddess will take on the form of the maiden. She acts as the God's playmate and they play in the fields to encourage the flowers to bloom.

Here is where beginner Wiccans might get confused. The Goddess has now taken on two forms simultaneously. She is both the playmate of the child

God (as a maiden) and the nurturing (mother) of the child. She will continue the year changing from two forms as needed in order to serve the life cycle of the God.

Beltane: May 1. The Maiden Goddess and the Sun God are now young adults. They are fertile and ready to procreate. For this reason, Beltane is viewed by Wiccans as a sacred night for sex. Fertility also represents the upcoming crops. The Sun God will impregnate the maiden here and she will turn from the maiden to the pregnant mother. The Goddess is now both the pregnant lover of the God as well as his nurturing mother.

Litha: June 20-23. The summer solstice. Litha is the peak of the Sun God's life, he is now full of strength and masculinity. Litha is when the Sun God and the pregnant Goddess will get married.

Lughnasadh: August 1. Autumn is upon the earth. The leaves are turning brown and the temperature is cooling. The Sun God is dying. The God will begin preparations for his death and make sure that his unborn child and the pregnant Goddess are taken care of. The Sun God knows that winter is upon the earth and it will be a challenge to survive it. He knows that his strength and light can only be renewed if he willingly offers himself up as a sacrifice. He will do this to become one with the earth to provide sustenance. His sacrifice will be the wheat that is harvested for the winter.

Mabon: September 20-23. Time with the Sun God has nearly ended. Preparation for his death and the winter are in full swing. Knowing of losing her son, the nurturing mother transitions into the crone. Her wisdom and experience will help guide us through the mourning of the Sun God.

Samhain: October 31. The Sun God dies. Many Wiccans believe that this is when the Sun God is referred to as the Horn God. He is animal-like, he is one with the earth.

During Samhain, the crone and the pregnant mother goddess mourn the God's death. Samhain is the start of the New Year for Wiccans and many Wiccans view Samhain as the most important Sabbat. Samhain is a day to remember those who have passed on, including ancestors, family and even animals that were either pets or used on a farm. Samhain rituals celebrate darkness.

Although it is considered the beginning of the year, it also marks the end of the previous year in which rituals celebrate and commemorate last year's harvest and the accomplishments that were made.

Samhain also represents a promise of new life. The pregnant mother holds the seed of the reincarnated Son God who will be born at Yule.

Yule: December 20-23. The Goddess gives birth and the Sun God is reborn, thus re-starting the cycle.

The Greater Sabbats and the Lesser Sabbats

The eight Sabbats are divided in half making four of them greater Sabbats and the other four, lesser Sabbats. The divide is as follows:

Greater Sabbats:

Samhain (October 31)

Imbolc (February 2)

Beltane (May 1)

Lughnasadh (August 1)

Lesser Sabbats:

Yule (December 20-23)

Ostara (March 20-23)

Litha (June 20-23)

Mabon (September 20-23)

The four lesser Sabbats mark the end of one season and the beginning of the next while the four greater Sabbats are the middle or the peak of the season. These days are considered days of power.

Esbats

Although the Goddess plays a key role in each of the Sabbats, they are mostly used to outline the life cycle of the God or the sun. The Goddess is represented by the moon, as she is the polar opposite of the God. Therefore, we celebrate the Goddess during **Esbats** which follow the phases of the moon rather than the sun.

As a reminder, the Triple Goddess is represented by three phases of the moon. The maiden is represented by the waxing moon, the mother by the full moon and the crone by the waning moon. Esbats take place whenever the moon is full, which means they occur twelve or thirteen times a year.

The Blue Moon Esbat

During each solar year, there will be either twelve or thirteen full moons. The thirteenth full moon (or Esbat) will occur once every two and a half years and this is referred to as the "blue moon". This Esbat is rare and is considered to have more power and energy than a regular Esbat. The presence of the Goddess during the blue moon is very powerful and is a great time for beginner witches or Wiccans to establish a connection with her. The blue moon is a time that Wiccans find very sacred and they will hold special rituals under the light of the blue moon.

My First Blue Moon Ritual

The first time I held my own blue moon ritual was truly astounding. See, as a Christian, I had never had a spiritual experience with a feminine deity. Since I am a woman, I always felt that side of my spiritual being was missing from my religious faith.

I went outside to perform my ritual under the moonlight and called upon the Goddess, hoping that I would be able to feel her presence. Although I couldn't feel her right away, a few minutes (or maybe an hour?) in and I knew she was there with me. I could feel her telling me that I was not lesser or weaker because I was not a man.

Without her power, the God would not exist and I felt myself understanding my role as a woman on this earth. Motherhood, fertility and nurturing kindness were all equally as important as strength, the need to provide and masculinity. If you are a woman, I highly recommend taking part in a ritual under the full moon. You will feel an overwhelming sense of belonging and understanding of your place on this earth.

If you are a man, I recommend performing this ritual even more. See masculine and feminine energy aren't limited to one gender or the other. There is a feminine side to you and if you have grown up Christian, that side of your being has likely been ignored for years. Making time to appreciate the Goddess and how her feminine energy lives inside you will help make you truly whole. At least that is my theory on the matter, every Wiccan is free to take their own path.

Reincarnation

Unlike Christians, Wiccans do not believe in the idea of heaven and hell but we do believe in an afterlife, or a place where the soul can live without the physical body.

As a witch on this earth, your purpose is to better yourself, better your environment and help others. You are to go through life's ups and downs, learn from your mistakes, collect wisdom and grow as a person. This is the same purpose that your soul has.

Your soul is meant to experience the physical world, die, reflect on the life it lived and then be reincarnated into a new physical life. The goal is that each physical life is lived better than the last. For this reason, we can assume that people who are immoral and treat others badly are "new souls" who have not yet lived many lives and learned how to be good.

The Afterlife

Every time your soul lives life and reflects upon it in The Afterlife, it will live a more moral and spiritually satisfying physical life the next time it is reincarnated. It's like your soul is on a mission to live the perfect physical life and it takes numerous tries for this to happen.

So what is the Afterlife? The Afterlife is a place (similar to the idea of heaven) where your soul can go and rest before it is reincarnated into a new physical body. Unlike heaven, however, this place is not a place where your soul will be judged. While you are in The Afterlife, you can communicate with the other souls, the deities and reflect on the physical life you just lived. If you lived a bad life, you will follow the guidance of the Goddess and the God in hopes that your next life will be more spiritually satisfying. Once your soul has satisfied the physical life's purpose, it will remain in The Afterlife for all eternity.

The God and Goddess (or Lord and Lady)

Wicca acknowledges both the masculine god and the feminine goddess. They both represent unique but essential characteristics and are seen as equal. Now for Christians, the deities in Wicca can be confusing, I know it was for me! This is because Christianity focuses on a very rigid set of beliefs but Wiccans have the ability to interpret things on their own.

Some Wiccans view the God and Goddess as two gods. Other Wiccans believe there are many different masculine deities which collectively would be referred to as the God or Horned God and that there would also be many feminine deities that all together would be referred to as the Goddess or Triple Goddess.

To compare this to Christianity, we can use God, Jesus, and the Holy

Spirit. In Christianity you would consider all three of those entities to be "God" but they can either be broken down into individual entities or referred to as a whole.

In Wicca, you have the ability to choose whether you want to refer to the God and Goddess as a whole or if you'd like to worship the individual deities and break them down further. I will outline the basic overview of the God and Goddess but I recommend delving deeper into this on your own.

Other Beliefs

The Rule of Three

The rule of Threefold means that whatever energies we put into the universe; it will be returned to us times three. This can include every day acts of kindness or negativity or a lifetime of treating people or a person in a certain way. Wiccans who do not practice magick or witchcraft still abide by the rule by the actions they choose to do and the decisions they make every day of their lives.

For Wiccans who do practice witchcraft, this rule becomes even more significant. Once you are able to create spells and harness your powers, you will be able to cause things to happen to people. You can use this power for good or bad but the Threefold rule states that whatever we put out into the world; it will come back to us threefold so mind what you do as it will come back to you.

The Elements

The elements are integral parts of Wicca. The elements: earth, wind, water, and fire are seen as the components that make up the earth as well as energies that make up living beings. This means that they are considered the root of all matter. The elements are often a large part of rituals and are used in their physical forms to purify a ritual circle.

Fire

Fire is an integral part of a comfortable human existence but we do not necessarily need it to survive. Fire gives us warmth in the cold, allows us to cook food and is a source of light in the darkness. For these reasons we should look to fire less as a survival element and more of a luxury in which we should offer our deepest gratitude. Fire is also one of the more dangerous elements and should always be treated with caution and respect. Fire is used in candle magic and also to create an environment for rituals and spellwork. In rituals, fire is represented in the form of burning objects, baking and lighting candles or bonfires.

Deity: the Sun God

Energy: Masculine (to will)

Tools: Candles, bonfire

Season: Summer

Corresponding Zodiac Signs: **Aries, Leo, Sagittarius**

Air

Air is a symbol of our intelligence and our ability to communicate with other humans on this earth as well as the spirits. Air is how some Wiccans have psychic powers and telepathy.

Unlike fire, air is crucial to our survival and reminds us of the importance of being connected with both earthly beings as well as spiritual beings. It reminds that we are very fragile and we can be transferred to the afterlife if we are without air for only a few minutes. Air is used in rituals by tossing objects into the wind, burning incense of aromatic candles. Air is used in spells that involve freedom, knowledge, traveling and psychic powers.

Deity: The Sun God

Energy: Masculine (to will)

Tools: Wand, incense, bell

Season: **Spring**

Corresponding Zodiac Signs: **Gemini, Libra, Aquarius**

Water

Water is the most versatile of the elements. It can be present in the form of a liquid, solid and gas and each of those states can be used to excerpt different magical qualities of water. Water is an integral part of our lives and is used to nourish ourselves as well as the earth in the form of plants and animals.

Water is a symbol of the subconscious, purification, wisdom and emotions. It is the element of love and femininity. In rituals, water is represented by pouring water over objects, making brews, and ritual bathing.

Deity: the Triple Goddess

Energy: Feminine (to listen)

Tools: Cauldron, cups

Season: **Autumn**

Corresponding Zodiac Signs: **Pisces, Cancer, Scorpio**

Earth

Earth is the foundation upon which all is built. As Wiccans, we take pride in our relationship with the earth and consider the earth a direct pathway to the divine. The more we take care of our earth, the more we honor the God and Goddess. The earth is a symbol of life. All life is born of the earth, grows and is nourished by the earth and then returns to the earth in death. The earth represents strength, abundance, prosperity, and femininity. In rituals, the earth is represented by salt, burying items in the ground, herbalism and crystals.

Deity: the Triple Goddess

Energy: Feminine (to listen)

Tools: Pentacle, a bowl of salt

Season: **Winter**

Corresponding Zodiac Signs: **Taurus, Virgo, Capricorn**

Wiccan Symbols

Just like Christians have the cross, Wiccans also have symbols that represent different aspects of the faith. Although there are many, I will cover the four main ones below.

Pentacle

The pentacle is a pentagram within a circle. It is the most common and traditional symbol of Wicca.

The Horned God

This symbol represents the masculine God as we can see his horns above his body. The horned God is also known as the Sun God.

WICCA

The Triple Goddess

This symbol represents the Triple Goddess with the phases of the moon representing each of her forms.

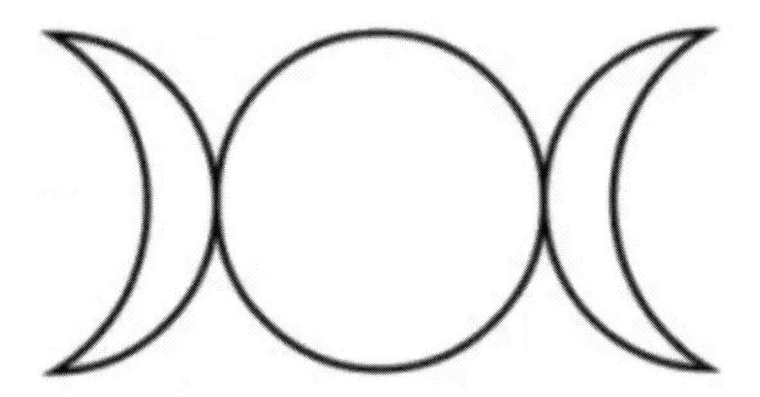

Wheel

This symbol represents the wheel of the year, and a cyclical view of time rather than linear. Each piece represents one of the eight Sabbats.

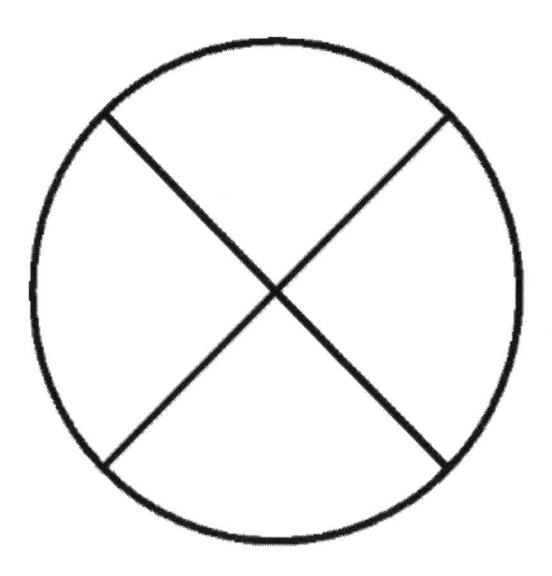

Chapter 3: Phases of the Moon

In Wiccan traditions, the phases of the moon are significant when it comes to casting spells. This is because Wiccans believe in the power and energy of the moon. For every phase, they perform a particular spell. They believe that certain spells work better during certain moon phases. For them, the waxing moon, the waning moon, the full moon, and the new moon all have different yet special magickal properties. This is the exact reason why they plan their spell casting accordingly.

During the waxing moon, spells for love, inspiration, friendship, freedom, happiness, and prosperity are highly recommended to be done. Positive magick or the magick that draws things to you is ideal to be performed. During this time, the moon turns from dark to full within fourteen days. So, if you want to cast a spell to bring love into your life, get you promoted at work, or make you more financially stable, you have to cast your spells when the moon is waxing.

During the waning moon, the opposite happens. The moon turns from full to dark within fourteen days. A lot of Pagan and Wiccan traditions perform baneful magick or the magick that gets rid of, destroys, or sends away things that they no longer want in their life during this time. When the moon is waning, that is the perfect time to cast spells against addictions and negative energies. It is also the ideal time to break curses and banish bad habits.

So, if you want to end a relationship, get rid of toxic people from your life, or reduce negativities such as financial debts and health issues, you should cast your spells during the waning moon. This time is also ideal for performing rites that get rid of hostile influences.

During the new moon, you can cast spells for love, romance, health, work, and new beginnings. During this phase, the moon becomes dark before it goes into the waxing phase once again after it waned for three days. However, you may find it quite difficult to see the moon during this period. It may look like a faint crescent of silver low on the sky.

Moreover, a lot of Wiccan traditions consider this period as a fallow time wherein individuals are expected to rest and rejuvenate before they begin to work on more intense magickal workings. Other traditions, however, regard this period as the best time to perform magickal workings that are related to wish fulfillment, mind and body purification, sacred space, and magick related to peace and inner harmony.

Then, there is the full moon. During this time, you are able to see the whole side of the moon. Many Pagan and Wiccan traditions perform magickal workings on the day when the moon is full, the day before it, and the day after it. In three days, they perform rituals that are focused on spiritual development and personal growth. You can use this period to cast spells for healing, intuitive awareness, wishes, predictions, and better relationship with the deities.

Chapter 4: Magical proprieties of the Lunar Cycle

Each moon phase is governed by very specific energies. These energies are known to have an effect on us, much in the way the moon effects the tides. A complete moon cycle, or a lunar month, lasts approximately 29-30 days. Thirteen complete moon cycles lead you through one complete turn of the Wheel of the Year.

For the purposes of this book, we'll divide each moon cycle into four periods. The waxing period starts 3 ½ days after the dark/new moon; it runs from the mid-crescent through mid-gibbous phase. The full period runs from mid-gibbous through mid-disseminating phase. The waning period runs from mid-disseminating through mid-balsamic phase.

The dark moon period lasts from mid-balsamic through mid-crescent phase.

The waxing moon period is the time when the moon starts as a slim 'fingernail' in the sky and grows fuller by the night. In magic, the waxing moon is a period used to bring desired things toward us. The waxing moon period corresponds to the mornings, when you wake up and start your day. It also corresponds to springtime, when everything seems fresh, hope springs eternal and possibilities seem endless.

This period is a time to start things. It's conducive to new beginnings, focusing on new goals and challenges. It's the ideal time to build, to begin a new project or routine, to move forward with things.

The full moon period starts about three days before the moon is full, continues through the day the moon reaches its zenith and continues for about three days after that. The moon is at its height of power in this period. In magic, the full moon is generally considered the most powerful for constructive or positive magic. The full moon is associated with the middle of the day, when activities are generally in full swing. It also corresponds to the season of summer, when nature is reaching its peak of fullness and inhabitants of the earth are at their most active.

If the new moon is when the engine starts coming to life and picking up speed, the full moon is when it's chugging along at full force. It's a time to focus on developing things you've started, on busting through roadblocks and leaping hurdles. The full moon is a time of illumination, when you can look and see what's going on around you more clearly.

The waning moon period starts about the fourth day after the full moon and continues until the moon shrinks back down to a sliver. Energies of the waning moon are ideal for bringing things to a conclusion. Magical goals for the waning moon period would usually be pushing things away. The waning moon is associated with the evening, when the sun is setting and the day is winding down. It corresponds to the autumn season, when we reap what we've sown, for better or worse.

This is a time for bringing things to a close, finishing up and shutting down. Give attention to any lingering problems, as it's a time to figure out some resolution. It's conducive to endings: that final push to reach the finish line or – if the case may be – knowing when to cut your losses.

The dark moon period starts with the balsamic moon, a thin crescent rising in the daytime. For about three days, it will continue to diminish, until it's a practically invisible orb that goes unnoticed in broad daylight and is hidden at night. Then a sliver of silver reappears and for three days grows back into the crescent, thus completing a full cycle.

The dark moon corresponds to night, the time for resting and recharging. It's also associated with the season of winter, when the seeds of the fallen fruits lie underground, waiting for the proper time to sprout. The dark moon is a time for reflection on what has been. It's a time to cut loose and let go of what was so that you can move on again when the time is right. The dark moon is a classical time for destructive or negative magic. It's a time to begin thinking ahead, to look toward the future with anticipation and cautious optimism.

It's also a time for going within.

Unlike the full moon when everything is illuminated, the dark moon is the time for delving deep into the shadows, for facing that which is misunderstood, and for recovering that which is deeply hidden.

Chapter 5: Moon's connection with Oceans

In contrast to our understanding of circadian biological rhythmicity, matching the solar day, our understanding of possible Moon-related—that is, circatidal and circalunar—biological rhythmicity has lagged seriously behind. Nowadays, however, cushioned by the fact that it has been scientifically established that some living organisms have adapted to indirect effects of the Moon through its influence on tides, even direct biological effects in response to, or in anticipation of, changing moonlight are being characterized and gaining in acceptability. In this book I will discuss these newly emerging aspects of the science of chronobiology, with examples from plants, but particularly among animals, with reference also to supposed lunar influences on human behavior, setting them against the mythologies attributed to the Moon throughout human history.

Repeatedly throughout history supposed Moon-related effects upon human life processes have been critically dismissed with understandable skepticism. Recently, however, evidence is building up, for a small number of animals, that clock genes related to the periodicities of the Moon and tides may be present in their genetic make-up alongside the more familiar circadian clock genes. If circa tidal and circalunar genes are present within some living organisms, might they be more widespread in the genetic make-up of animals and plants, and even in humans? If they are, perhaps the search for Moon-related rhythms in humans should now gain more respectability. At least one very recent study indicates that humans may indeed be inherently responsive to moonlight in the determination of patterns of sleep, paving the way for further scientific enquiry into the relationship between the Moon and the human condition. Humans have obviously adapted to the patterns of the solar day; are we now seeing that, less obviously, they have also adapted to the lunar day and month? If so should we at least remain open-minded that moonlight may have more of an impact on our lives than few in modern societies have previously been prepared to admit?

Chapter 6: Preparing for your Spells And rituals

You will need your book of shadows for rituals and nearly everything you do as a witch/Wiccan. Your book of shadows is a book that you fill with any and all things Wicca. What you put in it is completely up to you and I suggest starting it as soon as you begin studying Wicca. Here are some suggestions for creating your book of shadows.

I'm sure you're learning a lot from this book and you will continue to learn more and more as your journey continues. Your book of shadows is a great place to keep track of important notes and lessons that you learn along the way. You can include the Wiccan Rede, the Wheel of the Year as well as the various Wiccan symbols.

Your book of shadows can be filled with what you want to accomplish as a Wiccan and a human being. You can treat this as your "life to-do list" and its main purpose is to ensure that your path is always heading in a direction that feels right. Having these things in your book of shadows will also help you ask for guidance to achieve these goals when you are connecting with the deities during a ritual. You can continue to add this as you discover more about yourself as you get older.

Spells, crystal properties, herbal benefits

As you develop your witchcraft skills, you will need to take notes or keep charts to help you. Your book of shadows is where all of these things should be kept so that you can go back and refer to them quickly. I personally think it's nice to draw or make your own charts and guides. This allows the information to sink in and also keeps your book of shadows very personal and close to your heart. Just like witchcraft is an extension of your spirit, your book of shadows is an extension of your creativity.

Physical symbols

I think that a book of shadows is incomplete if it doesn't have some physical items in it. This means anything in the book that is not written text. You can include drawings, symbols of the earth such as leaves, feathers, stones, herbs etc. I also think that using physical properties are a great way to incorporate the elements into your book. For example, you can rub a page with dirt or light a page on fire to represent earth and fire. Get creative with this book as it is only limited by the limits of your imagination.

Should my book of shadows be kept a secret?

You must be getting used to this by now but everything that you do as part of your Wiccan journey is up to you! That being said, I personally recommend that your book of shadows stays a secret and that you do not share it with others. I think that a book of shadows is a deeply personal tool that witches use to keep their deepest and darkest secrets. If you know that your book of shadows is private and will never be shown to anyone, you are free to write absolutely anything in it - without any filters. To me, this is a truly magical experience because you're allowed to make mistakes, change your mind and change your values and goals without anyone holding you accountable. You can then look back on your book of shadows throughout the years and see how much you have grown as a person and a witch.

As a Christian, I hated confessing my sins to a priest because I couldn't understand why a human needed to hear that stuff. If I was truly asking for God's forgiveness, surely this could just be a conversation between him and I? This is why I keep my book of shadows very secret. It is a place for me to unleash all my desires and confessions without anyone needing to read it other than myself and the deities. I also recommend keeping a large book of shadows for your home and a smaller, pocket-sized one for you to take with you to coven meetings, rituals and just to have on you in everyday life.

A Wiccan Altar

Along with a book of shadows, every Wiccan must also have their version of an altar. This is a spiritual place where you will keep your tools and symbols of your Wiccan faith. There is no need for your altar to be permanently set up in your home but I find this is the most satisfying way to have an altar. That way you have a sacred place for all your tools and you can always go to it whenever you feel the need to connect with the deities.

However, if you do not have a family that supports your faith or if you don't have enough space in your home, you may want to keep your tools in a separate place and simply set them up when you're ready to perform a ritual.

I was a secret Wiccan for many years so I was unable to have an obvious altar, however, it was permanent because it was always set up in my room and I never took it down. I hid my altar in plain sight by setting up "ordinary" objects on my dresser. None of my items looked particularly "witchy" so they could easily stay on my dresser without my Catholic family taking any notice. On my altar, I had a few candles, picture frames of loved ones, an incense burner, and some crystals. I recommend setting up something like this if you have a family that isn't going to support you or you're not ready to come out as a witch just yet.

Just like the book of shadows, your altar design is up to you but there are a few guidelines that you can follow. I will outline them below.

Different purposes and tools for your altar

Meditation

Your altar is a place where you can go to meditate and visualize. You can have affirmations, meditation prompts, or photos that help take you to places that make you feel calm and in touch with your spiritual energy.

Connection with deities

Your altar should be a sacred place where you go to connect with the deities, therefore you should have symbols of the deities on your altar. Here are some examples of symbols that you can use for the deities:

- A black candle for the God and a white candle for the Goddess
- A painting or statue of the deities
- A necklace or other jewelry with the symbols of the Horned God and Triple Goddess
- Offerings that your deities accept
- And this list could go on and on!

Some people enjoy creating their own tools and symbols but you can also purchase items or have them given to you by other members of the faith.

Witchcraft

Your altar is a place where you will perform magick and perfect your craft, therefore you should keep all your tools here. Here is a list of common tools that witches nearly all witches will use:

Pentacle necklace

A necklace or amulet in the shape of the pentacle, the most common symbol of the Wiccan faith. The pentacle is used for protection.

Wand

Your wand can be made out of wood, metal or rock. Many people use wood from their birth tree to construct their wand. Your wand will be used for certain spells and rituals. Gardner stated that the wand was to be used for elemental spirits that were afraid of steel or metal which meant they couldn't be called upon using the athame.

Athame: A sword or knife that will be used in ritual.

Chalice

A cup or goblet that represents the Goddess. It is used to hold water, wine or other liquids that will be used in rituals.

Cauldron

Basically a mixing bowl used for making brews and burning oils.

Book of Shadows: Your book of shadows should be kept on or near your altar if possible. When I was a secret Wiccan I could not keep my book of shadows on my altar.

Personal items

In my opinion, no altar is complete without an item that has deep personal meaning to you. When you use an item with a strong emotional connection, your spirit can be pulled out of your mind when you're at your altar. It is a way to get in tune with your feelings and spirituality and away from your logical brain.

Depending on what kind of magick you like to practice most, your set of tools can include the items listed above as well as others such as crystals, candles for candle magic, herbs etc. There is no limit to what you can include with your altar, it should simply have a deep and personal meaning to you.

Rituals

Rituals are a series of acts that are performed to honor and connect with the deities. They may be performed alone or with a coven. If you are Christian, rituals are much like going to church in that you will say prayers, meet up with other members of the faith and perform certain acts and routines in order to get closer to God.

Rituals may be performed for a variety of reasons. Usually, they are performed to celebrate the Sabbats and the Esbats and also during significant life events such as the birth of a child or the passing of a loved one. Rituals are also used as initiations or self-dedications in order to welcome a new member of the faith.

Although rituals can be used to cast spells and create magick, you do not need to be a witch in order to partake in a ritual. This is because a ritual's main focus is to connect with the God and the Goddess. Even if you are not Wiccan, you can take part in a ritual with other Wiccans, just like a non-Christian would be welcome in a Christian church.

Casting a circle

Before a witch performs a ritual or does certain kinds of witchcraft, they must first cast a circle. Casting a circle is used both in solitary rituals and coven rituals. The purpose of the circle is to keep in the good energy that you will be working with and to keep out any negative energy or spirits that you do not want coming in and disrupting your work. It is often said by Wiccans that the circle is a form of protection and is essential for any witch who wishes to practice magick in a safe manner.

As a beginner, it's crucial to learn how to cast a circle because you don't want to accidentally let in a negative or dangerous spirit and you do not want to let out any negative energy should you make a mistake during the ritual or spellwork. Casting a circle is the best way to keep yourself and everyone around you safe.

Just like everything in Wicca, you may choose your own method of casting a circle but there are a few main points that will help you cast a proper one safely. I will outline these methods below. If you are a beginner, I suggest sticking to these points and as you get more advanced and do more research, you can look up more complicated circles or create your own.

Your circle may be marked out physically, such as with stones, twigs, candles or crystals but this is not necessary. If you choose to mark out your circle physically, you simply need to incorporate the placing of stones, salt or other material around your workspace or altar when you are doing "the casting". I will show you how to do that, as well as the other steps to casting the circle below.

The Casting

In order to make your circle effective, you must do more than simply make a circle with physical items. Casting the circle spiritually, as opposed to physically, is the essential part and it must be done to make sure all the negative and positive energies are where they should be. Casting a circle will be done in four steps:

Preparing the space: Firstly, you should prepare the space in which you wish to work by sweeping away negative energies. You can do this by waving your hands in a sweeping motion and using a broom to sweep away any dirt and debris from the ground. If you are performing a ritual outside, you don't need to sweep the ground but removing excessive leaves or dirt will be good.

Mark the circle: If you are going to physically mark your circle, now is a good time to do this. You can take your stones, candles other materials and mark a circle around your altar or workspace.

Cleansing the circle: It is best to cleanse the circle using a symbol of the four elements. Mix some salt and some water in a chalice and sprinkle the salt water around the circumference of your circle. You do this by dipping your fingers in the water and spreading it using a flicking motion. When you're done, use a candle and incense to cleanse the circle with air and fire. As you are doing the cleansing, you may call upon the elements to protect the circle. You can do this by saying "element of air, please protect my circle and my spirit" and repeat this line with the other elements.

Call upon the deity: Now that your work area is safe and purified, you are nearly ready to call upon the deity. However, before you do so, you'll need to make sure that your own mind has been purified and cleansed. You can do this by standing in your circle and meditating. Visualize your mind opening up and letting out a white light. This white light is a symbol of purity and it's your way of telling the deity that your mind is open and ready to accept their presence. Once this is finished, you may call about the deity and begin your ritual.

Initiation and Self Dedication

It is likely that the first ritual you partake in will be your initiation. This is when your Wiccan journey will become official as you will be initiated into the faith. Your initiation process will be unique to you and does not need to follow any hard fast set of rules. Just like everything in Wicca, it is up to you to decide the way that you want to be initiated. To be clear, an initiation is performed when you'd like to join a coven or a group of witches. A self-dedication is performed if you're by yourself meaning that you will be a solitary practitioner. There isn't one that is better than the other and you can also do both.

Coven Initiation

If you are initiated as part of a coven, you will need to follow the rules that they set out for you. Before being initiated, make sure that you agree with the values and the goals of the other members. This is an extremely important first step because coven initiation is taken very seriously, just like a baptism or other important declaration of faith with other religions.

The comforting part about this is that unlike Christianity where you are baptized and initiated into the faith without your knowledge, here you have the ability to make sure that you agree with all the values, practices and deities that will be part of your faith moving forward. Initiation is viewed as a very serious and binding promise. It is almost like a marriage, something that you intend to be a part of for the rest of your life. When you find a coven and decide to be initiated, be sure that you are entering yourself into a path you'd like to follow for the long term.

Oftentimes beginners are afraid to join or reach out to covens. I know I was a little nervous about practicing with others when I first started but you shouldn't be afraid! We now have the internet, so it is very easy to find other pagans and Wiccans that are willing to accept you into their communities. One great thing about practicing with others is that you can easily learn songs and dances that are an integral part of the culture but aren't so easy to learn online, and impossible to learn from a book!

Witchcraft, traditionally was never written in books or literature and was a set of traditions that was passed on via word of mouth. This is the most earnest and traditional way to learn witchcraft practices and there is nothing like learning from those who are already proficient in the craft. I know it may seem scary at first but meeting others who believe the same things you do is going to help your faith and help you feel as though you are part of something bigger, which you are.

Self-Dedication

Unlike a coven initiation where the rules and rituals will be laid out to you by the coven itself, a self-dedication is up to you and you can choose which rituals you partake in and when you partake in them. It is recommended that you initiate yourself into the Wiccan faith after you have a very robust knowledge of the values, deities and the purpose of the faith. Because of this, it is often suggested that you do not self-dedicate until you have been studying the craft for at least a year and a day.

That being said, I know some Wiccans who self-dedicated before they were studying for a whole year and a day. Because your path is completely up to you, this is perfectly acceptable however in my experience I find that it is a lot more rewarding to dedicate yourself to the faith after you have completed a year and a day to study. This is what I did and when I initiated myself under the full moon in the presence of the Goddess, knowing full well that I was completely leaving Christianity behind and was making a very informed decision, few words can describe the feeling that came over me that night. I felt complete joy, void of any guilt or self-doubt. I knew that I would be living the rest of my life as a Wiccan.

Because I had dedicated all that time to study the faith beforehand, I knew that I was committed and serious about this decision. My life had been given a new purpose which was to live a life of humility and dedication to helping others and my environment.

Spellwork

Just like rituals are similar to going to church, spellwork is similar to praying. It is a way for you to connect with the deities and elements in a more casual manner. You can cast a spell anywhere and at any time as long as it makes sense for the spell. You can cast a spell when you're just walking down the street, in school or as part of an organized ritual or spellwork practice.

Unlike praying, spells are usually cast with a certain goal or intention in mind. We have already discussed a spell above which was "casting a circle". This spell is used for protection and we can use spells for many different purposes. We can use spells to ask for guidance, to heal ourselves, to heal others, to manifest desires, change our environment etc. We are using intense focus so that we can manipulate the energies and elements to achieve the results we desire.

Remember that spellwork takes a lot of practice and studying to get right. If you want to cast spells, it's important to learn as much as you can and make sure you are in a safe and protected environment. Don't be frustrated if your spells don't work right away, it takes a lot of practice but once you get there – it's very fun!

Science and Magick

Magick (spelled with a 'k') is different than magic. Magick is what we use to describe the result of spellcasting, rituals and manipulating energies or substances. For example, if you cast a spell asking for money and the next day you win the lottery, winning the lottery was magick. Magic (without the 'k') is used to describe what is done by magicians who pull rabbits out of hats and who perform tricks on stage. Their magic is not real and is simply used for entertainment purposes.

Unlike magic, magick has a true impact on our world. One way that science has proven that magick exists is in the form of energies. For example, gravity is an energy that holds us down to the earth - this is magick. Inertia, light, sound and other scientifically proven energies are also magick.

Science has also proven magick is real through the use of substances because we can manipulate substances in order to reach a desired result. Witches will do this using teas and herbs but science has also done this with chemistry in order to create medicine. Whenever we use a natural substance or energy and manipulate it so that it results in our desired intention, we have made magick.

How to use spells to create magick

One way to create magick is to cast spells. You can learn different spells by looking online, reading books or creating your own. I wouldn't try creating your own spell until you have practiced a few others first. The easiest spell to cast is casting a circle which you probably did or will do during your self-dedication. This spell is the easiest to cast because you are simply using the elements and asking the deities for protection - this is magick that they will gladly and easily grant you. Other spells which ask for more ambitious results won't be as easy and will take some practice before they work.

Chapter 7: Altar and Tools

As in many other religions, tools are used to enhance and aid in rituals and worship. The tools themselves have no actual power, although they do hold powerful significance symbolically.

While using tools isn't an absolute must when practicing Witchcraft, they are good to have, even if only to help you focus your concentration and will. The most basic tools a Wiccan can start with would be elemental tools. What are those, you ask? Well, these are tools that represent one of the four life elements. For example, The Wand is for Air, The Pentacle is for Earth, The Chalice is for Water, and The Athame is for Fire.

You don't need to go out and buy a lot of these tools, or spend large amounts if you do get them. Many ordinary things around your house can become implements and substituted in as tools. If you choose, you can even make the tools yourself. Many believe that making the tools by hand means they become infused with some of your own personal power, thereby making it more effective.

However, you come upon your tools you should always cleanse them of any negative energy and prior influence before using them. In order to do this, you'll want to physically clean the item and then bury it in the ground at least a few days so that any negative energy can be purified and dispersed back into the earth.

Another cleansing method is to immerse your tools in natural water, such as a river, lake or sea. Leave the item in the water for a few hours before taking the tool out and drying it off. Don't use this method if water will ruin the item. Always use common sense when cleansing your tools. Once your tools have all been cleansed, you'll want to consecrate each one so that it's ready to be used for any magickal purposes.

Below I will go over a bunch of the different tools commonly used by Wiccans, along with why they're significant. This is by no means a complete list of tools. Just some of the main ones Wiccans should be aware of.

Pentacle

This is normally made from wood, stone, or copper and comes in the form of round shaped solid disc. The disc itself will normally have an engraving of a five-point star that is upright, enclosed in a circle referred to as a Pentagram. When a disc is decorated in this particular fashion it becomes know as a Pentacle.

Many traditions will add other spirits, elements, or deities as a source of additional power. A Pentacle is usually the centerpiece of a Wiccans altar and is usually what other items are placed on in order to be charged or consecrated. This tool represents Earth, and can be used at times to summon the Goddesses and Gods.

Athame

This is a Wiccans ritual traditional dagger. Normally it is a double-edged blade made of steel with a black colored handle. Most Wiccans will engrave the blade or handle with magickal symbols of elements, spirits, or deities to give it another source of power. This item is a command tool, it's used direct the power that passes through it. The Athame is often used to cast circles, consecrate items, charge objects, and cast away negative energy.

Most Wiccans do not use their Athame as a regular knife. It is used only for magickal purposes. In most traditions this elemental tool is associated with Fire, although in some it's connected to Air.

Chalice

This often represents the Water element. It's seen as symbolizing containment and is often used to help represent the Goddess and her womb. The base of the Chalice is symbolic of our material world around us. The stem of the Chalice is representative of our connection between the spirit and man. The opening or rim of the Chalice is used to symbolize the receiving of spiritual energy.

The chalice will normally be made of material from olden times. Shells, gourds, and horns were often used for holding sacred fluids during a ritual, and then eventually silver became the preference of most Wiccans as it's associated with the Goddess and the moon. The Chalice is used during rituals to hold blessed wine and water. Traditionally, many covens pass around the Chalice to all members so they can take a sip in a show of unity.

Wand

This is considered to be one of the main magickal tools of any Wiccan. Normally the Wand is crafted from a tree that is considered sacred. Some sacred trees are Elder, Willow, Oak, Peach, Apple, Cherry and Hazel. The Wand should be about a foot in length and nowadays is often tipped with gems and crystals.

The Wand is used as an invocation tool, used to help evoke the spirits, Gods, and Goddesses. The Wand is also used when bestowing blessings, charging objects, and drawing down the moon while during a ritual. For most Wiccan traditions this tools represents the Air element, although in a few it can represent the Fire element.

Broom

This is a ritual tool most Wiccans use as it is sacred to both God and Goddess. Traditionally, this tool is made of three separate kinds of wood. Birch twigs are used for the brush, Ash is used on the handle, and Willow is used to make the cord that binds it together. Birch is used because it purifies and draws a spirit into a person's service. Ash is used because it has command over all four elements and is protective. Willow is used because it is something that is sacred in the eyes of the Goddess.

The Broom has many purposes in Wicca, but its main purpose is to protect and purify. This tool is used to cleanse areas before any magick is practiced by sweeping any astral or negative energy away. Some Wiccans would also place this item under their pillows or beds for protection. Some Wiccans hung it over their doorways so evil couldn't enter.

Censer

This tool is used for containing any burning incense used during a ritual. It doesn't matter what type of censer a Wiccan uses. For instance, I've always just used a bowl that was filled up with sand as mine. This tool represents the Air element, and will usually be placed before images of the God and Goddess on an altar.

Book of Shadows

This tool is essentially a Wiccans workbook. Within its pages, rituals, invocations, guidelines, runes, spells, rules, poems, symbols, and chants are all recorded. This Book of Shadows is normally always written by the hand of the individual who owns it. Many covens will have newer initiates copy their teacher's book exactly by hand, then adding their own material as they continued to progress. In today's society, people often use technology and computerize their Book of Shadows.

I prefer the old Tradition of having a handwritten book. I think using a loose leaf book is best. This allows you to shuffle pages around when getting ready for a ritual. However, this is just my personal preference feel free to use whatever method you want when creating your own Book of Shadows.

Cauldron

Besides the broom, this is probably the item most connected to Witchcraft. The Cauldron is a container where germination, transmutation, and transformation can occur. This tool is symbolic of the Goddesses womb, and is the manifestation of fertility and femininity. All things are born out of the Goddesses Cauldron, and eventually, all things return to it. This item is also a symbol of the Water element and is often associated with inspiration, immortality, and reincarnation.

The practical purpose of the Cauldron is for making potions, brews, and containing smaller fires that will be used with spells. This item can also be used for divination or scrying, by filling it up with water and then gazing into it.

Traditionally, this tool is made out of cast iron and sits on three legs. A Cauldron normally has an opening that is smaller than the widest part. These items can come in any size and are a cherished possession of most Wiccans.

Bolline

This is the practical knife used by Wiccans. In the past, this was used for harvesting herbs and the blade was a sickle shape. Today, this is normally just a regular knife that can be used for carving and cutting. Bolline normally has a white handle so you can easily differentiate it from the black handle of the Athame.

This knife is used during any ritual function that requires a knife be used for mundane tasks like cutting flowers, cutting cords and carving symbols into candles.

Candles

A Wiccan ceremony isn't complete with candles. Many believe the candle represent either God or the Goddess. Some use it to indicate the Fire element. Candles are used in rituals to help symbolize concepts, people, and emotions. Candles are also used heavily in spell casting, with different color candles having different uses.

Crystals

These are powerful tools as they emanate and hold healing energy. Many Wiccans use crystals in spell casting, some carry them to absorb healing energy while others place them around their homes. Crystal quartz is often considered to be the most versatile crystal. It's a powerful energy amplifier and can hold the charge of any vibration. Other crystals have more specific uses. For instance, citrine is used for abundance, rose quartz is used for love, and onyx is used for protection.

Altar

This is the main component to any Wiccans tool set. In an ideal situation, you'll have a room that is designated specifically for your altar. These can be as simple or as elaborate as you'd like to make them.

The altar serves two purposes. First, it's an ideal spot to keep your other materials and tools. Second, it's the visual focus of your ritual magick work. Depending on the traditions you follow, you may want to have your altar facing in a specific direction. Place it wherever you think it should go. You want to be able to view it easily, where you'll also be able to have access to it and any other tools you'll be using.

The left side of an altar is normally reserved for the Goddess and the right side is reserved for the God. Tools sacred to each are placed on their respective sides. This means on the left side you'll place tools like the Chalice, Pentacle, Cauldron, and Bell. On the right side, you'll place tools like the Wand, Censor, Bolline, and Athame. Also on the right side you'll normally place a gold, yellow or red candle to represent the God. On the left side, you'll put a silver, green, or white candle.

Bell

This is a tool used in rituals for banishment and invocation. This is a feminine symbol of the Goddess and her creative force. This tool is often used to indicate the start of ritual by banishing any negative energy before beginning. It is also used in rituals to invoke the Goddess, and can be sounded to call forth Elementals and Watchers.

The Bell is also used to guard homes and ward off evil spirits or spells. They are normally hung on doors or placed inside a cupboard. When hung from some type of cord, a Bell comes to symbolize the soul of humanity suspended between earth and heaven.

Sword

This is another command tool. It's not often used, but may be necessary during some spells. The size, length, and style of the Sword are all personal preferences, just be sure you're able to easily wield the Sword you choose. This is also a Fire element.

Robes

This tool is the final thing I'll go over in this tools section. Robes are important as they can often be a fundamental piece of magickal gear. Robes can be either decorated or plain, and they can be any color you desire as long as that color gives you a more magickal feel.

Many Wiccans have more than one color robe and match them to the color of the candles used in the spells their working on. The idea of the Robes is to feel more at ease. The robes don't need to be fashionable, and of course, if you don't want to wear one you can wear something that works for you.

Chapter 8: Lunar Grimoire - Spells

In Wiccan traditions, the phases of the moon are significant when it comes to casting spells. This is because Wiccans believe in the power and energy of the moon. For every phase, they perform a particular spell. They believe that certain spells work better during certain moon phases. For them, the waxing moon, the waning moon, the full moon, and the new moon all have different yet special magickal properties. This is the exact reason why they plan their spell casting accordingly.

During the waxing moon, spells for love, inspiration, friendship, freedom, happiness, and prosperity are highly recommended to be done. Positive magick or the magick that draws things to you is ideal to be performed. During this time, the moon turns from dark to full within fourteen days. So, if you want to cast a spell to bring love into your life, get you promoted at work, or make you more financially stable, you have to cast your spells when the moon is waxing.

During the waning moon, the opposite happens. The moon turns from full to dark within fourteen days. A lot of Pagan and Wiccan traditions perform baneful magick or the magick that gets rid of, destroys, or sends away things that they no longer want in their life during this time. When the moon is waning, that is the perfect time to cast spells against addictions and negative energies. It is also the ideal time to break curses and banish bad habits.

So, if you want to end a relationship, get rid of toxic people from your life, or reduce negativities such as financial debts and health issues, you should cast your spells during the waning moon. This time is also ideal for performing rites that get rid of hostile influences.

During the new moon, you can cast spells for love, romance, health, work, and new beginnings. During this phase, the moon becomes dark before it goes into the waxing phase once again after it waned for three days. However, you may find it quite difficult to see the moon during this period. It may look like a faint crescent of silver low on the sky.

Moreover, a lot of Wiccan traditions consider this period as a fallow time wherein individuals are expected to rest and rejuvenate before they begin to work on more intense magickal workings. Other traditions, however, regard this period as the best time to perform magickal workings that are related to wish fulfillment, mind and body purification, sacred space, and magick related to peace and inner harmony.

Then, there is the full moon. During this time, you are able to see the whole side of the moon. Many Pagan and Wiccan traditions perform magickal workings on the day when the moon is full, the day before it, and the day after it. In three days, they perform rituals that are focused on spiritual development and personal growth. You can use this period to cast spells for healing, intuitive awareness, wishes, predictions, and better relationship with the deities.

Casting Spells During the Waxing Moon

The waxing moon is further categorized into the following phases:

Waxing Crescent or Crescent Moon

It is also known as the Moon of Regeneration. It is when the moon is forty-five to ninety degrees ahead of the sun. During this period, it is ideal for you to make plans, gather information, lay a foundation, and start to make a change in your life. You also have to aim to gather anything that may be necessary for you to achieve your goals. Now is the perfect time for regeneration. Strengthening the body and fortifying yourself are most effective during this moon phase. At this time, your body gets better at absorbing both positive and negative energies.

First Quarter or Waxing Moon

It is also known as the Moon of Caution. It is when the moon is ninety to one hundred and thirty-five degrees ahead of the sun. It also last for seven to ten and a half days after the new moon. During the first quarter, the Time of Warrior Maiden, which is represented by Minerva, Artemis, Athena, Bridget, and Diana, is remembered and celebrated. It is the time for intuition and instinct. It is also the time for motivation, luck, friends, and courage. In addition, it is the time for renewal and regeneration.

Waxing Gibbous Moon

It is also known as the Moon of Endings. It is when the moon is one hundred and thirty-five to one hundred and eighty degrees ahead of the sun. More than half of the moon is illuminated, although not fully, by sunlight at this period. When the moon is at this phase, it is best to prepare for the energy coming from the full moon. It is also the perfect time for you to tie loose ends.

Since the waxing moon is also the perfect time to cast spells for prosperity, you must use this opportunity to cast money spells and spells that can make you more financially independent.

The following are examples of money spells that you can cast. Your money spells will be more powerful if you cast them on a Thursday while the moon is on its waxing phase.

Money Spell

Materials:

Cauldron

Silver coin

Directions:

Fill your cauldron halfway with water. Drop the silver coin inside it. Place your cauldron in a location where the moon shines through the water. Place your hand into the water and sweep it lightly on the surface to symbolically gather the silver of the moon. As you do this, you have to chant or recite your spell three times. You can write your own spell if you want it to be customized. It does not necessarily have to rhyme, but it is better if you can use words that sound alike. When you are done with the chanting, you have to pour the water into the earth.

Money Tree Spell

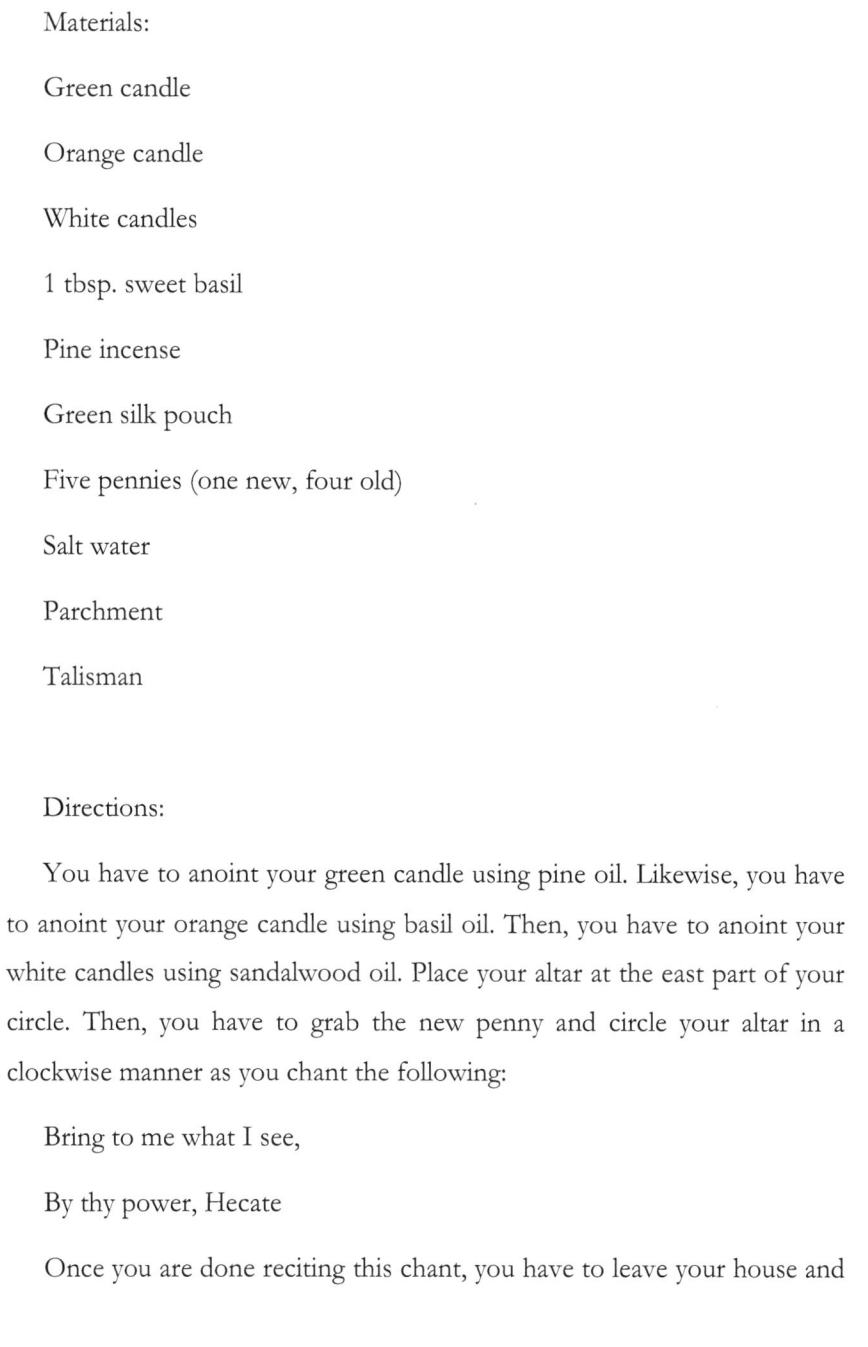

Materials:

Green candle

Orange candle

White candles

1 tbsp. sweet basil

Pine incense

Green silk pouch

Five pennies (one new, four old)

Salt water

Parchment

Talisman

Directions:

You have to anoint your green candle using pine oil. Likewise, you have to anoint your orange candle using basil oil. Then, you have to anoint your white candles using sandalwood oil. Place your altar at the east part of your circle. Then, you have to grab the new penny and circle your altar in a clockwise manner as you chant the following:

Bring to me what I see,

By thy power, Hecate

Once you are done reciting this chant, you have to leave your house and toss your new penny into the air. You also have to bury all five pennies in the spot where the new penny landed. As you do this, you have to chant the following:

I give the money, Hecate

Return to me prosperity.

I give thee five

Return by three

As I will

So mote it be.

After that, you have to go back to your altar and blow out your candles. Make sure that you repeat this ritual the following week on the same time and day. That time, however, you have to use your parchment and talisman. Light your orange candle and imagine money coming towards your altar. Dig up the coins you have previously buried and then place them on your altar. Next, you have to wash them with the salt water in the chalice and put the coins inside the pouch. When you put the coins inside, see to it that you put the old coins first. After that, you have to add in nine tiny pieces of rock salt before closing the pouch. Position yourself to the east and chant the following:

Bring to me what I see

By thy power, Hecate.

Altar power must it be

Earth and air

Fire and sea

Bring to me what I see

By thy power Hecate.

You have to wear the bag every day for seven days. Each night, you have to place it on your altar and visualize prosperity. On the seventh day, you have to place it in the east part of your home.

Money Spell Bottle

Materials:

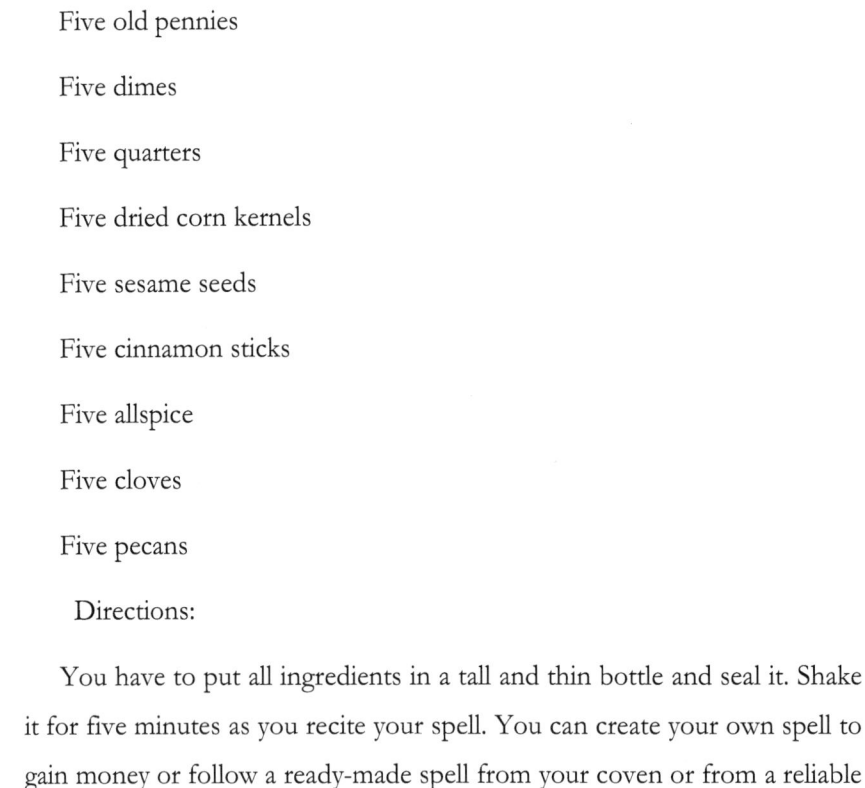

Five old pennies

Five dimes

Five quarters

Five dried corn kernels

Five sesame seeds

Five cinnamon sticks

Five allspice

Five cloves

Five pecans

Directions:

You have to put all ingredients in a tall and thin bottle and seal it. Shake it for five minutes as you recite your spell. You can create your own spell to gain money or follow a ready-made spell from your coven or from a reliable source on the Internet. Then, you have to put the bottle on a table inside your home. Whenever you are at home, you must place your wallet, checkbook, or purse near your money spell bottle.

Get a Job Spell

Materials:

Green candle

Paper clip

Banknote

Directions:

Get the candle and light it. Make sure that you hold both sides of your banknote near the flame. Then, you have to attach the banknote to a picture of you. Blow out the candle as you put your banknote and picture into your wallet or purse. Take it with you during your job interview. Good luck will then follow you and you will increase your chances of passing the interview, getting the job, and earning good money.

Shine at Your Job Interview Spell

Materials:

Yellow candle

Topaz

Directions:

This one is another spell to help you pass the interview and land your dream job. In this spell, you have to light the candle and hold the topaz near its flame as you chant the following:

Find me to be compatible in all ways.

Wear or carry the topaz during your job interview.

Love Attraction Spell

Materials:

Tea lights

Salt

Bath crystals

Lavender oil

Herbs

Rose quartz

Incense

Red pen

Parchment paper

Red candle

Cup

White-colored clothing

Directions:

You have to fill your bath with warm water and place as many tea lights as possible. Next, you have to add the bath crystals, salt, and lavender oil into your bath water. When your bath is ready, you can take a bath and clear your mind from negativity. Call upon your desired deity and ask him or her to cleanse you of all negativity. Take your time and meditate for a few minutes. Then, you have to thank the deity and finish your bath.

Next, you have to get the cup and fill it with your bath water. Get dressed and prepare yourself for the next parts of the ritual process.

Make sure that you wear white-colored clothing when you set up your altar. Put the rose quartz and herbs on it. Light the incense and write down your love wishes on the parchment paper. You have to write your wishes as if you have already received them and are thanking the gods and goddesses.

When you are done writing your love wishes, you have to anoint the red candle with the lavender oil. Place the parchment paper under the candle before you light it. Next, you have to meditate and visualize your wishes coming true. Finally, you have to put the parchment paper under your pillow and leave it there for thirty days.

Casting Spells During the Full Moon

The full moon is perhaps the best phase of the moon because high energy levels are present during this time. So, you can cast any spells, including healing spells and wishing spells more effectively. There are also Wiccans also use this time to do an Esbat ritual. During the full moon, you can celebrate with your coven and perform a ritual to hone your intuitive abilities.

The full moon is also known as the Moon of Celebration. It is when the moon is one hundred and eighty to two hundred and fifty-five degrees ahead of the sun. During this period, the moon is a representative of the Goddess as a Mother. So, if you are planning to do any major workings, you have to do them at this time since the power of the moon is at its strongest.

The following are examples of the spells that you can cast during the full moon:

Wish Spell

Materials:

Pint-size clear jar

Silver coin

Silver or white candle

Bell

Water

Directions:

You have to fill the clear jar with water and light the candle. Next, you have to drop the silver coin into the clear jar and allow the water to settle and be flat. Check out at the reflection of the moon in the water as you ring the bell three times. See to it that you speak out your wish in a loud voice. You can also ask the moon to bring you good fortune.

Healing Spell

Materials:

White candle

Directions:

This spell is very simple. You simply have to light your candle and gaze at its flame for about five minutes. Then, you have to recite your spell for healing.

Casting Spells During the New Moon

The new moon is the most ideal time to cast purifying and cleansing spells.

Then again, you have to take note that it can be quite tricky to do workings on the new moon because the moon is not that visible during this time. When the moon is at this phase, it appears as a faint silver crescent on the horizon. You barely see it on the night sky.

It becomes dark before it starts to wax again for about three days during the lunar cycle. In a lot of Wiccan traditions, the new moon is considered to be a fallow time, wherein one rejuvenates and rests prior to beginning more intense magickal workings.

In other Wiccan traditions, however, the new moon is a time to perform magick that is associated with fulfilling wishes. Some of the most recommended spells during this time include purifying and cleansing spells for the mind and body. You can also perform rituals for designating sacred space, as well as cast magick that is associated with peace and harmony.

The new moon is also known as Dark Moon and the Moon of Rest and Beginnings. It is when the moon is positioned between the sun and the earth. This causes it to appear hidden.

At this time, it is at zero to forty-five degrees ahead of the sun. It is actually the only time when the eclipse of the sun becomes visible. Also, it is most ideal to have new undertakings and new beginnings. Now is the perfect time for rest, new growth and love, giving of thanks, and regeneration. It can also be a starting point for getting rid of bad habits or starting projects.

In addition, it is an ideal time for getting engaged, putting ideas in motion, and creating long term plans for the future. While the waxing moon is the time for instinctual and spontaneous action, the new moon is the time for seeing your efforts and enjoying the fruits of your labor. Transitions may be more calmly accepted as compared to the other phases of the moon.

Tea Cleansing Spell

Materials:

Herbs

Water

Direction:

You have to put your favorite herbs in a cauldron or pot of water and then simmer for half an hour. Allow the wonderful aroma to fill your entire house. If possible, you must walk around your house carrying the cauldron or pot. This can help you spread the aroma around the house much better. You can also use the brew with a clean cloth to wipe or clean any part of your home that you want to be cleansed.

Broom Purification Spell

Materials:

Branch

Semi-precious stone or coin

Colored flowers

Directions:

Ideally, you should get a fresh branch for this spell. You can break off a branch from any tree before dawn. Make sure that you do not forget to thank the tree after breaking off one of its branches. You can leave a semi-precious stone or coin at its base as a token.

Next, you have to gather some colored flowers and tie it to the branch to make a broom. You have to sweep the floor of your home using this makeshift broom as you imagine the flowers absorbing all the negativity from the rooms in your house. When you are done, you can leave this broom at the

crossroads before the sun rises.

Self-Purification Spell

Materials:

White candle

Green candle

Black candle

Directions:

The white candle represents positive energy while the green candle represents healing. On the other hand, the black candle represents negative energy.

To cast this spell, you have to light the white candle and chant your spell for cleansing your body from negative energies. Next, you have to light the black candle and repeat the same spell. Finally, you have to light the green candle as you chant your spell of asking the elements of the earth, wind, fire, spirit, and water to help heal your body from negative energies. When you are done, you can relax yourself for fifteen minutes before you do chores or work for the rest of the day.

Casting Spells During the Waning Moon

When the moon is waning, it turns from full to dark. It becomes smaller and moves from the full moon towards the new moon. It stays on this waxing phase for about a couple of weeks. It is also during this time when the moon becomes a representation of the Goddess as a Crone.

When the moon is in its waning phase, it becomes ideal to cast spells for deep intuition and divination. A lot of Wiccans actually use this time to perform baneful magick or magick that eliminates, destroys, or sends away anything that you no longer want around.

Some of the most recommended spells during the waning moon include rituals for banishing negative habits, workings for smoothly ending a job or a relationship, magick for eliminating toxic relationships or sending away negative people, and any magick related to reducing illness, debt, and others. During the waning moon, you can also do a ritual to keep hostile people and influences away from you.

Waning Gibbous or Disseminating Moon

It is also known as the Moon of Retribution. It is when the moon is two hundred and twenty-five to two hundred and seventy degrees ahead of the sun. It is considered to be the Moon of the Earth Mothers. It is the best time for harvesting and beginning renewal. It is also the best time for reviewing endeavors and correcting mistakes, as well as settling disputes and making amends with other people. In many Wiccan traditions, the waxing moon is associated with mundane external matters while the waning moon is associated with subconscious enlightenment, which often leads to clarification of conscious values. Instinctual growth is brought about by the waxing moon while creative release is brought about by the waning moon.

Last Quarter or Waning Crescent Moon

It is also known as the Moon of Harvest. It is when the moon is at two hundred and seventy to three hundred and fifteen degrees ahead of the sun. During this period, it is ideal to release negativity by letting go of it consciously instead of simply banishing it. It is also the best time to focus on removing yourself from certain relationships, habits, and situations. See to it that you use this time to get rid of everything that causes an obstruction in your life. You also have to use this time to practice meditation, rest, recuperate, analyze yourself, and prepare for the energy of the new moon.

When the moon is waning, you can cast spells to keep negative people and forces away from you. It is ideal for banishing spells and protection spells.

Negative Energy Cleansing Spell

Material:

Lemon

Directions:

Put yourself in a meditative position, ideally sitting down. You have to hold the lemon on top of your head and imagine black smoke escaping from your body through your head. Imagine this smoke being absorbed by the lemon. You can chant or recite a spell as you do this. You can recite a spell to help your body become pure. You have to recite your spell seven times. Then, you have to burn the lemon and throw it out.

Protection Against Evil and Harm Spell

Materials:

Silver or blue wand or staff

Silver or blue glitter

Directions:

Ideally, you have to cast this spell outside of the house and amidst nature. You have to cast your circle and move around clockwise, starting from the west to the south. Then, you have tap or pound on the ground with your wand or staff as you chant the following:

I call thee, who guard the watchtowers of the (direction – West, North, East, South) to guide me through the darkness and ensure my safety.

Repeat this chant for all the four quarters. Then, you have to go to the center and chant the following:

In the shadows, evils hide

Ready to draw me from love's side

But with your help I shall be strong,

Banish all that do me wrong.

Send them away, send them astray

Never again to pass my way.

So mote it be.

Finally, you have to scatter the glitter around as you chant the final three lines. Close your circle when you are done with the ritual.

Banishing Bad Habits Spell

Materials:

White candle

Black candle

Green candle

Directions:

You have to light the white candle for purity, the black candle for banishment, and the green candle for health. Then, you have to meditate and think about getting rid of your bad habit. Finally, you have to make a firm decision to fully banish such bad habit.

Banishing and Cleansing Spell

Materials:

Athame

Water

Salt

Directions:

This spell is done to cleanse your home. You have to point the athame towards the sky and then towards the earth. Then, you have to point it horizontally as you walk in a circle and chant or recite your spell for getting rid of evil or negative elements. Finally, you have to sprinkle water and salt around the area.

Chapter 9: meditation and dreams

The purpose of learning to be a witch is to enhance your life. You can do this with magic. You can find yourself entirely engulfed in a new and more adventurous lifestyle. Enhancing your life with magic takes a lot of practice.

Magic is not something that comes easily to most people. It takes getting out of your head to achieve anything. Life enhancement is a big part of the

Wiccan culture, and that is what draws a lot of people to it. However, despite a lot of people being drawn to this religion, there are a lot of people that leave it as well, and that is because they are not willing to put in the effort when it comes to enhancing their lives. They expect just to say a few phrases and the magic happens. This is due in part to how the media portrays magic. Look at the popular television series Charmed. It shows three witches who fight evil, and all they do is use a few simple spells, and that is not reality. The same goes for most literature out there. Wiccans are portrayed as people who get together in the woods, say a few spells, wave a few herb sticks, and boom—magic. It is harder than these portrayals.

Spells take practice and require executing multiple times to master results. There are also several different parts to spells that you must master, once mastered; you get to move on to the next level and practice those spells for hours on end before you get any results. To become a powerful witch, you must put in a lot of time and be dedicated to your craft. The cost of being lazy will have you remain at the same level for ages.

You cannot expect life enhancement to make your life one of leisure. This is yet another reason people leave Wicca. They expect to be able to make their crush fall in love with them and to use magic to become rich, and that just doesn't happen—at least not right away. Those things take hard work and dedication.

People have also joined and fell off the wagon, by becoming black witches. They found out ways to make themselves rich, and force someone to fall in love with them. However, that magic comes at a price, and the price is not cheap. These people will literally sell their souls to a demon to achieve what they want. You want to stay away from these witches. If one were to die from a black witch, their soul would be tortured for all eternity. You will not be reincarnated; you will be sent straight to purgatory. Purgatory is where the spirits of people who have done evil things and used black magic go to in the afterlife. It is not where you want to end up. Your spirit will be torn to pieces every day until the end of time, and even though your body will be dead, you will still be alive to feel it because you are your spirit. Let those who join Wicca and turn to black witches' parish on their own accord.

Anyways, how do you enhance your life with magic? You connect with the earth. You connect with other people. You fill your life with things that will enrich you and bring you joy. These things are possible with magic. It may seem that magic can't do anything that you can't do yourself, and maybe there may be some truth to that. However, being in the Wiccan religion, it makes it a lot easier to do these things with magic, rather than without magic.

Here's how magic can help you enhance your life:

Making Friends - Friends are hard to come by, and even if you have a big group of friends, they may not be the best of friends to have. As humans, we are attracted to what is known as shiny people. These are usually the people that are fun to hang out with. However, these shiny people are generally not the best people to be around, as they seem only to hang around if you can do something for them. Humans are also easily drawn in by dramatic people. These people are the ones that are always loud, and always doing something that they shouldn't be doing. It is exciting, and it is fun. However, if they turn on you, it can be an unpleasant experience. These people can be toxic, and toxicity is the best way to ruin a friendship. You want to hang onto these people because you think that they bring a lot of joy to your life, but the truth is they are only dragging you down. Usually, people feel obligated at the requests of shiny people—starting to ring any bells? To spot a toxic friend all you should do is try to do something that you want to do for yourself or ask for a favor, and watch them try to drag you down or not participate.

This is where magic comes in. Magic will draw in the right type of friends so that you can make a lasting bond with them, and not have to worry about them walking out of your life because you reach a milestone in your life, and can't take them to the mall twenty times a week anymore. Instead, these friends will root for you, encourage you to be the best that you can be, and they will not bat an eye when you do something to improve your life.

Magic will help you find the love of your life and someone who will bring you soup when you are sick. You will attract the type of person who doesn't care if you are wearing your pajamas all day or wearing a $300 dress when you see them. These friends are hard to come by, and magic will fill your life with these friends. This way you can ensure that you are making friends with the right kind of people.

Help You Find True Love - True love is the hardest to find. You may fall in love several times in your life, and you may even get married, but chances are it is not everlasting love. Love is everywhere, and at times it can be easy to find. However, true love hard to find, because they are not looking for the right identifiers. They want excitement and butterflies forever, and while those are all well and good to have with your partner twenty years from now, the butterflies eventually fade, or they will not happen as frequently. When that happens, you want to be still able to wake up and kiss the person beside you good morning and feel good about it. If you don't, how will you ever love them for the rest of your life? Find someone who even when the butterflies fade, gives you a warm feeling in your heart, and makes you happy. True love is the love where you can argue all day, and then laugh and be happy for months on end. True love is waking up next to the one you love, and seeing them in their most vulnerable state, and loving them even more. This love is the love that people strive for endlessly, and it is a love that not a lot of people find. Some are tricked into thinking they found it because the butterflies last longer than usual, then they get married, and five years later, they get a divorce. This is because they just found someone that they lusted after longer than usual.

Enter magic. Magic will bring you someone who can make your heart race, and make you feel calm at the same time. It will bring you the person who will hold your hair when you are sick, and rub your feet when they are sore. It will bring you, someone, who will help with the dishes for the rest of your life. Someone who gets up with you at two in the morning to bake cookies when you can't sleep.

You want someone who is encouraging the Wiccan religion so that you can be yourself around them. Once you let go and let fate show you who you should truly be with, these spells will help take your relationships, and make them strong, and at the same time help you form a bond with someone to create an unbreakable relationship. Letting fate take over is the hardest part. You want to find someone who you like, but most people do not trust fate to make that choice because they already have someone in mind to be their forever love. They do not want to relinquish that control for fear of something going away. Are you going to fall in love with someone who is truly the one for you, or are you going to spend the rest of your life fighting with the person you married, and using countless spells to try to fix your relationship? The choice is for you alone, but with a little patience, and a little time, you will find the person that you have truly been waiting for.

Courage - If you are a person who is not particularly courageous in any aspect of life, do not fret. You are not alone. The average person has at least one area in their life where they lack in the courage department. This can range from being talking to strangers, or trying to make it up in the business ladder. There are many parts of life that require courage; it is impossible to be courageous enough for all of them on your own. For instance, you may be able to go skydiving, but the thought of talking to that gorgeous person who has caught your eye completely terrifies you. And that is okay because you can't be courageous at everything. Or maybe you are great at talking to people, and doing public speaking, but you are terrified to ride an elevator. There are different fears out there, and you cannot conquer your fears without courage. A lot of people overlook magic and how it can boost your courage levels up. Courage is important, and spells can make you a little stronger. As a witch, it is one of the most important things you can have because you are going to have to stand up to people. Whether it be to save an old tree from a company that wants to tear it down, or stopping a black witch from ruining someone's life, lots of acts require courage.

Magic can help, and it can bring you so much more than a little bit of courage. Magic can make you feel like you can take on the world. You will feel like you can do anything, and that is what you want. Just remember that the effects are not permanent, and you may have to reapply the spell a couple of times. Magic gives you the courage until you find it on your own, after a few times of realizing how great it feels to stand up to something that terrifies you, you will not need the spell anymore because you will be able to be courageous on you own.

Luck - Luck is hard to come by, and lots of people need it. You need luck when you are playing the lottery, and you need luck when you ask the love of your life to marry you, and that is something that not a lot of people think of either. Just like courage, luck is something that you need to get by in life. It is not always hard work that you should rely on because sometimes, hard work can only get you so far. Such as in a big law firm, where you and the partner's pet are vying for a promotion. You may do the harder jobs, and work the hardest, but they have the advantage of you because they are a favorite. In this case, a little luck may help. Luck can ensure that they are paying attention to your hard work, rather than having a clear winner picked out before the race even begins.

You can use a few simple spells to make talismans and good luck charms, as well as just cover yourself in an aura of good luck with some spells; these spells are generally not difficult. However, the more luck you desire, the stronger the witch you would have to be, because, the stronger the witch, the more powerful the spell. You also have to "reapply" less when you are more powerful. Even more, a reason to practice, right? Everyone wants to be lucky, so make sure to work on becoming the best witch that you can be.

A real-life scenario would be a job interview. You want to use these spells without abandon, because the more luck you have, the better off you will be in an interview, and you will hopefully land the job with ease. Don't get too cocky, even though you may apply and interview, if you are not a good fit, you may not get the job no matter how much magic you use.

Recall there is a major difference between confidence and being cocky. Confidence is knowing you can do the job. Being cocky is thinking that without any training you can do it better than everyone else. Cocky thinks that you are a shoe-in for a job you have never had any experience with. Confidence is knowing that you are a strong and quick learner and will be good at the job without any training. You want to be confident, yet humble. Know that you are not the perfect person for the job, but also know that you are the best candidate.

Clarity of Mind - Have you ever had a question that is burning in your mind or a decision that you had to make that was really hard? Did it take you longer than you care to admit to achieve what you wanted with these scenarios? That happens to everyone at some point in their life, and it is entirely normal. You want to have a clear mind, and it is harder to achieve than you would think. And, even if you clear your mind, a lot of times it is still hard to find a clear answer. You search and search, but there are pros and cons to everything. This makes it hard to find yourself the time to do what you want to do when you want to do it because you are still agonizing over making the decision or trying to figure everything out—decisions can be messy.

If you are having trouble figuring out where to go in life, you can use a spell to help you figure things out. There are many spells that help you open your mind to make the right decision, and a lot of it has to do with Divination. Yes, prophesying helps you make the right choices because you will be able to get an idea of what will be the outcome of your choice. There are spells out there to clear your mind, and there are spells to get the answers that you desire. These spells are the ones that you want to use to find your way in life and really make the right choices. Perhaps you are wondering if your spouse is cheating, and you do not know if you should pursue the matter. Do a spell and get the answers you are looking for. Don't feel guilty if they are not cheating. You are not going through their personal effects, rather doing your research before confronting them and that is what a rational person does.

Banishing Evil - Let's face it, a lot of times, we are surrounded by evil. This world is a demonic playground, no doubt about it. In these times, it becomes harder to find a pure environment, and a lot of times those who are good are under attack from the world. Have you ever felt like the entire world was against you, and even though the evil people seem to be living good lives, you are miserable? That is what a lot of people deal with when they try to lead decent lives because it seems that life does not want good in it and rewards evil. There are ways to keep yourself pure and keep your environment pure as well. Have a good place to do your magic. You want your mind to be pure and clean from attacks of other, evil witches as well.

There are several spells out there for purifying not only the area but your mind as well. One of the most common spell types for purification is known as smudging.

If you are regularly practicing, you should probably smudge your area before each spell, but if you are not practicing often, once a week or biweekly should suffice. Just make sure that you purify it before you do a spell. The purer you keep it, the more effect your spells will have on your life and evil forces will not be able to counteract your spells. There are several other spells that you can use to make sure that you are keeping your mind and environment pure from the evil that lurks around. Candles are essential to this (white candles especially). They give you pure energy in which to perform your spells. White candles act as a channel directly to the Goddess herself to help you keep other entities from answering your calls. Although most spells do not call for white candles, it is best to light one whenever you do a spell.

Healing - As you a Wicca beginner, you can relieve side effects and many other issues that dwell under and on top of the surface of one's skin. Mental illnesses are something that you can help with. While you cannot cure these diseases, you can help alleviate the symptoms of things such as depression and anxiety. You can also help someone who has PTSD sleep better at night. Magic when used to help people, including yourself, is wonderful. It also does not take a lot of magical strength to help alleviate the symptoms of illnesses, unlike with pain and suffering from a major physical injury.

Prosperity - Have you ever been unemployed and found yourself searching high and low for any source of income just to keep the lights on? It isn't fun, and nowadays it is getting harder to find jobs that are enough to pay the bills and keep food on the table. That is the downside of the world we live in. Jobs are becoming electronic and outsourced. And unfortunately, unless you live in a commune, you must have money to survive.

There are a lot of spells to help you have the upper hand with prosperity. It is a good idea to find a plethora of them to douse yourself with luck and prosperity if you are ever in need of it. The same goes with healing spells.

Chapter 10: TABLES OF CORRESPONDENCE

If the Sun is the outline of your self-portrait, the Moon is the color pallet. The Moon is arguably as important as the Sun within your birth chart. The moon sign describes how you feel emotions and how you express them to other people. The moon sign covers parts of you that you don't even realize are happening, little habits you do on a day-to-day basis. The moon sign shows your most basic needs for affection, and how you feel the most loved. Because of the Moon's connection with femininity and fertility, it also predicts an individual's relationship with the women in their life. This is different from the romantic relationship shown in Venus and is more likely to interactions with mothers.

Mercury

Mercury controls our intelligent side. It predicts our rationality or lack thereof. It gives us our skills in speaking, writing, or memory. Mercury often greatly affects how we learn or take in information. The knowledge of a child's sign in Mercury is very helpful in understanding how they are doing in school and how they could be helped.

Venus

Venus shows us how we love and feel the love of others. People often find that they may act very different in romantic relationships than in normal relationships. The planet Venus is a powerful planet due to the power we as a society give to romance and love. Not only does this planet affect your love life, but it also affects how you appreciate beauty. Your tastes in art and beauty can often be traced to your sign in Venus. This planet is also known for its hand in pleasure. As a result, this planet can be connected to what you like to do for fun. Due to the feminine strength of this planet, it also predicts what an individual would consider the "perfect woman". Within a woman's chart, this is often the type of woman they wish they were or strive to be, whereas, in a man's chart, this is the type of woman they are most attracted to.

Mars

Mars is most in control of physical action. Where Venus often has a hand in the spirit of a person, Mars is more attached to the actions of that person. Mars often predicts your sex drive and tendency to lust over love. Mars is the passion behind sex, the anger before a fight, and the energy before a race. Mars is the commitment to action before it happens. These are all very extreme examples, but Mars is an extreme planet. If you've ever made a rash decision that was out of your normal process, Mars may be to blame.

Jupiter

Jupiter is often considered in Astrology to be a sign of luck and optimism. Within your life, the strength of Jupiter in your chart can predict the luck or lack thereof you will experience in your lifetime. We as people experience luck in different aspects of our life – one who is gifted in wealth might not be gifted in beauty or vice-versa. So, while Jupiter is a sign of luck depending upon the constellation, it may be lucky to you in different ways. This planet also governs our philosophical views on the world and how we feel about deeper, less practical knowledge. This planet also predicts where you might devote much of your time in your life. That is, it expresses what sort of things you hold with higher importance than others.

Saturn

Not all of the planets promote good qualities of their sign. Saturn traditionally is considered the "evil" planet. While this isn't necessarily true, it is easy to see why people may believe this. Saturn is in charge of maintaining balance within the Zodiac. This can sometimes be translated into being "evil" because Saturn often has to deny the excess of the other planets. It is this denial that leads people to identify Saturn as evil because it can be interpreted as the destruction of dreams. This is, of course, a surface-level belief – if you look deeper, you can find that Saturn is the cause of motivation of the human spirit. The struggles and difficulties that Saturn can cause in a person's life are really seeds of motivation to spur an individual towards accomplishment and completion. Tough love is a better descriptor of Saturn's ruling than evil.

Conclusion

You have reached the end of this book, Wicca Moon Magic. We hope this book has giving you the opportunity to begin your studies in the magic and enlightenment of Wicca Moon Magic and we look forward to hearing from you if you enjoyed your time reading it. This book is just the beginning of what all you can discover out there in the world and what the religion of Wicca is all about. We encourage you to reach out to other Wiccans in your area to get their tips and insights into how to be a Wiccan and where you should start in your journey.

The next step is to continue your work. There truly is no end to the power and experience that can be accumulated on the Wiccan path. As you continue your journey, keep this book nearby for reference and inspiration. Whether you are working with a coven or working alone, the knowledge in this book is invaluable, even to someone who is adept in the magical religion of Wicca.

Let the Wiccan Rede be your guide in life. This does not have to be just your guide in Wiccan magic but also in life. Ensure that you do no harm to others, in your words and actions. Endeavor to live in harmony with nature by ensuring that you do not tip the ecological balance. Care for the Earth and other living beings is part of living harmoniously with nature.

As it has been repeatedly mentioned in the book, a whole lot of Wiccans choose to keep their path a secret. As you must have read, there was a witch hunt in history - something that led to a lot of Wiccans shying away from sharing their knowledge and wisdom. It is therefore very understandable if you choose to practice without particularly announcing your beliefs. Today, there are a lot of negative implications that surround Wicca and the name

"Witch." Since the myths and misconceptions have been debunked in this book, it would be great if you to share this book with anyone interested in understanding Wicca especially if they still have questions. As previously mentioned in the introduction part of this book, everything in this book is only an invitation that you may choose to deny or accept.

While we cannot guarantee a certain outcome, magic can increase our chances of attaining this desired goal. If you find that working alone is not yielding the desired goals, then find a coven or group to join. The quicker you find what works best for you, the quicker you will be on your way on the Wiccan path.

Magical practices aim to engage the earthly senses on an intimate level to allow our conscious mind to utilize a sort of 'sixth sense.' This sixth sense then, in turn, allows us to engage with other realms and beings that aren't readily seen with only five senses. These beings and realms were the homes and dwellings of our ancestors as they saw no difference between conscious experience and the experiences of dream realms and astral planes.

These practices are key to unlocking the secrets of humanity and ushering in the rebuilding of our spiritual evolution. Without magic, there is no progression for humanity's mind, Technology and science alone cannot push us beyond the heavens.

As you progress on your journey, keep in mind the Wiccan philosophy that as long as you are not harming anyone then do what you like. This is reminiscent of Crowley's 'do what thou wilt', this has become an umbrella philosophy more almost every magical community. A real magician will not be concerned with petty arguments over lineage or purity of practice, they will not segregate or discriminate, no, and they are beyond the earthly confines of prejudice.

Magicians also will not intentionally harm others if they are innocent, there is no need for violence or forceful magic to get your way. Be creative and always walk a righteous path that is full of love, discipline and understanding. These are the true virtues of magic and the essence of truth.

Finally, if you found this book useful in any way, a review on Amazon is always appreciated!

WICCA

Wicca Crystal Magic

The Ultimate Guide to Crystal Spells, Wiccan Crystal Healing and Rituals. A Book of Shadows for Wiccans, Witches, Pagans, Witchcraft practitioners and beginners.

ESTHER ARIN SPELLS

INTRODUCTION

Congratulations on downloading *Wicca Crystal Magic* and thank you for doing so. You have taken the important first step in discovering the art of Wicca Crystal Magic and what it takes for you to become a Wiccan yourself.

Crystals in the new age and Wiccan circles are used to mean an array of solid minerals. A substance that is inorganic in nature and formed when the geological processes take place underground is called a mineral. Every mineral has its own composition and energy that makes it unique. Every Shaman, Witch, and healer knows the energies that are present in different mineral stones.

The regular molecular structure that is formed by a mineral stone that creates a surface that is flat informs what we know to be crystals. The popular crystal is the clear quartz. True "crystal balls" are said to be formed by clear quartz. Other popular crystals are the amethyst and rose quartz. Interestingly, known stones such as the lapis lazuli, bloodstone, and jade are formed by the combination of several stones and are not regarded as true crystals. Amber and jet, which are also considered to be "crystals", are apparently organic substances that have been fossilized. It is for these reasons that to enjoy the gifts of the earth stones and crystals have been used in the place of each other.

This guide provides an overview of how the powerful energies of crystals can be harnessed on the vibrational level to create the changes you seek. You'll then be introduced to the most widely used crystals in contemporary magic, including their primary magical properties and tips on how to select and care for them.

The practical magic section in this volume includes simple spells that build on what you've learned about candle magic, along with new workings like crystal elixirs and talismans. And you'll quickly learn something else about crystals: once you've invested in a few of your own, you'll have tools you can use in spellwork again and again!

CHAPTER 1: History of Crystals and Stones

The magical power of stone has been recognized by people all over the world from as far back as 11,000 years ago, when the oldest known stone temple was built at Göbekli Tepe in Turkey.

The famous sites of Stonehenge, Newgrange, and other monuments in Europe and beyond are further testaments to our long history of relationship with this most fundamental building block provided by the Earth.

Stone's ability to shelter our early ancestors surely had something to do with the importance it held in the spiritual lives of the communities who built these mysterious structures. To this day, cairns—or piles of stones—are still used as landmarks on trails and coastlines, as well as memorials to the deceased and tributes to the unseen spirits of the natural world. Then there is the widespread tradition of making, carrying, and/or giving away "wishing stones," which are small enough to be carried in pockets and often have words like "love," "peace," and "luck" carved into them.

But there are certain treasures sourced from the Earth that hold particular power for contemporary spiritual seekers, including Wiccans and other Pagans.

Generally found inside larger masses of rock under the Earth's surface, crystals and other mineral stones are used in magic for everything from protection to divination to manifesting wealth and love.

This magical relationship with crystals and other stones also has a long history.

Quartz crystals were used as talismans by ancient Egyptians, Greeks, and Romans alike. Aboriginal people in the American Southwest have revered the powers of turquoise since the time of the Aztecs. Indeed, throughout time, in any culture where minerals and crystals were accessible, they were incorporated into the daily lives of those who knew to recognize their powers.

Those powers include healing, which is what crystals are best known for in the wider contemporary "New Age" culture.

Alternative healing modalities incorporate crystals and other stones in a variety of ways. One major use for crystals is Chakra balancing, acupuncture, color therapy, and other energy healing techniques incorporate crystals into their work.

Crystals work on the physical, emotional, and spiritual planes to effect positive change, rather than conventional medicine with its focus on the physical plane alone, so they are considered to be more holistic in their transformative effects than, say, an aspirin taken for a headache.

There is a wide variety of information available about the healing powers of crystals, for physical and spiritual imbalances of all kinds.

Because healing—physical, emotional, and spiritual—is often a goal of magic, there is quite a bit of overlap between what alternative healers know about crystals and stones, and what Witches know. Furthermore, it might be argued that crystals and stones are more suited for healing magic than non-natural objects, such as candles (though magic for healing can certainly involve candles or any other object).

Because of this overlap, the word "healing" will show up often in this guide, and much of the information about the magical uses of specific crystals will include their use in healing. However, this information is in no way intended to replace that which a trained practitioner in the alternative healing modalities would provide, and should not be used in place of needed medical treatment of any kind.

The focus of this guide is on the use of crystals and stones in magic, and will therefore pay more attention to the emotional and spiritual elements of their unique and special powers.

Of course, in Wiccan tradition, the use of crystals goes well beyond healing.

Indeed, they are often involved in many facets of spiritual and magical practice. One common use for crystals and stones is to mark the sacred circle before ritual begins—whether the ritual is performed by a solitary Witch or a coven. They are also used to honor deities, with specific stones sacred to particular gods and goddesses. In keeping with centuries of tradition, they are still used in amulets, talismans, and other "good luck" charms, as well as for scrying and protection.

Some magical tools, such as wands and pentacles, are decorated with crystals, and they can also be used to improve the energy of any indoor or outdoor space.

Finally, crystals and stones can be powerful components of spellwork, which is the focus of this guide. Before getting into any further detail, however, it's helpful to take a brief look at the terminology associated with crystals and other stones in order to get a better understanding of the physical makeup of these mysterious gifts from the Earth.

Crystal, Stone, or Rock? What's the Difference?

Many sources, including this guide, will use the terms "crystal" and "stone" interchangeably.

This is because the technical differences between the two, in terms of their physical makeup, isn't really significant when it comes to magic.

Actually, in many cases the more appropriate term is "mineral," as opposed to "crystal," since not every stone associated with healing and magic has the kind of orderly molecular structure that characterizes a "true" crystal.

To make things even more complicated, there are a few substances, such as amber, that don't qualify as either mineral or crystal but are considered to be powerful "stones" nonetheless.

Although it's not strictly necessary to understand the physical properties of these different substances from a scientific perspective, it can be helpful to know a little bit about why there are different terms, and what makes crystals and other stones more potentially useful in magic than other, more "ordinary" pieces of the Earth.

Minerals are defined as any inorganic substance that is formed naturally in the Earth's underground geological processes, through the interaction of heat, pressure, and fluid. Every mineral occurs in a solid-state at normal Earth temperatures and has a specific chemical composition. Gold, silver and copper are perhaps the most commonly recognized minerals. Minerals occur in a very wide variety of shapes and colors, and may be found as a single specimen, or in a mixture with other minerals. Almost all of the stones involved in magic and healing are composed of single minerals. Some of the most popular are hematite, malachite, and turquoise.

Many minerals have a specific molecular structure that forms a regular pattern, creating the flat surfaces and interesting geometric forms we tend to think of when we hear the word "crystal." Probably the most common type of crystal that people are familiar with is clear quartz, which is what true "crystal balls" are made from, and is used in watches, clocks, and many other electronic devices. Other forms of quartz—especially rose quartz and amethyst, are commonly available and useful for a wide variety of magical and healing purposes.

Any given solid piece of the Earth containing more than one single mineral is called a stone, or, alternatively, a rock. These two terms are essentially interchangeable, although "rock" tends to bring to mind more drab, less interesting objects than the word "stone." Rocks may be made of two or more minerals as well as organic substances, and they don't have a consistent chemical composition. Chunks of single minerals may be found in rocks, though it's more common to find microscopic grains of minerals instead.

Some of the substances used in magic and healing are technically stones—such as lapis lazuli, which is a mixture of lazurite and diopside. This may be one reason for the interchangeability of "stones" and "crystals" among magical practitioners. You won't find too many people, however, who will lump crystals in with "rocks," as the connotations just aren't the same.

As mentioned above, there are further exceptions to the "rules" of categorization when it comes to some stones.

Amber is actually fossilized resin from ancient trees, and jet comes from fossilized decaying wood. Then there's a geode, which is a cavity in a spherical rock that is lined with crystals or other minerals. The most commonly available geodes tend to be lined with amethyst quartz.

Finally, some sources will use the term "gemstones" to refer to both crystals and other minerals. This term is not rooted in science or magic, but is instead a category of particularly attractive and often rare minerals used in jewelry. Some minerals used in healing and magic, such as garnet and fluorite, are also considered gemstones. The more expensive gemstones, like diamond and emerald, are less commonly used in magic due to their cost.

Those interested in learning more about crystals and other stones, from both geological and physical healing disciplines, will find plenty of information available in print and online, but this knowledge isn't required for those seeking to draw on the magical properties of crystals and other stones.

As with any other form of magic, intuition and intention are the driving factors for transforming your reality through the use of crystals.

However, it is helpful to know their basic magical associations and emotional and spiritual healing properties, as well as whether they are projective or receptive—key qualities that determine their most effective uses in healing and magic.

These aspects of crystals and stones will be covered below, but first let's take a look at how these natural wonders make excellent tools of magic.

How Does Crystal Magic Work?

Crystal magic, like any other form of magic, is essentially the art of directing a specific intention into the Universe at the spiritual level in order to effect change on the material plane.

While crystal spellwork may make use of other tools, such as candles, herbs, charms, chants, etc., the main "ingredient" of this kind of magic will be one or more crystals or other mineral stones.

Crystals are a unique magical tool in that they occur in nature and are not made by human hands like candles, cauldrons, athames and wands.

They can be polished and carved into beautiful shapes, but are just as effective when left "raw" in their original state.

Although crystals and stones are made of inorganic matter, many healers who work with them believe them to be "alive," capable of communicating their ancient wisdom with us if we are open and receptive to their messages.

Even scientists speak of the process of crystal formation as "growing," since crystals start out small and then increase in size as new atoms are added to their structures under the Earth's surface.

The shape, size, and color of a given crystal's formation will depend on the temperature, location, and presence of other minerals, as part of an ancient and ongoing dynamic process of creation. If you've ever held a crystal and looked at it closely from several angles, turning it over and over in your hand, you've most likely felt the mysterious sense of wonder they evoke. They seem to speak silently of the infinite, creative, living power of the Earth.

Wiccans and other Witches understand that the power of crystals and stones is also in essence the same power inherent in other natural phenomena, such as the wind or a flowing river. All matter, visible and invisible, is essentially energy, and all energy is interconnected.

This core concept is found in both metaphysics and quantum physics, and while the exact ways in which energy communicates and ultimately transforms reality remain a mystery, we can use the power of our intentions in conjunction with the power of crystals to harness this interconnectedness of the Universe, both on the material and the spiritual plane.

Certain crystals, such as quartz and tourmaline, actually exhibit one aspect of their power through what scientists call the piezoelectric effect. When mechanical pressure is applied to these stones, such as through squeezing them or tapping them with a hammer, the stones give off an observable electric charge. It's this piezoelectricity that helps a quartz watch keep time.

Quartz and certain other crystals also exhibit pyroelectricity, meaning that they release an electric charge when exposed to a change in temperature.

Some healers who use crystals theorize that the stones' healing abilities stem from their piezoelectric and pyroelectric qualities, but in reality, only a few of the crystals most often used in healing and magic are known to exhibit these effects.

Nonetheless, every crystal emits its own subtle energy that then interacts with the energy fields of everything around it. Therefore, every crystal responds to the energy flowing through the human body, and when used appropriately helps to balance that flow and restore it to optimal conditions for good health.

Another way to view this concept of energy is through the Hermetic principle of the Law of Vibration, which states that all matter is in constant motion, even though most of it appears to be perfectly still.

At the subatomic level, everything is moving and therefore interacting with everything else. The rate, or frequency, at which any particular piece of matter is vibrating will determine how we perceive it with our senses, as well as how its energy interacts with ours.

Each crystal vibrates at its own precise frequency, which is determined by its physical makeup, and will affect other matter, such as the human body, in a particular way through these vibrations. The frequency of a particular crystal will also resonate with the frequencies of a particular condition or situation in life that we wish to change or manifest. For example, rose quartz resonates with the frequencies of friendship and love, and is therefore used in spellwork for these aims.

Colors are also vibrations of light, and resonate with different aspects of our existence (such as love, health, and money matters) according to their specific vibrations. The color of a stone will therefore often have a correspondence with particular magical aims.

Pink, the color of rose quartz, is a color with a harmonizing, loving vibration. The color and the physical makeup of this kind of quartz combine to make it a powerful force for drawing love into your life. Likewise, the color green has a vibrational resonance with abundance. Therefore, some green stones, such as bloodstone, are particularly good for spellwork involving matters of prosperity.

However, traditional color associations such as those used in candle magic are not always a key factor in crystal-centered magic. For example, citrine and pyrite, both primarily yellow in color, are highly associated with prosperity and wealth.

Finally, one more way to view the basic makeup of all matter in the Universe is as information, or consciousness.

The Hermetic principle of the Law of Mentalism states that at the basic level, everything is mental, that all of creation stems from the Universal Mind. Since thought is energy, the power of thought can shape our reality. It has been established that positive thoughts raise the frequency of one's energetic vibration, while negative thoughts lower it.

We can harness this power of thought and use it to send our intentions out into the universe through the energy field of the crystals we choose to work with. In this way, crystals and stones are conduits of energy. They can both bring healing energy to us, and send our positive energy to the spiritual realm to manifest real change in our lives.

Understanding what crystals are and why they make such great magical tools is the first step toward learning how to use them to manifest positive change in your life.

If you're reading this guide, you may already have one or more crystals in your possession, or you may just be simply feeling drawn to learn more about them.

In order to work crystal magic, you'll need at least one, though a good handful of a few different types is ideal.

In the next section, you'll find tips on choosing and caring for your crystals, as well as exercises and ideas for building a relationship with them for effective use in magic. We'll also take a closer look at 13 common crystals and stones and their magical uses. If you're undecided as to what kind of crystal to begin with, this information can help you narrow down your choices.

Chapter 2: Use of Crystals in Various Ancient Cultures

There is no one way in which to use crystals and minerals to the best effect. It is down to the severity of the illness and the personal judgment of whoever is guiding or using the stones. Each natural substance has a variety of uses which can affect the mental, emotional, physical and spiritual elements that make up a human being.

Stones can be placed close to or onto the body, using chakra points or simply placing them close to your skin; they may be placed around you or used as a tool of focus and guidance when meditating. The proximity of the crystal or mineral to the skin directly affects the concentration of the energy so if only subtle healing is required then it is entirely possible for someone to benefit from the stones without even realizing it is happening.

Before you begin to use a healing stone you should consider all the options and decide personally which type of healing is required and how it will be obtained based solely on the condition(s) being treated at that time.

Some highly effective techniques are listed below with full instructions following of any practices involved with the treatment:

1. Jewelry
2. Body Contact
3. Sleep & Environment
4. Bathing with Crystals

5. Meditating

6. Chakra Healing

Jewelry

Jewelry is an excellent way to ensure a stone is kept in close contact with the person who requires treatment. Whether it is in the form of a bracelet, necklace, earrings or a ring, the closer the stone to the skin, the more effective it will be. This technique is best suited to long term, ongoing treatment but it is important to ensure that the stone is cleansed regularly.

To gain a higher level of benefit, if the jewelry is situated close to or on a chakra point which corresponds to the affected area, (see following chapter for information on chakra points), then the energies will be directed to the desired area in a much stronger way, gaining a better result. Additionally, any area's which correspond with the stone itself, and that is not governed by that particular chakra, will still be stimulated and healed.

If you make your own jewelry then let your inner spirit choose the stone for you where possible. This is easier if you have a selection of the same stones. While every one of the stones will be helpful in your healing, if your sub-conscious, (spirit), chooses it then the healing benefits will be increased.

Body contact

Jewelry is not the only way a stone can be carried with you. Even something as simple as placing a stone in your jacket pocket will promote healing energy. You could choose to carry a small bag of stones, place one in your purse/wallet or a pocket or even attach them to clothing or your mobile phone. The closer it is to you, the stronger the impact but so long as it is close by you then you will reap the rewards of its energy.

Sleep & Environment

Placing crystals or minerals around your home will provide a constant, subtle healing energy. It will not be as effective as skin contact but even a crystal in the same room as you will provide a therapeutic benefit.

Consider where you are placing your stone and what you wish to achieve, for example, if you struggle to sleep at night, place stones with sleep-inducing or anxiety-relieving properties on your nightstand or beneath your pillow. If you struggle will concentration and or motivation, place one on your desk or close to you at your place of work. Symptoms of depression can also be relieved by keeping relevant crystals around your home.

Bathing

This may seem like a strange way to use crystal healing but try adding non-porous stones to your bath water or around your bathroom when you bathe.

Crystals and minerals are spiritually and emotionally cleansing, and when bathing we are generally in a relaxed state so a crystal bath can be highly effective. If placed into your bath water the healing energies and absorbed into the water giving an extra boost to their natural properties.

Meditating

Many crystals and mineral have naturally relaxing and calming properties in addition to the active healing energy they contain so using a stone while meditating can aid healing. As meditation involves opening up and connecting with your spirit, this boosts the effectiveness of the stones because your energy channels are already open and flowing well.

Holding or focusing on a stone during meditation will allow you to better guide the energy of the stone and, if you wish to take it one step further, you can use the meditation as an opportunity to charge the crystal with your own energy, strengthening the link and strengthening the focus of healing. If you later carry this stone with you then the effects on your ailments will increase in intensity, helping you to heal faster.

Chakra Healing

Now that you understand the way crystals work and how you can use them, you can begin selecting your crystals according to your specific needs. Below, we'll review the seven chakras and the crystals that correspond with each.

Crystals for Balancing Chakras

The crown/seventh chakra

The colors that correspond with this chakra are violet and golden-white, so it makes sense that the crystals used to balance the crown chakra are amethyst, Oregon Opal, and clear quartz. Some individuals also choose to use white calcite and white topaz near the seventh chakra. Diamond and sapphire are also popular choices for regulating the crown chakra's frequency.

The third eye/sixth chakra

Indigo is the third eye chakra's representative hue, so the crystals lapis lazuli, sugilite, and azurite all have beneficial powers when it comes to achieving harmony here. Sodalite and blue fluorite are other popular choices for regulating the sixth chakra.

The throat/fifth chakra

Recognized for its lighter blue corresponding color, the throat chakra has corresponding crystals which include sapphire, Angelite, blue lace agate, and aquamarine. Blue turquoise, calcite, and kyanite are other common crystals that work to balance the fifth chakra.

The heart/fourth chakra

Deeply associated with love, the heart chakra has a wide variety of corresponding crystals. Rose quartz is among the most popular, while watermelon tourmaline, aventurine, and moonstone are other known matches. In addition, many green-hued crystals, including emerald, green calcite, jade, and green tourmaline, are beneficial for this chakra.

The solar plexus/third chakra

This chakra, which is associated with the color yellow, has corresponding crystals that include citrine, yellow jasper, amber, topaz, yellow sapphire, and golden calcite.

The sacral/second chakra

The most common corresponding crystals for this chakra are red jasper, red garnet, ruby, carnelian, and red and brown aventurine.

The root/first chakra

Known for its deep, red hue, the first chakra benefits from bloodstone, red zincite, tiger's eye, as well as obsidian, onyx, and hematite. Smoky quartz is another matching crystal for this chakra.

Crystals for Multiple Chakras

In addition to the crystals listed above, which correspond with one particular chakra, there are additional gems that serve other specific purposes, which we'll discuss below.

Aligning the chakras

There are certain gems that work well specifically for aligning or opening the chakras. In particular, you should choose to use chrysoprase, pink kunzite, and kyanite.

Cleansing the chakras

Moonstone and celestite effectively detoxify all of the chakras. Green fluorite also has renewal properties that benefit each chakra.

Stimulating chakra energy

Use clear or white calcite to rev your chakras' energy levels, especially near the crown. Malachite is a great stimulate that has the greatest impact on the heart and throat chakras.

Turquoise can also elevate the vibrancies of all chakras.

Opening the chakras

Quartz crystal is an extremely popular choice for opening all of the chakras, especially for beginners. In fact, many crystal users keep quartz readily available to them at all times, and rely heavily on the wondrous benefits that this crystal offers.

Crystals that Target Specific Ailments and Issues

While using crystals to regulate specific chakras will benefit any ailments corresponding to those areas, you may still want to incorporate certain gemstones to heal recurring issues. If you experience any of the health troubles listed below, consider using the corresponding crystal to alleviate the problem. Keep in mind that you should still place the stone near the corresponding chakra from which the problem originates, and that not all crystals work the same for everyone.

Recurring headaches

The stones that work best to heal chronic headaches and migraines are amethyst, turquoise, amber, and lapis lazuli. Headaches can also be a result of an imbalance between the solar plexus and head energies, so if you notice a mild upset stomach accompanying your headaches, consider using moonstone or citrine to resolve the issue.

Sleeplessness

Oftentimes, inability to sleep is a result of another issue. For example, if you are unable to sleep because of constant worrying or stress, you might want to consider using rose quartz, citrine, or amethyst to help promote restfulness. If, however, you're experiencing nightmares, you may want to employ protective stones such as smoky quartz and tourmaline. In addition to using these during your healing practice, you may also want to place them at the foot of your bed while you sleep. Labradorite can also promote sound sleep, since it aids in protecting against unpleasant thoughts or feelings.

Depleted energy

Most crystals with yellow, orange, and red hues will increase energy levels. The most powerful of these are deep red garnet and golden amber or topaz. If you're looking for motivation that you can apply to your everyday life for practical purposes, consider using crystals with deeper hues, such as tiger's eye and jasper. You can also boost your entire chakra system by holding a clear quartz crystal in each hand and pointing them upwards, while simultaneously keeping a citrine crystal on your solar plexus.

Lack of concentration

Using quartz crystals is perhaps one of the best ways to achieve mental clarity. You can also use amber and citrine to stimulate your memory, while lapis lazuli can amplify thoughts. Amethyst also promotes clarity, and can help you to become cognizant of your own specific goals. If you need to study for a big exam, consider using fluorite, which helps to enhance brain functionality.

Placing the correct/corresponding stones on top of your chakra points will help with channeling the energy of the stone into the areas of your body which require the most healing. This will allow you to channel intense rivers of energy directly to the affected area and focus the energy of the crystal onto a specific point.

To gain the best results from chakra healing you should open your chakras, ensure they are free from blockages and spend a minimum of 10 minutes in a meditative state while the crystal(s) is placed on the correct chakra(s). Depending on the nature of the illness, you may need to do this on a daily basis for a short while.

The use of stones and crystals for magical reasons has grown in popularity in recent years. Many stones have planetary attributions and related herbs as well. These stones can be used for magical talismans, jewelry, offerings or even just carried around in your pocket for protection or other energetic uses. Our ancestors knew of these powerful stones and used them wisely for important magical endeavors. Whether for protection or to house energies or spirits, stones can add a nice dynamic to our practice, while also being beautiful aesthetically.

Consider our traditions of wedding rings and other meaningful jewelry. These metals and stones are used for distinct reasons, whether the general population knows it or not. Choosing stones and metals in your jewelry should be done with great care and not haphazardly carrying around energetic properties that won't benefit you. Diamonds are relatively universal, but the metal they are housed in and other added stones can potentially cause problems for some people especially if the stones are not properly cleansed.

Many New Age communities have been promoting the use of crystals for energetic cleansing and protective barriers for their homes. These techniques are often sold as a newly discovered practice, but we know the folly in this concept. Crystals and stones are formed over the course of thousands of years, comprising of one or many combinations of organic compounds. These crystals and stones all carry their own energetic signature that can be felt or harnessed by a skilled witch or magician. Along with the energetic signatures, these crystals also form physical patterns that are not only beautiful, but also affect their behavior and energy.

The stereotype of the fortune teller with their crystal ball like we see in movies and television shows is far removed from the reality of crystal healing and divination. Although you can very well use a crystal ball to divine and cast spells, it's not going to go over like the movies of course. Many people use the stones for scrying and divination, but there are many other uses too, from protection, planetary work, housing knowledge and even for casting spells or wands, stones and crystals have a lot to offer a Wiccan practitioner.

Not unlike plants and herbs, crystals are considered to be alive, maybe not in the scientific sense of life, but nonetheless alive in some way. Science has found that these crystals do give off measurable energy. Piezoelectricity is found in many stones and is readily used in many devices today, from cellular phones to electric guitar pickups. Striking stones with a hammer or exposing them to certain temperatures will release these electric charges. We know through science that humans are electrochemical in nature as well, this brings up the notion that everything is connected somehow, perhaps the electrical charges are the means that we share experience and existence with the rest of the universe.

There are many ways we can start a crystal magic practice as Wiccans. Crystals can not only be used on their own to house energy or spirits, but can be combined with other materials to create wands, scrying mirrors, fetishes, pentacles or even sculpted to create statues of deities. Crystals and stones also work really well with color correspondence magic. We know planets; herbs, deities and even certain holy days have color correspondences that align with the energy of certain things. There is no exception to this with stones, and in fact stones and crystals are a great way to bring color into your practice. Keep in mind that some stones are dyed a certain color, it will always be more effective to go the natural route, and there are plenty of colorful stones readily available.

Some people feel that for a full effect you have to use the most expensive crystals and stones. This is not particularly correct; you can have just as much success using a common red stone like carnelian as opposed to an expensive and pure ruby. Even a rough ruby works just as well. While diamonds, rubies, sapphires and emeralds are essentially the same chemical makeup, and tend to be purer with fewer compounds, they tend to be very expensive when they are cut and appraised. These expensive stones are usually harvested in negative ways as well. You do not need expensive stones to have a successful crystal magic practice.

There are thousands of different stones and almost all of them have been explored or used for spiritual or magical purposes. Just like many other practices some people are way more skilled in working with stones than others, be open-minded when approaching stones. And if you are having trouble opts for easy to use stones like clear quartz in your workings. We can't cover them all, but we can touch on a few of the more popular and readily available ones.

The Earth has produced a truly stunning variety of crystals and other mineral stones, many, many of which are wonderful tools in healing and magic.

Below is an introduction to 13 of the most popular and versatile stones used in various magical traditions around the world. Think of this group of stones as a sort of "Witch's starter kit" for crystal magic!

Remember, there's no need to go out and buy one of each kind of stone all at once, but, if you find yourself overwhelmed by the choices when you do seek to acquire a stone or two, you can use this list to help make a decision.

Here, you'll find information on each stone's appearance, key energetic properties, and common magical uses.

Quartz Crystal

The most abundant and arguably the most versatile crystal on the planet, quartz is the one most people associate with the word "crystal."

Usually clear, but also opaque white, quartz is used in many magical and non-magical objects including clocks, computers, prisms, crystal spheres and wands.

Clear quartz is a supreme aid in concentration, fostering intellectual clarity, new ideas, and strengthened focus. It increases awareness, helps with memory and filters out external distractions.

Interestingly, it is both helpful for sleep and for raising energy, as it has a somewhat hypnotic quality but also contains the full spectrum of light, which is seen when it's used as a prism.

Quartz is a great purifier, helping to eliminate negativity and restore positive energy in a person or in one's surroundings. It's useful in meditation and clearing out inner turmoil, replacing it with positive feelings and affirmations. It assists with perseverance and patience, bringing a sense of purpose and harmony to those who work with its energy.

Clear quartz is a very versatile stone, easy to "program" (or charge) with a magical intention for any positive purpose. It stores and concentrates the energy, retaining it for use in healing and magic at a later time.

This crystal serves to amplify the power of your intentions, as well as the power of other stones used along with it in ritual. It is particularly well-suited for communication with spirit guides, building psychic ability, communication with animals and plants, and recalling past lives. Many people use quartz in workings connected to strengthening intuition and spiritual development. It also works well for attracting love and prosperity.

Wearing or carrying a clear quartz crystal helps keep personal energy strong and positive, and the mind and heart open to guidance from the higher realms. It dispels negative energy from others in your environment. Placing quartz in the bath is a good way to unwind and clear your mind when facing confusing events.

Keywords: Clarity, Transformation, Manifestation

Zodiac Sign: Leo

Planet: Sun

Element: Fire

Amethyst

Another form of quartz crystal, amethyst is considered by many to be the most beautiful of magical stones.

It ranges in color from pale lavender to deep, very dark purple, and may be transparent or opaque. The color is created by the presence of manganese in clear quartz, and the variation in hue is caused by additional amounts of iron.

Amethyst frequently occurs in geodes, where it's not uncommon to see amethyst and clear quartz points clustered together.

In ancient Greece, amethyst was considered the "stone of sobriety," believed to help reduce the intoxicating effects of wine, and to this day is used in working to break addictions, as well as other unwanted habits and patterns. This is because amethyst has a very high vibration that helps people connect to their spiritual selves and find the balance between healthy indulgences and unhealthy overindulgence.

It is a stone of contentment, aiding in meditation and attaining higher states of consciousness and transforming negative energy into positive energy. It also helps enhance perception, on both intellectual and intuitive levels, and increases psychic ability.

In magic, amethyst is wonderful for clearing sacred space and maintaining a positive atmosphere anywhere it is placed. It is useful for healing rituals related to the addiction of all kinds, both physical and emotional (such as difficulty removing oneself from toxic relationships). It increases luck and prosperity by curbing the tendency to overspend, as well as promoting motivation. It's a good stone for creativity and any projects requiring imaginative thinking and focus. Amethyst has been used traditionally in Wiccan magic for dispelling illusion and to bring about psychic healing.

Wearing or carrying amethyst creates a protective shield against negative energies in your environment. Like rose quartz, amethyst near the computer can help relieve eye strain, and it's also a good stone to keep under your pillow for peaceful dreams.

Unpolished Amethyst is a good charger for other crystals, as well as healing energy for plants—places it in areas where plants don't tend to thrive to purify the energy and enhance their growth.

Keywords: Transformation, Higher Guidance, Protection

Zodiac Sign: Aquarius

Planet: Jupiter

Element: Air

Citrine

Citrine is a yellow variety of quartz, usually transparent and ranging in color from pale yellow to gold, but is sometimes found as an almost-brown honey color.

It has been known as "the Sun Stone" due to its bright color and often sparkling appearance, but the name "citrine" comes from the French word for "lemon."

Citrine is also good for helping to overcome negativity associated with having been ill-used by another person, either through direct manipulation or more subtle means. It can be hard sometimes to know whether some acquaintances are positive influences in our lives. Citrine can help illuminate which of your associations are worth keeping, and which to let go. It can do this for your own thoughts as well, by clearing out negative or unnecessary mental "chatter" to help you realign with your inner wisdom.

It reduces sensitivity to criticism and helps you let go of the past, clearing the way for new, positive thoughts and experiences.

Citrine is excellent in spellwork for manifesting and maintaining wealth. It is sometimes known as the "Merchant's Stone" and kept near the cash register of many businesses. It's also good for issues of communication in interpersonal relationships, and clearing and blocking negative energies from people around you.

Moonstone

Moonstone is named for its opaque, silver and white sheen reminiscent of the moon, although it can be found in a variety of colors beyond white—especially blue, gray, peach, and a multicolored variety called "Rainbow Moonstone."

Associated with the element of Water, it has a feminine quality that helps you tap into your inner wisdom and psychic abilities.

It is also known as the "Traveler's Stone" and has long been a talisman of safe journeys, though these journeys may be inward, soul-searching travels just as much as physical journeys to a far-away location.

This stone's affinity with the Moon makes it ideal for connecting to the regular cycles of and natural rhythms of life, reminding us that there is a time for all things, and that allowing for right timing is often better than trying to force things to happen on our preferred schedules.

It has a calming energy that reminds us to stay in the present moment and open up to the joy available to us when we let go of the chatter of the mind and listen to the heart instead. In a culture where we feel pressured to "know the answers" and "be in control" of our circumstances, moonstone helps us relax into the mysteries of the future, developing our intuition and staying open to possibilities we can't see yet with our rational minds.

In Wiccan magic, moonstone has been used to increase psychic abilities and clairvoyance, relieve stress and foster compassion, and for the ritual worship of triple moon-goddesses. It's also a good stone for spellwork related to female reproductive health and childbirth, as well as erotic love and kundalini energies.

Although it is ultra-feminine in its energy, it is not just a woman's stone—it helps men tune into their own feminine side and encourages them to open up to more creative thinking and emotional balance. It's also another good stone for encouraging restful sleep, particularly in children, and especially when on a trip away from home.

It is still worn as a talisman when traveling, particularly at night and/or on journeys over water. Some people keep a moonstone in the glove compartment of their car, and it is said to be good protection against road rage.

Key Words: Clarity, Higher Guidance, Intuition

Zodiac Sign: Cancer

Planet: Moon

Element: Water

Carnelian

With its rich red-orange-to-orange coloring, Carnelian was known to the ancient Egyptians as "the setting sun." Single pieces of this stone can actually include several shades between red-orange and golden yellow, and are sometimes streaked with white.

Used in Egyptian magic as protection against the evil eye, it was also carried by the Romans for protection and courage. Carnelian's energy is bold and joyful, encouraging and empowering, making it a great stone for any situation in which you need a strong boost of positive personal power.

Carnelian also has a grounding influence, helping to anchor us in the present moment and therefore make better use of the high-level energy it provides. It can calm anger and replace it with a new enthusiasm for life.

Its energy is good for endurance, motivation, courage, and passion—traits that bring success in whatever endeavor you're hoping to succeed in. It helps overcome procrastination and helps you move from the dreaming/planning phase of a project to the action required to get it done.

Creative types can benefit from carnelian's ability to move past creative blocks and manifest one's inner vision in the outer world, particularly when one's "inner critic" is the main obstacle. Carnelian helps those struggling with indecision to make a choice and act on it, bringing them closer to achieving their goals.

Wiccans have long recognized carnelian's assistance with grounding and aligning with one's spiritual guides, and it makes a good talisman against "psychic attack," or negative thoughts projected by others. It's also good for spellwork related to love and to invigorating a relationship with new sexual passion.

As a motivator and activator, it is said to attract prosperity and is good for money-making ventures. Some use it to guard their homes from theft, storms, fires, or other damage. It is also known as the "Singer's Stone," and can promote confidence in people performing on stage. Most often, however, it's worn to enhance desire, passion, and love.

Keywords: Grounding, Self-awareness, Creativity, Vitality

Zodiac Sign: Leo

Planet: Sun

Element: Fire

Bloodstone

Bloodstone gets its name from a myth about the crucifixion of Christ—

that some of Christ's blood fell on some green jasper stones. Some specimens may almost entirely lack the red inclusions, but holding bloodstone up to bright light can reveal colors not seen in ordinary light.

Bloodstone is a powerful crystal for blasting through negative, distracting, or excessive emotions in order to get to the truth of a situation. It helps to calm the mind and dispel confusion for better decision-making. Its energy is practical, strong, and grounding and good for helping you return to the present moment after too much worry about the future or regret about the past. This makes it a good stone for heightening intuition, as we can only really hear our inner wisdom when we are still and centered in the present.

Bloodstone has been used in magic to reduce emotional and mental stress, stimulate kundalini energy, and psychic healing. It is also used in rituals to honor the Goddess and for seeking information about past lives from dreams.

Many use bloodstone as an aid in banishing negative energy, as well as in weather magic—drawing on the power of strong wind or rainstorm to increase strength and courage or wash away unwanted habits or patterns. It's good for fertility and attracting money, and excellent for manifesting healing of all kinds.

Wear or carry it to increase mental clarity and calm the mind, and for strength when adjusting to change. As a booster of energy levels, bloodstone is also good for physical endurance, and makes a good luck charm for those involved in sports competitions.

Keywords: Clearing, Protection, Vitality

Zodiac Sign: Aries

Planet: Mars

Element: Fire

Jade

For nearly 6,000 years, jade has been a prized stone used in tools, ritual artifacts, and jewelry from ancient Britain to Central and South America to New Zealand and China.

This stone is normally green and mostly opaque, though it can be somewhat translucent and sometimes occur in shades of white, gray, and pink. It has traditionally been a symbol of tranquility, truthfulness, wisdom, and luck.

On the emotional and spiritual planes, jade is a great stone for helping you to tap into your authentic self—the self that knows what is best for you underneath all the emotional chaos that may be occurring during a difficult or confusing time. It helps with self-trust, and with clearing away past emotional experiences that cloud your ability to see the present circumstances objectively. It also helps you to be your real self in your interactions with others, rather than trying to present yourself in a way that you think will be pleasing to them.

For these reasons, jade has a very calming energy, and is an excellent help for unsettling situations in your life. It also leads to the ability to create better circumstances—in terms of relationships, health, wealth, and new opportunities—because you're aligning your goals with your authentic self. It can also help make difficult tasks feel easier to accomplish, increasing your sense of peace around work.

Jade is used in magical workings for protection and eliminating negativity, and tapping into our innate wisdom and courage. It is used as a "dream stone" to bring insight from the spiritual realms by placing it on the forehead at the location of the "third eye." Keeping it under your pillow can help you remember your dreams better.

As a green stone, the color of prosperity, jade can also be used in spellwork for abundance, and it supports the growth of plants. It supports new love, and harmony in business relationships as well as within the family.

Some people keep a piece or two of jade in their workplace to keep away unwanted negativity from coworkers. Keep a piece in your pocket to help recharge your energy and keep your immune system in good shape.

Key Words: Self-awareness, Transformation, Manifestation

Zodiac Sign: Pisces

Planet: Neptune

Element: Water

Malachite

Another stone revered by the ancients, malachite was used by the Greeks and Romans for ornaments, jewelry, and even in powdered form for eyeshadow. (This last use turned out to be a bad idea, since Malachite is toxic and should never be used in powdered form. Polished malachite pieces are the safest bet.)

Malachite is an opaque stone of deep, rich green with lighter green circular bands that cause many pieces to appear to have an eye. For this reason, the stone was believed in the Middle Ages to ward off negativity and enhance visionary abilities.

Malachite is considered a "Stone of Transformation," fostering spiritual growth during times of great change, or inspiring us to make important changes and take emotional risks. Its energy can help you break unwanted patterns that restrict your growth, such as avoiding social situations due to shyness or self-consciousness.

This stone helps build emotional courage and clarity, by helping we learn to recognize and then release old emotional wounds, especially those suffered in childhood. It helps with fear of confrontation, encourages the expression of feelings, and promotes healthy, positive relationships and empathy for others. Malachite is good for protection magic, particularly for people who get easily overwhelmed by the congestion of psychic energy in crowded places. It's good for all travel situations, and particularly aids in fear of flying. It absorbs negative energy, so holding it in the palm of your hand during difficult or frightening situations can bring immediate relief—but be sure to clean and clear it often if you use it for this purpose. As a green stone, it can be used in any prosperity spell, and is also good in workings for healing emotional wounds. In the workplace, it helps dispel energetic toxins from fluorescent lighting, electrical equipment, and unwanted noise.

Key Words:

Self-awareness, Healing, Clarity, Protection

Zodiac Sign: Scorpio

Planet: Venus

Element: Earth

Tiger's Eye

Tiger's eye is a beautiful stone of light to dark brown with gold highlights and dark brown to black banding, which, when polished, resembles the shimmering stripes of a tiger and creates a similar "eye" effect to that of malachite.

As an "eye stone," it was regarded by the ancient Egyptians and Romans as a stone of protection as well as "second sight," allowing its wearer to see beyond the physical limits of doors and walls.

The energy of tiger's eye is excellent for soothing and resolving emotional turmoil, as it helps you observe emotional patterns from a more distanced, objective standpoint. Witnessing the larger picture of a situation, including the viewpoints and circumstances of others involved, helps facilitate the release of emotions that may be blocking your ability to leave the situation behind and evolve into higher levels of consciousness.

Tiger's eye is helpful in this regard for its ability to help you separate fantasy (which arises from emotion) from the reality of the situation. This energy is also good for helping you gather focus and renewed energy when pursuing a goal, especially one that is relatively long-term and complex. It promotes courage, strength, and the ability to see things with true optimism.

Magical uses for tiger's eye include invigorating overall energy and physical health, as well as spellwork for courage and self-confidence. It's good in rituals related to emotional clarity and for protection and grounding. As a "reality" stone, it is also a prosperity stone—its grounding properties help curb temptations toward gambling or other impulsive spending, and improve the ability to attract wealth through practicality and focus.

Many people carry tiger's eye for good luck, as well as increased psychic "radar" to cut through any deceptions or illusions created by others. Additionally, this stone has been used by those with affinities for tigers and other big cats as a prayer stone for their conservation and well-being in the wild as well as in sanctuaries.

Key Words: Clarity, Balance, Vitality

Zodiac Sign: Capricorn and Leo

Planet: Sun

Element: Earth and Fire

Jet

One of the exceptions to the "rule" defining crystals and stones, jet is not technically a mineral, but is actually a type of fossilized driftwood that decayed under extreme pressure to become a form similar to coal. It is surprisingly light in weight and warms quickly in the palm of your hand.

Jet was mined as early as 1500 B.C., and was used in pendants and as beads in ancient times. It was believed to protect against illness and attacks from personal enemies.

As a stone of transmutation—having begun as one substance and ended as another, jet is a helpful stone for transitions. Its energy appeals to mental cloudiness, helping you ground and center in order to see clearly your best possible approach to changing circumstances.

When the future is unknown, it can be hard to maintain clarity of focus, as we become uncomfortable being unable to see exactly what's ahead. Jet helps clear the fog of this anxiety and sets us up to stay open to positive possibilities. This stone absorbs energy from negative thinking, and as such should be cleaned often if used for this purpose. It's also a great meditation stone, aiding in increasing spiritual awareness and healing from grief and sorrow.

Jet is considered one of the most protective magical stones, used for guarding a home against negative energies, and to banish unwanted spirits. It has been traditionally used to protect against damage from thunderstorms, and worn by the wives of sailors to protect their husbands at sea. It is used in spellwork to guard against nightmares, violence, and psychic vampires.

Hematite

Magically, hematite is used for protection, divination, and psychic awareness. It can be placed in the corners of a room, or even in the corners of a yard, to protect the space from negativity. It's good for grounding during spiritual work, keeping you connected to the Earth plane during your astral journey so that reintegrating into consensual reality is an easier, smoother process. Many Witches use hematite in spellwork related to confidence and willpower, and solving complex problems. As a divination tool, you can hold a large piece of hematite near a candle and watch the images created by the flame's reflection in the surface.

Of course, it's also great for preparing for magic. If you want to do some spellwork but are unable to get yourself in the right "mental space," try meditating while holding or wearing hematite for several minutes to calm the energy of the distracted mind.

Chapter 3: Crystals in Witchcraft

Agate

Agate is a variety of chalcedony which is, in most cases, formed in areas of volcanic activity. There is a wide variety of different types of agate available in an array of colors, many of which contain some form of banding which runs throughout the stone, although some contain natural patterning which is similar to varying forms of vegetation.

In general, agate can be used to create calm within and settle fears and anxiety. It is also a beneficial stone when confidence and inner strength needs to be increased. Agate, in all its forms aids in the stimulation of imagination, creative processes and intelligent thought.

Each variety of Agate possesses its individual healing properties in addition to the above

Amazonite

- Development of psychic ability, creative processes, intellect & intuition
- Balancing of self-esteem and self-belief
- Strengthens communication, inner strength, honesty & commitment

- Calming enhanced emotional states
- Eases all conditions which stem from nerves and anxiety
- Aids in removing symptoms which have developed from stress conditions such as heart palpitations and breathlessness.
- Heals and/or strengthens bones, nails, teeth and hair

Amber

Although amber is not officially a crystal or mineral, (it is pine tree sap that has been petrified and is often centuries old at least), it has many healing qualities and can be used in the same way as a stone. Quite often amber contains fossilized leaves, flowers, insects and other natural deposits than has become trapped in the sap.

Amber has many uses in healing and is a great all-round stone. It has the ability to absorb any and all diseased energy from the body, to help neutralize pain and settle a disturbed mind.

From the strengthening of the muscles in the brain and mucus-producing muscles to enhancing the memory and aiding in the control and development of emotional control and intellect, amber is an excellent stone to keep on hand.

Amber is also a strong stone for helping with stomach problems, all illnesses concerning the bladder, kidneys, liver and throat. Blood diseases are all helped with the use of amber along with any condition involving skin, bones and eyes.

Amethyst

- Strengthens willpower in the treatment of addiction
- Promotes inner strength and balance
- Increases courage
- Stabilizes energy levels
- Improves communication
- Pain relief, especially when concerned with headaches, arthritis and general muscle or bone pain
- Strong stone in the treatment of fibromyalgia and chronic fatigue illnesses
- Strengthens the immune system
- Mood enhancement
- Development of psychic ability

Aventurine

Blue

- Calming
- Balances emotions
- Improves communicative ability
- Enhances creativity and creative thought processes

Green

- Stimulates the imagination
- Enhances positivity
- Improves circulatory issues
- Sleep problems and insomnia
- Headaches

Orange

- Strengthens communications
- Enhances and focuses intellect
- Stimulates feeling of self-worth
- Aids imaginative thinking
- Helps to settle and balance the emotions following sexual trauma

Beryl

All color varieties of Beryl are beneficial when dealing with stress-related illness and anxiety. It is also helpful when treating illnesses relating to the circulatory system, liver, stomach, spleen, detoxification and the pulmonary processes.

Yellow (Heliodor)

- Improves the ability to feel compassion and sympathy
- Increasing understanding of others emotional state

- Promotes healing in all areas affected by the spleen, pancreas and liver
- Strengthens the ability to connect to higher self
- Aids in cleansing of all chakra points

Green

- Increases concentration and stimulates intellect
- Energizing
- Stimulates creative thoughts and actions
- Aids respiratory healing
- Promotes healing in all areas connected to the liver and eyes

Blue

- See Aquamarine

Pink

- Promotes empathy
- Improves patience and tolerance of others
- Aids transition of thought and emotional processes
- Enhances the acceptance of self and others
- Stimulates calm feelings & love of self and others

Aquamarine

- Increases intuition
- Calms the mind and emotions
- Aids in recovering from all aspects of mental health illness
- Increases self-belief and confidence
- Improves communication abilities
- Promotes creative thought processes

White (Clear)

- Strengthens and focuses intellect
- Aids in connection to the wisdom of higher self
- Aids in the expansion of perception
- Helps in the healing of stomach and intestinal disorders
- Detoxifying
- Strengthens self-confidence, willpower and mental ability
- Calms and balances the nervous system
- Aids in the healing of spine and bone problems
- Improves conditions relating to stomach ulcers, nausea, depression and eating disorders

Black Tourmaline

- Neutralizing of negative energies

- Calming and grounding excessive nervous energy
- Restraint of obsessive thoughts and behaviors
- Relaxing of fears and emotional instability
- Pain relief in arthritis
- Aids in healing of problems relating to the heart
- Boosts immune system

Bloodstone

- Strengthens courage
- Relieves depression and depressive tendencies
- Detoxifying
- Increases energy levels
- Calms anxiety and nervous tension
- Helps to ease flue, colds, infections and swelling along with all symptoms relating to these conditions
- Focuses thought processes

Blue Quartz

- Strengthens the mind so thought processes become clearer and thoughts are more streamlined

- Improves self discipline
- Reduces fears and anxious thoughts
- Stimulates courage
- Calms hyperactivity and overstimulation
- Helps in healing of the endocrine system

Carnelian

- Promotes feeling of courage and inner strength
- Aids in individual expression of both self and creativity
- Calms emotional instability
- Aids in healing of fevers, colds, hay fever, skin disorders, kidney problems and rheumatism
- Healing for skin conditions

Citrine

- Improves and promotes feelings of self-belief and confidence in self
- Strengthens willpower and conviction of thought
- Promotes happiness

- Helps to relieve symptoms of depression
- Settles the mind to encourage rational thought
- Balances mood
- Eases digestive upset

Clear Quartz

Clear Quart is a natural healing crystal and will help in all areas of mental, physical and emotional healing.

- Balances life force energies

Emerald

General all-round healing stone which can be used to aid healing through all chakra points.

- Improves respiratory system
- Heart function
- Eyesight
- Circulatory system
- Strengthens spine
- Detoxifying

- Pancreatic and thymus healing
- Improves and strengthens the immune system
- Aids in contact with higher self

Garnet

Garnet is a stone which can be used in the cleansing of each of your chakra points and to aid the balancing of energy flow.

- Increases self-awareness and confidence
- Increases the libido
- Calms emotions
- Reduces anger
- Removal of inhibitions
- Promotes healing of the respiratory system, circulatory system and heart, all aspects of blood, spine and bones

Hematite

- Reduces fever and temperature
- Promotes clearer thought processes

- Strengthens logic and problem solving cognitive processes
- Balances energy flow
- Improves sleep disorders and insomnia
- Calms the nervous system
- Aids in healing all blood related illness

Jade

- Calms the mind
- Removes negative energies
- Increases ability to remember dreams
- Settles irritability
- Release of stored emotional feelings helping to heal symptoms which have been caused by them
- Stimulates creative and imaginative thought
- Creates feelings of strength of self-belief
- Useful in fertility problems
- Strengthens bones and promotes healing in all areas connected to the kidneys and adrenal glands
- Detoxifying

Orange Calcite

- Lifts the mood and helps to overcome shyness
- Improves depressive thoughts and depression
- Increases sex drive
- Stimulates the imagination
- Strengthens resolve to carry out plans
- Increases confidence and creative and imaginative thought processes

Peridot

- Eases negative emotions
- Calms the nervous system
- Balances emotions
- Strengthens the body's natural healing ability

Pyrite (fool's gold)

- Increases mental ability
- Strengthens and focuses intellect
- Stimulates creativity and imagination
- Improves memory

- Balances the psychological state
- Enhances development of psychic abilities

Red Jasper

- Stabilization of the life force energy
- Calms the mind
- Strengthen control of thought processes

Rose Quartz

- Promotes calmness of mind and emotions
- Increases general happiness and mood
- Strengthens feelings of love of self and others in non selfish ways

Smoky Quartz

- Alleviates depressive thoughts and feelings
- Calms excessive emotions
- Absorbs negative energy
- Settles nervous energy

- Opens the mind to allow access to the subconscious self, (higher self)
- Aids in the healing of conditions relating to the stomach, reproduction, kidneys, water retention and pancreas
- Balances hormone production

Sodalite

- Aids cognitive processes promoting rational thought
- Strengthens communication abilities
- Stimulates intellect
- Promotes focus of mind to enhance ability to learn and recall
- Aids with sleep disorders and insomnia
- Strengthens healing of colds and flu
- Settles digestive disorders

Tigers Eye

- Strengthens practical thought processes
- Clears mental vision
- Strengthens willpower
- Calms ailments relating to the stomach
- Settles and balances the emotions

Selenite

Many metaphysical workers refer to selenite as their most important tool. It has been called "Satin Spar" because of its milky sheen that shines from its surface. Selenite can be found in most countries including the United States of America, Mexico, Greece, and Australia. People who want to profit from the healing properties of selenite need to look for the clear selenite stones that are fairly long that come from Mexican.

Selenite isn't known for its strength, but they are used to lighten the home's décor. The most luxurious one who uses this is the Santa Sabina that is located in Rome. All of the window panes are made completely of selenite. Because selenite is so soft, it is used in drywall, cement, soil conditioner, and plaster.

The stone was named for Selene, the Greek Goddess of the moon. This meaning is easy to understand as you can see it when it reflects the light. It sometimes appears to be a rock that has fallen directly from the moon's surface. It is formed from hydrous calcium sulfate; this stone is part of the gypsum crystal family. This crystal system forms in long columns. Before it is polished, you can recognize selenite by its fibrous striations that run the length of the stone. These crystals normally form in clay beds around hot springs. Because selenite dissolves in water, the healing properties of selenite are similar to those of water.

Even though selenite isn't strong, it is extremely powerful in its metaphysical abilities. The healing properties of selenite are about reaching higher planes and activation. It can connect to the third eye and crown chakras as well as those beyond. By radiating light energy, it can promote honesty and purity. It will force anyone who is holding it to be completely honest. Because it is so good at clearing energy blockages, it allows energy to flow like water. It can get the chakras in alignment and raise a person's awareness of higher planes.

Once selenite connects the crown and third eye chakra, it brings total purity and positivity. When the selenite's power flows into the crown chakra, it will activate, clean and open the energy. The chakra is going to feel totally purified. The person should experience no inhibitions, negativity, and have a liberated sense of self. This is the perfect stone to connect with your guardian angels and spirit guides. Because it can be programmed, it is the best facilitator to transmit information and advice that you might be looking for from your guide. It can connect you with your higher self where you will be accepting and open to symbolic messages.

The selenite can be used with other stones to manipulate and boost the effect you want. You can create a selenite spectrum by laying your selenite wand down and then place tumbled stones on top of it in the order of the rainbow. You can also use it to create energy grids in your home, or on your yoga mat to give your mental balance a boost while keeping your balance. Wearing jewelry made of selenite like a necklace can keep toxic energy away and keep your light from getting sucked by energy vampires.

There are many ways to use the healing properties of selenite during meditations and rituals. If you are meditating alone, you can place a selenite wand over your chest. Place one end pointing toward your crown chakra and the other end pointed toward your root chakra. You can say a mantra like: "I take in the light. I am the light." This will help you grasp the true meaning of selenite.

To use selenite in Reiki practices, you will need small stones to put on your chakra points and a wand. The wand needs to be used before you start Reiki healing to clear any tension and negativity within the person being healed. The person being healed will be lying on their stomach. You will hold the selenite wand above them and pass it over their body starting at their head and going to their toes moving it along the spine. After the Reiki healing is over, close the session by putting the small stones on the chakra point to balance and align their harmony.

Selenite can cleanse energy from other stones. If you feel that a specific stone's energy is getting dull, clear it by using selenite. You can lay the dull stones on top of a large block of selenite to recharge them. If you have a wand made from selenite, you can lay your other stones next to it for some time until their energy has returned.

Lapis Lazuli

Lapis lazuli is the most sought-after stone since it was discovered. Its coloring is a celestial blue that is still the symbol of honor and royalty, vision and spirit, and gods and power. It has always been a symbol of truth and wisdom.

During ancient times lapis lazuli was highly regarded for its beautiful coloring and valuable ultramarine dye that can be made from it. The Latin word lapis means "stone," and the Persian Lazhuward, means "blue." It is a rock that comes from many minerals that are mostly pyrite, calcite, sodalite, lazurite. Its coloring is a rich medium to royal blue with gold flecks. A lower grade of lapis which is a lighter blue with white instead of gold is called denim lapis.

Lapis lazuli is the most prized possession of Egypt. It is still being mined from the ancient mines that have been worked since 4000 BC and is still being mined today. It was referenced in the Bible as sapphire.

Lapis lazuli was also in King Tutankhamun's tomb. Other Egyptian queens and kings were also buried with lapis lazuli burial ornaments. It was used to make jewelry, pendants, scarabs, eye shadow, and medicinal elixirs. It was also ground into powder for dyes. Deep in the dry barren land of Egypt, this deep cobalt blue is in contrast to their dull desert hues. The gold flecks are like the stars in the night sky and they thought if they meditated on these colors, it would transform their lives. Royalty and priests' garments were dyed with lapis lazuli to show their status as gods.

In pre-Columbian America and ancient Persia, lapis lazuli is a symbol of the starry nights and a favorite stone on the Islamic. It was used as protection from the evil eye. Lapis was used in Greece and Rome as an ornamental stone. During medieval Europe, lapis lazuli resembled the blue color of the heavens. When this stone is processed and ground into powder, the result was an intense and expensive ultramarine color that was a favorite of Michelangelo, the painter. Buddhists used this stone to bring freedom from inner thoughts and inner peace.

Lapis is a great stone for psychologists, journalists, and executives. It can stimulate good judgment and wisdom. It helps historians and archeologists with their intellectual analysis. It helps lawyers solve problems. It can give writers and inventors new, creative ideas.

It can stimulate the desire for knowledge, understanding, and truth. It can help in the learning process. It is great for enhancing memory. This is a stone of truth, lapis encourages honesty of the written and spoken word, and spirit. Lapis grid could bring loving and calm communication in a home that has temperamental teenagers or children who have ADD, autism, or Asperger's syndrome.

If you are looking for fame in the public or creative performance field, carry or wear lapis lazuli to your auditions. In any workplace, it will attract recognition, success, and promotion in your field of expertise.

Lapis lazuli can activate the third eye's psychic centers and balances the throat chakra's energies. The third eye is the center of command and perception. It can direct our sight and daily awareness of the world around us. We relate to others through this chakra because our consciousness is found here.

It can balance both the unimportant and important. It sorts the meanings from impressions and date. It can command how the energy flows through our body. When the third eye is balanced, we will see clearly and understands the things we see. We will be able to interpret visuals when our perception is high. Our internal communications and thoughts inside us are vibrant and healthy. We will be open to new visions, dreams, and ideas. We can be quietly reflective and observant. We have the ability to control the flow of energy in all our chakras.

The throat chakra is the body's voice. It is a pressure valve that let the energy from other chakras to be expressed. If it is out of balance or blocked, it could affect the other chakras' health. If it is in balance, it will allow us to express what we feel and think. We will be able to communicate our emotions, beliefs, and ideas. If the throat chakra is open and balanced, we will be able to tell the world our truths. We will have an easy flow of energy in our spirit and body. The energy that comes up from our lower chakras will be able to continue on its path allowing the natural release of free expression. Blue crystal energy will balance and unblock the throat chakra. Dark shades of blue will carry the power of truth.

Tourmaline

All varieties of tourmaline help with the enhancement of mood and aid in the strengthening of self belief and confidence. They are also useful in the treatment of any ailment connected to the lymphatic system.

Blue

- Improves communication and speech
- Reduction in mental tension
- Aids in healing of thyroid problems and ailments of the throat

Pink

- Balances the emotions
- Promotes understanding and acceptance of self
- Transforms negative thoughts and emotions into positive ones
- Calming
- Improves strength of mind

Black & Green

- Regulates and balance blood pressure
- Reduces symptoms of stress and calms the nervous system.

Turquoise

- Turquoise is a healing stone which promotes full mind and body healing

- Strengthens communication
- Boosts the immune system
- Improves respiratory problems
- Strengthens healing in all areas jointly governed by the heart & throat chakras

Exactly what sensitivities do some crystals have?

Porosity

As mentioned earlier on, some crystals cannot get moist without getting destroyed. That is why you can only use other cleansing methods other than letting water run over them. In this regard, you need to take particular care on:

- The azurite; the halite; and the selenites because they are literally water soluble

- The lapis lazuli; the opal and also the turquoise as they are porous. With these ones, water is not exactly out of question, only that you cannot soak the crystals in it. So you can wipe them with something moist and then ensure you instantly dry them after the cleaning.

- As for the malachite, you need to use only cool water to clean it and then you instantly dry it afterwards.

Light sensitivity

Some crystals may fade if exposed to light for too long.

The ones that stand out in this regard are:

- The amethyst as well as the Rose Quartz
- The turquoise as it may just dry out

Heat sensitivity

Some crystals are disfigured when exposed to heat. These include:

- The amethyst, which, in mild heat, begins to fade. In fact, in extreme heat the amethyst practically loses all its color and turns colorless.

- The quartz, which tends to fracture when temperatures around it are fluctuating

- The lapis lazuli, which cannot take extreme heat

- The malachite, like the quartz, does not fare well when exposed to fluctuating heat conditions

- Tourmaline, which gets its color marred in extreme heat

- Turquoise, which fares badly under heat in general.

Sensitivity to scratching

In this category are all crystals that are metallic or are on a mineral nature. By name, you have the Calcite; the Celestite; malachite; Fluorite; the Rhodochrosite; the Apatite; and the Lapis Lazuli. There are also sodalite; selenite; turquoise; hematite; as well as the moonstone.

Chapter 4: Programming Your Crystals

Why do you want to have crystals in your possession, whether to wear as jewelry, use to decorate your house or even place in hidden strategic places within your home? Well, the answer to that question is what guides you in programming the crystals.

In programming your crystal, you are effectively making your intention or intentions get ingrained within your crystal. Remember as already mentioned, crystals are capable of absorbing energy the same way they emit energy.

Some of the intentions people have when they program their crystals include:

- Healing purposes
- Seeking protection
- Seeking spiritual guidance
- Attracting more love in your life
- Seeking prosperity
- Seeking to create harmony in your home or even working place

The list of intentions you could have can be much longer, but the most important thing to note is that a single crystal can bear more than one intention. That means that the same crystal you are programming to help you heal physically can be programmed to bring harmony into your home.

It is advisable to limit your intentions to four or even five when programming your crystals. And the good thing is that as long as you do not reprogram those crystals thereafter, or even clear them of the original intentions, those intentions remain intact and your crystals continue to serve you as you originally intended.

Crystal Programming Procedure

The presumption here is that you have already cleansed your crystals – cleansing must always precede programming.

Have your intention ready. Of paramount importance here is to avoid ambiguity or any confusion. If you frame your intention in a way that leaves it subject to different interpretations, it will be the same kind of confusion you will be transferring to your crystals. The energy in your crystals will only help your cause properly if the wording of your intention is specific and clear. That way the crystal energies will be focused and correctly directed.

The other important thing is that you need to guard against going wild. The implication here is that you just can't pick any crystal and begin assigning it intentions irrespective of its energy intensity and vibrations. Already it has been pointed out in this book that certain crystals are suitable for certain issues. Remember when it comes to personal issues, you have chakras working in tandem with your chosen crystals. All these are important factors you need to consider lest you go against the grain and achieve little success from otherwise great and precious crystals.

Just for example, if your intention is to calm your nerves and your environment, you will be better off programming an aquamarine or chrysocolla; or even any one of the green stones – or blue ones. And if you need your crystal to bring stimulation within and around you, you will be better off programming a ruby, a garnet, or any of the red crystals. Of course, if you want tempered stimulation you could go for the orange or even yellow crystals; say a carnelian or even a piece of citrine.

The Steps You Take in Programming Your Crystals

Just as in the cleansing procedure, you need to be in a quiet place with your mind fully focused on the intention you have for your crystals.

- Cozily hold your crystal in your hands
- Focus you gaze on the crystals
- Allow your energy to flow freely towards the crystals as you positively sense the energy from the crystals getting attuned to it
- You will reach a point where you and the crystals are in harmony with each other
- This is the instance to state the intention you have for the crystals – this time verbalizing it aloud. Remember clarity of intention is fundamental.
- You don't have to assume your crystals are programmed after stating your intention or intentions just once. A repeat process may be helpful. In fact, you are advised to repeat your intention a couple of times until your intuition tells you that the programming is well done.

Ways to Activate As Well As Re-Energize Your Crystals

Just as in cleaning, you need to be conscious which crystals are delicate, which ones are porous, which are those that can easily fade and so on. That way you will choose the best and safest method to activate and re-energize each set of crystals. And, of course, any crystal that is metallic, porous or with some water content will fare badly if soaked in salty water.

Crystals that you should not soak in salty water include the angelite; the calcite; the carnelian; hematite; lapis lazuli; the labradorite; the lodestone; marbles; moldavite; the opal; pearls; the pyrite; as well as turquoise.

Is This the Complete Process of Preparing Healing Crystals?

Answer – no. You need to dedicate them; program them; activate them; and also charge them. By the time you are through with the process, your healing crystals will be clear energy channels and will be in the best of conditions to help in healing.

How to Dedicate Healing Crystals

- Dedicating healing crystals basically means affirming to them that nothing short of positive energy will penetrate them.

- You will be making a commitment that you are going to see to it that the crystals are used only for good and never for anything evil.

- Note that you need to have your full focus on those crystals that you are dedicating, as you make those commitments.

The impact of your dedication is:

- To ensure that no negative energy clings to your crystals at the time of dedication and thereafter.

- To ensure that nobody and nothing will manage to interfere with the positive energy of your crystals, and as such the crystals will be protected from all negative influences.

Crystal Dedication Procedure

- Seek out a quiet place and sit down
- Have your crystals safely cupped in your hands as you sit
- Close your eyes
- Embark on taking deep, slow but regular breaths
- You know why you are undertaking this procedure, so focus on your crystals accordingly, even with your eyes closed. This means that you are making a deliberate effort to focus your inner energy on your crystals.
- In the quiet, allow yourself to sense the energy from your crystals
- Visualize some bright white ray beaming from the world around you and engulfing your crystals
- Visualize Mother Earth's own golden energy, with all its grounding properties, surrounding your crystals
- Visualize both energies merging and swirling together in harmony and having the effect of giving each other balance.
- Feel the positive energy and abundance of love filling you up
- Now allow yourself to direct that intense love to your crystals
- It is now time to make a focused statement of intent in your mind – so declare in deep commitment that those crystals you are holding will be used only for the utmost good.
- After that statement you may open your eyes. Look at your crystals and focus on them.
- With your eyes open and your focus still on the crystals, do repeat

the mental commitment that you made a while before of using the crystals only for the utmost good.

- To bring your dedication to due conclusion, say: May it be so.

Helpful Items to Have When Activating Your Crystals

Items that can enhance your crystal activation process include lavender; cedarwood; nag champa incense; an incense holder; and candles or even match sticks.

Here is the simple but useful crystal activation process:

- Make your setting conducive for crystal activation and energizing
- The place needs to be somewhat dim, with only some candlelight
- It needs to be quiet
- Right in front of you, place one unlit candle
- At the same front, place a stick of incense
- Sit down with crystals well held in your hands
- Take slow and deep breaths
- Focus on the fact that you want the crystals activated and re-energized
- Visualizing your crystals radiating bright light that surrounds you in full protection.

- You may also wish to visualize that radiant light seeking into the body of someone who is feeling unwell, and effectively clearing the entire person's hurt.

- Now make a point of lighting the candle before you using a single match

- Then use the lit candle to light your incense.

- While tightly holding the candle in one of your hands, direct your mind to focus on your intent.

- It is now time for you to visualize the flow of strong positive energies around you

- Begin by imagining the flow of healing or even protective energies traversing through your hand and entering the crystals you are holding.

- Then sweep the crystals over the candle flame as well as over the nice scented smoke of the burning incense.

- As you visualize the crystals taking in the positive energy from both sources, visualize its glow becoming brighter, second by second.

- Keeping your crystals well cupped in your hands, visualize their energy pulsing

- At this time when your visualizing your crystal's pulse, visualize too your crystal turning to the color that is associated with your purpose and intent.

- In this regard, if what you intend for your crystals is to raise your confidence, you will visualize your crystals adopting red; for protection you will visualize blue; and so on.

Now that your crystals are well re-energized and ready to discharge their role of protecting and healing you, you may wish to put them safely in your pocket or in your pouch – that is, if you are interested in personal healing and not necessarily purifying and harmonizing an environment. However, even when wrapped or enclosed somewhere, it is an added advantage to you if you took time to touch the crystal periodically. That direct touch gets you receiving direct energy from the crystal to you.

Is That the End of the Story as far as Crystal Re-Energizing Goes?

No – once in a while you could place your crystals some place where they can sap some energy from the sun or even the moon. Of course, you must consider those crystals that risk fading when exposed to strong sunshine. Those ones you can expose to early morning sunshine as it is not usually scotching. Otherwise they are better being laid out in moonlight. Some people also choose to place their crystals on the window sill for a while to get recharged by the sunlight. Do have in mind that the sun discharges strong energy whereas the moon discharges energy that is gentler. So do make your choice according to your need.

Remember Mother Earth also has its natural energy that can do your crystals a lot of good. So, you may wish to bury your crystals in the soil for a couple of days to get re-energized. If outside is not convenient, your flower pot can do the trick – just bury your crystal there for, say, three to seven days.

Proper Way of Storing Crystals

If you want your crystals to retain their luster and energy vibrations, you need to handle them with care and love. You need to avoid exposing them to long periods of sunlight otherwise they are likely to get faded. Some of the safest ways to store your crystals include:

- Enclosing them in a pouch
- Wrapping them using a silk scarf

Choosing and Using Crystals in Spellwork

In order to provide opportunities to deepen your acquaintance with some of these stones, the spellwork in the following section draws exclusively from this list.

However, as you set out to bring new crystals into your life, always go with your intuition. If a stone not on this list calls to you, then by all means, listen!

Likewise, if you're looking for a particular stone, like jade for example, but don't feel connected to any of the available jade stones in the shop, it may not be time for you to work with jade—or the jade for you may be elsewhere.

It's also possible to make substitutions in many of the spells, since it's often the case that a handful of stones are equally suitable to any given purpose. This is especially important to remember if you're on a budget that doesn't have room for a new crystal. Remember, magic should never be a cause for financial stress—in fact; it should be a means of creating more abundance!

The next section will introduce you to a few different types of crystal magic, from simple "charge and carry" spells to using crystals in ritual baths, and joining the power of crystals with magically charged candles and herbs.

Because of the mineral and energetic nature of crystals, some of the spellwork requires caution, so be sure to read instructions carefully!

Remember also to spend some time with the stone(s) you plan to work with in your magic. The power of spellwork is much more effective when you have a strong connection to the tools you work with, and this is especially true when working with these natural gifts from the Earth. So approach this work with reverence for the living energies of crystals, and, just as importantly, have fun!

Introduction to Crystal Spellwork

As mentioned in the first section of this guide, Wiccans and other Witches use crystals in their magical and spiritual work in a variety of ways.

They may be used in the creation of ritual tools, such as using a crystal point as the end of a wand or bejeweling the handle of an athame, to keep the energy of sacred space in balance, or to amplify spellwork simply with their presence.

Below, you'll find a few of the various ways crystals can be used as direct agents in magical work. There is traditional-style spells involving one or more charged crystals along with other spell ingredients and spoken incantations, as well as more "hands-on" work with crystal charms, and even magically charged drinking water!

But before trying any of the workings below, there are a few things to keep in mind.

When you take a closer look at Crystals from different directions you will begin to see the Witchcraft energy of these stones. They have been used as a talisman and to make jewelry for many years. These stones create an aura of the stone being a symbol of creativity, representing the living power of the Earth and infinity. Crystals are used for their healing powers and their ability to increase the energy in physical spaces. They are also used as a source of alternative healing.

Crystals in the new age and Wiccan circles are used to mean an array of solid minerals. A substance that is inorganic in nature and formed when the geological processes take place underground is called a mineral. Every mineral has its own composition and energy that makes it unique. Every Shaman, Witch, and healer knows the energies that are present in different mineral stones.

The regular molecular structure that is formed by a mineral stone that creates a surface that is flat informs what we know to be crystals. The popular crystal is the clear quartz. True "crystal balls" are said to be formed by clear quartz. Other popular crystals are the amethyst and rose quartz. Interestingly, known stones such as the lapis lazuli, bloodstone, and jade are formed by the combination of several stones and are not regarded as true crystals. Amber and jet, which are also considered to be "crystals", are apparently organic substances that have been fossilized. It is for these reasons that to enjoy the gifts of the earth stones and crystals have been used in the place of each other.

One of the known ways of practicing Crystal Initiation simply is by charging a stone with an intention and having it with you as the day progresses. Crystal spell is cast by individuals to be used situations that seem challenging. Such situations could be those that require communicating something important as well as situations that require people to draw agreements thereafter. Lapis Lazuli is a crystal stone that is referred to as "a stone of truth." The name is derived from Persian and Latin and it means "blue stone." The Lapis Lazuli helps with effective communication with others and yourself. Blue as a color symbolizes the throat chakra whose association is the expression of one's true voice. Negative thoughts and words from other people can also be thwarted by the Lapis Lazuli. The stone sends the negative energy back to its senders. Having a Lapis Lazuli that is charged enables one to be confident and have the general peace of mind in a conversation that might be challenging. When charging a lapis stone, if one puts either amethyst or clear quartz, the lapis will receive an energy boost.

To cast this spell one would need one piece of lapis lazuli stone, 1 yellow or white candle and 1 or more optional pieces of either amethyst or clear quartz crystals

Instructions are:

If using amethyst or crystal, place it first at the front of the candle while lighting the wick. Take the lapis lazuli stone and place it in both of your hands, with your eyes closed, take in deep breaths. Take a moment to visualize feeling a sense of relief after having a potentially challenging conversation. After that, visualize the positive energy that you experience while visualizing the result of the conversation and feel it flow into the stone. While doing that proclaim this statement or another similar one

"I communicate clearly and effectively from the essence of my true self."

Once you get a strong feeling about the stone being charged enough, take it and place it next to the amethyst or clear quartz if you were using one of them and leave them by the candle as it burns for the next one hour at least. Once this is done, your stone is now able to guide you in any potentially charged conversations.

Crystals and stones have powerful energies and are the reason why they are used in initiation.

The amethyst enables one to have a clear purpose and is violet in color.

The bloodstone is green in color and has gold or red flecks has energies that promote prosperity and physical healing

The carnelian crystal is used to thwart negative energies away and is either orange or red in color. It also enables one to be courageous.

The citrine has magical properties of renewal, useful dreams and is yellow in color.

The hematite is grey, black or grey and has the magical properties of aiding with problem-solving and also strengthens one's willpower.

Jade is a black crystal that has the magical properties of protecting one from negativity and helps during the transition of grounding and centering.

The blue or dark blue lapis lazuli has the magical properties of divination and altered consciousness.

The malachite is a green crystal with bands of dark black and green and has the magical property of aiding with emotional courage during a person's significant transition and enhances spiritual growth.

The moonstones are usually either a pale blue or white in color that has the magical properties of enhancing the reception to initiation, creativity and is supportive of intuition.

The quartz crystal is clear or white in color and has the magical properties of promoting spiritual growth, healing, and clarity.

The rose quartz is pink in color and has the magical properties of enhancing friendship, love, and emotional healing and wellbeing.

The tiger's eye has the magical properties of energy and protection and is brown, tan or gold with bands of black in color.

Chapter 5: Guidelines for Successful Spellcasting

Spellcasting is for anyone who wants to practice magic and the craft. It only takes a little bit of practice and some experimentation to feel comfortable and confident with any spell. Because there are so many different kinds and so many different ways to cast, this chapter will serve as an overview of guidelines to cast spells safely and effectively to get you on the right path.

As you are reading, you will appreciate how much you may already know about spells and casting. So much of this is innate knowledge and intuition, and as you grow your spiritual practice, you will learn how to be guided by your intuition so much more through all of your individual endeavors with magic.

The main thing with any spell is to be safe and to have fun while you set your clear goals and intentions. All spells are about the energy you put into them to create a positive outcome. Starting on the right foot with spellcasting will make all the difference on your journey.

Safe Spellcasting

Enjoying your spell work is easy, especially when you are taking the right precautions. Even when you aren't using any potentially dangerous tools or implements, it is still a good practice to go into your work with a mindset of feeling prepared, protected, and safe. Having a standard protocol for your witchcraft and spell work will help you remain respectful of yourself and all the energies that you choose to incorporate into your process.

Safety with Tools

You will find that a lot of the tools in this book and any that you find online or in other books will have a list of things you will need to accomplish the spell. Some of these tools will include flame, candles dripping hot wax, smoke for smudging, blades for cutting and other sharp tools for specific acts of manifestation, and many more.

The tools that you use will help you harness the energy and manipulate in the way that is required to achieve the final goal and outcome of your spell. All tools are sacred to your practice and should be properly cared for. Safety with tools isn't just about safe handling, which you will want to make sure of; it can also be about safe energy.

Consider how often you will be using these tools and how much energy they will accumulate over time. Cleansing and purifying your tools is an easy and effective way for you to keep your tools in a higher state of vibration and clarity for use in spell work. Sometimes, the energy of something can feel "off," and you aren't sure why. This can happen with your tools for Wiccan spell work, and a "funky-feeling" tool can cause you to fumble and could even cause some injury.

Safe handling of candles, matches, fire, blades, and smudging sticks is always highly recommended. Make sure you have the right dishes and containers to keep your candles standing upright and your smudge stick away from anything it could set fire. You may also want to make sure your altar and ritual space is well-ventilated while you use smoke for purification.

Practicing proper tool safety is a must, even when it means clearing and purifying the energy of your tools and implements regularly, to prevent them from collecting unwanted energies that could mar your spells and incantations or them make difficult.

Fire Safety

Fire safety should go without saying, but it bears mention here. However, fire comes into your rituals and spell work; it must be respected for the energy that it carries. Fire is a power of creation and destruction and has always been here to give us life and sometimes take it away. The reality is, fire is dangerous, and it needs to be used wisely.

Many spells call for candle magic for the lighting of sacred smoke and for burning of intentions, messages written on paper, and herbs. The use of fire and burning things is a very holy and magical practice and will give a great deal of power to any spell work you choose to do when performed safely.

When you are using fire in your spells, take necessary precautions:

- Use a sturdy candle holder for every candle.
- Keep your candles out of strong winds and away from things that can easily burst in flames.
- If you are letting your candles burn down, then you will need to monitor them or make sure they are in a safe container.

- Have a dish for your smudge sticks to lay them in while they burn out, as well as your incense.

- Use a cauldron or fire-safe bowl to burn your written words on paper, herbs, or other items. You may even want to do your burning outside during spells, depending on the space and ventilation.

- Keep flammable items away from anything burning until the flames are put out.

- Fire is powerful, and so is the magic it adds to your spell. Use it wisely, and it will help you to manifest your goals and spells very effectively.

Harm None

As you have already read in Chapter 1, an essential aspect of the Wiccan philosophy is that you will cause no harm to another while you practice magic. This is a potent tool to help you stay safe from causing damage to yourself and others while you cast.

The Threefold Law states that anything you do can return to you three times, meaning your energetic impact through rituals and spells will return to you three times over. That is incredibly powerful energy to return to you, and if you are casting to bring more wealth and abundance into your life, that would be a good thing. However, if you are casting a spell to make someone fall out of love with another person to fall in love with you, that is harmful to not only one, but two people. It will come back to you at some point by the power of three, according to Wiccan beliefs.

However it returns to you, it will likely feel bad and unpleasant, and so for the safety of your feelings and those of another, it is best to state the Wiccan Rede of "harm none," before you cast any spell to make sure you are not going to bring any hurt to you or another. This is a powerful way for you to engage with magic more positively and beneficially to the good of all.

Spiritual Safety

Preparing to cast a spell requires an opening to all of the energies and a connection with spirit. Becoming wide open as a channel of energy during your spells and incantations requires some protection on your part to make sure you only include positive and light vibrational energies into your spellcasting.

Sometimes, when we are doing our work, we forget that we can easily open to all different kinds of nature, both dark and light and that it will be necessary to consider protecting yourself from anything that might have a negative impact or effect on your energy or your spells.

All this means is that you set an intention of protection and invite only positive energies into your circle and your spell work. Some might even call upon a specific deity to act as a guardian during their spells to help them stay focused and keep any unwanted energies at bay.

Another excellent method of creating spiritual protection is through the casting of a circle (more on that later in the chapter).

Personal Safety and Well-Being

Your personal safety and well-being can have a significant impact on your ability to cast magic well and safely. If you are overworked, overtired, ill, or unhappy, it may not be the best time for you to be doing any casting work. That energy will carry through in your spell and can have an impact on your manifestation. If your spell involves helping you out of those states of mind or being, then make sure you are gentle and nurturing and that you are performing your spells at a moment of optimal health to achieve your goal.

Your personal safety is just as important as the concept of harming none. Make sure you are in the right mindset and emotional state to perform magic. Remember, what you cast can return to you threefold, so whatever your intentions are, make sure you are in a good head, heart, and body space to perform your spell work.

Grounding and Centering for Spellcasting

Success with spellcasting isn't just about safety and what tools you might use; It's also about how you prepare your mind, body, and spirit. The idea behind grounding and centering is that you ask yourself to unite with your authentic energy and power to call upon the work you want to do accurately.

Calming the mind, focusing on your intentions, and getting aligned for your magical purpose are a massive part of how to successfully cast. If your mind is wandering and thinking about what you are going to need from the grocery store, then you won't be focused on your power for manifestation. A lot of people will sometimes consider the centering process as something very akin to meditation.

In general, meditation is an all-encompassing term that essentially asks you to clear your mind and stay focused on the moment you are in. Meditation is another way to describe the centering process to help you ready your energy to make magic.

Grounding is another term to help you understand the quality of vibration—or energy—that allows you to stay within the power of Earth and her abundant fuel for magic. To ground yourself is to connect to the floor of everything, everywhere. You ground into the floor of your body and mind, and you also ground into the energy of whatever deities you are supporting.

Grounding helps us to siphon any excess energy into the ground and then pull the available power endlessly from the Earth through us. It is a way to help the direction of your energy flow so that you feel supported, balanced, and prepared for whatever spell or ritual you are about to perform. In many ways, the grounding and centering process is what directs your intuition, instinct, and power into what you are working on. It is a focus of energy on all levels.

Not everyone will ground and center before casting, and if you were to compare results of spells from someone who does and someone who doesn't, you might be surprised to find that there is more return for those who are practicing their groundedness before and after casting a spell.

For many who practice Wicca, the grounding process can occur with the casting of the circle, as this activity has very stabilizing, opening, and centering qualities. Before any spell, if you want to have greater success with manifestation, it is crucial to prepare your energy to work with it according to your wishes and goals. Some people will use a circle of protection while others might use a specific meditation, incantation, or poem. You can also use crystals and stones that are specifically for the purpose of grounding, and using incense and smudging can have a very centering and grounding impact.

You will need to determine the right method for you, and if you want to have success with your spells, consider a grounding and centering ritual before you get started to make sure your energy is in right alignment with your spell's purpose.

Casting a Circle: How and Why

Casting a Circle is one of the most common aspects of practicing with Wiccan spells and all kinds of Pagan ritual and witchcraft. First, let's talk about why you want to cast a circle before you start a spell. Then, you can see exactly how it is done.

A circle in Wicca and witchcraft serves multiple purposes. It is specific energy to help you feel safe and protected, while it calls upon the elements, directions, and spirit to help you in your work. Traditionally, the circle is your gateway to magic and will always keep you in alignment with the energy of nature. Here, within the circle, you will find the support you need to accomplish your goals from all directions of the Universe.

You should always cast a kind of circle, even if it completely simple, like spinning in a circle to acknowledge energy around you that will shield you from outside forces. A circle is an energetic bubble that holds your power and your magic inside. It can be a way to keep you spiritually safe, only inviting in the energies you want to work with.

Many will use a candle, an object from nature, or an altar tool to mark each direction with one of the four primary elements. The fifth element, spirit or ether, is what is above you. In Wicca, it can pertain to the God/Goddess energy you call upon to worship in your work.

The purpose of your circle is to protect you and also to empower you while you cast. It is a connection to the divine and promotes the gateway and opening for manifestation while it holds you in the balance of all life.

Basic Circle Casting - Opening a Circle

Use creative visualization to help you picture your circle and the protective shield that will surround you and your work. You can see it like a glass orb, a tent, or a colorful light surrounding you. The size of your circle depends on the amount of space you need to work your spell.

Use a compass if you don't know what way is north.

1. From the north position, use your finger or some other kind of tool to point in front of you or to the floor at the north of the circle. You can say something like this: "As I open to the divine powers that be, I call upon the power of the North and the Earth element to protect and guide me. And so it is."

2. Now, move clockwise to the East and say something like this: "As I open to the divine powers that be, I call upon the power of the East and the Air element to protect and guide me. And so it is."

3. Continue clockwise to the South and say: "As I open to the divine

powers that be, I call upon the power of the South and the Fire element to protect and guide me. And so it is."

4. Continue to the West position and say: "As I open to the divine powers that be, I call upon the power of the West and the Water element to protect and guide me. And so it is."

5. Return to the starting position of the North and hold both hands above you, either clasped together and your fingers are pointing up or using a tool of your choice. Then connect to the element of spirit and say: "I call upon the energy of the Universe and [insert preferred deities or other energies of spirit] to aid me in my magic. And so it is."

You can change the format according to your preferences and add any other information that feels the most grounding, opening, and balancing for you. Use creative visualization to picture guardian and ancestors with you, or use crystals and gemstones to create the entire circle, laying them out on the floor around you. How you choose to cast your circle must be a regular part of your preparation for a successful spellcasting.

When you are finished with your spells, you can close your circle by moving backward through the circle, counterclockwise and repeating words of gratitude to each direction and element for being with you in your practice.

The Steps of a Basic Spell

There are a few steps to help you cast spells successfully. You only need to know a few things to get you started, and all of these critical points and tips are what makes the difference between a prosperous manifestation and a flimsy spell.

1. Set Your Intention

Before anything else can happen, you have to know the reason for your spell. What is the outcome or goal? What are you trying to accomplish? Be specific and clear when determining the point of your spell work so that there isn't any confusion between you and the universe.

2. Find Your Tools and Ingredients

With most spells, you are going to need a few things to help you manifest that abundance. It could merely be a candle and a crystal, or it could be an elaborate mixture of herbs and a more delicate process that takes a while. Whatever you need for your spell, you want to make sure you have the right tools to help you cast your intention into the energy of the Universe.

3. Decide the Timing

Timing can matter, as you will learn in the later chapters. Some spells need the power of the full moon, while others might need to occur at high noon under a bright summer sun. When you perform your spell, it can have an impact on the quality of the energy you are working with in conjunction with the intentions of your spell. Most spells that you find online or in books will tell you if there is a specific timing, and as you create your own, use your intuition about when a good time will be for a specific intention.

4. Prepare the Language

Most spells encourage and incorporate the use of particular and specific wording to help you establish your goals and intentions. Every word you speak in a spell carries great meaning and energy toward your spell becoming manifested. It is vital to prepare your choice of words ahead of time so that they are direct and in clear communication with all that is around you and working with you.

5. Organize and Design

With all of these components decided upon, you will then need to organize it into a usable format so that when you are performing the spell, it flows in the right direction. Decide when to light the candles, when to burn the incense, and so on. You will know precisely how it needs to flow as you are working with it.

When you are looking at the spells in this book, you will find that they incorporate all of these components to help you organize the way to cast your magic spells. These steps will help you create your spells. The more you practice the Wiccan spells you find in these pages, the easier it becomes, and the better you will be able to understand the basic steps behind every spell.

These guidelines and tips will help you in all of your spell work. Safely performing your work while maintaining a healthy attitude and groundedness will bring you a more significant return and success with all of the spells that you cast. Going into the next chapter, you will learn more about the popular spell book for a Wiccan or Witch and why it will be so valuable to your spellcasting. Your Book of Shadows is the number one book of spells, and having your own is a part of the fun and magic of Wiccan spellcasting.

Chapter 6: Crystal Spells

This is the chapter you all have been waiting for. Here you will find lots of different spells that will utilize these all-powerful gemstones. Get your intentions ready and get started.

A word to the wise, though, you should never do a spell just because it sounds fun. You should always do one because you have and intention and believe that it will help you bring that intention to life.

Communication Talisman

You need:

- Yellow or white candle
- Amethyst or quarts – optional
- Lapis lazuli

If you are using, put the amethyst or quartz in front of your candle and then light the candle. Holding the lapis lazuli in your hands, close your eyes and take a few deep breaths. Picture yourself feeling satisfied and relieved with how you communicate with people. Imagine all of the positive energy of this flowing out of your hands and into the crystal. Now, say: "I communicate effectively and clearly from the essence of who I truly am."

Once you feel that your stone is charged enough, place it next to the amethyst or quartz and let it sit with the candle as the candle burns for at least an hour. You can now carry the lapis lazuli with you to add in communication.

Self-Empowerment Spell

You need:

- Citrine, rhodonite, amethyst, or rose quartz
- Yarrow
- Orange or lemon essential oil
- Light or matches
- Red candle

Begin by anointing the candle with your chosen essential oil and then sprinkle it with or roll it in the yarrow. Now, light the candle. Focus completely on the flame of the candle and on raising your energy.

Pick up the crystal and then wave it through the flame of the candle and then say: "I am love, I am power, I am enough, I am joy, I am good." Make sure that you will pop the word "am." Continue to chant this for as long as you are able to. Keep this chant in your mind every day to remind yourself of your personal power. Keep this crystal on you when you need extra confidence. You can also take a moment to visualize the flame of the candle and chant the mantra whenever you need to.

Protection and Cleansing Charm Bag

You need:

- Sage essential oil
- Candle holder
- Matches
- Black candle
- Lavender buds – optional
- Lavender essential oil
- Dried rose petals
- Dried thyme leaves
- Jet or black obsidian stone
- Dried sage leaves
- Piece of white or black ribbon
- Square of black fabric

Begin by casting your circle however you choose to. Take a moment to clear and relax your mind. Next, anoint your candle with some of the sage oil, and then roll it in the thyme and sage leaves.

Light your candle and picture yourself feeling protects, cleansed, and pure. As the candle burns, let the smoke to waft over the fabric, ribbon, and everything that will go in it. Do this and say the following three times:

"Cleanse my soul, I ask of thee, cleanse me of my negativity. Wishes and energy, thoughts and deeds, cleanse them all, so mote it be. As you cleanse, protect my soul to, through night and day, and the morning dew. Protect me from harm and negativity, cleanse it now, and leave only purity. It is done."

Once you have said these three times, and everything has been passed through the smoke, blow the candle out and then put everything in the middle of the piece of fabric and then draw up the edges and close it with the ribbon.

Do the same thing every day until the candle has completely burned out. Bury the leftover wax in the dirt. Keep your charm bag with you and repeat the candle process if you start feeling as if you need a boost.

Love Spell

You need:

- Piece of red cloth
- Light or matches
- Heatproof container
- Piece of paper with your list of attributes you want out of a significant other
- Iron filings
- Lodestone
- Red candle

Begin by lighting the candle and then place the lodestone beside it and say, "This stone is me."

Now, take your list and then say: "This is my (boyfriend/girlfriend/partner) who (read your list in present tense)." Make sure as you do this that you visualize all of this coming true.

Once you have read through your list, light it with the candle flame and let it burn. You can place the paper in the heatproof dish for it to burn so that you don't get burned. Add some of the iron fillings to the dish with the ashes and stir them together. Lay the lodestone on the cloth and cover with the ash mixture as you say: "What I want, comes to me." Say these three times.

Wrap the cloth around the lodestone and ashes as you say: "As I will, so mote it be." Place your little bundle into a safe space.

Sleep Spell

You need:

- A piece of parchment
- Smoky quartz
- Lavender sprigs

You need to start this spell by getting your bedroom ready. Put on some fresh clean sheets. Dim the lights and make sure it is quiet so that you can help you focus on your spell and will help you to fall asleep. It wouldn't hurt if you took a bath first as well.

Sit comfortably on your bed as you hold onto the piece of smoky quartz. Make sure you aren't sitting on your pillow. Take a few moments to focus on the energy of the stone and let all of your troubles disappear. After you feel grounded and calm, let your eyes close while saying the following chant three times as you are holding onto the stone in the right hand and moving your wrist in a slow clockwise circle: "The moon is up, I hold its piece, the silver dust will guard my peace."

After you finish saying this for the third time, wrap the stone and the lavender in some parchment and lay it next to your bed. Now go to bed.

Don't get discouraged if this doesn't work for you on the first night. It can take three nights to really get this spell working for you.

New Year Ritual

You need:

- Small jar
- Quartz
- Chalice of water
- Black candle
- Citronella or sage incense
- Paper and pen

Pick a place where you can sit or stand comfortably that is quiet to create your holy space to start your ritual. You can also just do this at your altar. Begin by focusing on your breath to calm your soul and mind. Once you feel you are at peace and relaxed, you can continue.

On the paper, write out what you intend on doing during the coming year.

Do you want adventure, joy, friendship, love, or financial abundance? Write out general and brief statements. The Universe is going to bring you the things that are the best for you, so try not to focus a bunch on the specifics, but it is a good thing if you start feeling excited as you write.

Next, you will bring in the elements.

Light your incense and then say:

"Lord and Lady, God and Goddess, I give you my thanks for everything I have. With air, I cleanse the past to prepare for a prosperous new year for the highest good. So mote it be."

Allow the incense to fill up the room as heaviness and negativity begin to leave your energy field. Picture a rainbow forming around you and growing bigger and brighter with each breath you take. Say: "Thank you."

Light your candle. While you do this, start to think about what you have done through during the last year, and try to focus on getting rid of the energy baggage you could be carrying. Watch as it disintegrates and changes into the fire. Then picture the fire bringing energy back into your life. Say: "Lord and Lady, God and Goddess, I give my thanks for what I have. With Fire, I ignite the future to prepare for a prosperous new year. For the highest good, so mote it be."

Allow the candle to burn until you have made it through the ritual.

Say: "Thank you."

Now, pick up the chalice and fill it up with water. Hold it in your hand and let your energies to blend and merge with the energy of the water. Feel grateful for the water and all of its life-giving and purifying properties. Pick the chalice up and say: "Lord and Lady, God and Goddess, I thank you for all that I have. With Water, I vitalize the future to prepare for a prosperous new year. For the highest good, so mote it be."

Drink the water and focus on how your body feels energizes, revitalizes, and cleansed. Say: "Thank you."

Now, pick up the paper and the quartz and wrap the stone inside the paper. It will help you to manifest your wishes. Hold this as you say: "Lord and Lady, God and Goddess, I thank you for all that I have. With Earth, I manifest my wishes to welcome a prosperous new year. For the highest good, so mote it be."

Sit this inside the jar and make sure you place it someplace safe where it won't be disturbed. Say: "Thank you."

Take the time, now, to thank all of the elements for being with you and helping you and then send them away by patting the ground or floor three times. Spend a little bit of time picturing what you want, having already been, manifested. Feel all of the joy and calmness inside of you. Hold onto those feelings as you close your ritual and go about your year.

Friendship Spell

You need:

- Yellow or orange candle
- A teaspoon of dried allspice
- Carnelian
- Orange pouch

Before you start your spell, really take the time to figure out what kind of friendship you would like to bring into your life. Do you want a small group of close-knit friends or a lot of friends? What about their personalities and hobbies? What kind of qualities or values do they need?

Take as long as you need to on this step so that you get the friends that you want.

Next, cleanse all of the objects that you are using. This could be through visualization or smudging. Start by casting your circle and doing any prep work that you need to, like meditating or calling your spirit guides.

Then, light the candle. Sit everything else out in front of you. Place the carnelian in the middle of your pouch and make a circle of allspice around it.

Shut your eyes for a moment and picture yourself surrounded by all of your friends. These are all positive people that you like to be with. Make this come to life in your mind's eye and really focus on the positive feelings that your friendship brings. Once you have these strong feelings, place your hands, palms down, over the spices and crystals. Picture these feelings like a gold light moving out of your heart, through your arms, and then down your palms, filling the objects with the light. Picture your objects soaking up all of this golden light until they are pulsating with its energy.

Put everything inside of the pouch and close it. Pick up the candle and draw three circles above the pouch in a clockwise direction as you say: "True friendships, come to me, as I will, so mote it be."

Thank everything you called into you spell and close your circle.

Carry this pouch with you wherever you go to attract the friends you want into your life.

Glamour Spell

You need:

- Makeup or jewelry you want to wear
- Cotton ball or pad
- Micellar water
- Rose quartz
- Red candle
- Palo Santo stick
- Small mirror

Start by lighting the Palo Santo and use it to cleanse your workspace and all of the items that you are going to be using. Next, cast your circle in order to keep all of the energies housed into your sacred space.

Now decorate your sacred space with the mirror and any extra rose quartz that you may have. Place a rose quartz into your micellar way and then say: "Pasithea, Aphrodite, see my wishes shine through brightly."

Pick the mirror up in your non-dominant hand, left hand for right-handed people and vice versa. Now gaze upon the part of your face that you would like to change. Say: "My (state the part you want to change) is seen only by me. I create the canvas for others to see."

As you are still looking at yourself, dip your piece of cotton into the micellar water. Say: "Now a canvas, I wipe it clean. Only what I visualize shall be seen."

Start wiping the potion over all of your face, making sure that you pay more attention to the part that you would like to change. As you are cleansing, let your vision go a bit blurry, like you do when you are crying.

Gaze into the mirror and see what you would like other people to see when they see you. Make sure that you can see all of your face intact as well. After you are satisfied with what you are visualizing, say: "What I see will be seen by all, until I let my glamour fall. And it harms none, so mote it be."

Lay your mirror down and thank Pasithea and Aphrodite and then close your circle.

This glamour will take several visualization processes and it will take a lot of energy to keep up. Every time you look in the mirror, take a moment to visualize your glamour. Those who don't know you that well will notice your glamour first, and then with time, people who are close to will be able to see it as well. Eventually, it will become second nature.

Lammas Ritual

You need:

- Palo Santo or sage
- Lodestones
- Aventurine
- Carnelian
- Tiger's eye

- Rosehips
- Sandalwood incense
- Brown candles
- Golden candles
- Dark green candles
- Cornucopia fills with veggies and fruits

Start out by cleansing your space with the Palo Santo or sage. Next, you need to set up your space. In the Air space, place the tiger's eye around the corner candle, like a grid. Think about all of the ideas that you have had during the year so far.

Then in the Fire corner, place the carnelian crystals around the corner candles, like a grid. Start to think about the passions that you have gotten to start during the year.

Then in the Water corner, place the aventurine crystals around the candles, like a grid Start to think about all of the times that you have been strong in the face of emotions during the year so far.

Then in the Earth corner, place the lodestone around the candles, like a grid. Start to think about all of the times where you have grounded yourself so that you can make the best decisions during the year. Think about any financial successes that you have had as well.

Then place your cornucopia on your pentacle plate in order to amplify the energies of abundance in every part of your life.

Now place the candles listed above to your altar wherever you see fit.

Place the rosehips in a mug and pour boiling water over them. Enchant the tea with all of the energies of health and prosperity. Now, cast your circle in whatever way you would like.

Once your circle is cast, say: "Today, today, on Lammas day, I celebrate the goodness that has come my way. Blessings of love, happiness, wealth, and truth, blessed Lammas, cheers to you."

Now light your Lammas candles and drink a bit of your tea, then say: "Blessed mother, blessed father, and Lammas God Lugh, I drink to you and ask from you, teach me something new."

Continue to sip on your tea and let yourself to enter a meditative trance. Feel all of the sensations of your spirit and body. Allow all of your senses to open up and pay attention to any messages that are sent to you. Let yourself meditate on the meaning of Lammas and ask to receive a symbol of what you should learn or do between now and Mabon.

After you have finished your meditation, thank the God and Goddess and God Lugh. Now you can close your circle.

Friendship Charm Bottle

If you can, do this spell during a full or waxing moon, on a Friday, and in the hour of Venus.

You need:

- Pink, brown, or yellow candle

- Three drops of lemon juice
- Three sun-dried lemon slices
- Three lemon seeds
- Six coriander seeds – or other friendship herbs
- Tiger's eye
- Pentacle plate – optional
- Cauldron – optional
- Scissors
- Black pen
- Yellow paper
- Glass jar with lid
- Palo Santo or Sage

Start by cleansing yourself with the Palo Santo or sage and then cast your circle in your favorite way. Using the same smudge, cleanse all of the items that you are going to be using in your spell. Picture all of the items being surrounded by a yellow light and know that every one of the items will bring new friends into your life.

Sit the jar onto the pentacle plate or your altar if you aren't using the plate. Picture, that as you fill it with items, that your life is also being filled with new friends. Imagine yourself as being happy.

Cut the sheet of yellow paper into strips and one each of the strips write one quality or trait that you would like your new friends to have. While you write these things down, say these things out loud and picture the friend that you are creating with these qualities. It is very important that you never, ever, write down a specific person. You are trying to bring the person to you that will be the best fit for you, and it may not be the one you believe is the best for you.

One at a time, pick the strips of paper up, say the trait, picture the friend, light it on fire, and let it burn away into your cauldron. Continue to picture the person as the strip of paper burns. Then place the ashes inside of the jar. Continue with all of the strips. If you do not have a cauldron or heat-proof bowl, you can simply fold the piece of paper and then unfold to release its magic and place it inside of the jar. If you are using the folded paper method, one-fold is for a single friend being called into your life, multiple folds will bring more than one friend.

Now, add in the lemon seeds, one by one, while you say: "Into this jar, I drop this seed to manifest into my need. I wish that my number of friends will grow, based on the qualities I've placed below. So mote it be."

Place the tiger's eye stone into the jar and say: "Tiger's eye to keep away false friends, and allow me to see the friends who will be loyal until the end. So mote it be."

Add the coriander and say: "Coriander to invoke Universal love, a love that has been absent from my life. So mote it be."

Place in the lemon slices and say: "A lemon slice, the color yellow, place into this bottle to show just how much the fruit called our friendship will grow. So mote it be."

Next, add in the lemon juice and say: "Lemon juice, meant to preserve, serve the purpose you were meant to serve. Preserve this friendship, every little drop, let us remain good friends until time stops. So mote it be."

Finish off the spell by place the lid onto the jar and seal it with some wax from the candle. Take a moment to visualize the amazing friendship you have just created as you see a pink or yellow light surrounding the bottle. Close your circle and thank anybody you have called in and know that the spell is complete.

Confidence Spell

You need:

- Clothes in orange, red, or yellow – optional
- Solar anointing oil
- Tiger's eye crystal
- Yellow or gold candle

Place all of your tools in the middle of what will become your circle. Start by meditating on what you would like the spell to do for you. Make sure that you are crystal clear about what you want the outcome to be, such as, what areas of your life do you need more confidence? How would you want to act in different situations? Specifics will improve this spell.

Now, you can cast your circle and then sit in the middle of it so that you are facing south. Pick up the candle and anoint it with the solar oil as you say: "I call upon the energies of the Sun and Earth to help me find my confidence and worth."

Now, light your candle and sit it in front of you. Pick up the tiger's eye and let your hand cup around it. Gaze at the flame and picture a golden light shining over you. Have this light become vibrant and beautiful. This is all of the unconditional love that the Universe has for you. As you allow this golden energy to wash over you, see yourself in the eyes of the God and Goddess. See them loving you like a parent would their child. They love you simply because you exist. There are no conditions attached to that love. Feel your heart expanding with this energy. Watch as the light continues to grow bigger. It starts to fill the circle and then spills out into the entire room. Take as much time as you need to in order to visualize this.

After you feel that the room is completely filled with this light, open up your hands and begin to feel the tiger's eye taking in all of this energy. Watch as the golden light pours into the crystal until it is all held within it.

After you are finished, close your circle and carry your tiger's eye with you and use all of its energy whenever you need some unconditional love by holding it and meditating for a moment.

Love Spell for the Full Moon

You need:

- Pink yarn
- Red cloth
- Rose quartz
- Moonstone
- Two apple seeds
- Ground cinnamon
- Dried basil
- Pink candle

- Red candle

Before you begin, make sure you take a moment to clarify what type of relationship you are looking to have. Make sure that you are clear on what your desire is. This can take some time. It is also a good idea to figure out how you feel about it and not allow yourself to get hung up on the details. For example, instead of listing out all of the traits you want them to have, write down that you want to be attracted to them. Also, think about how you want to feel in the relationship.

Get your items together and then cast your circle. Light the candles and spread the red cloth out in front of you. Pass the moonstone through the flames of the candles and then sit it on the cloth. Repeat this for the rose quartz.

Pick up the apple seeds, and say: "By the light of the moon, I now plat these seeds of love."

As you sit these seeds onto the cloth along with the crystals, start seeing all of the soft pink energy coming from the crystals and nourishing your seeds with their loving energy. Sprinkle everything with some cinnamon and basil. Pull the four corners of the cloth together so that everything is wrapped inside, and then wrap the pink yarn around the bag three times. Tie the bag with three knots and say: "So mote it be."

Close your circle and carry your charm bag with you to attract the one you love.

Quit Drinking Spell

You need:

- Amethyst
- Glass of water
- Black string
- An empty alcohol bottle that has been washed and has a lid
- A pen
- 10 to 15 small paper pieces

Take a bit of time, before you start, to think about why you want to give up alcohol. If you have an actual physical addiction, you should speak with your doctor first because quitting cold turkey can endanger your health.

Now, write down all of the reasons for stopping drinking on each slip of the paper.

Now, cast your circle and take a few moments to meditate until you feel calm and clear-minded. Pick up a piece of paper and read it. Then, you need to affirm the opposite of that, as if you have stopped drinking. Then bask in how this would feel if it were true right now. Picture yourself as being a non-drinker and rejoice in a healthy and happy feeling. Place the paper into the bottle. Continue to do this until you have gone through every piece of paper. Next, tie the black cord around the neck of the bottle and tie three knots.

Pick up the water and picture white light coming out of it. Slowly drink that water, and feel all of that light pouring into you with every sip. Feel it bless and purify you.

Pick up the amethyst and cup it in your hands. Feel all of this white light spinning through your body. Feel it becoming stronger and then feel it flow into that amethyst. Picture the crystal pulsing with the energy. Sit in meditation for a little bit, until you know that you are done.

Say: "I am a non-drinker. So mote it be."

Feel that this is a true statement. You can now close your circle. You can dispose of the bottle either by burying it or throwing it out. Carry the amethyst with you. If you feel like you need to drink, have a glass of water instead.

Chapter 7: Crystal Healing. How Crystals Influence and Enhance Your Life

By now, you have learned and experienced some of the ways that crystals can enhance different areas of your life. Another way to use crystals and stones in your day-to-day activities is for healing, on a physical, emotional and spiritual or psychological level. Crystals help to amplify and channel energies of all different sorts, and by selecting different stones, we can choose exactly which of those energies to amplify, and where to channel that energy, depending on the type of healing to be done.

While not a substitute for medical care, crystals and semi-precious stones can be used to enhance the body's natural powers of healing, and give medical results a boost.

Physical Crystal Healing

Using crystals to heal physical conditions is often as simple as choosing and purifying your stone, charging it with your intention, and dropping it in your pocket or purse. Just touching or holding your crystal throughout the day can often have dramatically positive effects. You can also use healing crystals by dropping one (or even a few) into your bath water for a soothing and healing experience. Before introducing your crystals to water, however, always be certain that they are water-safe. Some crystals can break, dissolve, or even release toxins when introduced to water and other liquids or when immersed. Those crystals and gemstones that should not come into contact with water have been denoted below, where possible, but this should not be substituted for careful research of your own. Always check to be sure your crystals are safe to be used in or with water if you choose to use them in this way.

Amber is a wonderful healing stone, used for easing the symptoms of colds, arthritis, bladder and kidney issues, as well as problems associated with the liver. While amber can be immersed in cool water, it should not be soaked for long periods of time, or introduced to hot water. Toxins trapped within this stone could be released when hot water comes into contact with it. Amber dust should not be inhaled either, as it may also contain toxins that are harmful to ingest.

Amethyst is a general pain relieving and detoxifying crystal. This gemstone is also used to alleviate insomnia, and to aid in the control of diabetes. While water immersion won't hurt this gemstone, any dust from it can contain toxins, and should not be inhaled.

Aventurine is another all-around healing stone, and is particularly effective in aiding in the healing of sinus problems and issues with the lungs. Red aventurine is often used for equalizing blood pressure. This gemstone is fine to be used in bath water, but should not be consumed (in a gem elixir, for example) because it contains aluminum.

Bloodstone is used to draw toxins from the blood and aid in the healing of circulatory issues. This beautiful stone is also used to combat anemia, and bolster the immune system.

Carnelian is a crystal that promotes cellular growth, to aid in the recovery of many ailments, and especially wounds, and is also used to fight the symptoms of seasonal allergies. While immersion in regular or purified water is fine for carnelian, introducing it to, or immersing it in salt water can cause it to crack.

Citrine is yet another all-around general healing stone, and aids with the healing of digestive issues. Like all types of quartz, citrine is just fine for water cleansing, but any dust from these stones should not be inhaled as it may contain toxins.

Emerald aids in lowering high blood pressure, and helps to sooth nausea. This crystal can be used for gem bathing, but should not be used for elixirs because it contains aluminum.

Hematite stones are often carried by people suffering from joint pain to sooth these symptoms, and can be used to help fade bruises. Because tis stone contains high amounts of iron, it should not be ingested in elixirs. Hematite should not be left in water for long periods of time, as this may induce rusting and cause this stone to fade quickly.

Malachite is often used to combat asthma, itching, and to fight infection. This stone may break in hot water, and can release toxic amounts of copper if used for elixirs. Malachite dust is also highly toxic and should not be inhaled.

Moonstone is highly prized for easing the pains of childbirth and the symptoms of P.M.S. This stone is sacred to many Goddesses, and is used to alleviate many health problems specific to females, such as the symptoms of menopause. While not adversely affected by water, it could become dull if left immersed for long periods of time, and moonstone dust may contain aluminum or other toxins.

Moss Agate is a beautiful gemstone, and is used most commonly for combatting the effects of hypoglycemia as well as stomach ulcers. Most agates are water-safe.

Obsidian is often used as a general detoxifier, and is also used to alleviate pain and cramping. This helpful gemstone has also been used to strengthen the spine and back, and even slow or reverse hair loss. Obsidian can be immersed in water, however, extreme temperatures may cause it to break or crack.

Rose Quartz, aside from being a general healing stone, is also known to heal matters of the heart. This pink quartz not only helps to heal relationship problems, but is useful in fighting fatigue, and healing kidney, and heart issues. While being a gemstone that can be immersed safely in water, it should not be ingested in an elixir because it gets its color from toxic iron and titanium, for this reason, rose quartz dust should not be inhaled.

Ruby has long been used to improve vitality, energy, and circulation. This red crystal is also used to fight impotence and constipation. Ruby contains aluminum and should not be used for gem elixirs, but can be used in gem baths, and cleansed with water.

Sapphires promote cellular production and regeneration, ease disorders of the blood, and help to clear up issues involving the eyes and vision. Because Sapphires get their color from aluminum, they should be avoided for use in gem elixirs.

Smokey Quartz has long been effective in fighting disorders of the skin, including warts, and is often used to fight infections. Being a member of the quartz family, this crystal can produce toxins in any dust formed from it, and should not be inhaled.

Sodalite helps to improve the metabolism, raise low blood pressure, and combats diabetes. This stone can be used in gem baths, and purified with water, but should not be used for gem elixirs, because of its aluminum content.

Turquoise is often used to ease respiratory problems, strengthen bones, and boost the immune system. Turquoise has high levels of both aluminum and copper, and should not be ingested, or inhaled in dust form. It has also been known to fade when immersed in water.

Emotional Healing

Conditions such as anxiety, stress, self-control, lack of willpower, and emotional imbalances, while not being physical maladies are still conditions that require healing. For these ailments, crystals and gemstones can be an invaluable tool in any treatment regime. If your crystals are water-safe, drop one (or a few) into your bath water for a powerful surge of healing energy. A crystal "lay-out" is another great way to enjoy the powerful healing vibrations of your gemstones. For a crystal lay-out, lie comfortably in a quiet room, and place your crystals on the areas of your body that you feel need the most healing attention. For instance, if you've been suffering from stress headaches, place a gemstone on your forehead, or your stomach if you just can't stick to that diet without suffering hunger pangs, for mood swings, try a crystal right over your heart. If you are familiar with the chakras, you can also place a crystal over the appropriate chakra that corresponds to your problem. Remain prone like this for at least five to ten minutes, while you enjoy the resonating, healing vibrations of your crystals. A nice addition to your crystal lay-out is to light some soothing incense, or a favorite scented candle to improve the healing ambience.

Norse runes, used for divination as well as introspection and self-healing, are often carved into gemstones for added healing benefits, because the runes themselves point out the areas in our subconscious that are demanding attention, a rune set carved into a crystal or stone that you particularly resonate with can be a powerful and personalized healing tool in your arsenal.

Below are some crystals to help you heal on an emotional level. Remember to double-check to make sure your crystal is safe to use in water, either for gem bathing, or gem elixirs.

Aquamarine will help to calm aggression, sooth feelings of anger, and help to even out and center your emotions. This crystal is generally fine to use in water for purification, and bathing, as well as in elixirs.

Black Tourmaline helps to ground and center emotions in order to combat social anxieties. Carry this stone with you when you feel you may be in a stressful situation, and need some extra emotional support. Black tourmaline contains aluminum, so should not be used in gem elixirs.

Blue Lace Agate helps to improve self-esteem and self-confidence, calms anxiety, and has the added benefit of improving communication. Almost all agates, including blue lace agate, are water safe gemstones.

Carnelian improves self-confidence, and promotes higher levels of self-worth. As previously noted, this crystal should not be used with salt water.

Howlite helps to calm aggression and quiets feelings of anger. This milky white stone also helps to remove feelings of negativity, as well as negative energy. While this stone can be used in gem baths, it should not be ingested in elixirs because of its boron, boron oxide and borate content.

Lepidolite calms fears and helps to improve overall mood. This crystal helps to alleviate anxiety and social anxiety, and actually contains lithium, which is found in anti-anxiety medications. This crystal is not water safe, and will flake apart if immersed or wet.

Malachite works to improve willpower, while bolstering self-control and self-discipline. This is not a water-safe stone, as noted in the physical healing section.

Moonstone is a gemstone that is particularly effective in healing issues specific to women. This stone is often used for relieving stress, and improving emotional balance, and is also used to equalize hormonal issues. Moonstone should not be used in gem elixirs.

Pearl is known to calm all sorts of emotional turmoil, and is helpful in combatting the effects of P.T.S.D. While pearls are water-safe for gem baths and purification purposes, they can lose their luster in water, or break when exposed to temperature extremes. These gemstones should not be used in gem elixirs because they may contain bacteria or other water pollutants from their formation process.

Rose Quartz is an overall emotional healer and balancer. This pink crystal helps to increase feelings of self-love, and bolsters confidence while promoting feelings of self-worth. As previously mentioned, rose quartz dust may contain toxins, and while this crystal is water-safe, it should not be used for gem elixirs.

Sodalite is a soothing stone that helps to ease panic attacks, and calm the mind. This gemstone can be used in gem baths, but should not be used for elixirs. Sodalite is a great stone to carry with you in its tumbled form for when fears and anxiety rise up. Use this stone in your lay-outs, and in gem baths, but not in gem elixirs.

Tiger's eye is an overall calming stone, and works to help balance emotions. This is also a wonderful stone to meditate to, with its enchanting bands of color. This gemstone should never be used for gem elixirs, or used in its raw, un-tumbled form because it is a fibrous form of asbestos, and highly toxic when in its raw form.

Mental/Spiritual Healing

Psychological and spiritual health is the highest level of crystal healing. From improving your life situation and cleansing Karma, sharpening your powers of perception, empathy and intuition, and even deep-rooted psychological issues from your past, crystals and gemstones can resonate on our highest levels of consciousness and help us to create positive healing changes in our lives. Meditation with your crystals is one way to accomplish this. You can place your stones in an area where you can view them during your meditation or hold them in your hands, while sensing and feeling the soothing and rejuvenating energies of your gemstones resonating around you, and mingling with your own energies. Many people even make gem elixirs by allowing their crystals to soak in purified water for a time, and then drinking the elixir like a daily tonic. Before you make a gem elixir, however, make certain that your crystals are safe to ingest, and don't contain any harmful toxins that will be released into your elixir. If in doubt, or if you discover that your crystal of choice is not safe for ingestion, set your purified water next to your crystal for 24 hours or longer to allow the water to absorb the gemstone's healing vibrations safely, without direct contact. Often, simply placing crystals around your living space so that their energies permeate your home can create a positive effect on your health in general, and your mindset in particular. Healing crystal rituals are also a great way to achieve healing on multiple levels, from the physical to the highest levels of our consciousness and spirituality.

Amethyst is well-known for increasing psychic abilities, and this clear, purple stone is also used for increasing the powers of perception, and enhancing the intuition. As noted earlier, this crystal can be used in water for bathing, as well as elixirs, but amethyst dust may be toxic, so avoid inhaling it.

Black Tourmaline helps to clear the aura, and can transmute negative energy that has built up within a person, to be used in a positive fashion. While safe for gem baths, black tourmaline contains aluminum, so should not be used for gem elixirs.

Carnelian is a motivating crystal, and boosts creative energies, while promoting problem-solving abilities. This allows the user to find new inventive solutions to the problems they face in their life situation. This crystal is safe for use in water, but should not be used with salt water, which may cause it to crack or break.

Citrine increases your sense of security, helping you to feel safe and comfortable in your life with the added benefit of helping to improve your financial situation. As with the rest of the quartz family, do not inhale dust from this crystal. Citrine is, however water-safe, and can be used for gem elixirs.

Clear quartz acts as a deep cleanser for the spirit, or soul. This crystal also enhances the memory, and deepens the consciousness, allowing us more insight, and improving mental clarity. Clear quartz also acts as an "amplifier" for any other gemstone, boosting their energetic vibrations. This gemstone is safe for use in water, but quartz dust may contain toxins, and should not be inhaled.

Dumortierite allows a person to let go of illusions and fears, in order to understand, and face life lessons more effectively. This stone also increases intuition. Dumortierite contains aluminum, so is not safe to use for gem elixirs.

Hematite wards against negativity in your life, as well as negative emotions that plague you. This soothing helpful stone helps to keep your emotions and thoughts well-grounded, increasing productivity, and boosting your mental clarity. Because of its iron content, hematite should not be used in gem elixirs, and can rust if left in water.

Labradorite raises consciousness, and helps in the development of intuition and perception. This stone also helps the psyche to adapt during difficult transitional phases in life. Labradorite contains aluminum, so is not safe to use for gem elixirs. This gemstone will dissolve in water so should not be water purified, or used in gem baths.

Lapis Lazuli stimulates mental clarity, giving problem solving skills a boost, and increasing perception. Lapis, while safe to immerse in water for gem baths, should not be ingested in elixirs because it contains copper, sulfur, and may contain toxic pyrite inclusions.

Sugilite purifies the aura and provides protection from psychic attacks. This stone also helps to connect one with their true life's purpose when used during meditation and rituals. This gemstone contains aluminum, making it unsafe for consumption in gem elixirs.

Tree Agate helps to ease negative thoughts and equalize personal energy. This beautiful member of the agate family is also used to revitalizing and rejuvenating the spirit. Tree agate is a water-safe stone, and can be used in gem baths and elixirs.

When our energies are flowing unimpeded, and we are free of negative energy, we can allow our bodies and minds to heal on every level of our being. In order to accomplish this, you may wish to try opening up your chakras, and healing crystals are especially powerful tools for this purpose. Although stagnant, negative energies can reside within us for long periods of time, creating blockages in our lives in many areas and on many different levels, with just a little persistence, a chakra cleansing is not only possible, but quite easy to perform. Start with one chakra at a time, and perform the opening ritual for each one, for seven consecutive days, opening and adding a different chakra each day.

There are seven chakras, each one being associated with a different location in or on the body, a color, and areas of influence in our lives. Allow 15-20 minutes to clear a chakra using your healing crystals, more if you feel the need, don't worry, you won't be timed! If you begin to feel uncomfortable, or lose focus during a cleansing/opening, simply remove your healing stone, purify it, and start over at a different time. Clearing the chakras of energy that has resided within for a great deal of time takes persistence, but is well worth the effort! This exercise will allow you to remove and equalize any imbalances on the physical, emotional and spiritual/mental levels, creating opportunities for new, fresh, creative energy, beneficial changes, and powerful healing in all aspects of your life.

1. Root/Base

The Root chakra allows us to feel grounded. Represented by the color red, this chakra controls our passions, and is located at the base of the spine. When the Root chakra is blocked, you may experience pain in the lower back or legs, and feel tired, listless, or find yourself feeling a lack of motivation. Opening this chakra creates a renewed sense of vitality and empowerment. To open your Root chakra, use a red colored healing crystal, such as ruby, red jasper, or bloodstone, and place it between your thighs, near the groin. Meditate on your passions, foundations, or simply a general feeling of warmth, while you visualize the color red.

2. Sacral

Orange is the color of the second, or Sacral chakra, which is located two inches below the belly button. This chakra represents creativity, and helps us to be accepting of others. When this chakra becomes blocked, feelings of dependency, frustration or confusion may be experienced, along with low hormonal levels, or swelling in the body. To open this chakra, place an orange healing stone, like carnelian, dark citrine, or tangerine quartz above the pelvic bone, and visualize the color orange, while focusing your thoughts on your creativity.

3. Solar Plexus

The third chakra is represented by the color yellow, controls how you see yourself in life, and controls the intellect. Located at the upper abdomen, when this chakra is blocked or closed you may experience feelings of fearfulness, or find yourself being overly controlling. A closed third chakra may also lead to a lack of emotion and problems with digestion. Opening this chakra also leads to opening yourself to happiness, new ideas, and joy, as well as the ability to let go of things you don't need to control. In order to open this chakra, place a yellow healing stone, such as citrine or amber, two inches above the navel while visualizing the color yellow, or the bright rays of the sun, while you meditate on your manifestation abilities, and your center of power.

4. Heart

This chakra is located in the center of your chest and is represented by the color green. It controls your ability to love and accept others. When the fourth chakra is closed, you might feel anger jealousy and bitterness, and experience fluctuations in blood pressure or heart rate. Opening the Heart chakra lets you relax and accept new relationships, as well as sustain existing ones, and can allow you to more easily experience love and forgiveness. Open the Heart chakra by placing a green or pink healing crystal on the breastbone. This combination of colors is used for the added benefits of soothing, mending and nurturing the Heart, in order to restructure and open this very important chakra. Concentrate on opening up your heart, to let in soothing and healing energies, while letting go of any anger you harbor, while you visualize the colors green and pink. Stones to use for opening the Heart chakra can be either green or pink, for instance, malachite, emerald or aventurine for green, or rose quartz (especially effective in soothing and healing matters of the heart) or pink tourmaline for pink. Watermelon tourmaline will also work for this chakra, being both pink and green.

5. Throat

Obviously located at the throat, this chakra controls communication and expressing one's self. Blue is the color that represents the Throat chakra. When this chakra is blocked or closed, you might find yourself at a loss for words, or have difficulty expressing yourself effectively. This can lead to feelings of loneliness, or feeling misunderstood, and can manifest in stiffness of the neck or a sore throat. Opening up the fifth chakra can allow you to communicate more effectively and be more expressive, and you may discover an improvement in your oral health, including your teeth, gums, as well as an opening of the nasal and sinus passages. To clear the Throat chakra, visualize the color blue, and place a blue healing gemstone on the larynx, such as sodalite, aquamarine or turquoise, and focus on the power of your words, clear communication, and positive speech.

6. Third Eye

The sixth chakra, represented by the color indigo, is located on the forehead, in between the eyes. A closed sixth chakra may lead to stiff necks, an inability to focus, and an overactive mind. Clearing this chakra leads to heightened intuition, a clearing of the mind, and greater problem solving abilities. To open the Third Eye, place a purple crystal, like amethyst, lapis lazuli, or iolite between the eyebrows, and think of the color purple. Concentrate on your intuition and mental clarity.

7. Crown

The crown chakra is located on top of the head, and is represented by the color violet. If you are experiencing bouts of clumsiness, feeling out-of-sync, or find yourself trapped in overly rigid thought patterns, try clearing out this chakra. Opening the Crown chakra leads to feeling more flexible, both physically and mentally, and can give you more clarity in your world views. To open up the seventh chakra, place a light hued amethyst, or clear quartz crystal above your head while you visualize a pure, white light. Focus on your Higher Consciousness, and your connection to the Divine and/or Spirit.

Progress through opening your chakras by laying one healing stone each day, starting with your Root chakra, and adding the next consecutive one each day. After the first week of opening a new chakra each time, try and open your chakras at least once or twice a week for a powerful, full body, mind, and spiritual cleanse. To keep your energies flowing well and your natural healing powers working effectively, you can also open up chakras in varying order, or numbers whenever

Conclusion

You have reached the end of this book, Wicca Crystal Magic. We hope this book has giving you the opportunity to begin your studies in the magic and enlightenment of Wicca Crystal Magic and we look forward to hearing from you if you enjoyed your time reading it.

This book is just the beginning of what all you can discover out there in the world and what the religion of Wicca is all about. We encourage you to reach out to other Wiccans in your area to get their tips and insights into how to be a Wiccan and where you should start in your journey.

The most important thing, is to make sure that you listen to the stones before you buy them. Whether you plan on using them in spells or to keep them on you to use their powers, they will work better for you if you make sure that you are connected to them. Crystals are an amazing source of energy and power. Utilizing them can provide you with so much in your life.

Always remember that the true meaning of being a Wiccan is to become more connected with the earth and living in peace with the energies of the nature around you. Once you have gotten to this harmony you should see that you are in the right frame of mind to begin your incantations and ritual casting.

Finally, if you found this book useful in any way, a review on Amazon is always appreciated!

WICCA

Wicca Herbal Magic

The Ultimate Guide to Herbal Spells and Magic Healing Herbs for Rituals. A Book of Shadows for Wiccans, Witches, Pagans, Witchcraft practitioners and beginners.

ESTHER ARIN SPELLS

INTRODUCTION

From the beginning of time evidence has been found that support the use of herbs as a form of natural medicine. This includes the likely hood that herbs were used during biblical times. In this book you will find a plethora of information starting with explaining what exactly an herb is all the way to ways to use these herbs in your Wiccan spells. In between this front and back you will also find lists with common herbs. These lists include magical qualities, old fashioned names, and medicinal qualities. You will learn how to raise your own herb garden and what to do with the contents once you have successfully raised the crop.

Use this book as a guide on introducing yourself to the world of herbs and magical medicine. Take precaution when using herbs because while a multitude of them can help there are just as many that can cause harm. As a principle of Wicca and of medicine, your priority should be to do no harm.

There are guides on writing your own spells included and how to do this. It is important as a witch to make sure that you are putting as much of yourself into your magic as you can. Use this guide as the beginning of a journey into self-discovery. Find the herbs and other materials that fit your taste as well as your wallet. Let this overview slowly introduce you into the history of Wicca and the use of herbs medicinally and magically.

And remember to always practice your magic wisely!

CHAPTER 1: What Is A Herb?

An herb is classified as any plant with leaves, flowers, or seeds that are used in the production of perfume, food (garnishment), flavoring, or medicine. It is from the Latin for herba which was used to describe grass crops and herbs in that time. Herb and spice usage can be traced as far back as prehistoric times and were often used as trade currency. Is there a difference between an herb and a spice though?

Herbs

Herbs are most often the leafy part of the plant. They are typically found in whole or chopped form even though they can be dried or fresh when used. Herbs are not known for having a strong aroma since they are the leaf and it does not hold in the essential oils like other parts of the plant. As a rule, most herbs do not come from plants with a woody stem. There are exceptions to this rule though, bay leaf and basil are examples of this because they are aromatic leaves and not stored or served as a spice. In a medicinal form herbs have three functions:

- To detoxify the body
- Regenerate organs
- Enable self-healing

Herbal Adulteration

The three components that factor what is a legitimate use of herbs in medicine are properly identifying the herb, the quality of the herb, and the purity of the herb without any modifications. The easiest form of herbal medicine to adulterate is fine powders. Herbs and spices are a multibillion-dollar industry and demand have been on an upward trend for quite some time now. Through testing of samples, it is becoming apparent that fillers are present in herbs and spices being mass-produced and distributed. An example of this is testing done on oregano. There were trace amounts of other herbs and leaves found in the samples that included olive leaves, sumac leaves, and hazelnut leaves. These filters decrease the natural abilities of herbs because they alter the natural state.

Spices

Spices are the part of the plant minus the leaves. This includes the seeds, stem, and bark if applicable. These components are typically dried and crushed. They have a high aromatic value because these parts of the plants are high in essential oils. Spices are often used as disinfectants and for food storage preservation.

History of Herbs

Herbs are mentioned throughout history, even in the book of Genesis in the Bible. The Bible includes multiple references to herbs and how to use them. Through the years to come, documentation has gotten better regarding the use of herbs. There is evidence that herb gardens were present in the middle ages in Europe and that schools of Egyptian herbalists have been present since 3000 B.C. This is where students delved into the experimentation of herbs being used in cooking, cosmetics, and medicine. The Sumerians soon followed by documenting their discoveries using herbs for medicinal use. By the time we get to the Greeks, around 700 B.C., we can see how they heavily utilized herbs and spices in daily trade. It soon became apparent that herbs could be used for medicinal purposes and Hippocrates, who later became known as the father of medicine, had a record of around 400 herbs used during his time.

In Medieval times families would primarily cook with herbs because they were easy to grow and inexpensive to purchase. A lot of herbs were grown for both culinary and medicinal purposes. Mugwort was only grown for its medicinal properties though due to its smell and was often used to make foot ointments. Herbs were used in a lot of ways during this time period. From a painkiller to fumigation, herbs held significance especially during the time of the Black Death. Herbs were experimented during this time hoping to aid in healing this plague.

Settlers who came from Europe to America brought seeds with them to recreate their herbal gardens in the new world. They learned new cultivation techniques from the Native Americans who already inhabited the area. These herbs were an important role in medicine for the settlers because there wasn't always a doctor readily available for illness or ailments. The settlers used trial and error with these herbs and their healing capability. Soon word of mouth got around to other settlements about how herbs could be used for this and for that and the use of herbal medicine spread through the new world.

As we head toward our more recent history, synthetic pharmaceuticals were introduced at the start of the 20th century and it caused a huge decline in the use of herbs and natural medicine practices. During the 1960s people were becoming more self-aware and were growing more concerned about what they put in their bodies, this started the influx of herbal medicine rising back up.

Today's society has kept on the trend of being self-aware and are even more observant about what is being put in the human body. A lot of pharmaceuticals are even using herbs as a base for their medicines. The incline that herbal medicine is making is not a trend that will fade away any time soon. All over the world people are beginning to see what it means to seek a natural approach to what ails them.

Christianity and Herbs

Christianity is a vast religion comprised of multiple denominations. With these many viewpoints comes a lot of controversy on such a simple subject. There are some denominations that believe that herbs are a gift from God. That God put these herbs and remedies on Earth to be utilized in healing and such should be done.

On the other hand, there are some who believe that using these herbs is a sin and that if healing is to be done, it will be done by God's will. One thing that cannot be disputed is that plants, herbs, and spices show up all over the Bible.

Aloe	Psalms 45:8, Numbers 24:6
Dill	Matthew 23:23
Mint	Matthew 23:23
Coriander	Exodus 16:31
Hyssop (herb that was known for being sacred and for cleansing)	Exodus 12:22, Psalms 51:7, John 19:29
Rue	Luke 11:42

| Wormwood | Jeremiah 23:15, Revelation 8:11-12, Proverbs 5:4 |

There are many Christians that struggle with the idea of herbal medicine not being a sin though. Most of the religions that rely heavily on herbs in their practices tend to revolve around nature, which is not the foundation of any Christian religion. There is the theory that as long as all glory be given to God for herbalism, then it is not a sin.

Buddhism and Herbs

Buddhism focuses on five cosmic elements: air, space, fire, earth, and water. It is believed that all things come from these elements and is the basis of all Tibetan medicine, including the use of herbs. Doctors are trained in the art of classifying the herbs used in their medicines. These herbs are classified by tastes and potencies, which can be altered by the region in which they grow.

The six herbal tastes include:

- Bitterwater & air
- Saltwater & fire
- Sourfire & earth
- Astringentearth & air
- Sharp fire & air
- Sweetheart & water

The eight potencies include:

- Astringent

- Light
- Spicy
- Oily
- Coarse
- Cool
- Heavy
- Dull

These combinations are used to treat diseases usually in the opposite of their onset. For example, if you have something with a fever, it will be treated with something comprised of herbs in a cool manner. The majority of these are delivered via teas. Each tea can have twenty to thirty different herbs in them and treat a wide range of ailments from indigestion to menopause.

Islam and Herbs

"Allah did not create a disease for which He did not also create a cure." - Prophet Mohammed

Muslim faith depends on the Quran and the Sunnah for all their guidance in life situations, much like Christians use the Bible as a rule book for their lives. Islamic use of herbs is in the form of teas, ointments, syrups, and infusions. At the present time there are about 250 plant species used in Arabic medicine. All treatments in Islam are "Medicine of the Prophet" and seen as a gift. Traditional therapies used by religion today are:

Black Seed (aka Black Caraway or Cumin)

The Prophet Mohammed told followers that this would help cure everything except death.

Honey

The Quran 47:15 considers honey a blessing and a gift and it could possibly derive from the antibacterial properties that honey possesses.

Olive Oil (from olive tree)

Good for heart health and skin elasticity due to high concentrations of vitamin E

Ayurveda

The practice of Ayurveda is derived from Hindu books. These knowledges were called Vedas. Of the four Vedas, the last one, Atharva Veda, included treatments using herbs, mantras, and potions. This practice believed that the body could heal itself if nurtured correctly. Plants and herbs were revered in the highest of regard. Plants were equated with love and power from the sun, which in turn, nourishes our bodies as well.

Taoism and Herbs

Taoism is the root of what is now known as traditional Chinese medicine. It centers on the yin and the yang balance of the body. While a traditional medical diagnosis may bring up a cause, Chinese medicine may treat the underlying imbalance. Herbalism is often used in tandem with acupuncture and herbs are generally never used solo. Most Chinese herbal medicines combine a vast number of herbs and spices that work together. The method of delivery can be as simple as a tea. Capsulated formulas as well as tinctures can also be used.

Astragalus	Used for diarrhea, night sweats, improvement of immune function, heart conditions. Considered one of the most important herbs in traditional Chinese medicine	Should not be administered to people who have had a transplant, children, people who are autoimmune deficient, or pregnant/nursing mothers.
Ginkgo Biloba	Believed to help in the prevention of Alzheimer's Disease, Anxiety, Depression, Asthma, High Blood Pressure, and Glaucoma	May have the possible side effects of skin reactions, diarrhea, dizziness, headaches, and muscle weakness. Can interact with a number of prescribed medication and should be discussed with a doctor prior to implementation.
Ginger	Has been used for centuries to treat Nausea, Morning Sickness, Irritable Bowel Syndrome, Muscle Pain, and High Cholesterol.	Can cause heartburn, indigestion, and gas. Should not be used by someone with Gall Bladder Disease. Should not be used by someone taking a blood thinner due to interference with

		blood clotting factors.
Gotu Kola	Proven to help cognitive function and anxiety, help with blood circulation, and help speeding up the healing process on wounds	Not recommended for someone with liver disease since it's metabolized by the liver. Limit sun exposure. Can cause upset stomach, drowsiness, and headache.

Classification of Herbs

Theophrastus, a Greek philosopher, divided the plant world into three distinct categories. This included trees, herbs, and shrubs. He then took the herb category and subcategorized them into three more categories: pot herbs, sweet herbs, and salad herbs. Due to selective breeding of plants in the 17th century, pot herbs became known as vegetables due to being "too big for the pot".

Pot herbs include:

- Basil
- Lemon Balm
- Mint
- Oregano
- Chives
- Parsley

Sweet herbs include:

- Lemon Verbena
- Violets
- Mint
- Bee Balm
- Angelica

Salad Herbs include:

- Basil
- Parsley
- Dill
- Thyme
- Chives

Below is a breakdown for the various ways herbs can be used and what category they fall in. There are a lot of herbs that are versatile and span multiple lists due to their unique qualities.

Culinary Herbs – Used for cooking and garnishment	Rosemary, Basil, Thyme, Parsley, Oregano, Tarragon
Herbal Teas – Used for drinking to cure ailments	Rooibos, Cannabis Tea, Arrowroot Tea, Ginger Tea, Labrador Tea
Sacred Herbs – Religious uses	Myrrh, Mugwort, Yarrow, Hyssop
Medicinal Herbs – Used in treatments	Chamomile, Ginger, Echinacea, Feverfew, Maidenhair, Gingko, Goldenseal
Herbal Cosmetics – Natural make up alternatives	Aloe, Henna, Saffron, Elder Tree, Neem, Lavender
Strewing Herbs – Used in the Middle Ages as insecticides, astringents, and smell	Juniper needles, Oregano, Sweet Woodruff, Lemon Balm, Chamomile

Chapter 2: What is Herbalism?

The exploration and study of how herbs can be used medicinally and therapeutically is called herbalism. Herbalism covers a broad spectrum of medicinal studies that include herbal medicine, botanical medicine, and herbology. It is often referred to as phototherapy as well. Someone who practices herbalism is referred to as an herbalist. An herbalist will take all parts of the plant and study the possible uses for it, they do not waste any materials. Herbalism is used to promote health improvements and preventing illness by using natural methods. The use of herbal medicine also offers a more affordable approach to healthcare by using things that are made naturally verses the synthetic blends put on the market today. This is what makes the usage of herbs unique, each herbal supplement is self-regulated and provides exactly the amount necessary. Herbalists believe that herbs and plants are superior and offer the most when they are in their raw form.

To become a licensed herbalist who can practice herbal medicine, the American Herbalists Guild suggests taking a course program at a school of herbal medicine for 1600 hours. They also require a 400-hour clinical study requirement before a certification is awarded. Should an herbalist decide they want to pursue a ND (Doctor of Naturopathic Medicine) they will also have to obtain a bachelor's degree in this program. In the United States, however, there is no certificate or license that is obtainable, so you do not have to meet any requirements to become and herbalist. Most states do require that an herbalist get a business license to sell herbs.

History of Herbalism and Herbalists

Herbalism history goes as far back as the history of herbs. This history is also closely related to the history of medicine itself. There is evidence in artifacts that have been recovered that document herbalism as well as herbs themselves. Some of the most notable herbalists, their time period, and their finds/practices are below.

Chi'en Nung/Shen Nung	Xia Dynasty (Dynasty that "preceded" all other Chinese dynasties)	Mythological Chinese figure that is rumored to have taught the culture medicinal practices including herbalism and acupuncture.
Hippocrates	460-377 BC	Known as the father of modern medicine, he was the first to speculate that Gods were not responsible for healing illnesses and that nature was to thank.
Theophrastus	371-287 BC	Wrote two books on botany and was considered the father of botany. (Botany is the study of all things plant like)

Pedanius Dioscorides	40-90 AD	Wrote a five-volume compilation on herbs and herbal remedies called *De Materia Medica* which was popular for over 1500 years.
Nicholas Culpeper	1616-1654	Doctor and herbalist who believed that everyone should be able to access herbal medicine. Wrote a book on herbal medicine.
Joseph Banks	1743-1820	Led Australian exploration that led to the collection of plant species for the Royal Botanic Gardens in Kew.
Johannes Moldenhawer	1766-1827	Responsible for detailed description of the parts of a plant.

Herbalists believe that the body is a vessel that can heal itself. They also believe that herbs are what ignite that possibility in a body. Looking beyond the disease or illness, they treat the body for the imbalance they feel caused it in the first place. Herbalists today use recipes that have hardly been changed from ancient recipes due to the proof that they work.

Western Medicine Versus Traditional Chinese Medicine

Western Medicine is the use of pharmaceuticals and other "unnatural" means to treat symptoms and illnesses. The goal of western medicine is to eliminate the source of the disease which in turn heals the person. The body is seen as a machine that must be mechanically fixed as the part needs it.

There used to be a time when religion and medicine mingled closely together, but over time a separation has driven the two of them apart. Some cultures still regard the two inseparables, however, western medicine has completely driven a wedge in between the two. Western medicine treats the body with doctors who prescribe pharmaceuticals or perform procedures and let the clergy and chaplains fulfill what the soul needs.

Adversely, Traditional Chinese Medicine, also dubbed eastern medicine works on treating the whole person and improving their health not just putting a band-aid on the issue. This type of healing is also called holistic medicine. Holistic medicine came from the separation of magical and herbal practices. Natural sources, herbs for example, are used in treating illnesses and symptoms.

Almost all eastern medicines still intertwine the medical with the spiritual. They create a bond between doctor and patient which helps the patient put their faith in the doctor, especially if they share the same religious values. It is this trust that allows herbalists to continue in their quest for all-natural remedies.

Concepts and Beliefs Regarding Herbalism

Terry Willard, author and herbalist, brought forth the concept that herbs have their own personal structure. Almost like humans are more than living things, he believed that herbs were more than just plants. They are not only unique in composition but in personality as well and it takes realizing this to truly understand their energy and how special they can be.

Another herbalist Lesley Tierra made the assertion that herbs are made up of multiple personalities that mimic those in the Chinese culture. The energy from herbs correspond with the hot/cold energy, the four directions, and the five tastes. These are a balancing act for the body's natural equilibrium.

With that principle in mind, it supports the Chinese foundation of Yin and Yang. That all things are codependent on each other. When the body is out of alignment with the Yin and the Yang, that is when illness sets and must be rebalanced and harmonized by using herbs to equal out the underlying cause.

Wildcrafting

In conjunction with herbalism, many Wicca are also turning to wildcrafting. This is a timeless practice that is comprised of going out and finding herbs and plants in their natural habitat. Wildcrafting is for the witch who already enjoys growing their own herbs but desires a more natural approach for their harvest.

It is important to always seek permission to pick from the wild. There are some herbs that may look very inviting, but if they are close to being endangered, you do not want to deplete the supply. Checking with the local Department of Agriculture is a good way to see what grows in a specified area and what you should avoid picking. Make sure to take a handbook and guide of local plant life. Something that is prominent in one area may not be included in another. It is important to know what the plants and herbs look like in your region. Never pick from the first patch you see. Instead seek out a hidden patch or one that is not necessarily visual to the regular passerby.

Go with the intent in mind of what you are looking for. Do not just randomly pick herbs that you have no physical use for. Only pick what you are going to use and never more. Bless the herb and the area while taking the herb. Throw down seeds for new growth or offer another gift to rejuvenate the life you just took. It is extremely important to wildcraft both ethically and responsibly.

Homeopathic Medicine

Homeopathic medicine is another form of natural medicine, much like herbalism. The difference is the methods in which it is delivered. Homeopathic medicine also includes minerals and animal products, but still rely heavily on the use of plants and herbs. Homeopathic remedies are comprised of the principle that what makes one person healthier may make an ill person better. The herbal principle does not follow this same pattern. Herbs in homeopathic medicine are diluted using serial dilution. Vigorously shaking the concoction between each dilution strips away the toxicity of the herb and intensifies its herbal makeup. Most of the herbs used in homeopathic medicine are dried out parts of the herb or plant that aren't typically used. Most homeopathic remedies are only available via tablets, creams, and syrups. Herbals have a wider variety of transportation. Unfortunately, there is not enough enough research on the effectiveness of homeopathic medicines to confirm nor deny just how effective they can be.

Chapter 3: Wicca and Herbal Medicinal Magic

Wicca, which can also be categorized as Pagan Witchcraft, is a pagan religion that is more modern. It was brought into the spotlight in the 1950's by Gerald Gardner but the infrastructure has been passed down by secret text and teachings as well as taught by word of mouth. There is some controversy regarding the teachings due to there being no core authority figure to oversee it. There are multiple denominations, which are also called traditions, and they each have their own lineage. Despite all the variations of Wicca beliefs, Gardner did publish books alongside Doreen Valiente that outlined the basic foundations that were passed on to those who followed their teachings.

Wicca is most often duo theistic. This means that there is worship of not only a Goddess but a God as well. The celebrations of Wicca follow the moon (Goddess) and sun (Horned God) cycles. Although it is not a necessary requirement to identify as Wicca, magic is often practiced.

After her claim of being a hereditary witch in the 1940's, Sybil Leek rose to fame and popularized Wicca by writing as a regular for a popular magazine. Laurie Cabot taught classes at Salem College in the 1960's and was known as "The Witch of Salem". She later founded the Witches League of Public Awareness in 1986.

In 1986 Wicca became a federally recognized religion. Herbert Daniel Dettmer, who was already incarcerated at the time, was denied ritual objects in which he requested for worship. When this made it to court, it was granted protection under the First Amendment just like other religions.

In 2005, United States Army Sgt. Patrick Stewart was the first recorded Wiccan in history to die in combat. When the family requested a pentacle be placed on his tombstone, the Veteran's Administration refused to allow this. A court case came about due to the refusal to allow the religious symbol and is now a recognized symbol and accepted by the Administration.

Currently there is no way of telling how many practicing Wicca there are in the United States. Many do not publicly share their beliefs. It is estimated that anywhere between three hundred thousand and three million people are practicing some form of Wicca in the United States.

Wicca Religion and Medicine

Medical professionals who follow the Wiccan faith must keep true to tradition. The holy days for the Wiccan are called Sabbats. These are ruled by moon cycles and deities. Esbats are for the full moon or the new moon. Greater Sabbats include Samhain (October 31), Imbloc (February 2), Beltrane (May 1), and Lammas (August 1). Lesser Sabbats are Ostara (Spring Equinox on or around March 21), Litha (Summer Solstice on or around June 21), Mabon (Fall Equinox on or around September 21), and Yule (Winter Solstice on or around December 21).

Burials in Wicca religion are more of a personal choice. Most Wicca prefer to not be embalmed. Most prefer being buried at sea or cremation in place of traditional burials. A lot of witches will come sit with the deceased member until after the wake ritual has passed. A window is generally left open in the room where the body lies so that the person's spirit can seek easier escape to the "Summerlands", which is the Wiccan equivalent to Christian afterlife.

Like a lot of other religious groups, Wicca don't view prayer as the only form of healing. They believe in using magic as an essential part of the healing process. Because of the vast traditional lineage of the religion, there are no set guidelines when it comes to healing but some of the more common ones are below:

Amulet or Talisman

Small objects (crystal, ring, medallion) that are inscribed with writing or symbols and should be kept, in most cases, with skin contact of the person who is ill. These should be touched by no other person without consent from the person it is for or a high priest or priestess.

Candle

When the candle is lit, it symbolizes the life force of the patient and should be kept burning until the procedure has concluded.

Anointment

Blessing with oil or water

Using a magical tool

This can include, but is not limited to, a wand, athame, or crystal. They are passed around the person's body.

Chanting

Generally used in conjunction with a magical tool, it is the use of repetitious words, generally a spell, being cast upon the person who is ill.

Divination

Using things like astrology, runes, and tarot cards to explore the illness

It is common practice for Wicca to not seek out medical professionals until they have treated themselves. It is usually at the point when nothing else has worked that they see a formal doctor for the illness. It is becoming more popular for the Wicca to question vaccinations and some are even refusing them. Blood transfusions are not against the religion either. These types of treatments are decisions to be made at the personal level.

It is a Wicca belief that anyone who possesses a part of them has the power to do harm unto them. When being treated in a hospital it is not uncommon for a witch to request any bodily parts that have been removed so that no one else can cause harm upon them by possessing their appendage. This can go for something as little as a tooth and as big as a severed limb. Adversely it is hard for the Wicca to accept an organ transplant. The body is more than just a temple for the Wicca it is where they harness their energies and powers for their magic. When needing a transplant, a ritual may be performed to cleanse the body, accept and include the new organ, thank the donor, and restore magical balance.

The Wicca see death, not as an end, but as the beginning of a new life. They believe in reincarnation and help spirits pass on to their new homes. That is why it is not unheard of that the religion would not be opposed to euthanasia. They do not want prolonged life if they cannot enjoy it. Most likely you will find a DNR (Do Not Resuscitate) with a Wicca. They do not want to have a heartbeat and not be able to enjoy the quality of life as it only prolongs the transition onto another plane or place.

The overall distinction in the Wiccan religion is that decisions rely mainly on the individual witch and their belief on the issue. When it comes to childbirth some witches prefer home births and some let nature take course. There is very little to no genetic testing prior to birth and most prefer not to use artificial forms of baby making. If there is something wrong after birth, testing will be done to see what can prevent it the next time. Wicca women prefer natural means of birth control because reproduction is viewed as their responsibility. Condom usage is high among the religion. Children of Wicca are taught at a young age what reproduction is and how to control it.

The Eight Sabbats

Wicca and Pagans follow an annual cycle of the year known as the Wheel of the Year. It is comprised of all eight sabbats and has been heavily influenced by the history, folklore, and magic of the religion. All sabbats incorporate nature in some aspect.

Samhain is traditionally held on October 31. This is when celebrations centered around the cycle of life, death, and rebirth take place. Samhain is seen as a chance for Wicca to reconnect with their ancestors whom have passed on. The veil between living and dead is dropped for this short time and communication is increased with the spirit world.

Yule is the winter solstice. It is celebrated around December 21, when the winter season comes to season. This is a time for celebration with the ones you love and to celebrate the sun starting its return to Earth.

Imbloc is held February 2. This is when the winter is typically most frigid. The Goddess Brighid, deity of Celtic belief, reminds the Wicca that spring will soon be here. Her fire and fertility remind us that new beginnings will start soon.

Ostara is the spring equinox which falls around March 21. This is when the celebration of the vernal equinox takes place and the promise that new blooms will soon be emerging because of the rising temperatures.

Beltrane is traditionally held on May 1. This celebration is when Earth opens up to the fertility God and they bring forth the promise of healthy livestock, crops, and nature in general. This is the celebration in which new life is promised.

Litha is the summer solstice and takes place around June 21. This is the longest day of the year. It is important to spend as much time outdoors during this time to take in the magic of the sabbat. This is when you absorb the sun and take a chance to reconnect with nature.

Lammas is traditionally held August 1. This is the beginning of the early harvest season. This is when Wiccans take the moment to appreciate what has been sown and the abundance that has been brought forth from the Beltrane celebration.

Mabon is the autumn equinox and takes place around September 21. This is when celebrations to honor the second harvest take place. This is the time when thanks are given from what blossomed from the other seasons. This is also when acceptance of the dying soil takes place and that cold weather approaches and the new cycle starts.

Wicca and Herbalism

Most Wiccans hold true to the belief of earth, air, fire, water, and spirit; the five classic elements. Most Wicca is considered an earth-centered religion, where nature is held in high regard. The Wicca believe that herbs have magical healing powers and utilize them in their rituals and spells. Much like any other spell, the right herb must be used to maximize results.

Like all cultures and religions, herbalism has its place in the Wiccan religion as well. Most true Wicca practitioners find themselves well versed in which herbs can heal and highly advise knowing the difference between which are good, and which can cause harm. When starting the craft of magical herbalism, it is important to take your time. Do the research required to learn the herbs and become one with them. Feel them with your spirit and invite their power in.

For centuries herbs have had their place in Wiccan history. From the very first recorded witches to the more modern witches of today, both medicinal and magical, herbs have held their own important place. Shakespeare used some of these phrases in one of his plays that are still commonly used today when talking about witches and their spells. Generally, the terms are used in a joking matter and misconstrue the actual meaning of herbs and plants and their place in medicinal and magical history. There was never an "eye of newt" but it is believed to have been mustard seed during that time. Witches in older times would use overly vivid terms to describe herbs and flowers used in their spells and potions to scare common folk. This was to create a hysteria and get people to leave them to their magic. Below is a list of these herbs and plants and their secret names:

Actual Name	Secret Name
A Mulberry Tree's Milk	Blood of a Goose
Adder's Tongue Fern	Snake's Tongue
American Valerian	Lady's Slipper
Asafetida	Devils Dung
Ash Weed	Goat's Foot
Avens	Golden Star
Balmony	Snake's Head
Bear's Breeches	Blood from a Shoulder
Betony	Lamb's Ears
Bistort	Dragon Wort
Black Haw	King's Crown

Blooming Splurge	Snake's Milk
Bluets	Innocence
Breast Weed	Lizard's Tail
Buckthorn	Bone of an Ibis
Bugle Weed	Wolf Foot
Bulbous Buttercup	Frog's Foot
Bulbous Violet	Snow Drop
Burdock	Beggar's Buttons
Burdock	Fox's Clote
Calamus	Dragon's Blood
Chamomile	Blood of Hestia
Carob	John's Bread
Cedar	Blood of Kronos
Chamomile	From the Loins
Chinese Sumac	Tree of Heaven
Clover	Semen of Ares
Club Moss	Stag's Horn
Club Moss	Wolf Claw
Cockhold	Beggar's Tick
Coltsfoot	Bull's Foot
Coltsfoot	Horse Hoof

Common Agrimony	Holy Rope
Common Daisy	Eye of the Day
Common Plantain	Cuckoo's Bread
Common Plantain	Englishman's Foot
Common Stonecrop	Mouse's Tail
Conoglossum Officinale	Dogs Tongue
Daisy	Eyes
Dandelion	Pig's Snout
Dandelion	Priest's Crown
Dill	Semen of Hermes
Dill Juice	Tears of a Baboon
Dill Seed.	Hairs of a Hamadryas Baboon
Earth-apple	From the Belly
Elder sap	Blood
Elecampane	Elf's Wort
False Unicorn	Unicorn's Horn
Field Clover	Rabbit's Foot
Five-leaf grass	Five Fingers
Fleabane	Semen of Hephaistos
Foxglove	Bloody Finger
Foxglove	Fairies' Finger

Foxglove	Lady's Glove
Fraxinella	Burning Bush
Fringe Tree	Old Man's Beard
Fumitory	Earth Smoke
Fungus on Elder or Elm	Jew's Ear
Garlic	An Eagle
Germander Speedwell	Bird's Eye
Germander Speedwell	Eye of Christ
Goldenseal	Eye Root
Goose grass	Everlasting Friendship
Goose grass	Gosling Wing
Great Mullein	Cuddy's Lungs
Great Mullein	Hare's Beard
Great Mullein	Jacob's Staff
Great Mullein	Jupiter's Staff
Ground Ivy	Cat's Foot
Hart's Tongue Fern	Hind's Tongue
Hart's Tongue Fern	Horse Tongue
Hawk Weed	Mouse's Ear
Heart of Wormwood	Hawk's Heart
Holly	Bat's Wings

Horehound	Bull's Blood
Horehound	Eye of the Star
Horehound	Semen of Horus
Houseleek	From the Foot
Houseleek	Jupiter's Foot
Houseleek	Semen of Ammon
Indian Pipe	Fairy Smoke
Irish Tops	Butcher's Broom
Kansui Root	Wolf's Milk
Knotweed (grass)	Sparrow's Tongue
Lady's Mantle	Bear's Foot
Leopard's Bane	Pig's Tail
Lupine	Blood from a Head
Lupins	Blood from a Head
Magnolia	Cucumber Tree
Maidenhair Fern	Hair of Venus
Maidenhair Fern	Maiden's Hair
Marguerite	Ox's Eye
Marjoram	Joy of the Mountain
May Flower blossom	Ladies' Meat
Mugwort	Felon Herb

Mullein	Graveyard Dust
Mustard Seed	Eye of Newt
Mustard-rocket	Semen of Herakles
Nine Hooks	Lady's Mantle
O'Cedar	Kronos blood
Ox-eye Daisy	Great Ox-eye
Periwinkle	Hundred Eyes
Purslane	Blood of Ares
Quickset	Gazel's Hooves
Reindeer Moss	Blood Leather
Rosemary	Dew of the Sea
Royal Fern	Heart of Osmund
Shepheard's Purse	Mother's Heart
Shepheard's Purse	Shepherd's Heart
Silverleaf	Queen's Delight
Snap Dragon	Dog's Mouth
Snapdragon	Calf's Snout
Southernwood	Lad's Love
Spearmint	Erba Santa Maria
Spira Root	Lady's Tresses
Spurges	Fat from a Head

Starwort	Devil's Bit
Tamarisk Gall	Blood of an Eye
Toadflax	Toad
Tormentil	Flesh and Blood
Turnip leaves	Lion's Hairs
Turnip Sap	A Man's Bile
Vegetable Ivory	Negro Head
Vervain	Enchanter's Plant
Vervain	Herb of Grace
Violet	Serpent's Tongue
White Hellebore	Semen of Helios
White Plantain	Squirrel's Ear
Wild Geranium	Chocolate Flower
Wild Geranium	Crow's Foot
Wild Geranium	Dove's Foot
Wild Lettuce	Blood of a Titan
Wormwood	Blood of Hephaistos
Yarrow	Bloodwort
Yarrow	Devil's Plaything
Yarrow	Knight's Milfoil
Yellow Archangel	Weasel Snout

| Yerba Santa | Holy Herb |

Solitary Verses Coven

At some point in your Wiccan journey you may find yourself questioning where you belong. If you are part of a coven you may feel like you need to veer off on your own to discover your craft or you may find that you are at a crossroads in your growth and not sure where to go on your own. There is no right or wrong way to practice your craft. Some people thrive better with a support system and others are disciplined enough to practice and grow on their own.

- Establishing a routine

o When working on your own if you can develop a good routine that does not let your education, meditation, and ritual work go unpracticed then there is no problem with being a solitary witch.

o If you need the extra push and a set routine shared by others, then the support of a coven might be the way to go. Having the support to practice and further educate yourself and others will help you prosper in your craft.

- Book of Shadows

o In both circumstances, either solitary or coven, documentation is important. Keeping a record of spells, rituals, herbs, and other important information is important in passing on and keeping magic alive.

- Meet new people

o Even if you decide to practice as a solitary witch, it doesn't mean that you cannot associate and learn from people who share your same interests. There are a lot of groups out there who meet that are Wiccan or Pagan but do not belong to a formal coven.

- Ask questions and never stop learning

  o Whether you decide to practice on your own or with a group, never be afraid to ask questions regarding the craft. Never stop learning new things either. A successful witch is not defined based on his or her Book of Shadows or the size of their coven. It is based on the amount of information they hold and the discipline they hold for the craft.

Drug and Alcohol Use

Just like in any religion drug and alcohol abuse can be a problem among the Wicca community. Most of the programs available for recovering addicts are centered around Christian or Catholic religions and do not cater to those of Wiccan belief. Most recovering addicts in the Wiccan world find themselves turning to their circle for support. It is amongst most of the religion that the belief is that a person must take personal responsibility for their choices and accept the consequences that come from them.

This is not saying stone the sinner; this is saying allow them to ask for help and support them in finding the answers they need to find to heal.

Due to the increase in drug and alcohol problems plaguing mankind today, a lot of rituals are steering clear of even using wine in their rituals. "The 12 Step Witch" has taken the traditional twelve step program and made it functional for the Wiccan religion. There is support for recovery in all walks of life, all you have to do is ask.

Chapter 4: Herbs – Medicinal Qualities

Herbs have always had their place in medicine. The first medical schools were founded on the principles of using herbs to heal medicinally. The term we use today to describe most medications, "drugs", comes from a word used to described drying. This was how medicines were made in ancient times, from drying herbs. This is where the term originated. Today it is estimated that one in three adults have tried herbal treatments. The big decline in herbal medicine came after the Black Death when nothing being used was solving the problem. This is when toxin laced medications started making an appearance.

The oldest medicinal practice still alive today is using herbs to treat illness and ailments. Some of the most popular methods of delivering these medicinal herbs are through teas and oral medications. Sublingual tinctures have become a popular method in more recent times, especially with CBD oils. This helps maximize absorption levels.

Herb	*Latin*	Description	Medicinal Uses
Angelica Root	*Angelica archangelica*	During first year only grows leaves, second year it grows larger producing a flavorful stem and roots with green flower clusters	Relieves tension headaches, helps buildup of phlegm due to asthma or bronchitis, diuretic qualities. Use caution because large quantities can be toxic.
Basil	*Ocimum basilicum*	Tender and aromatic, leaves can range from green to purple and be sized larger like lettuce to a half inch in size	Stomach problems, kidney conditions, common cold, insect bites
Bay Laurel	*Laurus nobilis*	Leaves are thick, green, glossy in appearance	Arthritic aches, back pain, sore muscles, earaches, sprains
Blessed	*Cnicus*	Hair covered leaves;	Strengthens liver function,

Thistle	*benedictus*	yellow flowers produced surrounded by spines	aids in prevention of hepatitis, helps with migraines, gallstones
Borage	*Borage officinalis*	Course in texture, fine hairs on leaves and stem, star shaped blue flowers	Fever, cough, depression, adrenal insufficiency, prevent lung inflammation
Caraway	*Carum carvi*	First season produces flowers, second season produces seeds	Digestion issues, stomach spasms, phlegm production, urine control, kill bacteria in body
Catnip	*Nepeta cataria*	Scalloped heart-shaped leaves, blue flowers	Insomnia, migraines, anxiety, flu, fever, intestinal worms, colic
Chervil	*Anthriscus cerefolium*	Resembles the light green leaves of parsley, produces	Fluid retention, digestion, eczema, gout, cough, high

		white flowers	blood pressure
Chives	*Allium schoenoprasum*	Grow in clumps via bulbs underground, long hollow leaves, pink flowers in summer	Digestive health, blood circulation, improves appetite
Cilantro	*Coriandrum sativum*	Finely cut leaves, penetrating odor and flavor	Measles, antioxidant health, removes poisonous metals from body, toothache
Comfrey Leaf	*Symphytum*	Bristle-like lower leaves with winged stalks of leaves on top	Nutritious and good for healing sprains, sores, and fractures, Soothes upset stomach
Dill	*Anethum graveolens*	Fine feathery leaves, color range from blue green to a dark green, little yellow flower clusters	Cough, colds, fever, hemorrhoids, cramps, sleep disorders, inflammation

Epazote	*Chenopodium ambrosioides*	Weed like in appearance, green leaves that have sharp looking points, produce small flowers that are yellow green in color	Stomach ailments, anti-diabetic properties present
Eucalyptus Leaf	*Eucalyptus globulus*	Long, slender, oval shaped leaves, wax-like in appearance with a gray to blue-green color	Kills germs and infections, stimulates the heart, helps congestion in the lungs
Feverfew	*Tanacetum parthenium*	White flowers with yellow middle, aka bachelor's buttons	Migraine treatment, reduces nausea
Fennel	*Foeniculum vulgare*	Resembles dill with fine textured leaves, clusters of yellow flowers in	Digestion problems, colic, respiratory infections, cholera, bedwetting, vision

			late summer problems
Garlic	*Allium sativum*	Flat leaves, hardneck and softneck varieties	Lowers cholesterol, lowers blood pressure, common cold
Lavender	*Lavendula angustifolia*	Bushy with needle like leaves that are blue green to gray in color, spikey flowers either lavender or white	Antiseptic properties, insomnia, depression, anxiety, restlessness
Lemon Grass	*Cymbopogon citratus*	Gray-green color, grass-like appearance	Digestive tract spasms, high blood pressure, mild astringent, rheumatism, fever
Lemon Balm	*Melissa officinalis*	Light green, shaped like an arrow, coarsely textured with fine hairs, flowers that bloom may be white, yellow, or	Reduces stress, promotes sleep, eases pain and discomfort

		pink	
Lemon Verbena	*Aloysia triphylla*	Narrow leaves, glossy sheen, white flowers	Muscle spasms, fever reducer, indigestion
Lovage	*Levisticum officinale*	Dark green leaves, yellow flowers in summer	Pain and swelling, prevent kidney stones, urinary tract infections
Marjoram	*Organum majorana*	Velvet feeling leaves, grayish green color	Digestive problems, coughs, runny nose, liver disease, gall stones, ear pain
Mint	*Mentha*	Spread aggressively, violet flowers, small green leaves	Upset stomach, bile production, indigestion, supports healthy cholesterol levels
Nasturtium	*Tropaeolum majus/ Tropaeolum minus*	Trails and climbs/ Bush-like (both have leaves that resembles the leaves of	Expectorant, anti-fungal, antibiotic properties

		a water lily and orange flowers)	
Nettles	*Urtica dioica*	Stinging hairs on stem and leaves, green in color, grows in dense clumps	Used for skin disorders, allergies, anemia, and is an expectorant
Parsley	*Petroselinum crispum*	Rosette curled or flat green leaves	Kidney stones, asthma, cough, urinary tract infections, high blood pressure
Passionflower	*Passiflora incarnata*	Creeping vine with white and purple flowers, grows orange berries	Aids in sleep, relieves nerve pain, alleviates hysteria
Pau D'Arco	*Handroanthus impetiginosus*	Made from inner bark of Tabeuia trees	Antibiotic and antiviral properties, relieves gastrointestinal issues, arthritis, skin conditions, and bronchitis, it is a sedative

			and a diuretic
Oregano	*Organum vulgare*	Leaves are green and gray in appearance, produces small white or purple flowers	Acne, dandruff, urinary tract disorders, menstrual cramps
Rose Petals	*Rosa Centifolia*	Aromatic, multiple color ranges, soft to touch	Helps clear headaches, mouth sores, dizziness, cramps, and is a great used in tonic for heart and nerve health
Rosemary	*Rosmarinus officinalis*	Dark green needles for foliage, white band on underside of needles	Muscle pain, boost immune system, improve memory, hair growth
Sage	*Salvia officinalis*	Pebble-like texture on leaves, grey sheen to green leaves, spikey purple flowers in	Digestive issues, depression, over production of saliva, memory loss

		summer	
Scented Geranium	*Pelargonium graveolens*	Both flowers and leaves come in varieties of colors, sizes, and shapes	Astringent properties, poor circulation, nausea, tonsillitis, ring worm, lice
Sorrel	*Rumex scutatus*	Shiny green leaves, resemble lances	Inflammation in respiratory tract, bacterial infections, pain relief
Tarragon	*Artemisia dracunculus*	Small green flowers, dark green leaves that are twisted and narrow	Toothache, digestion, start menstruation, promote sleep
Thyme	*Thymus vulgaris*	Small oval leaves, gray-green sheen, flower clusters range from white to lilac	Diarrhea, arthritis, sore throat

Medicinal Teas

The key to making a beneficial tea is to brew it correctly. You should never put your herbs in boiling water because this kills the flavor and the medicinal quality of them. The proper steeping is also a key factor in making a proper tea. You can use a French press or even pantyhose (clean of course) to place your herbs in to steep. Make sure you keep these in hot water, which is heated to just below the boiling point, for at least ten minutes.

Make sure that you know your herbs and their medicinal qualities before using them. Never exceed the recommended dosing for them either, some of them can be toxic. Do you research before making a tea on your own due to the medicinal qualities and interactions that some herbs can have with each other and pharmaceutical medications.

Rose Hip Tonic

12 ounces water

4.5 teaspoons rose hips, dried and crushed

Bring water to just below a boil. Steep rose hips for twenty minutes. Add honey for added flavor.

Headache Relief

4 ounces white willow bark

6 ounces peppermint leaf

6 ounces chamomile flower

Bring 12 ounces of water to just below boiling point and steep blended herbs together for at least twenty minutes. Make sure to drink while still warm.

Comfortable Digestion

Large amount of fresh peppermint leaf

.75 tablespoon ginger, sliced

.75 tablespoon honey, optional

Put herbs into a pot and add 32 ounces of hot water just below boiling. Steep for twenty minutes, depending on desired strength. Strain herbs and drink while warm.

DIY Herbal Tea Blends at Home

When trying to come up with your own herbal tea blends, it is important to ask yourself why you are making this at home. Are you just trying to be creative and experiment with flavors or are you looking for something to help with an illness or an ailment? If you are seeking something for medicinal purposes it is important to seek out what might be the underlying cause of your symptom. Treating the underlying cause may completely rid your body of the symptom that was ailing you. An example of this would be insomnia. If you are losing sleep because of stress, an herb specialized in treating insomnia may not treat the stress your body is under, thus leaving that symptom once the herb has worn off. Instead it would be more beneficial for a body to treat the stress and allow the insomnia to melt away with it.

Once you have done the required herbal research, start with your primary medicinal herb as the largest quantity. Next pair this with other herbs in the same group, but ones that offer complementary flavors. Steep these for at least twenty minutes in close to boiling water.

Examples of complementary pairings:

Lemongrass and rosemary

Lemon, honey, ginger, turmeric

Hint of cinnamon, elderberries, honey, blueberries

Using Herbal Salves and Balms

Herbal salves are used primarily for joint pain, drawing out infections, and smoothing skin. These are comprised of herbs steeped in oil, generally for longer periods of time to draw out their essential oils. They are then mixed with a small amount of base, generally beeswax, to solidify the mixture. The primary composition of a salve is herbal. Herbal balms are much like salves in composition, only tend to be comprised more of the wax than the herbal oils. Both are beneficial, but you will receive a larger medicinal quality from the salve.

Natural Over the Counter Alternatives

Most of the herbal medicines we see on the shelf today at the pharmacy are known as over the counter medications. These basically mean that you do not need to have a prescription to obtain them. These supplements are typically cheaper than going to the doctor and being prescribed pharmaceuticals that can cost even more than the appointment did. The only problem that people do not think about with purchasing supplements over the counter is the possibility of interactions. The most important thing to do is research before putting anything in your body.

Dangerous Herbs

Keep in mind that not all herbs are safe for consuming in little or mass quantities. Some may not even be safe for touching. It is important to know which ones to avoid. Know what they look like, know where they grow, and know who they affect. Some herbs only effect pregnant women. Others will only harm children and animals. Some herbs are safe in a small dose but if a larger quantity is used it can cause illness or even death.

Pregnant Women

- Basil can cause spontaneous menstruation
- Black cohosh causes miscarriage
- Angelica, pennyroyal, and catnip can induce contractions

Pets

- Chamomile can make your dog or cat have explosive diarrhea
- Foxglove can elevate your pet's heartrate and can even cause death
- Tobacco can ultimately cause death in your pet. Less severe side effects are paralysis, vomiting, and abnormal heartrate. (I would just keep this one away from them in general)

Children

- Licorice root in large doses (more than four grams) can cause tiredness, loss of potassium, cardiac arrest, and headaches
- Uva ursi can cause kidney failure in children under twelve

- Mistletoe, both leaves and berries, are highly toxic and can be lethal if ingested
- Goldenseal can cause brain damage in newborns, because of this a breastfeeding mother shouldn't even take it

Herbal supplements that can cause problems

- St. John's Wort can make some medicines less effective. Can increase the chances of sunburn. Has been known to cause headaches and dry mouth.
- Kava can cause irreversible kidney damage to someone who drinks or already had kidney problems.
- Arnica taken internally can raise blood pressure and cause shortness of breath. Liver damage, coma, and death have occurred.
- Black cohosh can cause liver failure
- Feverfew causes issues with the bodies blood clotting ability

Chapter 5: Herbs – Magical Qualities

Herbs are believed to have their own gender, elemental ruler, and planetary ruler. They are harvested and used because of their essence and vibration in the magical world. Growing and harvesting your own herbs for personal use can be beneficial because your own personal energies can influence their utilization. There are many ways that Wiccan use herbs in their magic. Some forms of herbal transportation include:

Incense

Herbs can be burned or smudged. Smudging, using the ashes of the burnt herb, can be used to clear negative vibrations and energies from a person or area. Burning herbs as a ritual can clear a room via smoke. Smoking can also help in the facilitation of altering a person's consciousness.

Smoked

Herbs can also be smoked. This is made up of a mixture of herbs and possibly a filler like natural tobacco. This is so that you can draw in the smoke and absorb it internally. This is often seen done by Native American cultures, but Wiccans participate in it as well.

Sachets and Charms

Herbs used in conjunction with the correct color and/or materials that are placed in a small bag are considered charms and sachets. These can be burned, carried on a person, or buried to name a few.

Healing or Ritualistic Bath

By placing a sachet in a bath of water, the herbs emitted can create a ritualistic setting or be used for healing purposes. An example of this is using eucalyptus for easing cold and flu symptoms.

Oil

To prepare an herbal oil, you place herbs in desired oil base and let it steep for a few days. After straining the herbs from the oil, it is left with the essence of the herb in the oil and it can be used for healing, anointing, or cleansing. This can also be used to infuse cooking by using cooking oils and herbs.

Tea

Herbal teas are most prominently used in herbal medicines. These are when herbs are steeped in water, could be hot or cold, and ingested by a person. These teas are usually comprised of multiple herbs mixed to achieve a desired medicinal state. In magic, herbal teas can be used to alter a person's consciousness and promote trance-like states.

Boundary

Herbs can be used in magic to help create a boundary and can be sprinkled around your home, alter, or magic circle to help ward off negative energies.

Herbs are a gift from nature and should be used as such in the growing, harvesting, preparation, and use. There is an amount of respect that should be paid to all living things and this includes plant life. A lot of herbs get the classification of "weed", and this is just an unfair judgement. Dandelions have a plethora of medicinal and magical properties but is labeled with the unfair assumption that it is just a weed.

Herb	Gender	Planetary	Element	Magical Qualities and Uses
Angelica Root	Masculine	Sun	Fire	Used as an incense for protection and exorcism; Can sachet for protection; Removes hexes and curses; Smoking can create a barrier against negativity and fill you with positive energy
Basil	Masculine	Mars	Fire	Used in love and prosperity spells; Carry on person to promote wealthy attractions; Crush and sprinkle over sleeping mate to help fidelity; Ritual bath use can let in a new love or cast out an old one
Bay Leaves	Masculine	Sun	Fire	Used in potions for clairvoyance and wisdom; Place under pillow to promote visions and prophetic dreams; Carry on your person

				to ward off evil
Blessed Thistle	Masculine	Mars	Fire	Use for purification practices; Breaks hexes; Removes unwanted malevolent influences; Strew to cleanse rooms
Burdock	Feminine	Venus	Water	Used in incense for protection; Healing incense for the feet; Carried on person for protection; Burn for room purification
Bramble Leaf	Feminine	Venus	Water	Powerful herb used for protection; Used in invoking Goddess Brigit whom presides over poetry, smith craft, healings and sacred wells; Attracts faerie spirits

Cacao (Chocolate)	Feminine	Venus	Water	Effective in potions and spells for love; Used to satisfy restless spirits; During seances it attracts loved ones who have passed
Camellia	Feminine	Moon	Water	On the alter, blossoms in fresh water can attract wealth and prosperity; Expresses gratitude
Caraway	Masculine	Mercury	Air	Can be used to ward off Lilith and other spirits seeking to do harm; Can help attract a mate; Can ensure faithfulness; When used in food it can bring forth lust
Carob	Masculine	Mars	Fire	Used to deter poltergeists; Attracts spiritual helpers; Aids in prosperity and protection

Catnip	Feminine	Venus	Water	Used to increase bonds psychically with animals; Used as a tea can induce happiness and relaxation; Burn dry leaves for love spells; Increases psychic abilities in meditation
Chamomile	Masculine	Sun	Water	Can attract money and wishes; Used in sleep for relaxation; Bathe children in bath with chamomile to ward off evil; Breaks curses cast against you
Cloves	Masculine	Jupiter	Fire	Used in incense to ward off negativity, stop gossip, attract money, and gain luck; Repels negativity when worn
Cumin	Masculine	Mars	Fire	In conjunction with frankincense it can provide protection when burned; Use with salt and sprinkle to

				ward off evil and bad luck; Steep in wine to bring forth lust; Used in love spells
Comfrey Leaf	Feminine	Saturn	Air	Strong protection while traveling physically and astral realm; Great for warding off any kind of negativity
Damiana	Masculine	Mars	Fire	Used as a tea to invoke sexual magic; Creates a mild aphrodisiac; Used in lust spells; Good for male enchantment
Dandelion Leaf	Masculine	Jupiter	Air	Great for divination; Calling upon wishes; Calling out to spirits; Used in tea form, the root helps to bring out stronger psychic power
Dill	Masculine	Mercury	Fire	Can bring protection to the home if hung over doorway; Used in love spells; Used in lust spells, you can

				bathe in it to become desirable to whomever you choose
Eucalyptus Leaf	Feminine	Moon	Air	Cleanses spaces from unwanted energy; Useful in dream pillows for sleep; Attracts healing vibrations
Fennel Seed	Masculine	Mercury	Fire	Curse and possession prevention; Attracts healing, courage, virility, longevity, strength, and vitality; Use for purification purposes
Feverfew	Feminine	Venus	Water	Wards off sickness and keeps up immune system; Carry in suitcase for protection while on trips; Great for spiritual healing; Helpful with love and protection

Name	Gender	Planet	Element	Properties
Flax Seed	Masculine	Mercury	Fire	Absorbs negative energy; Carry in sachet in purse/wallet to attract wealth and money; Used in protection spells
Galangal Root	Masculine	Mars	Fire	Aids with money, psychic ability, and luck; Great for strength and courage, as well as warding off legal issues; Powder form is burned to break spells; Protects when worn in a sachet on the body
Galangal Root	Feminine	Moon	Water	Used to heal; If worn can attract love; Burned in Moon incense to increase spirituality
Ginger	Masculine	Mars	Fire	Before performing a spell, eat to increase energy; Helps with love, power, success, and power

Holly Leaf	Masculine	Mars	Fire	Used in dream magic; Enhances wishes; Keeps away evil spirits and poison; Used for protection
Hyssop	Masculine	Jupiter	Fire	Purification herb; Burned in incense to bring dragon energy; Often categorized with the serpent and dragon
Mandrake Root	Masculine	Mercury	Fire	Promotes love, protection, fertility, and money; Makes magic more intense when charged (put under pillow for three days of full moon while you sleep); Powerful visionary herb
Mugwort	Feminine	Venus	Earth	Brings forth prophetic dreams when used in dream pillow; Burn in combination with wormwood or sandalwood for scrying; Leaves can help with scrying when

				placed around magical objects
Nettles	Masculine	Mars	Fire	Removes or sends back curses when worn; Used in baths for purification; Laid around house to ward off evil
Nutmeg	Masculine	Jupiter	Fire	Strengthens clairvoyant energy; Carry on person for luck; Used in prosperity and money spells
Orris Root	Feminine	Venus	Water	Used to find and hold on to love; Hung around the house for personal protection
Pau D'Arco	Masculine	Pluto	Fire	Most beneficial during waning Moon; Can empower the herb by drawing down the Moon directly

Passionflower	Feminine	Venus	Water	Used in love spells, can heighten libido; Encourages peace, balance of emotions, friendship, and prosperity
Pennyroyal	Masculine	Mars	Fire	Tote around in green bag for money and business attractions; Burn for protection while meditating and traveling astrally; Helps negative thoughts against you go away
Peppermint	Masculine	Mercury	Fire	Promotes sleep with visionary dreams; Supporting herb for purification, psychic powers, love, healing, and sleep
Rose Petals	Feminine	Venus	Water	Great for love spells; Promotes joy of giving; Great support herb in spells for love, healing, luck, psychic powers, and

				protection
Rosemary	Masculine	Sun	Fire	Use in incense for love and lust; Can be used for mental powers, protection, exorcism, and healing; Promotes youthfulness
Sage	Masculine	Jupiter	Air	Used in healing and wealth spells; As an incense it is purifying when smoke is expelled to the four corners of the room to rid and repel negative energy, which is great for moving into a new home; Promotion of immortality and wisdom
Scotch Broom Leaf	Masculine	Mars	Air	Sacred tree used in protection and purification spells; Burned to calm winds; Scattered to exorcise the evil spirits; Smoke can put

				someone in a meditative state
St. John's Wort	Masculine	Sun	Fire	Sacred herb used by druids for protection and exorcism; Promotes health, strength, protection, happiness, and divination; Burn to rid negative thoughts and energies
Star Anise	Masculine	Jupiter	Air	Used in incense for meditation, increase of psychic powers, and protections; Used to keep away nightmares; Used as a good luck charm
Tobacco Leaf	Masculine	Mars	Fire	Smoke can allow communication with spirits; Smoke also purifies space; Great offering for spirits
Thistle Flower	Masculine	Mars	Fire	Used in protection spells and spells for financial blessings;

				Produces joy, energy, protection, and vitality when carried in an amulet; Counteracts hexing
Thyme	Feminine	Venus	Water	Used in healing rituals; Burn to summon good health; Wearing increases psychic ability
Valerian Root	Feminine	Venus	Water	Put in bath for dream magic and sleep protection due to its mild stimulant quality; Keeps harmony in the home; Drink teas for purification
Yarrow Flower	Feminine	Venus	Water	Used in spells to dispel negative energy and melancholy; Repels negative influences when worn in amulet or sachet; Purifies the blood

Four Thieves Vinegar

Four thieves' vinegar is popular among folk magic and spells. It is speculated that during the plague, four thieves teamed up and were among some of the healthiest men around. They concocted a brew in which the base was vinegar and then they each contributed an herb, hence, four thieves' vinegar. This is used primarily in banishing and protection spells.

To make four thieves vinegar you need to find your base. You can use something as common as apple cider vinegar, but red wine vinegar is growing in popularity. No matter what you use, it needs to be a vinegar base. Next you will take four garlic cloves. Peel and mince these and add them to the vinegar. Next you need to choose four herbs to add to the jar since each thief added his own to the mixture. Popular selections are cayenne, lavender, rosemary, sage, mint, coriander, and thyme. Again, these are any four that you feel you need to choose. Add these to the jar with the vinegar and the garlic and close the lid tightly. Allow this to remain closed and sitting for four full days. Make sure you shake the mixture once each day. After the fourth day it is ready for use in spell casting.

Four Thieves Oil

There are some people who cannot stomach the smell or the taste of vinegar. For those of you who fall into this category, never fear, there is four thieves just for you.

To make four thieves' oil you need to select an oil base. Typically, something like jojoba is used because it will help the essential oils from causing skin irritation. Choose four essential oils to add to the carrier oil. You can use any combination and any amount, but make sure to choose only four. Popular essential oils are clove, eucalyptus, lemon, oregano, rosemary, and cinnamon. Make sure to swirl often after adding to make sure there is equal mixture in the carrier oil.

Herbs for the Home

There are a lot of uses for herbs that have been discussed, but one that is simple, and anyone can participate in is cleansing and protecting the home with them. You do not have to be Wiccan to believe that herbs have cleansing and protective powers. You can bundle and burn them to smudge a home from spirits or bundle and hang them in various locations. Each herb brings its specific scent and energy to an area.

Sage

Sage is traditionally a bundle and burn herb used in home cleansing.

Apple

If you hang apple branches and blossoms in the home, it enhances love magic.

Chamomile

Chamomile is an herb for protection and purification. If you hang this in your bedroom it will help promote restful sleep. Hang it on a door to repel a magical attack.

Hyssop

Hyssop is good for magical self-defense. This can be accomplished by hanging it on the door or spreading it out along the perimeter of your home.

Hanging it inside the home can also help starve out negativity.

Patchouli

Patchouli branches bundled together are great around windows and doors to keep negativity from entering.

Rosemary

Hang bundles of rosemary on your door to keep unwanted persons from entering. You can also burn in an incense to cleanse negativity around you.

Smudging

Smudging is a highly effective way to cleanse a space and a technique that is frequently used by Wicca. You can make your own smudge bundles at home. You can use herbs you have growing in your garden, go wildcrafting, or even purchase herbs for this purpose. You will need scissors, string, and your herbs to accomplish a successful smudge. Use a piece of string that is about five feet long to start. Arrange your herbs so that they are all in the same direction, leaves on one end and stems on the other. Use the string to wrap the herbs in a crossed pattern so that there are no loose ends hanging out. Work from the stem, then down to the leaves. Work this backwards as well ending with the stems. After you have created the stick, hang it up to dry. This can take several days depending on weather and number of herbs. Once dried it can be stored until needed for use in ritual.

Chapter 6: Growing a Green Witch Garden

It is important in Wicca spells to use herbs grown by the witch casting the spell. While not necessary, it helps put personal energy in the spell. Gardening by the Wicca is a way of connecting with Mother Earth and deepens the connection with nature. Herbs are a staple in the Wiccan culture. You don't need to have a large garden; it is possible to cultivate herbs in your windowsill. Make sure to keep the tie with nature and never use harsh chemicals on your plants, use only natural means to keep pests away. Sometimes using garlic or onion can help naturally keep the bugs from ruining your bounty. Use rainwater to keep with the reusing of resources in your garden.

Getting Your Ground Ready

Your garden will be your place of solitude. It is important to remove all impurities from the area. Building your garden may take a lot longer than simply planting some seeds. The first step you need to take is to replenish the nitrogen to your soil. This can be accomplished by planting various legumes and beans in the area you anticipate using. The first season of your garden is to take all chemical dependencies away from the soil. Growing some tobacco plants is also a good idea for the first year of your garden because they are a disease-resistant plant and strong.

Find Your Place

Find yourself a good spot in your garden area to create a meditative spot or an altar. This will allow you to spend time in your garden and reflect on your self-healing as well. This is also your place to allow your energy and power to fill your garden, giving it your own unique touch. Herbs filled with your own personal power are more useful in spell casting. One way of finding your own niche in your garden is to find a large stone to place in it and meditate upon. Add some plants that can double as a screen of sorts. This will give you the privacy you need to truly meditate and become one with your gardening spot.

Choosing Things Pretty and Green

There is no actual rule as to what plants, flowers, or herbs belong in a witch's garden. The contents of your garden are based on your own specific needs. Primarily your garden should contain what you need for your spells as well as any medicinal purposes you see yourself needing. Below you will find a list of recommendations for supplying your garden.

Rosemary

This herb is low maintenance. It does well with plenty of sun and minimal watering. This is an herb that can be grown in a small area as well such as a pot on a balcony or windowsill.

Calendula

Simple to grow from seeds. It produces an edible flower that can be put in a salad.

Basil

This is another easily cultivated herb. It requires no special care and is full of essential oils.

Mint

This is found in the majority of witch gardens. This herb grows rapidly and can take over any area if it is not maintained. It is best grown in a pot and away from other herbs to avoid takeover.

Sage

This herb requires full sunlight but doesn't need lots of water. Easily maintained and can be in a bed or a pot, which ever suits you.

Lemon Balm

Best cultivated in partial shade. This is good for attracting butterflies and bees.

Other commonly found plants and herbs include:

Yarrow

Foxglove

Poppy

Nasturtiums

Nightshade

Belladonna

Peppermint

Nettle

Hellebores

Comfrey

Henbane

Wolf's Bane

Patchouli

Tips for Choosing Your Plants and Maintaining

There are many things to think about when planning your garden. Take into consideration your surroundings. There are many plants and herbs that are poisonous to children and animals, so it is important to take care in choosing what and where your plants are located. You may feel it best to not even include some of them in your garden just to be on the safe side. It may be best to grow things like mandrake, poppy, and belladonna some place segregated from the rest of the regular garden so that it can be highly guarded against accidental ingestion.

Harvesting time is another area to take into consideration when planting. It is sensible to make selections that can be harvested year-round so that there is always something growing and being harvested. This adds not only a variety visually but texture to your garden that makes it pleasing to the eye and the mind.

Adding mulch or compost in your garden is a good way to eliminate a lot of weeding that may need to be done. It helps release minerals into the soil and roots of your plants and herbs as well. Compost is also a good way to stay away from pesticides. Placing hot compost around and in your garden can keep your plants healthy.

It is important when you begin a garden to see it through. Communicating with your plants and herbs are what help it thrive. Recent studies have proven that talking to your plants can make them more fruitful and boost their health. Just as communicating is important, it is also important to bless your garden. This starts at the seed level and takes place typically at night. This is how you ask for guidance from the universe and its energies to aid in the growth of your garden.

Seed Blessing

Materials:

Soil

Flowerpots

Four Candles (Represent the four corners)

Wand

Green Marker

Seeds

On your alter, place the items. Walking clockwise, cast a circle. Pointing downward with your index finger speak:

Creation comes from the arms of Mother Goddess.

Creation comes from the light and strength of our God.

Creation is the human spirit's mission.

I swear from my lips this oath, and a circle is born from my hands.

Earth returns, Air returns, Fire returns, Water returns.

Land's gifts also return.

Behold this circle has been cast.

Remember to ask for blessings from each of the corners as you call upon them.

(Light candle representing North) Northern Elements; Bless this ritual with a rich and comforting soil.

(Light candle representing East) Eastern Elements; Bless this ritual with gentle rain and a breath that is sweet.

(Light candle representing South) Southern Elements; Bless this ritual with a warm and caressing sun that will bring forth creation.

(Light candle representing West) Western Elements; Bless this ritual by bringing water that is pure and energy that will transform.

Using your wand, give each seed pack three taps while saying:

The dark half of the year is now passing

As the Earth grows warmer, so do the days become light

Spirit of the seeds I summon thee

Stir, swell, and ye awaken

You are planted in this Earth

Grow and bear new fruits

Be blessed!

As you do this make sure you are visualizing in your head what this seed will bring forth. Use this time to give the seeds wisdom and bestow upon them what you are hoping to accomplish with them. Next you need to use your marker to mark the pots (or on your identification markers for the plants and herbs) with a Birkana rune. This is a letter B that has points instead of curves. This symbolizes new beginnings. Plant and water your seeds. Thank the God and Goddess for their gifts and dismiss your corners. Make sure that you tend and look after your seeds closely and transplant outdoors once frost threats subside.

Harvesting by Moonlight

Using the moon's cycles for planting and harvesting can make your yield more plentiful. Planting and growing during the new moon phase can promote faster growth due to increased sap production. This is beneficial for plants that have a shorter life span, like annuals and biennials.

During the waning moon, it is the best time for perennials and plants with longer life spans due to the decrease in sap production. This makes pruning and harvesting easier due to the dryer conditions. This is due to the light decrease in the moon during this time.

During the last phase of the moon it is best to not plant anything but instead work on your soil quality. This means you should work on your composting and mulching to improve your growth in the coming new moon cycle.

Chapter 7: Harvesting and Preparing Herbs

Harvesting and herbal preparation are dependent on some key factors. A lot of harvesting depends on the herb and plant's personal chemistry. Some herbs are ready for harvesting earlier in a planting cycle than others. You must be well versed in the composition of the plants and herbs you are working with in order to know the part to harvest and when to harvest it. Preparing your herbs for their method of deliverance, medicinally or magically, are dependent on their harvesting factors as well.

Harvesting

Know what you have planted! Not understanding your herb is the biggest mistake made when harvesting. If you are working with an herb that is the leaf of the plant, you need to make sure you know when to pluck the leaf from the plant. Make sure the leaves are tender when you are harvesting them. The best time to do this is when the dew is still fresh on the leaves. Do not rinse your leaves. This removes a lot of the aromatic oils and lessens effectiveness. If you harvest too late, it can taste bitter.

Herbs that are harvested for their blooms are best done when right before the bloom has fully opened. This ensures their potency. This is especially true in flowering herbal plants like chamomile, lavender, and borage.

Harvesting herbs that are grown for their seeds is best done when the seed pod is beginning to change color. This is rule goes for dill, caraway, fennel, and coriander. The seeds are at their peak freshness during this phase.

Root herbs, such as ginseng, should be done at the end of the summer. It is also feasible to do this at the beginning of the fall season as well. This is when these sorts of herbs are most viable and at their peak of freshness.

Make sure that you are harvesting frequently. Therefore, it is of the utmost importance to pay attention to your gardens. Knowing when each type of plant was planted, and its growth cycle is important. By pruning your plants, you are encouraging new growths. This keeps the vitality of the plant high. A lot of plants such as oregano, mint, chives, basil, and parsley grow back even quicker because they thrive with constant pruning and harvesting.

Annual herbs can be harvested right up to the first frost. It is at this point where they will die out and need to be replanted during their normal growing season. Perennials, on the other hand, need to be cut off at least a month before the first frost occurs to ensure their growth in the next season. This will help stimulate growth.

Herb	Inside	Outside	Days to Mature	Frequency of Growth	Amount of Light
Basil	Anytime	March-August	70	Annual	Full
Catnip	4 to 8 weeks before last frost	April-June	75	Perennial	Full
Chives	Anytime	April-May	80	Perennial	Full
Coriander	2 weeks before last frost	March-August	65	Annual	Partial

Dill	October-April	March-August	60	Annual	Full
Lavender	Anytime	April-May or October	2 years	Perennial	Full
Lemongrass	February-March	March-August	75	Annual	Partial
Mint	Anytime	April-May	N/A	Perennial	Partial
Oregano	Anytime	April-May	85	Perennial	Full
Parsley	Anytime	March-August	80	Biennial	Partial
Rosemary	Anytime	April-May	85	Perennial	Full
Sage	Anytime	April-May	70	Perennial	Full
Stevia	February-March	April-May	100	Perennial	Full
Thyme	Anytime	April-May	80	Perennial	Partial

Preservation of Herbs

A general green thumb rule, herbs are better tasting when they are fresh. It does not take long after harvest for an herb to lose their strong aromas and they tend to deteriorate rather quickly. That is why preserving them is an important step in the process.

Short Term Storage

For short term storage of your herbs, you can simply use a glass of water for your herbs with longer stems. This is much like you would do with a bouquet of flowers, but this method will not hold them for an extended amount of time and with each passing minute you are losing out on quality. Some heartier herbs like rosemary and thyme can be preserved for a little longer period in your refrigerator. Wrap them in a damp paper towel and stick them in your vegetable bin in an open bag. Do not forget that the longer they sit, the less flavor they will have.

Long Term Storage

If you harvest your herbs and don't plan on using them quickly, a process you might consider is drying your herbs. By drying herbs, they can last two to three years, but have the best quality when used within a year of drying them. If you wait longer than a year, quality cannot be guaranteed nor can freshness. Using a dehydrator, oven, or even the sun is not recommended for drying out herbs because too much of the flavor is lost during this process.

Low moisture herbs like rosemary, dill, thyme, and sage can be dried by gathering a whole bunch by the branch and rinsing them gently. Tie them together in smaller bunches and hang them upside down. Do this in a dark room that is dust-free and has a good ventilation system. This process can take up to three weeks to accomplish. After they have dried you simply remove the leaves from their stems and put them for storage in airtight containers. You do not need to crush or grind them until you are ready to use them so that you do not hinder the integrity of them.

Higher moisture herbs like bay leaf, lemon balm, mint, tarragon, and basil tend to mold if not dried in a quick manner. Remove the best leaves from the stems at hand and use a frame covered in netting or on a drying rack in a single layer to ensure even drying. Make sure to turn frequently during the first few days, this will ensure they dry in about a week. These can be stored the same way as low moisture herbs.

Freezing herbs is another method of long-term storage that can be used for preservation. Wash the herbs you wish to preserve and pat them dry. Lay them out in a pan in a single layer. Place this pan into your freezer. Thinner herbs will freeze quicker than thicker herbs, so it is best to only freeze one kind at a time. Once they are frozen through, they can be stored in an airtight bag or container that can be kept in the freezer. Make sure that you are using something that is made specifically for freezing to prevent freezer burn. Freezing does not offer the same quality of life as drying herbs does. It is best to use the herbs within six months of freezing for the best quality.

Making Tinctures

Tinctures are becoming the most popular mode of herbal transfer. You can make tinctures with multiple bases. One of the most popular tinctures used today are CBD oil. CBD oil is used for treating anxiety, stress, aches, pains, and other ailments. It is made from cannabis. The FDA, however, has only approved three components of the cannabis for use in mass distributed CBD oils: cannabidiol, nabilone, and dronabinol. It is not recommended to try to make a tincture of CBD oil on your own. Some methods of making tinctures are more potent than others and keep longer. Here are some solvent examples of making effective herbal tinctures:

Alcohol

Alcohol is one of the most effective and highly used solvents for herbal tinctures. This includes one hundred proof vodka, rum, and brandy. These alcohols are good for stripping the essential oils and medicinal qualities from the herbs. They are resistant to the possibility of contamination and can keep the same herbal potency for over five years.

Vinegar

Vinegars that are used should be raw and unfiltered. The most common used vinegar is raw apple cider vinegar. Herbs should be introduced into a warm vinegar to maximize potency. These should be used within the first year of straining to maintain freshness and viability. These are not nearly as potent as tinctures made from alcohol.

Vegetable Glycerin

This is best found in organic form and must be food quality. Think about the fact that you will ingest this, you want it to be of the finest quality. This is the form used most often with children due to the sweet taste of it. It is not as strong as a tincture made from alcohol, but not everyone wants to consume alcohol. This should be mixed with a sixty percent oil and forty percent water ratio. These tinctures have a longer shelf-life than ones made from vinegar. They can hold for up to three years.

Using a Tincture

Using a tincture solution is a very easy form of taking medicine. Using a dropper. Measure out the desired amount of the solution. Place the tincture, using the dropper, under your tongue. This is also referred to as taking medicine sublingually. Allow it to sit under the tongue for a few seconds before swallowing. If necessary, rinse the mouth out to remove any bitter tastes that may linger from using the tincture.

There are six types of tinctures that are available commercially:

Propolis

Produced by bees, used for healing acne and wound care

Cannabis

Used for treating seizures, aches, depression, and anxiety

Elderberry

Antioxidant qualities, reduces inflammation

Turmeric

Antioxidant with anti-inflammatory qualities

Benzoin

Used to treat skin issues but only topically

Echinacea

Used to boost the immune system

Tincture Recipes

General Method

For this method you will need:

Sixteen ounces of one hundred proof vodka, quart-sized jar, two ounces of chopped dried herbs (four ounces if using fresh)

On the new moon, place your herbs into the jar. These should be finely chopped. Pour in the vodka until it is about two inches above the herbs. Stir to combine, then place the lid on the jar and shake it vigorously. Leave the jar to rest in a warm place to steep in the sunlight. Shake at least once or twice daily. Strain on the full moon or leave to steep for up to six weeks. Pour mixture through fine mesh to separate the liquid from the plant matter. Keep stored in a cool place in a glass bottle. Attach a label with the contents and date.

Cold and Flu Tincture

For this recipe you will need:

Solvent (alcohol, vinegar, glycerin) of your choosing, quart-sized jar, fresh or dried herbs. For this specific tincture you will need two ounces of dried echinacea root, one-ounce fresh horehound, one-ounce fresh sage, one-ounce fresh lemon balm.

Finely chop all the listed herbs and amounts and place them in the jar. Add the solvent to the glass. The solvent should over the herbs and rise at least an inch above them. Put the lid on the jar and shake until they are well combined. Set the jar in a warm place with direct sunlight. Steep for two to six weeks. The longer the steep the more potent. Remember to shake this daily. After the determined period of time, strain the plant matter from the solvent. Place the solvent in glass bottles in a cool place to be stored. Attach a label with the contents and date.

Migraine Tincture

For this recipe you need:

Solvent, quart-sized jar, four ounces of fresh herbs (three parts lemon balm and two parts feverfew)

Finely chop the herbs and place them in the jar. Add the solvent until at least an inch above the herbal mix. Shake vigorously to mix up the tincture solution. Set the jar in a warm and sunny place for up to six weeks. Remember to shake it daily. Strain the herbal matter from the liquid matter. Put the liquid in a glass bottle and store it in a cool place. Attach a label with the contents and the date.

Tincture Dosages

At the onset of symptoms, an adult dose of a tincture solution is a quarter to a half of a teaspoon of the solution to be taken every thirty minutes to an hour until the symptoms subside.

Children's dosages are a little different. Using "Young's Rule" to dose the tincture, add twelve to the child's age. Divide the child's age by that number. This will give you a decimal. If a child is five years old and you add twelve, that gives you seventeen. You then take the age, which was five, and divide it by the number seventeen. This will give you the result of twenty-nine percent. You would give the child a dose that is twenty-nine percent of the adult dose.

Chapter 8: BEGINNER SPELLS

Before starting any spells or practicing any magic, it is best to find which one is best suited for your situation. Make sure that you have done your research and have all the requirements for your spell or healing present before starting anything. Think of your spell as a recipe and follow it as it is written. Be advised of the Rule of Three while practicing your magic. This is also referred to as karma or three-fold karma to most practicing Wiccans. What energy you dispel into the world will come back times three to you. So do not take lightly what you practice.

To start out simple in your practice of Wicca, it is best to start with a simple gesture. Spells of intent that can be simple and easily modified for more personal results are the simplest form practiced. Examples of these may seem mediocre but when done correctly and with the best of intentions, they can have immense benefits.

For best results, make sure that you have good intentions. You must believe in the spell you are using and think upon it often. This will ensure the best results.

Money:	Spell: Use a mixture of basil and baking soda to sprinkle on your carpet before you vacuum your floor. This will increase the money flow in your household.

	Spell: Using a cinnamon stick, roll plastic or paper money toward your body to bring wealth upon yourself.
	Spell: Make an aromatic mixture of cinnamon, allspice, and nutmeg by simmering and allowing the aroma to fill your home.
	Charm: Take a square piece of paper and draw an infinity symbol on it. Fold this paper toward you and store it in your wallet. Doing so will increase your wealth.
Protection:	Spell: Take quartz crystals and bury them on the four corners of your property facing outward. This will protect from evil.
	Spell: Dry ginger and hang it in your kitchen to stop evil spirits from entering.
	Spell: Sprinkle dried chili or cayenne peppers around your house, doing so will keep harm away.
	Spell: Around the outside of your home, plant thyme to act as natural wards against evil and harm.
	Spell: To keep unwanted persons from entering your home, put ground up cayenne pepper under your doormat.

	Charm: To ward off energies intent on harm, carry around a peach pit in your pocket.
	Charm: To strengthen your mind, carry a walnut.
Dream:	Spell: To ensure good dreams, either eat a pinch of thyme or place a bit of it under your pillow before bed.
Healing:	Spell: Juniper berries carried on your person can keep illness away.
	Charm: Placing garlic in your home can keep illness from entering.
	Charm: Carry ginger in your coat pocket during the winter to stop from getting a cold.
	Spell: Inhale peppermint to thwart hiccups.
	Spell: Slice and onion and place it under the bed of someone who is ill. This will soak up the illness.
Love:	Spell: Give your partner half of a cut apple to ensure a lasting relationship.
	Spell: Use watermelon as an aphrodisiac to attract a mate.
	Spell: Place pepper inside a piece of cotton to bring back a love that is lost.
Purification:	Spell: Use salt on your floor before vacuuming or in your mop water to purify a room.

	Spell: Bathwater with a mixture of apple cider vinegar, epsom salt, and baking soda can purify the body.
	Spell: Cutting an onion in half and placing it in different locations in your home can cut negative vibes.
	Charm: Carry black tourmaline to remove and purify energies in your space that could be harmful.

Important Tips for The Beginner

Preparation

Make sure that your spells define your intent. By defining your intent, you are making your spells personal. They have a specific reason and are not just a blanket fix to something. The key to this is being focused on what you are trying to say. If you must ramble to explain your intentions, then you are not focused on your cause enough. Always remain positive in your spell casting. Stay away from negative connotations in your text. Do not overwhelm yourself with an overall goal. Sometimes it might be easier to break down the bigger picture to meet your overall goal.

Find or write your own spells to accommodate your goal or outcome. Make yourself familiar with the spell you choose. This does not mean that you must memorize it and know it by heart, but you should be familiar with what you are saying, and it should roll off your tongue naturally and not be forced.

Make a list of the materials and supplies that you need and have them ready and on hand for the spell you are wishing to cast. Beginner to advanced, this is important.

Make sure your area, altar, or room is cleansed and purified before starting. There should be no contaminating factors, this includes distractions. Make sure that all your worldly obligations are taken care of and you can be at peace during your time.

Prepare yourself for the experience. The day that you cast your spell should include meditation and self-centering activities.

State of Mind

Leading up to your spell (days or weeks, whichever applies), make sure that you keep your thoughts positive. Try to refrain from worrying about whether it will work or not and keep anything away that will bring down your vibes.

The place you need to be during your spellcasting is the ALPHA state. This is when magic and energy are most conducive. During states of relaxed awareness during meditation is when this is achieved. This is when you are in the zone most and focused on the prize.

Make sure that after you cast your spell you remain in the positive. The best piece of advice is to simply not reflect or think back on your spell at all and let it do its own work.

Linked Intentions

While in the ALPHA state it is important to reflect on your intentions. You can do this one way or ten ways, it really doesn't matter, if you are solely focused on why you were casting the spell in the first place.

Say your intentions out loud so that you can hear it.

Surround yourself with visual stimulations, scents, tastes, objects that secure your goal.

The harder you visualize your overall goal, the stronger your intent.

If the spell requires it, use your intent to strengthen the bond between you and the object.

Energy

Once you are focused and fully set on your intent, it is time to start raising the energy. If done correctly, your energy flow should gradually increase. Most of the energy you bring in will be drawn from external sources around you. The length of time it takes to reach the crescendo of your energy will depend on your own self. This can take five minutes, or it can take five hours. It depends on yourself.

Once you have reached your crescendo point, you need to direct and release that energy build up. This can be done in many ways. Shouting, stomping, orgasm, breaking things, or even gestures can all be signs of release.

Make sure that when you come down you are grounded. This can be an exhausting time. Coming down can be as simple as expelling the last of your energy into the Earth below your feet.

Channeling

Once you have cast your spell it is important to create a channel to help it reach its depth and potential. This is simply done by putting yourself in a situation where the energy can manifest and take effect.

Preparation (Spirit)

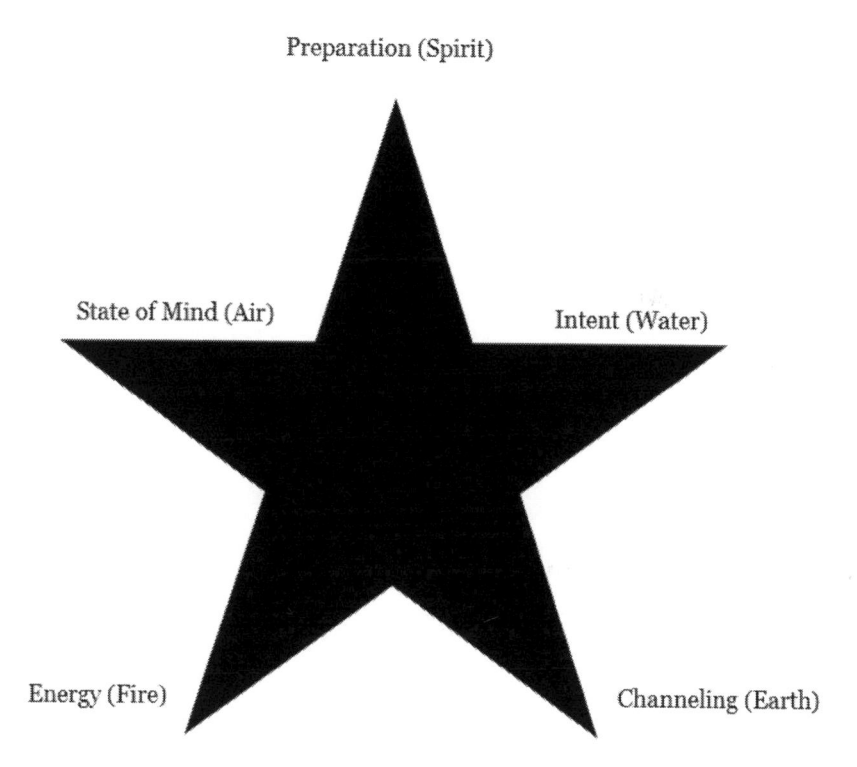

State of Mind (Air)

Intent (Water)

Energy (Fire)

Channeling (Earth)

Blessings

When something new happens in your life, blessings are the best way to start them off on a positive note. Things like moving into a new home, finding a new job, and meeting someone new are examples of life-changing events. By blessing these events in life, Wicca brings only the positive of outlooks onto it. Blessing and blessing spells can be done by anyone looking to improve their outlook on new beginnings in their life. New homes require sage burning at an integral time of day important to your home, in most circumstances it is at four o'clock because it is right before gathering the family in one room. This is done by asking for a blessing from each corner.

Blessing a person requires a lot of visualization. If you don't think you can visualize the person well enough it is ok to use a picture of them as an aid. You simply sip a drink and meditate about the person. See them with large blue space above them and see them prospering. See them moving through life with only the best of intentions. You see the stars that are starting to form in your vision and as one reaches the peak of explosion it drops a bead of moisture around the person you are blessing. This is your energy engulfing them.

Blessing a relationship should be done during a full moon, and you do not need the other person present. These kinds of blessings are most effective if there is a long-term bond between you and your mate. All the edible ingredients needed in this blessing have a symbolic purpose.

Bake a fresh loaf of bread (this represents gifts from fertility, peace, and prosperity)

- Hold this bread to the full moon and ask for a blessing on your relationship

Break off some of the bread and cover it with:

- Cinnamon (clear communication)
- Butter (physical attraction and kindness)
- Honey (true love)

You may now eat this and share with your partner if present. Do not cut it with a knife though because cutting would represent severing the relationship.

Using the Moon's Phases

During the full moon it is most beneficial to work spells for healing, connecting with a Goddess, magic that you are working on to increase your skills, and spells for mental intuitiveness. This phase totals three days. It is the day before the full moon appears and the day after.

During the waning moon, spells that center around banishing negativity and ending things are best during this moon phase. This phase of the moon lasts approximately fourteen days and is when the moon goes from full-back to dark. The new moon is a hard one to work during. Sometimes you can't see the new moon to know if it has appeared or not. This is the time for cleansing spells and spells for filling yourself with peace and harmony. For around three days after the waning cycle has completed and it is completely dark is when the sliver of the new moon will start to appear. This is believed to be the time for rejuvenation. During the waxing moon, the moon is going from dark to light again. This also lasts around fourteen days as the approaching full moon comes to light. The best spells to cast during this time are workings of positive magic. This includes love spells and wealth.

Blue Moon

A blue moon is more than just an old saying to describe something that doesn't happen very often. While this may be true in part because blue moons do not happen very often, it's not the point of this section. A full lunar cycle is calculated to take twenty-eight days from the full moon to the end of the waxing moon. Every calendar month has at least twenty-eight days in it, which facilitates the regular moon phases. Every month (except February, unless it is a leap year) has more than twenty-eight days in it. The moon does not simply put its cycle on hold during this time waiting for the next cluster of twenty-eight days. All these extra days add up and around every twenty-eight cycle there are enough days accumulated and an extra moon appears in the same month. This is the phenomenon of the blue moon.

For example, let's say that the cycle begins at the beginning of January, the model looks something like this:

Month	Number of Days	Moon Phase	Difference	Accumulated Total of Days
January	31	28	3	3
February	28	28	0	3
March	31	28	3	6
April	30	28	2	8
May	31	28	3	11
June	30	28	2	13
July	31	28	3	16
August	31	28	3	19
September	30	28	2	21
October	31	28	3	24
November	30	28	2	26
December	31	28	3	29

December will end up being the month with two moons, or the blue moon. This is because all the extra days throughout the year have added up to equal a moon cycle.

While the blue moon has no recorded historical significance, it is believed that during this phase of the moon there is more clarity and energies are higher during this time. This is a bonus moon phase for practicing your magic.

Chapter 9: Intermediate and Advanced Spells

Intermediate and advanced Wiccan spells start out with the same basic framework as the beginner's spells, but the entire structure ends up being a bit more complex. In order to practice intermediate and advanced spell work, a ritual schedule must be established.

- Set up an altar and cleanse your space, this includes the clothing you will be wearing during the ritual. Make sure your cakes and ale (libation) is ready.
- Ritual bathing
- Opening of the circle
- Ritual performance
- Libation
- Closing of the circle
- Tidying up

Altar

When getting your altar ready for your ritual, spell casting, make sure you have all your essential tools ready and organized. This includes anything you will need before, during, and after the spell casting. Cleanliness is an essential step in preparing the altar. Not only does this go for the altar itself, but for you and the room around it. Make sure the clothes that you are going to wear for the ritual are clean and consecrated. Lay them next to the altar prior to performing the ritual. Make sure your libation is ready and laid out at the altar as well. While ceremoniously it is cakes and ale, it does not have to be. Food and drink will suffice, but make sure to have it ready.

A basic list of things you may need for you altar include:

- Small bowl of water
- Censer with incense that you can freely move
- Wand
- Athame
- Staff
- Bowl of salt
- Ritual cup (with drink)
- Pentacle
- Plate (for cake or other food)
- Anything else specifically stated for ritual

Sample altar layout:

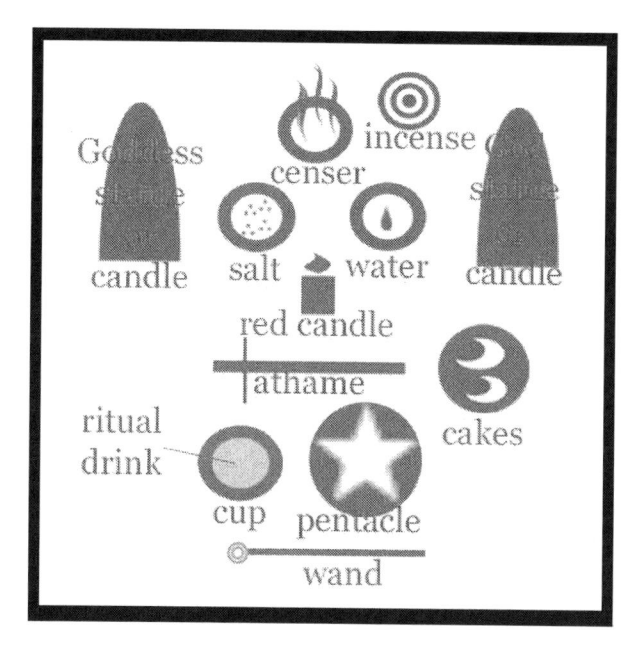

```
Goddess     incense
candle   censer   candle
         salt  water
         red candle
         athame
ritual                cakes
drink
cup    pentacle
         wand
```

Cleansing

To consecrate and cleanse your area do the following:

Place the incense with the censer in the altar's center or on the pentacle. Using your index finger say this while drawing a pentagram over it:

I consecrate and cleanse with burning incense to be the Representative of the Air Element. Bless us with your essence and clarify this circle.

Next take the small bowl of salt and put it in the center of the altar or on the pentacle. Using your index finger say the following while drawing a pentagram over it:

I consecrate and cleanse this bowl of salt to be the Representative of the Earth Element. Bless us with your stability and clarify this circle.

Place the red candle in the center and say the following while drawing the pentagram over it:

I consecrate and cleanse this candle's flame to be the Representative of the Fire Element. Bless us with your passion and clarify this circle.

Put the bowl of water in the center and draw the pentagram over it while saying:

I consecrate and cleanse this bowl of water to be the Representative of the Water Element. Bless us with your intuition and clarify this circle.

Place salt (three pinches) in the water and put it back in its spot.

Ritual Bathing

Ritual bathing will be based on the ritual performing. Herbs added or soaps used should reflect your intentions. During this bath is when you focus and meditate on what you are accomplishing with your spell. This is your mental preparation time prior to putting on the clothes you plan to wear during the ritual.

Opening the Circle

To open (cast) your circle, take your wand in hand and start with the North quarter. Imagine you are drawing the Earth's energies up and the universe's energies down. Walk around the circle once and repeat:

Circle of Power, I conjure you, by my Word and by my will.

Circle of Power, I conjure you, between worlds as a boundary.

Circle of Power, I conjure you, give a space that is sacred for worship.

Circle of Power, I conjure you, protect us from energies that are negative.

Circle of Power, I conjure you, contain within me the energies raised.

So be the powers above, as be the powers below, I cast this circle.

While you take in the energy cast, envision it as a bubble that surrounds your area. Let it cut through anything in its path. This is your circle of energy engulfing you.

Calling Upon the Elements

Hold up your hands, turn to face the North and call out:

The powers of the North, the powers of Air,

From your winds, send me knowledge and wisdom

In which to enlighten and bless in this circle.

Powers of the North, I welcome and hail you.

Hold up your hands, turn to face the East and call out:

The powers of the East, the powers of the Earth,

May I acquire stability and growth from your fertile ground

In which to strengthen and bless this circle,

Powers of the East, I welcome and hail you.

Hold up your hands, turn to face the South and call out:

The powers of the South, the powers of Fire,

Bring me your spark of inspiration and courage

In which to bring passion and bless this circle,

Powers of the South, I welcome and hail you.

Hold up your hands, turn and face the West and call out:

The powers of the West, the powers of Water,

Wash me over with your sensitivity and intuition

In which to transform me and bless this circle,

Powers of the West, I welcome and hail you.

Cakes and Ale (Food and Drink)

After all the ritual celebrations, observances, and workings are done, place your ritual cup in the middle of the altar. Using your finger draw the pentagram over it in the air. Take the cup in both hands and say:

Earth brings forth the seed;

Seed brings forth the plant;

Plant brings forth fruit;

Fruit brings forth juice (or whatever drink);

Juice (or whatever drink) that is partaken by human;

Human will one day return to the Earth;

Lifting the cup high speaking:

Lord and Lady bless this drink

Great cycle of life in which I partake.

Take a sip of the drink and pour some on the libation dish.

Take the cake (or food) and place on the libation dish that you just poured your drink on. Sit it in the center of the altar and draw the pentagram over it. Call out to it:

Earth sprouts planted seed;

Planted seed sprouts the plant;

Growing plant brings forth grain;

Grain supplies the bread;

Bread is partaken by human;

In which will return to the Earth one day;

Lift the plate high.

Lord and Lady bless this libation

For I partake in the cycle of life.

Take some cake (food) from the dish and eat.

Closing the Corners (Quarters)

Working in a counterclockwise manner, start with the West when closing the quarters. Each time you change and face the direction, call out:

West:

Powers of Water, the Western powers;

I thank you for the presence in my circle today,

Deep mystery and intuition, you have shared,

I bid farewell, hail the powers of the West.

South:

Powers of Fire, the Southern powers;

I thank you for the presence in my circle today,

Courage and inspiration, you have shared,

I bid farewell, hail the powers of the South.

East:

Powers of Earth, the Eastern powers;

I thank you for the presence in my circle today,

Growth and stability, you have shared,

I bid farewell, hail the powers of the East.

North:

Powers of Air, the Northern powers;

I thank you for the presence in my circle today,

Knowledge and wisdom, you have shared,

I bid farewell, hail the powers of the North.

Open but never broken is this circle.

After the ritual is completed and the quarters have been closed, it is now time to clean up the altar

Chapter 10: Spell Book

Common Wiccan Terminology

Term	Definition per Wicca
Altar	Ritual area that has been cleansed and set up with various tools and items pertinent to the spell
Amulet	Object worn on the body to deflect negativity
Athame	Double edged ceremonial knife
Book of Shadows	Book of spells and rituals relevant to the witch who owns it
Centering	Focusing energy and thought on a specific point
Chalice	Ritual cup
Channeling	Allowing another spirit to use you as a vessel to speak
Chanting	Repetitious words or phrases said over again
Charm	Object charged with energy
Circle	Group of witches gathered to perform a ritual
Cleansing	Removing negative energies
Coven	Group of witches with like standards and beliefs
Craft	Another term to describe Wicca

Elements	Universal building blocks- Earth, Air, Fire, Water
Pentacle	Object that has pentagram engraved or embossed
Pentagram	Five-pointed star
Spell	Ritual performed with a specific intent in mind

BEGINNER SPELLS

Dreaming Charm

Items needed:

New Moon

Spell:

When the new Moon appears in the sky, go out after dark and look up to it. Chant to the new Moon:

Hail all the new Moon

On this night, bestow upon me a vision

Who my spouse and lover shall be

The next person you encounter in your dreams will be the answer to the spell.

The Augury of Flowers

Items Needed:

Nosegay of flowers from your love

Vase

Spell:

Keep the flowers in a vase of cold water for twenty-four hours. After this time as passed submerge the flowers in near boiling water for three hours. Carefully remove the flowers from the hot water. If they perish then the love was false. If the flowers revive and bloom, then the love is true.

Lucky Amulet

Items Needed:

Full Moon

Green Silk Cloth

Tree

Frog-shaped Item

Spell:

On a Friday night, during the full moon, bury the frog-shaped item under the tree. Keep this there for twenty-one days. At the end of this, dig the frog up at exactly midnight. Clean the frog and put it in the moonlight for the next three days. Hold your hands above the frog and say:

By the name of four

Earth and Air

Fire and Water

Prosperity I bring, show me where my treasures are and provide help in operations

Carry the frog around on your person. When you want to be lucky, use the green silk cloth to rub it. The frog will help you with anything that comes your way.

Protection Stone

Items Needed:

Red candle made of wax

Stone

Spell:

In a dark room, light the red candle. Sit holding the smooth, rounded stone that is sized smaller than a clenched fist. Breathe deep and with rhythm and call out:

Faith and prayer, I believe in your healing and ask you to begin your mighty work in the life of (insert name here).

Please surround (insert name here) by reaching down and enabling peace and strength. Give (insert name here) confidence that through you all things are possible. Shelter (insert name here) from the lies around him/her and allow the healing to begin.

Place the stone next to the red candle and allow it to completely burn out. Collect the stone the next day and place it next to (insert name here).

Bring Back Good Health

Items Needed:

White, Green, and Orange Candle (one of each color)

Container to put the candles in

Glass with water in it

Photo or personal object

Spell:

Form a triangle in the container with the candles. In the center of this triangle, add the photo or personal object. Sit the glass of water next to the candles. One at a time, light the candles and say:

Throwing all pain and negativity in the water, I light this candle for recovery so that I may receive the energy of healing fire.

After lighting the final candle, go to the sink with the glass of water and throw the negativity (water) in it. Put the candles out and store them in a safe space until you are healthy again. At this point light the candles again and let them burn completely out.

Blessed Water

Items Needed:

Water (clear)

Salt

Bowl

Spell:

Boil water for at least three minutes to consecrate it. Pour the water into the bowl and lay hands over it saying:

Creature of the water with negativity both seen and unseen, I exorcise thee. Blessed in the name of the Goddess.

Next take ahold of the salt and say:

Creature of the salt with negativity both seen and unseen, I exorcise thee. Blessed in the name of the Goddess.

Put the salt into the water and stir it clockwise three times.

I consecrate this water in the name of the blessed Goddess. Allow this water to purify all it may touch.

Evil Eye

Items Needed:

Water in a deep dish

Olive Oil

Spell:

Have the person under suspicion of the evil eye wet their index finger in the oil. Take the oil and then pour three drops into the water. If the person has an evil eye the droplets will disperse. If the droplets are kept intact then there is nothing to fear. This process can be repeated to ensure true results, but no more than three times in a one-week period.

INTERMEDIATE SPELLS

Happiness and Longevity in a Relationship

Items Needed:

Three pink candles

Rose petals

Favorite perfume

Incense

Rosehip oil

Small glass bottle

Spell:

Do this spell in the morning after fasting. Light the pink candles and the incense. Picture you and your love having fun and completely head over heels in love with each other. Use the perfume to anoint the rose petals. Slightly kiss each one of the petals and say this as if in prayer:

Come to me fruit of love and immortality. The spice. The rind. The leaf. The love.

From all four quarters I see you smiling when I close my eyes.

I call this in the name of the Goddess.

Leave the petals somewhere safe to dry out. Once they are fully dry crush them and put them in the small glass bottle with some of the rosehip oil. Use a stopper in the bottle so none of the oil spills out. Give this to your lover. It is their job to put this somewhere safe.

Attracting a Love

Items Needed:

Five white candles

Matchstick

Object of the person you fancy

Rose petals

Spell:

Place unlit candles in a circle that is at least one foot in diameter. Place the object of the person you fancy in the middle of this circle. Speak softly the following:

Fruit of love and immortality bring forth to me happiness and joy. Expedite love and honor and goodness.

Use the single matchstick to light the candles going in a clockwise pattern. In front of the candles kneel and focus on the object intensely. Think only of this person that you are trying to enchant. Utter their name thirty times while only focusing on the object in the middle of the circle.

Use the rose petals and sprinkle them over the object that is still in the middle of the circle. Chant the following while you do this:

North, South, East, and West. Grant me all your power for I honor you.

At the end of the chant blow out the candles. Safely store the rose petals for at least one month.

First Date Magic

Items Needed:

Photo of the person

Spell:

Place your lips on the photo of the person you are wanting to date. Make sure it leaves a kiss mark. Place the picture inside your right shoe. Wear this shoe on your date with this person.

Wand

Items Needed:

Razor

Blessed water

Hazel rod

Spell:

Take a hazel rod that has grown for at least one year's time and write "Yxarpa Inamef Xara" on it with the razor. Bury this next to an oak tree for ten days. Dig this up on the tenth day and clean it off with the blessed water. If you touch the person you love with this hazel rod, they will instantly love you back.

Ring of Luck

Items Needed:

Round table

White cloth

Glass of water

Four purple candles

Matchstick

Ring

Spell:

After filling up on supper, return to your room privately. Place the cloth on the round table with the glass of water centered on it. Place all four candles around the glass of water. Drop the ring into the glass of water. Use the single matchstick to light the candles going in a clockwise pattern. As you do this, say these words:

Cleansing fire that can execute my desires, I summon you to be the subject of all my commands. Bring forth wealth and happiness. Expedite with honor, goodness, and love. By the four elements I summon thee.

Keep repeating this chant until your palms begin to tingle. Blow out all four candles and go to bed. After you awake the next morning, take the ring from the glass and throw the water into the closest body of water. Wearing this ring will bring you good luck. This can be repeated as often as necessary but only if using the same ring.

Lucky Numbers

Items Needed:

Scissors

Pencil

Paper

Box

Blessed water

Spell:

Using the scissors, cut up the paper into smaller slips of paper. Use the pencil to write any numbers you want on these slips of paper. You can write as many as you desire. Put all the slips of paper into the box face down and say this incantation:

Mihi prosint numera per Dominum Deum nostrum!

Sprinkle blessed water over the paper inside the box and cover it. Give the box a shake to distribute. Take off the cover and place in the moonlight. This must remain in the moonlight for an entire night uncovered.

In the morning, cover the box back up and shake it gently. When you open the box, you will see numbers facing up that were not there before. These are your lucky numbers.

Lucky Coin

Items Needed:

Rhubarb root

Pouch made of linen

Moon

Tree

Coin

Spell:

Grind the rhubarb root into a powder substance. Place this powder and the coin inside the small linen pouch. Put this pouch on a string around your neck and wear it with it touching your skin.

In the light of the moon, find a tree. Walk clockwise around this tree nine times and say:

Good fortune, wealth, and prosperity I ask one wish of thee be granted.

In the morning keep the coin but throw the powder from the pouch into the river.

Attracting Luck

Items Needed:

Dry laurel leaves

Dollar bill

Piece of yellow thread

Yellow candle

Fresh laurel leaf

Spell:

Cleanse the candle and light it. Grind the dry laurel leaves into a powder substance. Roll the dollar bill out and pour three drops of wax and powder into the middle of the dollar bill. Place the fresh laurel leaf on top of this. Roll all this up and tie off with the yellow thread. Place this amulet where you keep your money.

Healing the Aura

Items Needed:

Chalk

Bowl

Rose petals

Four white candles

Amethyst

Jar

Spell:

Make a circle on the ground using the chalk and write "MIARFE OFIRG" inside of the circle. Put the bowl in the middle of the circle and place the candles inside the circle but around the bowl. Light them in a clockwise pattern. Catch one of the rose petals on fire using the flame from the first candle. Once it has caught fire, place it in the bowl and allow it to burn itself out. Repeat this using each of the candles and a separate rose petal. Take the ashes from these petals and place them in the jar. Give the amethyst to the person with the aura in need of healing. Say silently:

In this situation, there is no illness that you cannot heal.

Bring me understanding of your plans and excite me with them.

Our hope is for your healing and we thank you and ask your guidance and wisdom.

After this place the amethyst in the jar and removed the words written in the chalk. Keep this jar safe and the person should start to feel better.

Spirit Crystal

Items Needed:

Crystal

Cup

Clear plastic

Blessed water

Salted water

Spell:

Place the crystal in the cup with a touch of blessed water on it. Cover the cup with the clear plastic and place the cup outside in the moonlight after sundown. When the dawn comes, take the crystal from the cup and wash it with the salted water to purify. Hold tight to the crystal with both hands and close your eyes. Use this incantation while doing this:

Leave my presence diseases and illnesses, I command.

The price has been paid and no pain, nor death, nor sickness, nor fear show ever rule over anyone in this room.

Put the crystal in the drawer of a sick person and they should feel better once the energy has been omitted to the room.

For Strength

Items Needed:

Bowl

Blanket

Spring water

Salt

Incense

Laurel leaf

Spell:

Fill the bowl with spring water and place in the sunlight for four hours. Lay the blanket out in the moonlight being careful not to expose the water in the bowl to it. Have a seat on the blanket and light the incense. Sprinkle the salt into the bowl of water. Put the laurel leaf into the water and swirl it over the smoke from the incense. Recite this chant while doing this:

Oh, Goddess and God, hope will renew our strength.

We shall soar on wings like eagles.

We will run and not grow weak.

We will walk without being faint.

Pick up everything and place the laurel leaf under the pillow of the person needing strength from illness.

Maintenance of Good Health

Items Needed:

Blue candle

Red candle

White candle

Small knife

Spell:

Using the knife, write your name on all three candles. Place them in a triangle on the ground.

When lighting the white candle say loudly and clearly:

This candle shall protect me from disease

As you light the red candle say loudly and clearly:

This candle shall bestow upon me more strength

As you light the blue candle whisper:

This candle shall always prosper good health

Avoiding Someone or Something

Items Needed:

Pencil

Paper

Bottle

Rubbing alcohol

Clove of garlic

Small linen pouch

Spell:

Use the pencil to write specifically on the piece of paper that you are trying to avoid. Be extremely specific when doing this. Roll up the paper and stick it down into the bottle along with the garlic clove and fill it with the rubbing alcohol. Sit the bottle in a sunny spot for an hour. Take the garlic out of the bottle and let it dry in the sun. Crush the garlic clove into a fine powder and place it into the linen pouch. Always carry this pouch on your person.

ADVANCED SPELLS

Attraction Spell

Items Needed:

Waxing moon

Pencil

Wandering star

Small piece of paper

White candle

Spell:

This spell should be performed during the waxing moon. Take the piece of paper and cut it into the shape of a heart. Use the pencil to write down the names of you and your significant other or whom ever you wish, in the center of the heart. On the other side of the heart write the word "ABRAXAS". Right before midnight, seek out the wandering star. Once you find it, place the heart on the ground, name side up, and step on it with your right foot and left knee on the ground. Light the white candle in your right hand and while looking at the brightest start say the incantation:

Beautiful moon and beautiful star,

I conjure you.

Brilliant light I hold in my hand,

By the air that I breathe,

By the Earth that I touch

Swiftly bring these names together in which are written.

After reciting these three times, blow out the candle out and take the paper and place it under your left shoe. Stay for the one written on the paper to come and find you.

Apple Potion

Items Needed:

Apple

Two small pieces of paper

Drop of saliva

Three hairs from you and three from your love

Myrtle leaves

Myrtle twig

Laurel leaves

Spell:

On a Friday morning before the sun rises, pick an apple from a tree. In your saliva write the names of you and your love. On the other paper write "CNIDO" with your saliva. Unite three of your hairs with three of the hairs from the one you love. Remove the seeds after cutting the apple in half. Put the pieces of paper in the place the seeds once were. Tie the apple back together with the intertwined hairs. Use the myrtle twig like a tourniquet to secure the halves. Wrap the apple with the leaves of myrtle and laurel. Have someone place this apple under the pillow of your love.

Gaming Luck

Items Needed:

Parsley sprigs

Small metal pitcher

Glass of whiskey

Nutmeg

Lavender oil

Small bottle

Spoon

Spell:

Place the parsley sprigs and a pinch of nutmeg into the metal pitcher. Pour in the whiskey and stir it with the spoon while adding a few drops of lavender oil to the mixture. Pour the liquid from the metal pitcher to the small bottle and close it tightly. Attach a small sprig of parsley to the bottle and rub the bottle and parsley together while asking for good luck when placing a bet.

Sunflower Amulet

Items Needed:

Sunflower

Blessed water

Tooth

Laurel leaf

Spell:

Pluck a sunflower during the sign of the lion (the month of August). Use the blessed water to clean the tooth. Wrap the tooth with the sunflower and the laurel leaf. Carry this to be spoken to with kindness, instead of harsh tones.

Visions

Items Needed:

Fresh egg from a black hen

Clear water

Transparent vase

Spell:

Take an egg straight from a black hen. Break the egg and fill the vase with water. Put the vase in the sun during midday in the summer and say the following:

Glory to the Goddess and God who rule this place.

In which ever part of the world, North, East, South, West,

Open our eyes and execute our desires.

Using your index finger, agitate the water to make the egg turn. Let this rest for a moment then look through the vase at the egg and your answers will become visible.

White Candle Protection

Items Needed:

White Candle

Amber oil

Spell:

Anoint the candle with the amber oil. Carve the word "PROTECTION" into the candle and burn it for ten minutes at a time each day until it has completely burned out. To protect someone else follow the same procedures, only on the other side of the candle carve their name.

Ritual to Kick a Bad Habit

(As a side note for this ritual, this does not replace the habit. This simply helps aid your energy and strength. You cannot do acts that interfere with making this ritual beneficial. In this example, you cannot go buy a pack of cigarettes and say that it did not work. You are putting yourself in the situation to fail.)

Items Needed:

Ginger

Cinnamon

Charcoal

Chili powder

Sage

Representation of the item you are trying to kick the habit of (For this it will be a cigarette pack)

Matches

Bowl

Red candle

Black candle

Ritual:

Get the alter together in your ceremonial manner. Cast your circle, call your corners, do whatever it is that you do to prepare for a ritual. Typically, it is best to use the waning moon because you are trying to rid your life of something and rituals for ridding are best done during this moon cycle.

Light the red candle and say:

Red symbolizes strength and power. I can use these to kick this habit. Hour by hour and day by day.

Light the black candle and say:

Black color is used to represent sending things away, which will empower me to end this today.

Grind together the cinnamon, chili powder, and ginger until they form a fine powdery mix. Put the charcoal in the middle of the bowl and pour this mixture on top of it. Light the charcoal. This will create quite a nice fire. Begin tearing the empty cigarette pack into small pieces. Picture all the negative leaving your body. Watch the nicotine leave your body and your dependency on it grow smaller. See your lungs changing from a dark color back to healthy.

Put these torn pieces into the bowl with the charcoal and light them with the match. While you are watching this burn, say:

I shall burn what shall no longer have control over me. Set free from the addiction I shall be.

Light the sage on fire and smudge your area. This will cleanse you and your body of the effects this habit held over you. Pay special attention to the area with the burning cigarette pack and say:

I have strength within me and no more doubts, I use this sage to cleanse you out.

Put the sage in the bowl to burn out with the rest. Take the time at this point to reflect on the addiction and habit and how going forward you are free from it. Envision this with all of your energy and focus.

Once this has burnt out, blow out your candles. Close your corners. Close your circle.

Banishing Bay Leaf

Items Needed:

Pen

Bay leaf

Spell:

Go to a river or a stream. Sit and meditate for a while on what it is you are trying to banish from your life. Make sure to spend an ample amount of time focusing your energy on this. Write down what it is you wish to banish on the bay leaf using the pen. Continue to hold the leaf in your hand and think about it even deeper. When you feel like you have taken the correct amount of time focusing all your energy on this wish, let the leaf fly from your hand and into the water. Watch it as it is taken down stream. Say the following incantation:

My problems I release

No longer will they plague me

WICCA

No longer are they welcome in my life

Let them be carried away along with my wish

Taken down stream upon the bay.

Chapter 11: Spell WRITING

Spell writing should be specific to the person writing the spell. By doing so, they are more effective and meet personal needs. Even if you are following a traditional spell, it should be constructed and tailored to fit your style and needs. Writing your own spell is almost like writing a good novel. There are specific parts to the story that need to be filled in and included for it to be successful.

Make your intentions clear.

Decide what it is that you are trying to accomplish with this spell.

Make sure the timing is right for your spell.

The moon is a very important key in spell casting. Make sure to use the correct moon cycle for your spell to reach its full potential. Full moons and new moons are the best times for spells and magic.

Much like the weather, there is a season for your spell casting.

There is a time to plan, a time to plant, a time to grow, and a time to reap or harvest.

Decide which tools will be necessary to carry

out your spell.

Don't forget to make sure that the tools you choose are cleansed and blessed prior to using them for your spell work.

Write down your words.

You can make your words stronger by writing them down so that they can be remembered or chanted. Chanting them will make their energy stronger.

Make sure you are following the rules.

Make sure that your spell is morally and ethically sound. Keep in mind that Wicca abides by the three-fold karma.

Keep in mind that it is not a necessity to use tools or even an altar while practicing or using spells. While these items may intensify the power, it is not a deal breaker if you do not have them. You can also collect your spells in a book and keep them organized. This is called many things, but in Wicca it is referred to as a Book of Shadows

Book of Shadows

A Book of Shadows is a tool used by the Wiccan and is sacred. Just like all other sacred tools, it must be blessed along with all your other tools. It is also believed that all rituals and spells should be handwritten into your Book of Shadows so that your energy transfers on to its pages. This also helps you memorize its contents.

Making your Book of Shadows is as easy as getting a blank notebook to begin copying your information into. A lot of witches are using a three-ring binder for this because pages can be rearranged in a way that is more conducive to magic. Using sheet protectors is also a great way to prevent candle wax and other items from your altar from ruining your pages!

This is your sacred book and it should be treated as such. You should make it your own and design your cover page the way you want it. Fancy or plain, it doesn't matter if you put yourself into it. It does not matter if it is written in code or in plain English. There is no guideline for creating a Book of Shadows other than to keep it growing with new spells, charms, and information. Make sure to cite your information though in case you need to go back later for more research. Using divider tabs is also a good way to organize your information.

Important things that are universally accepted in a Book of Shadows:

Laws and traditions of your coven, if you practice with one. While there are no overall rules, most covens follow rules passed down from previous coven members. It is important to include these in your Book of Shadows so that you can pass them down as well.

- Write a dedication. If you are in a coven this would be where you include your initiation ceremony or your dedication to a specific God or Goddess. This can be a long essay style dedication or a simple sentence proclaiming your dedication within your coven or on your own.

- Include a section on your dedicated God or Goddess. You could even include others you find interesting. This is a good place to keep information regarding different spiritual paths based on Deity.

- Creating a reference section with your own personal tools is helpful. Tracking the moon phases as they pertain to you. What herbs, colors, and crystals you have used and their meaning. Candle colors and meanings could go here as well. It is like your map for where you have been magically.

- Sections that include your circle casting, divination, sacred texts, and experiments within these are good to add. Making notes and learning from successes and failures is an important part of your growth magically.

- Magical recipes and other kitchen witch side notes are exceptional in a Book of Shadows. This is where you can keep your directions for making oils, teas, and other magically healing concoctions.

- Lastly spells. Keep track of your spells in your Book of Shadows. Separate the ones you have written from the ones that have been passed down to you. Make notes legibly so that future generations can learn from what you have to offer.

Basic Protection Techniques-No Ritual Required

There are some methods of protection that do not need to have an incantation to activate their powers. These are things that in spell writing can be useful when making your own spells. Knowing their own natural and elemental powers can enhance your magic.

Salt

Salt has natural protective qualities against negativity and evil. Salt can be placed around in a circle to prevent someone from entering it with malintent. A line of salt can also be placed in doorways and windows to stop someone with negativity from gaining entry.

Iron

Iron is used as an evil repellant. It can be placed at the door of your home to help keep unwanted visitors away. This is also why it is said that spirits cannot cross a railroad track, because of the iron creating a protective barrier.

Pentacle

The pentacle is the representation of the elements and is regarded as a symbol of protection.

Silver

If the silver has been formed for a pentacle it does not need any special magic to enchant it, it is a strong protector on its own.

Fire

There are some spirits and entities that fear fire. Simply lighting a candle can be a line of defense and protection against them.

Light

Some lesser known demons are sensitive to light and it can deter them. Unfortunately, this method does not protect from higher ranked demons.

Gemstones

Tiger's Eye can be used to reflect a person's negative energy

Amethyst blocks spells of manipulation

Magnetite can entrap lesser known demons

Onyx captures and cancels out negative energy

Incense

Good quality incense of sandalwood, patchouli, myrrh, and sage can make the air unbearable for some negative entities and can serve as a form of protection from them.

Plants

Saffron and Thyme protect and deter flying spirits that are associated with the Air element

Rosemary repels evil spirits that are elemental to Water

Burnt sage is very cleansing of negativity

Lilacs planted near will deter aimless and wandering spirits

Thorn covered branches placed in windowsills have the same effect as placing salt as a protective barrier

Myrrh can strengthen any spell or talisman by simply incorporating it

Broom

Sitting a broom by the door of your house can deter weaker spirits from entering. It falls to the ground as an alarm when stronger ones enter.

COMPLEX GUIDE OF HERBS AND MAGICAL USES

Below is a list, sorted by magical use to aid in spell writing. This can help you decide which herbs you may need for your spells, especially if it is a multifaceted spell. Using one or multiples of these does not ensure that the spell will work. A lot of herbal magic is comprised of learning what works with your energy and with your intent. Don't give up because you chose to do a love spell and it didn't work. Sometimes it is all about how you word something and how much energy and focus you pour into it. Never become discouraged but always try again.

Magical Qualities	Plant/Herb
Anti-Lightning	Mahogany, Mountain
Astral Projection, Visions **TOXIC**	Belladonna
Beauty, Healing, Psychic Powers, Protection	Yerba Santa
Beauty, Love	Maidenhair
Binding, Health	Knotweed
Calling Spirits	Sweetgrass
Cat Magic, Love, Beauty, Happiness	Catnip

WICCA

Changing Sex, Healing, Luck	Persimmon
Chastity, Health, Divination	Camphor
Chastity, Protection, Love, Divination, Sleep	Lettuce
Courage	Ragweed
Courage, Love, Psychic Powers, Exorcism	Yarrow
Courage, Protection, Health, Love, Divination, Exorcism	Mullein
Courage, Psychic Powers	Borage
Destroy Sexual Drive ***TOXIC***	Hemlock
Divination	Ground Ivy
Divination	Meadow Rue
Divination, Fertility, Love	Fig
Divination, Wishes, Calling Spirits	Dandelion
Eloquence, Anti-Theft	Aspen
Employment, Luck, Protection, Money, Travel	Lucky Hand
Exorcism, Love, Protection, Lust	Devils Bit
Exorcism, Prophetic Dreams, Healing,	Heliotrope
Exorcism, Protection	Arbutus
Exorcism, Protection	Sloe
Exorcism, Protection	Tamarisk

Exorcism, Protection, Beauty	Lilac
Exorcism, Protection, Chastity	Fleabane
Exorcism, Protection, Healing, Lust	Nettle
Exorcism, Protection, Healing, Prosperity, Sleep	Elder
Exorcism, Protection, Healing, Visions	Angelica
Exorcism, Purification, Love	Avens
Exorcism, Purification, Protection	Asafoetida
Fertility	Agaric
Fertility, Chastity, Fishing Magic, Happiness	Hawthorn
Fertility, Garden Magic, Mental Powers, Money	Grape
Fertility, Health, Love, Protection	Geranium
Fertility, Love	Chickweed
Fertility, Lust	Carrot
Fertility, Money	Wheat
Fertility, Potency	Palm, Date
Fertility, Potency, Prosperity	Banana
Fertility, Prosperity, Love, Luck	Nuts
Fertility, Protection, Mental Powers	Mustard
Fertility, Protection, Wisdom, Meditation	Bodhi

Fertility, Wishes, Health, Wisdom	Sunflower
Fidelity	Magnolia
Fidelity	Vetch, Giant
Fidelity, Hex Breaking, Love	Chili pepper
Fidelity, Love, Lust	Yerba Mate
Halts Gossip	Slippery Elm
Happiness, Lust, love, Exorcism	Witch Grass
Healing	Adders Tongue
Healing	Henna
Healing	Mesquite
Healing Heartbreak, Protection, Invisibility,	Amaranth
Healing, Fertility, Money	Dock
Healing, Fertility, Protection, Exorcism, Money	Pine
Healing, Health	Goats Rue
Healing, Health	Sorrel Wood
Healing, Health, Mental Powers, Exorcism, Love	Rue
Healing, Love, Mental Powers	Spearmint
Healing, Love, Protection	Lime
Healing, Love, Vision, Meditation	Hemp
Healing, Money	Golden Seal

Healing, Money, Protection	Blackberry
Healing, Peace, Fertility, Potency, Protection, Lust	Olive
Healing, Protection	Eucalyptus
Healing, Purification	Tobacco
Healing, Purification, Money, Protection	Cedar
Healing, Sleep	Hops
Healing, Wishes, Luck	Jobs Tears
Health, Healing	Groundsel
Health, Healing, Sleep, Psychic Powers,	Thyme
Health, Longevity	Tansy
Health, Mental Powers, Infertility, Wishes	Walnut
Health, Money	Sassafras
Health, Power, Protection, Strength,	St. John's Wort
Health, Protection	Figwort
Health, Protection	Larkspur
Health, Protection, Healing	Anemone
Hex Breaking	Hydrangea
Hex Breaking, Sleep, Protection	Datura
Hex-breaking, Courage, Success	Wahoo

Hunting	Parosela
Hunting	Yellow Evening Primrose
Image Magic, Money, Protection	Bracken brazil Nutbrown
Immortality, Longevity, Wisdom, Protection, Wishes	Sage
Invisibility, Bullet-Proofing	Edelweiss
Legal Matters	Hickory
Legal Matters	Skunk Cabbage
Legal Matters, Money, Protection,	Cascara Sagrada
Longevity, Health, Healing	Life Everlasting
Longevity, Purification, Love, Friendship	Lemon
Love	Apricot
Love	Aster
Love	Bachelor's Buttons
Love	Bedstraw, Fragrant
Love	Beet
Love	Bleeding Heart
Love	Chestnut
Love	Dogbane
Love	Dutchman's Breeches
Love	Elm

Love	Indian Paint Brush
Love	Lady's mantle
Love	Liverwort
Love	Lovage
Love	Orchid
Love	Pimento
Love	Quassia
Love	Senna
Love	Spiderwort
Love	Spikenard
Love	Tamarind
Love Attraction ***TOXIC***	Henbane
Love, Divination	Cherry
Love, Divination, Knot Magic	Dodder
Love, Divination, Luck, Money	Orange
Love, Divination, Peace, Happiness	Meadowsweet
Love, Divination, Protection, Healing	Willow
Love, Exorcism, Longevity, Fertility, Wishes	Peach
Love, Exorcism, Wealth, Flying, Protection	Basil
Love, Fertility, Luck	Daffodil

Love, Fertility, Youth, Peace, Money	Myrtle
Love, Fidelity	Rye
Love, Fidelity, Peace	Skullcap
Love, Friendship	Love Seed
Love, Happiness	Adam & Eve Roots
Love, Healing, Garden Magic, Immortality	Apple
Love, Healing, Happiness, Wind Raising,	Saffron
Love, Healing, Protection	Barley
Love, Hex Breaking, Luck, Money, Anti-Theft	Vetivert
Love, Hunting	Fuzzy Weed
Love, Longevity, Money	Maple
Love, Luck	Strawberry
Love, Luck, Health, Psychic Powers	Sumbul
Love, Lust	Sugar Cane
Love, Lust	Yohimbe
Love, Lust, Beauty	Avocado
Love, Lust, Fidelity	Licorice
Love, Lust, Mental Powers	Vanilla
Love, Lust, Mental Powers, Money, Protection	Periwinkle

Love, Lust, Money	Snakeroot/black
Love, Lust, Protection	Southern Wood
Love, Manifestations, Protection, Healing	Balm of Gilead
Love, Money	Sarsaparilla
Love, Money, Prophetic Dreams	Jasmine
Love, Money, Success, Power	Ginger
Love, Peace, Healing, Spirituality	Gardenia
Love, Power	Gentian
Love, Protection	Papaya
Love, Protection, Divination	Orris Root
Love, Protection, Exorcism	Leek
Love, Protection, Exorcism	Mallow
Love, Protection, Exorcism, Potency	Dragons Blood
Love, Protection, Happiness	Hyacinth
Love, Protection, Psychic Powers	Elecampane
Love, Protection, Purification	Bloodroot
Love, Protection, Purification	Parsley
Love, Protection, Purification, Peace,	Vervain
Love, Protection, Sleep, Chastity,	Lavender
Love, Psychic Powers, Healing, Love, Divination, Luck, Protection	Rose

Love, Rain Magic, Love, Divination	Pansy
Love, Respect	Joe-Pye Weed
Love, Sleep, Purification, Protection	Valerian
Love, Spirituality	Aloes, Wood
Love, Success, Healing	Balm, Lemon
Love, Wishes, Healing, Beauty, Protection, Lust	Ginseng
Luck	Be-Still
Luck	Cabbage
Luck	Wood Rose
Luck Money	Snakeroot
Luck, Change	China Berry
Luck, Fertility, Anti-Lightning, Protection, Wishes	Hazel
Luck, Healing, Money, Protection	Calamus
Luck, Image Magic	Straw
Luck, Love	Male Fern
Luck, Money	Moss
Luck, Money, Chastity	Pineapple
Luck, Protection	Cinchona
Luck, Protection, Dream Magic, Hex Breaking	Huckleberry
Luck, Protection, Love	Houseleek

Luck, Truth	Bluebell
Luck. Happiness	Banyan
Lust	Cat Tail
Lust	Maguey
Lust, Harmony	Dulse
Lust, Love	Cardamom
Lust, Love	Endive
Lust, Love	Pear
Lust, Love, Divination	Hibiscus
Lust, Love, Visions	Damiana
Lust, Luck	Daisy
Lust, Luck, Love, Money, Wishes	Grains of Paradise
Lust, Psychic Powers	Deer's tongue
Manifestations, Astral Projection	Dittany of Crete
Meditation	Gotu Kola
Mental Powers	Savory, Summer
Mental Powers, Happiness	Lily of the Valley
Mental Powers, Lust, Psychic Powers	Celery
Mental Powers, Psychic Power	Eyebright
Money	Blue Flag
Money	Cashew

Money	Fenugreek
Money	May Apple
Money	Oats
Money, Divination	Goldenrod
Money, Employment	Pecan
Money, Exorcism	Fumitory
Money, Fertility, Lust	Patchouli
Money, Healing	Horse Chestnut
Money, Love	Moonwort
Money, Love	Pea
Money, Love, Luck, Healing, Exorcism, Travel, Protection	Mint
Money, Love, Success, Happiness	High John the Conqueror
Money, Luck, Healing	Allspice
Money, Luck, Protection	Irish Moss
Money, Prosperity	Oregon Grape
Money, Prosperity, Wisdom	Almond
Money, Protection, Beauty, Psychic Powers, Healing	Flax
Money, Protection, Hex Breaking	Squill
Money, Protection, Prophetic Dreams, Sleep	Cinquefoil
Money, Psychic Powers, Protection	Honeysuckle

Money, Repelling Monsters	Honesty
Money, Sleep, Love, Purification	Chamomile
Money, Spirit Calling	Pipsissewa
Money, Success	Bergamot, Orange
Money. Lust	Sesame
Peace, Protection	Loosestrife
Peace, Sleep, Friendship	Passionflower
Potency, Lust, Luck	Caper
Prosperity, Anti-Hunger, Money	Alfalfa
Protection	Ague Root
Protection	Blueberry
Protection	Castor
Protection	Chrysanthemum
Protection	Feverfew
Protection	Foxglove
Protection	Gourd
Protection	Grain
Protection	Lady's slipper
Protection	Liquid amber
Protection	Liverwort
Protection	Molukka

Protection	Papyrus
Protection	Plot Weed
Protection	Ragwort
Protection	Snapdragon
Protection	Spanish Moss
Protection	Wax Plant
Protection ****TOXIC***	Hellebore, Black
Protection, anti-hunger	Norfolk Island Pine
Protection, Anti-Lightning, Luck, Dream Magic, Balance	Holly
Protection, Anti-Theft	Larch
Protection, Anti-Theft, Love, Exorcism, Health	Juniper
Protection, Breaking Love spells	Lily
Protection, Chastity	Cactus
Protection, Chastity	Witch Hazel
Protection, Ending Relationships	Turnip
Protection, Escape, Happiness, Legal Matters	Celandine
Protection, Exorcism	Boneset
Protection, Exorcism	Peony
Protection, Exorcism	Pepper
Protection, Exorcism	Solomon's Seal

Protection, Exorcism, Healing, Money,	Onion
Protection, Exorcism, Healing, Spirituality	Myrrh
Protection, Exorcism, Love, Money	Clove
Protection, Exorcism, Purification and Cleansing	Birch
Protection, Exorcism, Spirituality	Frankincense
Protection, Exorcism, Wart Charming,	Bean
Protection, Exorcism, Wishes, Legal Matters	Buckthorn
Protection, Fidelity	Rhubarb
Protection, Gambling, Luck, Power, Employment	Devils Shoestring
Protection, Healing	Bittersweet
Protection, Healing	Ivy
Protection, Healing, Exorcism, Lust, Anti-Theft	Garlic
Protection, Healing, Exorcism, Spirituality	Sandalwood
Protection, Healing, Hex Breaking	Wintergreen
Protection, Healing, Purification	Fennel
Protection, Health	Carob
Protection, Health	Pimpernel

Protection, Health, Money, Healing, Potency, Fertility, Luck	Oak
Protection, Hex Breaking	Toadflax
Protection, Immortality, Luck, Love, Sleep	Linden
Protection, Invisibility	Wolfs Bane
Protection, Lock-Opening	Lotus
Protection, Love	Raspberry
Protection, Love	Venus Flytrap
Protection, Love, Happiness	Quince
Protection, Love, Happiness, Health, Money, Healing	Marjoram
Protection, Love, Hunting, Fertility, Health, Exorcism	Mistletoe
Protection, Love, Lust, Mental Powers,	Rosemary
Protection, Love, Money, Fertility, Health	Mandrake
Protection, Love, Prophetic Dreams, Purification	Mimosa
Protection, Luck	Aloe
Protection, Luck, Hex-Breaking, Wishes	Bamboo
Protection, Luck, Love, Lust, Wishes, Peace, Healing	Violet

Protection, Lust	Radish
Protection, Lust, Health, Anti-Theft, Mental Powers	Caraway
Protection, Lust, Health, Money,	Galangal
Protection, Mental Powers, Exorcism,	Horehound
Protection, Moderating Anger	Alyssum
Protection, Money	Bromeliad
Protection, Money	Gorse
Protection, Money	Rattlesnake Root
Protection, Money, Lust, Luck	Dill
Protection, Power	Ebony
Protection, Power, Divination	Roots
Protection, Prophetic Dreams,	Marigold
Protection, Prosperity, Sea Rituals, Health	Ash
Protection, Psychic Powers	Althea
Protection, Psychic Powers, Healing, Purification, Strength	Bay
Protection, Psychic Powers, Money and Love Spells	Acacia
Protection, Purification, Love	Betony, Wood
Protection, Purification, Youth	Anise
Protection, Rain Making, Luck	Heather

Protection, Rain, Fertility, Money	Rice
Protection, Sea Spells, Wind Spells,	Bladder wrack
Protection, Sleep	Agrimony
Protection, Strength	Mulberry
Protection, Strength, Healing	Carnation
Psychic Powers	Stillengia
Psychic Powers, Fertility	Bistort
Psychic Powers, Healing, Protection, Power, Success	Rowan
Psychic Powers, Luck	Star, Anise
Psychic Powers, Manifestations, Lust	Mastic
Psychic Powers, Mental Powers	Mace
Psychic Powers, Prophetic Dreams	Buchu
Psychic Powers, Protection	Grass
Psychic Powers, Protection, Love, Calling Spirits	Wormwood
Psychic Workings	Urva Ursa
Purification	Shallot
Purification	Turmeric
Purification, Exorcism	Horseradish
Purification, Exorcism	Sagebrush
Purification, Healing, Protection	Pepper Tree

Purification, Hex Breaking	Thistle, Holy
Purification, Love	Lemon Verbena
Purification, Prosperity	Alkanet
Purification, Prosperity	Benzoin
Purification, Protection	Euphorbia
Purification, Protection	Hyssop
Purification, Protection, Wind Spells, Divination	Broom
Purification, Sleep, Love, Healing, Psychic Powers	Peppermint
Purification, Wisdom	Iris
Rain Making	Toadstool
Rain Making, Protection, Luck, Riches,	Fern
Raising the Dead	Yew
Removing Obstacles, Invisibility, favors, Frigidity	Chicory
Repel snakes, Lust, Psychic Powers	Lemongrass
Riches, Courage, Strength	Tea
Snake Charming, Fertility	Horsetail
Snake Enraging	Thistle, Milk
Snake Removing	Centaury
Spirituality, Protection	African Violet

Spirituality, Purify Negativity and Evil	Arabic Gum
Spirituality, Success, Healing, Power,	Cinnamon
Strength, Courage, Protection	Master Wort
Strength, Protection, Hex Breaking, Healing	Thistle
Strength, Protection, Peace	Pennyroyal
Strength, Psychic Powers, Protection,	Mugwort
Strengthening Spells	Echinacea
Success	Winters Bark
Transmutation, Protection, Purification	Yucca
Travelers Luck, Peace, Lust, Love	Eryngo
Tying Dog's Tongues	Hounds tongue
Understand Animal Languages	Cloth of Gold
Victory, Protection, Money	Woodruff
Visions, Protection, Luck	Kava-Kava
Wishes	Beech
Wishes, Protection	Dogwood

Conclusion

You have reached the end of this book, *Wicca Herbal Magic*. We hope this book has giving you the opportunity to begin your studies in the magic and enlightenment of Wicca and we look forward to hearing from you if you enjoyed your time reading it. This book is just the beginning of what all you can discover out there in the world and what the religion of Wicca is all about. We encourage you to reach out to other Wiccans in your area to get their tips and insights into how to be a Wiccan and where you should start in your journey.

Reading it cover to cover does not help it all sink in and make you an expert. Now is when you practice. Write your spells and practice them. This is when practice makes perfect. None of this will happen overnight. Learning to harness your own energies and magical abilities take time and trial and error. During this phase you must learn who you are and what you are hoping to bring from all of this.

You may never be a walking herbal dictionary, but you can have the reference tools on hand and even create your own guide as to what has personally worked for you. Consider this your foundation, the floor level of which you will build your craft upon. Honing into your inner skill as an herbalist may take time, but if you feel that is your calling, do not take it lightly. Make sure to follow the ways and traditions of herbal magic medicine and heal using your energies.

There is a lot of historical information included and may seem like a lot but the most important part of getting a firm foundation is making sure the contents are in an equal ratio. You cannot build your craft without knowing where it comes from or the traditions poured into it. Learn from those before you and allow yourself to grow outward in your search for herbal magic.

Always remember that the true meaning of being a Wiccan is to become more connected with the earth and living in peace with the energies of the nature around you. Once you have gotten to this harmony you should see that you are in the right frame of mind to begin your incantations and ritual casting.

Let's hope it was informative and able to provide you with all of the tools you need to achieve your goals whatever they may be.

Finally, if you found this book useful in any way, a review on Amazon is always appreciated!

WICCA

Printed in Great Britain
by Amazon